THE PEOPLE OF ARISTOPHANES

Walzer
November 1962

Plate I

TYPES OF OLD COMEDY

The People
of Aristophanes

A Sociology of Old Attic Comedy

VICTOR EHRENBERG

Haec res agetur nobis, vobis fabula
PLAUTUS

SCHOCKEN BOOKS · NEW YORK

First SCHOCKEN PAPERBACK *edition 1962*

*This edition is published by arrangement with
Harvard University Press*

To
MAX *and* MARY CARY
HAROLD *and* MARION MATTINGLY

Library of Congress Catalog Card No. 62-13137
Printed in the United States of America

PREFACE

THIS paperback edition has given me the opportunity of making a number of corrections in my book, most of them very small. Only occasionally have I added references to more recent literature. Though in all essentials a reprint of the second edition of 1951, this can be regarded as an improved edition. I am very glad indeed that it is now published in the United States where I have been a Visiting Professor in 1958 and hope to lecture again in 1962. It is to my American friends that I dedicate this edition.

The book was written during the years of distress and the emigration to England from Prague, where I had been professor at the German University from 1929 to 1939. It was published in 1943. For the first as well as the second edition I enjoyed much help and useful criticism from many friends. Both editions and the Italian translation (*L'Atene di Aristofane*, 1957) met with applause and criticism by reviewers. I have learned a good deal from all of them.

The Preface to the first edition ended with the following words which I should like to repeat, as they seem equally suitable today: "To write history and to live history are two very different things. Deeply grateful for guidance and protection during these years, I feel more than ever the inadequacy and insufficiency of my work. History has become our fate; to live up to it is indeed difficult."

V. E.

London (England),
October 1961.

CONTENTS

LIST OF ILLUSTRATIONS

THE illustrations are not intended to give a survey of the archaeological material connected, in one way or another, with the contents of this book. Their sole purpose is to brighten the book by a few selected specimens of works of art which in a language more impressive and illuminating than that of words show what the Athenians were like. Many of the illustrations belong to an earlier period than that of Old Comedy; nevertheless, they illustrate the essential facts. In the following list I have mentioned the books or papers from which each copy was taken, or to which it seems appropriate to refer; acknowledgments are due, for the permission to print the illustrations, to the *Journal of Hellenic Studies* and the following publishers: Les Belles Lettres, Paris; F. Bruckmann, Munich; W. de Gruyter & Co., Berlin; Schroll & Co., Vienna; R. Oldenbourg, Munich; H. Schoetz, Berlin.

QUOTATIONS AND ABBREVIATIONS

Aristophanes' extant plays:
After V. Coulon's edition (*Coll. Budé*), quoted without the poet's name:

A. = Acharnians	F. = Frogs	Pl. = Ploutos
B. = Birds	K. = Knights	Th. = Thesmo-
C. = Clouds	L. = Lysistrate	phoriazousai
E. = Ekklesiazousai	P. = Peace	W. = Wasps

Fragments are quoted after Kock, *Comicorum Atticorum Fragmenta;* a new edition with pleasant English translations, though many hypothetical supplements: J. H. Edmonds, *The Fragments of Attic Comedy*, I-IIIA (1957-1961).

frg. = Aristophanes. The other poets by name, partly abbreviated, in Kock's order.

adesp. = of unknown author.

D (behind number of fragment) = J. Demiańczuk, *Supplementum Comicum* (1912).

P (behind number of fragment) = D. L. Page, *Greek Literary Papyri* (*Loeb Library*), I (1942). The fragment 1 Mazon of Kratinos' *Ploutoi* — not printed by Mr. Page on account of its bad state of preservation — was re-published by R. Goossens, *Rev. ét. anc.* XXXVII (1935), 425.

Euripides' fragments (*frg.*) are quoted after Nauck, *Tragicorum Graecorum Fragmenta²*, some papyri after Page (P; see above).

Translations:
Some are original, others are by the following translators, whose renderings I have sometimes altered so as to bring them closer to the Greek.

Aristophanes' plays: B. B. Rogers.

Fragments: G. Norwood (in his book *Greek Comedy*) and J. M. Edmonds

The following books are quoted by the author's name only:

A. M. Andreades, *A History of Greek Public Finance*, I (1933).

A. Boeckh, *Staatshaushaltung der Athener* (1886³).

H. Bolkestein, *Wohltätigkeit und Armenpflege im vorchristlichen Altertum* (1939).

G. M. Calhoun, *Business Life in Ancient Athens* (1926).

P. Cloché, *Les classes, les métiers, le trafic* (1931).

M. Croiset, *Aristophane et les partis politiques à Athènes* (1906; Engl. translation 1909).

H. Francotte, *L'industrie dans la Grèce ancienne* (1900-01).

P. Geissler, *Chronologie der altattischen Komödie* (1925).

G. Glotz, *Ancient Greece at Work* (1926).

A. W. Gomme, *Essays in Greek History and Literature* (1937).

G. M. A. Grube, *The Drama of Euripides* (1941).

A. E. Haigh, *The Attic Theatre*, third edition by A. W. Pickard-Cambridge (1907).

J. Hasebroek, *Trade and Politics in Ancient Greece* (1930).

F. M. Heichelheim, *Wirtschaftsgeschichte des Altertums* (1938).

A. Meder, *Der athen. Demos zur Zeit des peloponnesischen Krieges im Lichte zeitgenössischer Quellen* (Diss. München, 1938).

H. Michell, *The Economics of Ancient Greece* (1940).

G. Murray, *Aristophanes* (1933).

R. A. Neil, *The Knights of Aristophanes* (1901).

G. Nicosia, *Economia e Politica di Atene attraverso Aristofane* (1935²).

G. Norwood, *Greek Comedy* (1931).

L. Radermacher, *Aristophanes' Frösche. Sitzungsberichte Wien* 198 (1921).

R. L. Sargent, *The Size of the Slave Population in Athens* (Univ. of Illinois Studies in Social Science, vol. XII, 2, 1924).

W. Schmid [and O. Stählin], *Geschichte der griech. Literatur*, part I, vol. IV (1946).

M. N. Tod, *A Selection of Greek Historical Inscriptions* I (1946²), II (1948).

U. v. Wilamowitz-Moellendorff, *Aristophanes' Lysistrate* (1927).

E. Ziebarth, *Beiträge zur Geschichte des Seeraubs und Seehandels* (1929).

INTRODUCTION

THIS book is an attempt to give a historical and sociological account of Athenian life, based on, and illustrated by, one kind of literature in particular, namely Old Attic Comedy. Such an approach may appear unusual, but the method, I hope, can be justified. The 'people' mentioned in the title of the book are not the characters who carry the plots of the comedies, but the people of Athens. If there were any doubt about this, the sub-title should make it clear. I understand sociology as a branch of historical scholarship, and not of systematic philosophy. 'A Sociology of Old Comedy' has to be justified from two points of view, that of sociology, that is to say, of the present position of the study of Greek social and economic life, and that of the peculiar value of Old Comedy as a historical source.

With regard to the former of these two considerations, the following facts may be briefly recalled. It was about the 'seventies of the last century that the social and economic history of Greece and Rome first became a subject of special research, and, very soon, a separate and independent branch of classical studies. It was a real discovery that the Greeks were not only lovers of freedom, wisdom and beauty, the Romans not only soldiers and statesmen, but that they had their social and economic problems, much like those of other ages, and especially, so it seemed, like those of the nineteenth century. The existence of slavery, the occurrence of social wars, and other similar facts were, indeed, already known to earlier scholars. Our attempt to define more precisely an epoch in historical writing necessarily ignores, but does not conflict with, such points of general knowledge; in principle, the definition is true.

The new discovery, though apparently obvious, was in fact a genuine discovery. For the first time, the importance of social and economic conditions in ancient life was recognized. Ancient history, which till about the middle of the century had been either political or else idealizing and aesthetic (when indeed it was not purely antiquarian), now came under the influence of the materialistic outlook which dominated the historical conceptions of the time. Hitherto only August

Boeckh, far ahead of his time both as historian and epigraphist, had found for ancient historians the beginning of the path to social and economic history.[1] Neither Grote nor Curtius, the best representatives of the political and idealizing schools respectively, led in that direction. Greek history (with which alone we are concerned) had no Mommsen. It was for the time being at a standstill and needed an impulse from outside. The ideas of political economy, and the prevalent interest in modern social and economic history, provided that impulse.

The change of outlook was as productive as it was significant. Even earlier, attempts had been made to free history from a too rigid antiquarian outlook and to make it live by actualizing and modernizing the past. Mommsen's *History of Rome*, with its passionate vivacity and its splendid style, was a brilliant example of this kind of writing. The general tendency to modernize the past coincided with the particular tendency of economic history. The historians of antiquity now learnt to investigate entirely new spheres of life, and it is easy to understand that at first in formulating their problems they adopted the methods of their teachers, the writers of modern history and the political economists. The outstanding importance of economics in the political and social life of their own day made historians suppose that economics had a like importance in antiquity. The details of economics in the ancient world were interpreted, and the general conception of its history was expounded, in the spirit and terms of contemporary circumstances. Almost all the features of the modern social system were discovered in Greece and Rome: industry and factories, wholesale trade and large ship-owners, capitalists and proletarians. Such, until a short time ago, was the view of ancient economics held by historians, for instance, in Germany, France and Italy. In England and America, it was in some measure corrected by natural common sense.[2]

The prevailing view was challenged by a political economist,

[1] It is interesting to note that also the discussion of fundamental aspects of ancient economic history began as early as Boeckh. He attacked (I, 65) Heeren's opinion, who denied, in the same way as the modern group of scholars we shall describe later, that there was any mutual influence between State and trade.

[2] Compare Sir Alfred Zimmern's *Greek Commonwealth* (1931[5]). Though its approach to the subject is primarily aesthetic, this outstanding book is a very valuable attempt to make clear the special character and importance of Greek economics. Cf. *Gnomon*, I (1925), 144f.

K. Bücher. His prolonged and vigorous opposition, however, had no great effect on historical writing, for it was founded mainly on the very extreme and one-sided theory of Rodbertus, and this theory — that in ancient times there existed no other economic unit than the self-contained household, the *oikos* — undoubtedly runs counter to the facts given in our sources. Later the great sociologist Max Weber put forward a wider and perhaps more profound theory. He distinguished two types, that of the political and that of the economic man, representatives of the ancient and modern world respectively, and this theory gave a new and fruitful impulse to historical research. A new generation of scholars, deeply impressed by it, set themselves to re-examine the foundations of economic history. In addition, they were convinced that it was their general task not to modernize the past, but to keep distant ages in proper perspective, that is to say, to understand and interpret every historical phenomenon, as far as possible, in the light of its own conditions and its special way of existence.

Very soon, however, the pendulum swung in the opposite direction. The chief conclusion then reached was the primitive nature of ancient economics embodying an entirely 'unmodern' way of life, except, to some extent, in the Hellenistic and the later Roman ages. Professor J. Hasebroek asserted the primitive character of Greek trade and industry, and arrived at the conclusion that economics were, in the Greek world, of almost no importance at all. In his view there was no real connection between politics and economics, between the State on the one hand, and trade and industry on the other. The human type of ancient Greece and Rome, the *zoon politikon*, the 'political animal', once postulated by Aristotle, and reconstructed in

---

[1] Naturally, I do not wish to say that Aristotle and M. Weber meant exactly the same. 'Political' in Aristotle's meaning is 'part of' or 'bound to the Polis', which is town and State at the same time. If he does not take the word in our sense, he neither talks only of "dem in Stadtform lebenden Wesen". The relevant books of Bücher, M. Weber and others are quoted in Hasebroek's two books: *Staat und Handel im alten Griechenland* (1928), and *Griech. Wirtschafts- und Gesellschaftsgeschichte bis zur Perserzeit* (1931). In the Anglo-Saxon world Hasebroek's ideas have been largely rejected or ignored, but the short and lucid paper of L. R. Lind (*Economic Man in Ancient Athens. Class. Journ.* XXXV (1939-1940), 27ff.) is entirely under his influence.

M. Weber's definition of the *homo politicus*, the 'political man', became, in Hasebroek's restricted view, the historical citizen, the *polites* of archaic and classical Greece.[1]

The two views were not merely different interpretations of certain historical facts. They embodied two different principles, two methods of assessing the place and importance of economics in the life of antiquity. Whereas the older generation over-estimated their importance, Hasebroek and his pupils denied them almost all significance. The two principles may be briefly, though perhaps over-simply, summarized thus: according to the one, the facts of economic life had the same nature and importance in the past as they have at the present day; for human economics at all times follow the same or at least similar laws. The other maintains that economic circumstances in different ages differ entirely both in their nature and in their importance. Since among ancient peoples they were on the whole primitive, their practical importance was negligible.

The need to steer a middle course between the two extremes has for some time past been recognized by many scholars, and, from various points of view, much good work has been done. To some extent, all this work culminates in the two lengthy volumes of Prof. Heichelheim's *Wirtschaftsgeschichte des Altertums* (1938). He gives a wide general survey, based on an extensive knowledge of archaeological and numismatic evidence on the one hand, and of economic theories on the other. Although Heichelheim keeps clear of the methods which led to both the extreme views we have described, his work lacks, in a way, historical 'differentiation'. By this I mean that the special character of an age or a people, the peculiar atmosphere of its life, are ignored, presumably of set purpose, because the author writes from the standpoints of economic theory as well as of universal history. I gratefully acknowledge what I have learnt from his book as well as from writers like Glotz, Andreades, Oertel, Bolkestein, and many others.[1] I owe to them much more than is expressed by the

[1] A full bibliography up to about 1926 is given by Mr. M. N. Tod to his excellent chapter in the *Cambr. Anc. Hist.*, vol. V (1927). Since the publication of Heichelheim's work, Professor H. Michell has published a useful, if somewhat unhistorical, survey of Greek economics, and Professor M. Rostovtzeff, in an interesting chapter of his great work *Social and Economic History of the Hellenissic World* (1941), has dealt with the fourth century B.C.

few quotations in the notes. But I do not believe that their work has made my own attempt superfluous, in particular since it is not meant to rival them in their special fields.

This book deals only with a short period of history, but on the other hand, is not restricted to purely economic problems. It tries to give a cross-section of the whole of Athenian life. Economics naturally play their part, and indeed one of increasing importance; but in order to see this part in the true light of history, it is of little help to deal with economics as an isolated subject, as the contents of *Wirtschaftsgeschichte*. The author hopes that this consideration will serve to justify his undertaking, since he must admit that he is no trained economist. The method of the book is not entirely new, and is in part familiar to every historian; it departs, however, from the usual methods of modern research in one respect. It need hardly be mentioned that in the author's view, too, it is essential, in the preliminary stages, to collect all the relevant material from every available source and to draw from it all possible and reasonable conclusions; but this is not always enough. Too often, as a result, we are offered as a reconstruction of life what is in fact no more than the sum of single facts, sadly lacking in general atmosphere.

We are concerned here only with the problems of classical Athens. Our possible sources are, first, archaeological evidence; secondly, numerous inscriptions and coins (single pieces and hoards); in addition, speeches delivered in court, some theoretical treatises and pamphlets, and a great mass of quotations from comedy as well as other general literature.

Historical conclusions from archaeological evidence are always somewhat dangerous, unless they can be checked by other sources. The clear facts and figures of coins and records are, beyond doubt, a most valuable source, reliable and matter-of-fact. But do they correspond to the real facts? To invert a famous phrase, *quod est in actis, non est in vita* — or at least one may say, *in vita esse non certum est*. Single facts, even though they may be entirely true and exact, do not take on life until they become part of a greater unit; until they do so, they may often be interpreted *in duas partes*. Statistics can, and often do, give uncertain and misleading results, because the classifications which they adopt are often too wide, and so do not always reveal the true significance of the facts. This is the more likely

to happen when the material is so incomplete and of so incidental a nature as that available for ancient times.[1]

Other sources are inadequate in a different way. All literature that deserves the name, whether poetry or prose, is a work
of art — in Zola's famous definition: 'un coin de la création vu
à travers un tempérament'. But quite apart from this inherent
nature of all literary sources, there are particular circumstances
that make for historical ambiguity. The forensic speeches, for
instance, are preserved without the supplement and corrective
of the counter-pleas. They provide important material,
addressed as they were to an audience of ordinary citizens, and
bound to agree with their standards and ideas. But this very
dependence of the orators on the minds of their audience, and
the necessity to plead and not to describe impartially, can also
cause serious misrepresentation.[2] Still, the background picture
of a case in court, though the light is always turned on a small
section only, must be at least as true to the facts as that of
comedy.

The theoretical treatises are necessarily subjective, and it
is impossible, beyond a certain point, to separate what is said
from the writer's purpose or the points he wishes to prove.
No doubt, the political and sociological dialogues of Plato, or
Xenophon's *Poroi*, embody ideas which were meant to be put
into practice, and it would be wrong to take them as merely
Utopian. Nevertheless, these books do not give a picture of
reality. All these sources, just as much as Ps.-Xenophon with
his violent sarcasm, can and must be used as contributors, but
only as such. In particular, they will help to decide whether in
some doubtful cases the evidence of comedy is distorted or not.

We should note another point. Questions of history, in so
far as they are questions of human behaviour, are ultimately
questions of psychology, and this aspect becomes even more
important when we try to interpret facts known to us only
from scanty and fragmentary tradition. In considering the
nature of Greek economics and Greek society we have to find
out not only the facts of external life, but the psychological
reactions to them, both of individuals and of society. We have

[1] Cf. A. H. M. Jones, *Ancient Economic History* (Inaugural Lecture, London,
1948).
[2] F. R. Earp, *The Way of the Greeks* (1929), 10ff, is right in stressing also the
different reliability of the various orators.

to discover the way in which a single man, or men in general or men in a particular group, think and act in regard to their economic circumstances. Only then will these circumstances take on real life. Here, in order to avoid misunderstanding, I should like to make it clear that these psychological reactions are themselves facts, not abstract reconstructions nor an attempt to explore the 'depths of the unconscious'. We do not ask for documentary correctness (it is not available), but for truth and reality. Our task is to make clear the 'atmosphere' created by the social and economic conditions of life, and to characterize, in its variety and its unity, the people who lived in this atmosphere. That does not mean a sum of single facts, but the total of life in which each single fact lives and grows and dies. This is, of course, an ideal goal, and I do not pretend that this attempt will succeed in reaching it; but the goal should be kept in sight.

Every source will answer some of our questions better than other sources, and some worse. We have therefore no right to neglect any of them, and I do not propose to do so. But if we find a fairly full and satisfactory picture of our subject in one kind of source, it is justifiable and even advisable to base our own description on it, and only to correct it and fill the gaps from other evidence. This is actually the method used by every modern historian when he has to follow in his narrative the lines drawn by one of the great Greek or Roman historians. Our position is only slightly different. We do not want a narrative; we want a mirror reflecting real life.

Possibly even those who have accepted my arguments so far will hesitate when I say that the source to which our quest for reality leads us, is Old Attic Comedy. For what kind of literature is less concerned with reality than the fantastic comic drama, 'still damp from its origins of vine and country'?[1] The nature and spirit of comedy we shall try to discuss, in part at least, in the following chapters, but at this stage it seems desirable to show the direction our arguments will take, and to turn for a moment to the second of the two considerations which we raised when outlining the scope and method of this book, that is to say, the peculiar value of Old Comedy as a historical source.

We shall best grasp and comprehend the 'atmosphere' of

[1] A. Bellessort, *Athènes et son théâtre* (1934), 297.

which we have spoken, if we can do so at all, when a source answers our questions without intending to do so. Perhaps the greatest and most real difficulty in all historical writing is to find out and reproduce what in our sources is implied but not said, or is said only unconsciously. Matters which were taken for granted as self-evident to the author and his contemporaries are never directly referred to at all. Such hidden facts lie in every source, and many of them will probably lie hidden for ever, though in some sources they are more difficult to recover than in others. For example, in forensic speeches on a commercial subject, the economic circumstances are themselves the 'case', they are the primary concern of the speaker, and are therefore moulded consciously and deliberately. It is my belief that nowhere but in comedy are the facts of social and economic life given merely as a background and to create an atmosphere. We must, of course, take into account all possible sources of error, such as comic exaggeration and distortion, unreal and impossible events, 'typical' persons and topics. Even so, we have in comedy excellent evidence of many real facts, above all of those relating to the general conditions of life which form the background of the comic plot, a background self-evident to poet and audience.[1]

Our object, therefore, is something quite different from an attempt to draw from comedy new information on political events or conditions, nor do I consider a comedian as one who gives expression to fixed political views. It has rightly been observed that the very fact of his being a comedian compelled the poet to be 'against the government' — whatever government it might be.[2] Aristophanes did not write his comedies to fight democracy. The question has often been asked whether he had any higher purpose at all than only to entertain his audience. In recent times, the interpretation of the true nature of Old Comedy has oscillated between two extreme views which regarded the comedian either as a mere jester or as a serious educator and critical moralist.[3] There is much to be

[1] Cf. J. Burckhardt, *Griech. Kulturgeschichte*, IV, 280: '*Aristophanes, welcher, sobald er von bestimmten Einzelnen redet, der stärkste Verleumder sein darf, kann, wo er Handlungsweisen überhaupt schildert, nur Sachen gesagt haben, welche jedermann kannte und kenntlich fand.*'

[2] Cf. G. Kaibel, *P.-W.* II, 985.

[3] The discussion between the two extremist views has been going on for several generations. Recent examples are provided by the following dissertations,

said for the view that he was 'not a politician, but a dramatist, an artist, a man whose purpose is to give us a picture . . . not to advocate a policy'.[1] But a great artist has views of his own, and the picture he paints will be more than clownery. I am convinced that it is possible to find an interpretation between the extremes. For us, however, the important question is not so much how far comedy is 'serious', but rather how far it is realistic. The danger that threatens a purely aesthetic outlook of the critic is that he will tend to separate the poet from real life, from the 'political' life of an Athenian citizen, and to deny the reality of the background, which is, in fact, needed to contrast with the unreal fantastic picture of the play.[2]

Reality in its essence means here the people, real life is the life of the people. We have no other source which springs so directly from the people as comedy, and which describes the people in equally vivid colours as the basis of social and economic reality. As a political factor, the *demos* is generally laughed at in comedy, and appears more or less unreal and fan-

---

which also contain good surveys of earlier literature on the subject. J. Schmidt, *Aristophanes und Euripides* (Greifswald, 1940), V. Frey, *Die Stellung d. att. Tragödie u. Komödie zur Demokratie* (Zurich, 1946), and, on the other hand, the careful and elaborate study by A. Meder. He assumes — in accordance, it is true, with W. Jaeger, *Paideia*, I, 457ff — that the comic poets intended to be 'der Sammelpunkt der offentlichen Kritik' (p. 19); that is, to say the least, a wild exaggeration. Even Gilbert Murray's view that Aristophanes was 'a partisan pacifist' (*JHS*. LXIV, 1944, 1) goes too far. Cf. below, ch. XI.

[1] A. W. Gomme, *Cl. Rev.* LII (1938), 97ff, also the same author in *Athenian Studies presented to W. S. Ferguson (Harvard Studies*, Suppl. I, 1940), 212.

[2] I quote a few passages pointing to the same view. W. Vischer (*Ueber die Bedeutung der alten Komödie als geschichtlicher Quelle. Kleine Schriften*, I, 459ff) writes: '*Da der Boden der Komödie der der Wirklichkeit ist . . ., so ist die Komödie für Sitten, Gebräuche und Einrichtungen aller Art eine wahre geschichtliche Fundgrube.*' W. Jaeger, *Paideia*, I, 355 (German edit. 450): 'The most complete reflection of his own age, far surpassing any other type of literature or art in fullness and accuracy.' Or G. Lowes Dickinson, *Letters from John Chinaman*, 93: 'Since his plays are concerned with the actual stuff of Athenian life, its political and religious controversies, war and peace, science and scepticism, the old times and the new, he gives a more vivid picture of that life than any other author.' In spite of statements like these, very little has, in fact, been done to draw the necessary conclusions. A good economic historian like Bolkestein (199), once again, repeats that the study of comedy is essential; but even he, though he frequently quotes from comedy, does not know any other testimony of the '*Gedanken- und Gefühlslebens des arbeitenden Teils des griechischen Volkes*' but the remarks of Sokrates in Xen. *mem.* II, 7.

tastic. The people who, in fact, speak through comedy (we shall try to prove it in detail in the following chapter) are the people both on the stage and on the seats, the performers as well as those who listen and look on.[1] We, too, can hear the people's voice if we listen to comedy. Here the reality of the people is not displaced by the myth, sacred or rationalized, as in tragedy, nor largely lost in the aloofness of the political historian as with Thucydides or in the abstractions of philosophy.[2] In comedy it may be hidden, but it is never destroyed. The play stands in between and blocks the view, but behind and beyond the play is life, quiet or vivacious, above all and unquestionably real. This is what we seek to uncover. We shall not do justice, alas! to the poets as they deserve, either as dramatic or as lyrical poets, or even as comedians. This follows from the nature of the case, and once and for all, let me apologize to their memory and to the reader.

The importance of economic questions in comedy is well understood. Some scholars have even tried to prove that Aristophanes was an expert in economic theory, familiar with the laws of modern political economy.[3] This is surely wrong. Nobody, indeed, believes that the poet was himself an economist, but he is said to have known the laws of economic life, most of which were not discovered before the nineteenth or twentieth century.[4] Did he, perhaps, study books on political economy? Impossible. From the *Poroi* of Xenophon we know

---

[1] It is the unqualified closeness of Old Comedy to the real life of the people that makes any comparison with modern musical comedy or with a Gilbert and Sullivan opera so inappropriate. Mr. Punch is a nearer relation.

[2] A friend, headmaster of a well-known Public School, wrote: 'It seems to me that it is an extremely good idea to turn from the literature in which Athens is depicted as more than life size to comedy where her geese are ducks instead of swans.'

[3] Cf. besides R. Gonnard, *Rev. d'économie politique*, 18 (1904), 53ff, the interesting book of the Italian economist G. Nicosia, the only specific work on the subject known to me. The author aims more at economic theory than at historical reality; but I agree with his statement that Aristophanes grants us '*la visione del momento economico nelle sfere della produzione e del consumo.*' I was unable to see a more recent book by the same author: *Aristofane e il pensiero politico greco* (1939). — In a paper by Y. Urbain, *Les idées économiques d'A.* (*L'Antiquité Class.* 8 (1939), 183ff), the poet is actually represented as engrossed in certain economic theories and laws.

[4] Cf. Urbain, 199: '*La théorie de la valeur développée par cet auteur a été formulée — entre 1830 and 1870.*'

the nature of theoretical economic literature in his day; though this pamphlet is based on some general suppositions, its author was not even aware of the possibility of economic rules and laws, much less of their existence.[1] Nor can we suppose that more scientific works on the subject, now lost, were current, for some traces of them would survive in the works of Aristotle, who wrote so much on *oikonomia*. This is an *argumentum ex silentio*, but by the analogy of political literature it holds good. Moreover, no one familiar with pre-Aristotelian (or even Aristotelian) speculation and science will be surprised by the absence of economic theory. Modern scholars who attribute such theoretical knowledge to Aristophanes argue roughly in this fashion. When the poet states some single fact, or refers to an event, of economic life — for instance, that during the war arms are easier to sell than agricultural tools, and that after the war the position is reversed[2] — he is supposed to allude to a familiar economic law, in this case that of supply and demand. Granted that Aristophanes' judgment on economic facts was sound, and that his view of them frequently agrees with the results of modern theory, this proves nothing more than that he was a shrewd and interested observer of life. Nobody will deny this nor indeed that his interest in economics was characteristic of him and his time.

This is part of the value of Old Comedy as a source of social and economic history, a use to which it has long been put. Even from this point of view, however, the subject has never received full treatment, and many new quotations may be added to those already current. More important is the fact that comedy has not yet been adequately used as a source which unconsciously illustrates social life, and which provides something more than single facts. The picture which in the end it will provide cannot be complete, and, as we have said already, other contemporary sources must and often will be taken into consideration.[3] But they remain subsidiary. They must never be allowed to interfere with our real aim, the re-

---

[1] The book is, however, not Utopian. Many of its ideas are, if not actually practicable, certainly intended to be so. Cf. K. von der Lieck, *Die xenophontische Schrift von den Einkünften*. Diss. Cologne, 1933.

[2] P.1198ff.

[3] The generation of Plato, Demosthenes, and Hypereides lies outside the limits of our period. Cf. next chapter, first section.

creation of the 'atmosphere' which can be found only in
comedy.

Lysias, for example, and others of the earlier orators will
provide many interesting facts of everyday life confirming as
well as supplementing the evidence of comedy. Ps.-Xenophon
and Thucydides are essential witnesses, however different
their attitudes. Xenophon and others have something to add,
as have epigraphic and numismatic sources. But there is
among the subsidiary sources one which probably gives a
deeper insight into the mind of the Athenians than any other
evidence. Tragedy is the chief source for our knowledge of
the intellectual, literary and religious developments of the
fifth century. Although there is no reason for including here
all of it, there is a strong cause for doing so in the case of
Euripides. He was the true contemporary of Old Comedy in
spirit as well as in time. He was one of the main targets for
Aristophanes' wit and scorn, but he was at the same time a
most influential factor in shaping Aristophanes' own mind
and art. The comedian's attitude to men and gods, his technique in inventing intricate plots, his scheme of 'saviours' who
brought rescue and salvation — all this and more was at least
partly a debt to the tragedian who was closest to reality, whose
characters 'speak in human fashion', and whose plays treat the
myth as a human affair.[1]

Comedy, however, will be the leading source, because it can
supply what no other source contains. On this foundation it
is legitimate to build our reconstruction of reality, or at least
such parts of reality as are recoverable by us. Often, it is true,
we may not be able to add much to a picture that was well
known before. Sometimes we may find more and can lay stress
on neglected or overlooked facts; thus we may be able to shed
new light on familiar problems. Sometimes new questions will
be asked, and tentative answers may be given. In a field like
this, the chance of really new and important discoveries is
limited, but the mere fact of a full synthesis, the attempt to

---

[1] F.1058, frg. 3 D: ἀνθρωπικὸς μῦθος. — Since in general we do not aim
at exploring Euripides' own views, but those of his time, we can use utterances
by any of his characters, though the exigencies of the plot have to be taken
into account. It is, on the other hand, because of the very different nature of
Sophokles' poetry and thought that we do not propose to use his plays in any
detail.

build up from innumerable pieces the whole picture, should
be worth while. It will open new vistas and views, although
even the most careful investigation cannot hope to illuminate
everything. We must always bear in mind what the chorus-
leader in the *Peace* tells himself and his audience, and therefore
us, his posthumous audience, also: 'There is a lot we don't
know.'[1]

I hope I have made it clear that this book is not a book on
Aristophanes or on Old Comedy. They are its main sources,
not its subject, although it is impossible to make good use of
any source, and particularly of one so complex as Old Comedy,
without seeing it as an entity of its own, and without judging
its reactions in the light of its own nature. This book is
intended as a contribution to the social and economic history
of Athens, and if our emphasis on comedy causes us to overlook
some facts — none, let us hope, that are essential — this deficiency ought to be more than compensated for by the unity
and uniformity of our main source, and resulting from that,
the greater unity of the picture we are trying to draw.

---

[1] πολλά γ' ἡμᾶς λανθάνει, P.618.

CHAPTER I

OLD COMEDY

It does not lie within the scope of this chapter to give a complete and general characterization of what is called Old Attic Comedy. Questions, for instance, relating to the development of artistic form, or the religious and social antecedents of comedy, though they may arise incidentally, are not fundamentally relevant to our inquiry. The three questions, or groups of questions, with which it is proposed to deal in this chapter, are: (1) The unity of Old Comedy, (2) The poet and his audience, (3) Reality in comedy.

I. THE UNITY OF OLD COMEDY

How far is it legitimate to regard the period of Old Comedy as a coherent period in Greek life and history? Old Comedy began before the middle of the fifth century B.C. with Kratinos and Krates — except for a few predecessors of Kratinos, who remain mere names to us.[1] Its end came with a process of internal change which began towards 400 B.C. So far as we know, no one of the important comic poets of the fifth century produced any play later than about 385. The Alexandrian division into Old and New Comedy, which was based on the recognition of decisive differences of form and content, does not seem to have fixed a definite year as a boundary between the two kinds of comedy. It was the later grammarians who, in distinguishing a Middle Comedy, limited it to the period from 404 to 338 (or 336), thus including the two latest extant plays of Aristophanes. These dates are indeed landmarks of political history, but in dealing with comedy we cannot accept the division without reservations. There can be no doubt about the gradual change in comedy after 404, but it is too rigid and artificial to separate from the earlier period the later works of such poets as Aristophanes and Platon, the bulk of whose works belongs to Old Comedy, both in date and character. In general, the whole question of these lines of demarcation, which are in fact zones of demarcation, is of little importance.

[1] The few extant fragments are in part not genuine. Cf. Geissler, 16.

It may be remarked, however, that Antiphanes, the first poet who certainly belonged to Middle Comedy, produced his first play about 387, while the latest poets of Old Comedy, such as Strattis and Theopompos, began writing about 410, so that, with no gap in production, there was yet a clear distinction between two generations.[1] For our purpose, at any rate, it is proposed to regard the period of Old Comedy as covering the years 455-385, and as a period, though not usually so regarded, of a real and demonstrable unity.

At first sight, the history of Athens in those years is not easily conceived as a unity. The period begins with the conclusion of the Persian Wars, and the temporary conclusion of the wars between the Greek States; at its very start stands the removal of the treasury of the Confederacy from Delos to Athens. All this made possible the fifteen peaceful and powerful years of the Periclean Age. Those years were followed by the great war and the collapse of Athens. Then began the struggle which is typical of the fourth century: the varying rivalry of the Greek States, and their varying dependence on foreign powers. But up to 387, this dependence had not yet been formulated in strict and binding terms, and the great influence of Persia on affairs in Greece in the decade following 403 was not dissimilar in character to that of the preceding ten years. The position was finally stabilized by the 'King's Peace', by which Persia guaranteed the autonomy of the Greek States; in a sense, that year 387 was the end of one chapter of history and the beginning of a new one.

The events of the whole of this period of seventy years may be seen as the changing aspect of one picture, the picture of the State and people of Athens, and of her empire. The changes, it is true, were profound, and the year 404-3 stands as a landmark in the process of decline and subversion. It is understandable that many scholars believe that the interruption by the *débacle* of the lost war was more important than all traces of possible continuity. The dualism of the fifth century had broken down and with it the relative balance of power within the Greek world. However, the end of a war is not necessarily the end of an epoch. The results of the war, its aftermath, can be considered as belonging to a period of transition. To the very end, the Athens of the Peloponnesian War had been,

[1] See the Chronological Table, p. 374ff.

in a sense, the Athens of Perikles and the Aegean realm. The Athens of Thrasyboulos and Konon showed altered features, but, in a quick and most impressive political recovery, it was concerned to re-create the great traditions of the past; and, further, the events of this period were closely and inevitably connected with those of the last years of the war. The many law-suits which arose out of the events of 411 and 403 are one typical symptom of this fact.

It we turn from the political history of those seventy years to literature and art, which best express the spirit of the age, we have a similar, though somewhat different picture. Aischylos died in 456-5. Sophokles had by then won several victories, but his greatest plays were still to come. Euripides, in 455, produced a play for the first time, so far as we know. Both died in 406, and tragedy survived only in a weak and negligible form. In the spheres of both politics and tragedy, there is a profound parallelism in development. The deeper significance, however, of these dates in the history of literature is brought out by other facts. Soon after 450 Protagoras, and, about the same time, Anaxagoras, had come to Athens, and with them philosophy invaded Athens.[1] Perikles formed his circle of friends in which a new spirit was incarnate. The sophists coined a new type of thought, creed and speech, which, in the succeeding generation, developed into ethical radicalism. This 'age of enlightenment' created the great intellectual experience which culminated in Sokrates. Herodotos, who, about 450, was occupied with his journeys and the writing of some of his *Logoi*, was already influenced by the new spirit; Thucydides was permeated by it. Contemporary with the great war, and its historian, he probably died a few years after 399, the year in which Sokrates was put to death. Sokrates himself represents a turning-point. His pupils, each in his different way, founded on his thought and life as well as on the work of the sophists a new epoch in the development of the human mind.

The parallelism in the development of architecture and art is evident. The building of the Parthenon began in 447, but the work of preparing for it must have been going on for several years. In 437 the Propylaea were begun. The Parthenon was almost finished in 432; the Propylaea remained a

---

[1] J. S. Morrison dates Protagoras' first arrival in Athens between 460 and 454, but his reasons are not fully convincing (*Cl. Q.* XXXV, 1941, 5).

torso, though only because the original plan was reduced for ritual and religious reasons. During the war the Erechtheion was being built. From the most perfect example of Doric architecture the buildings of the Acropolis had proceeded first to the harmonious union of Doric severity and Ionian lightness, and then to the Maidens' Porch, which, though perfect in its own way, must be regarded as decoration rather than pure architecture. In this process of architectural development, a certain internal dissolution is obvious, though one which certainly does not involve decline. The Long Walls and those of the Peiraeus, after their demolition in 403, were rebuilt in the 'nineties, and afterwards much activity was shown in building. But its purpose and its significance were altered, and a decisive part was now played by private architecture. Sculpture meanwhile went through the development from Pheidias to Praxiteles. These names stand out at each end of a process of change which can be best illustrated by the manner in which the gods were represented. Whereas the statues of Pheidias embodied Olympian majesty and power, the Parthenon frieze already shows the gods, though taller than men, sitting at their ease among human beings. With Praxiteles they became an image of human perfection and perfect humanity. 'Man is the measure of everything.'

What is the significance of these familiar dates and facts in the sphere of intellectual and artistic development? Above all, they prove the continuity in change. They prove that the break of 404 was not a complete break, that indeed in all the change a great tradition lived on, and that the early fourth century, though it opened new roads, was also a fading away of previous times. The dates and facts, however, prove something more. In the same decades in which Athens fought the fight for her empire, and finally for her existence, she experienced the great break which destroyed Attic Tragedy, and created Attic Philosophy. This means, in fact, that the operation of one general process united the years we have fixed as the life-time of Old Comedy. Individualism and rationalism conquered man and State, and it is the dynamic experience of this process which gave to the age its most exciting features. With all its changes, the age of Old Comedy was a unity, and neither political history nor the developments of literature, art and thought prevent us from accepting this unity.

Does the internal development of comedy correspond to the external situation? Here, too, the break of 404 may be considered of the same importance as in the general process we have been discussing. But there were more than two generations of comic poets, and also different types of comedy. Is it permissible to regard the whole as a single unit? Apart from the eleven plays of Aristophanes, which are preserved, we have nothing but fragments. In a few instances they are enough for some kind of reconstruction of the plot, or at least of parts of it, in most cases they are isolated passages; so that our knowledge of Old Comedy is only fragmentary, and we have to rely in part on the views of ancient writers who had access to many of the plays now lost. We learn, for instance, that the work of some of the comedians, or at least that some of the comedies, lacked the political character which is so strong in most of Aristophanes' plays. Krates appears to have been the creator of a form of comedy which was mainly concerned with private life or with fairy tales. Pherekrates and a few others followed him in this. But according to ancient tradition Old Comedy was dominated by the three great political poets: Kratinos, Eupolis and Aristophanes.[1] The works of theirs of which the dates can be fixed were written during the periods from 455 to 423, 430 to 411, and 427 to 386, respectively, so that they cover the whole period of Old Comedy. Like these three most of the other comic poets wrote political plays full of personal invective and aggressive satire. The lists of the victors in comedy, incomplete though they are, show clearly that this kind of comedy was far more popular with the Athenian public than the mild and sober fun of Krates and his like. If everything extant is taken into account, and also the fact that the eleven comedies of Aristophanes bear witness to an astonishing versatility in one poet, it will be seen that almost all possibilities are, if not exhausted, at least touched on. In spite of the fragmentary character of what is preserved we are entitled to assume that we know Old Comedy as a whole.

It is, therefore, unnecessary to stress the variety of the poets,

[1] Cf. Horace, *sat.* I, 4, 1; Quintil. X, 1, 65f. The triad of comedians was probably formed by analogy with the tragic triad. But the idea will have been right, as will also the generally accepted view that Aristophanes was the greatest of all the comedians. However, we cannot make comparisons as long as we have no complete play of either Kratinos or Eupolis.

though the chronology must certainly not be neglected. The table at the end of this book shows the general distribution of the comedies and other sources. Two important points, among other things, emerge from this table: the overlapping of the three (or more accurately: two and a half) generations of comic poets, and the fact that the bulk of our material belongs to the years after 431. In some cases, it is true, the date of a fragment is essential for our conclusions. But there was a strong traditional element in the development of Old Comedy, and the facts at our disposal justify us in assuming that the developments of all its seventy years are adequately represented by Aristophanes' working life.

Our subject is the forms of social life, in which the process of change operates much more slowly than in political history. The effects of war and defeat, the social transformation of political leadership, and other changes, are to be observed; but it will be seen that the great outlines remain constant. The relative position of agriculture and trade, for instance, was not quite the same in 400 as in 450, but this does not imply a change of fundamental importance, and the same is true in many other cases. On the other hand, the all-embracing process of change, which was the specific sign of the age, and which culminated in the break of 404, was inevitably reflected in all the individual phenomena of social life. It must be left to detailed treatment to prove that our line of reasoning and interpretation is not forced upon the facts. Naturally, we do not assume that the social life of Athens underwent no change in the course of seventy years, but there are surely many aspects of it where the change was very slight, and we shall not seek to demonstrate the contrary if the evidence of our sources points to a certain general uniformity.

2. THE POET AND HIS AUDIENCE

Every performance of a comedy in Athens was based on a number of social facts.[1]   The poets of Old Comedy were Athenian citizens.[2]   Practically nothing is known of their social

[1] Cf. in general the book of Haigh, which in many sections is not yet out of date.

[2] It is a mistake to assume that Aristophanes was a metic (so, e.g., after others, van Leeuwen). His relation to Aigina (A.653f and schol.) is not to be interpreted in this sense. Cf. Coulon, *Introduction*, p. IIIf. Wilamowitz, 40.

standing, but, as far as we know, none of them belonged to the nobility. On the other hand, from the fact that Euripides alone, and none of the comic poets, was derided because of his alleged low origin, we may assume that none, or at least none of the better known comic poets, came from the lower classes.[1] How far we can generalize when a poet's poverty is mentioned, is less certain. At least one of the comic writers was compelled by poverty to sell some of his comedies to rich people who performed them as their own.[2] Aristophanes, who had an estate in Aigina and left the production of some of his plays to others who thus received the remuneration for a victory, must have been well off.[3] Other evidence points to other than comic poets. A bad tragedian like Sthenelos is frequently derided on account of his great poverty.[4] Kinesias, on the other hand, a poet of lyric choruses, declares that he is much sought after by the tribes.[5] That is, of course, a boast; but as a rule it seems quite possible that many popular poets made a good deal of money. A somewhat obscure statement informs us that Simonides and even Sophokles were very eager to make money by their poems.[6] The poets who took part in the tragic or comic *agon* received public remuneration, but we have no idea of the amount, though it was certainly in proportion to the poet's place in the result of the *agon*.[7]

A poet who intended to produce one of his plays, had to ask for a chorus to be assigned to him, and the task of assigning choruses was the function of the chief archon for the Dionysia, of the *archon basileus* for the Lenaia.[8] It might happen that a

Norwood, 202. When Eupolis (357) turns to the audience and complains that 'foreign poets' are preferred, this has the same value as the occasional accusation by a comedian that Phrynichos was a foreigner (schol. F. 13). One poet of parodies, Hegemon of Thasos, seems the exception to the rule; later, in the time of Middle Comedy, the poets included several non-Athenians. Among the tragedians there were some foreigners, such as Ion from Chios and Achaios from Eretria.

[1] Euripides' mother a greengrocer: A.478, K.19, Th.387, F.840, cf. adesp. 16.

[2] Plat. 99.

[3] In the case of his first plays, the reasons were different — partly the poet's youth and partly political fear. See below, p. 25f.

[4] W.313, frg. 151, Plat. 128.   [5] B.1403f.

[6] P.697ff. But cf. T. B. L. Webster, *Introduction to Sophocles*, 12.

[7] F.367; cf. schol. E.102, and in general, R. C. Flickinger, *The Greek Theater and its Drama* (1936⁴), 268f.

[8] K.513, F.94, Kratinos 15. — Aristotle, *Ath. pol.* 56, 3. 57,1.

good poet went away empty-handed, while some obscure bung-
ler was awarded the chorus; but generally, under the control
of public opinion, the better poets were chosen, and the
'chatterboxes', the 'degraders of their art', only got a chorus
once in their lives.[1] The payment of the chorus, which always
consisted of citizens, as well as the total cost of the equipment
of the play and the festive meal which followed the performance,
was the responsibility of the choregus; only the actors were
chosen and paid by the archon, that is the State.[2] The duty of
the choregus was not confined to the mere payment of money,
but involved weeks of painstaking preparation and care.[3] This,
however, the choregus left for the most part to the poet and his
helpers. Even a choregus who was always victorious did not
necessarily understand anything about the technique of the
musical part or of producing a play. There were good and bad
choregi. 'Have you ever seen a choregus meaner than him?'[4]
The chorus might have to wear dirty rags and get poor food.[5]
A dinner after the performance was due to the members of
the chorus: 'The meat of the grouse is best to eat after a victory
on the stage.'[6] When the chorus of the initiates in the *Frogs*
are satisfied with the breakfast they have had, this refers to the
men of the chorus rather than to the Athenian procession to
Eleusis.[7] It is well known that the choregy was one of the
liturgies which were undertaken as a kind of moral obligation,
and at the same time regarded as an honour by wealthy men;
it was open at the Dionysia to citizens only, at the Lenaia to
metics also.[8] As a rule, however, a comic choregy was far
cheaper than that of a tragedy. Naturally, the costumes of the
chorus were simpler, and the artistic task was probably less
difficult, though the comic chorus in its own way would aim

[1] Kratinos 15. — P.801ff, F.92ff.

[2] A.886ff, 1154ff. — Strattis 1. This practice was probably introduced about
the middle of the century; cf. K. Schneider, *P.-W.* III A, 506. Later there was
also an *agon* of comic actors at the Χύτροι, the last day of the Anthesteria, and
this contest was used to select actors for the Great Dionysia (Plut. *vitae decem
orat.* 841 F, *IG.*[2] II/III 2325, p. 675a; cf. Haigh, 31).

[3] Antiphon VI, 11ff, cf. frg. 115, Plat. 213, which may refer to a large house
in which rehearsals took place.

[4] Eupolis 306; cf. Isaios V, 36.   [5] frg. 253, Pherekr. 185, Kallias 21.

[6] A.1154ff, frg. 433.

[7] F.376.   [8] Schol. Pl.953, cf. Lysias XII, 20.

at equal perfection and the comedians claimed that they had
to solve more difficult problems than the tragedians.[1] Great
statesmen were proud of being victorious with a chorus. But
gradually the liturgies became a heavy and unwelcome burden
to the rich, and a source of income to at least part of the people.[2]
The chorus, not the actors, not even the plot, was of chief
importance (see Plate II). The expressions 'to perform a
tragedy' and 'to dance a chorus' could be synonymous, and
the dramatic competition could take its name from the *thymele*,
the altar around which the chorus danced.[3] Athens needed
the poet, says Dionysos when he has descended to Hades, in
order that the city, saved by the poet, 'might maintain her
choruses'.[4] When the chorus declined and eventually became
a merely incidental feature of the play, the connection between
comedy and the people became increasingly weaker. 'The
chorus was suited to the Agora, but not to the fireside.'[5] The
comic mask, 'the comic bogey', is a symbol of comedy, and it
is significant that such masks — both tragic and comic — were
hung in the temple of Dionysos.[6] 'The man is dancing, and
all is well with the god.'[7] Not the 'theatre', but the cult made
the performance possible, and gave it meaning.

The poet was the *chorodidaskalos*, the teacher and trainer of
the chorus; the 'comic poet' was the 'comedy teacher', and in
this quality the true servant of the Muses, just like the 'tragedy
teacher'.[8] This means that he himself wrote the words and

---

[1] See below, p. 37.

[2] Ps.-Xen. I, 13. Later, probably for a number of years from 406-5 onwards,
the choregy was divided between two men (συγχορηγία), until the declining
importance of the chorus reduced the expenses; perhaps the general economic
situation had also improved to such an extent that the liturgy of single choregi
could be restored (about 394), and even the number of comedies performed at
one festival increased from three to the traditional number of five (in 388). Cf.
K. J. Maidment, *Cl. Q.* XXIX (1935), 1ff.

[3] frg. 873, adesp. 57.   [4] F.1419.

[5] Maidment, 8.   [6] frg. 31, 131.

[7] Phryn. 9. In reading the words: ἀνήρ χορεύει καὶ τὰ τοῦ θεοῦ καλά we
remember the famous chorus in Sophokles' *Oedipus Rex* (895ff): . . . τί δεῖ με
χορεύειν; . . . ἔρρει τὰ θεῖα, also *Aiax* 701: νῦν γὰρ ἐμοὶ μέλει χορεῦσαι, and
Eur. *Kykl.* 156. Lobeck (*v.* Kock) compared the Latin proverb: *saltat senex,
salva res est.* That, of course, would give a much more profane meaning to the
words. Mr. Edmonds even takes τὰ τοῦ θεοῦ as 'the weather', and compares
Theophr. *char.* 25, 2 (cf. also P.1141). The fragment seems to be too small to
make any one of these interpretations certain.

[8] A.628f, P.734, 737, B.912f, Th.88.

rehearsed the music and the dancing of the chorus. There was a special kind of dance for every chorus, appropriate to the character it represented in the play, and there were different melodies suited to the various songs, for example, the exit song of the chorus.[1] Thespis and Aischylos are said to have themselves planned the figures of the dances for their choruses; indeed, the drunken old man in the *Wasps* actually challenges the tragic poets to a competition in dancing, and the Muse is warned not to admit certain bad tragedians who were equally bad dancers.[2] The rehearsal of a chorus asked for an almost military discipline,[3] but even so it cannot always have been simple to teach the men who formed the chorus to sing and dance correctly. Some of them may not have been very musical, and it is doubtful whether the wine always had, as the poet hopes, the necessary effect.[4] Sometimes there was considerable strain between poet and chorus; certain tragedians are said to have been hated by the choruses, and Kinesias was called 'the chorus-killer'.[5] The poet was content if the chorus fulfilled their task sufficiently well.[6] Sometimes the poet himself was his own chief actor, and at least he instructed the actors.[7] These, and perhaps the musicians also, though citizens, were more or less professionals.[8] But the poet was composer, dance-master, producer, probably also the technical manager who gave his orders to the technician about the working of the various stage-devices such as the *ekkyklema*, which occasionally went wrong.[9] Thus, the task and the responsibility of the poet were immense. We can understand that Aristophanes did not produce his first plays, his 'maiden's children', himself.[10] Being very young, he

---

[1] F.1028f, frg. 678-9, Plat. 130.—ἐξόδιοι νόμοι, Kratinos 276.

[2] W.1479, frg. 677. — W.1480f. — P.781ff, cf. W.1497ff.

[3] Xen. *mem.* III, 5, 18. [4] adesp. 468.

[5] K.400f, Kallias 13. — ὁ χοροκτόνος, Strattis 15.

[6] The word is μετρίως, and used as it is by the chorus when leaving the stage at the end of the play (C.1510, Th.1227), it may refer to the extent rather than the quality of the singing and dancing.

[7] Cf. Anonymus, Kaibel, *Com. Gr. Frg.*, p. 7f. For the early tragedians see Aristotle, *rhet.* 1403b, 23.

[8] W.1275ff. There are only very few suggestions in Old Comedy of the growing importance of the actors; the most significant is the mere fact of an *agon* of the protagonists, which was introduced during our period (cf. Schneider, *P.-W.* III A, 500ff). For the later development cf. in general H. Bulle, *Festschrift für J. Loeb* (1930), 5ff.

[9] P.174, Th.265, adesp. 750. [10] A.628f, K.512ff, C.529ff.

did not feel equal to the task. But he also employed a special
'producer' on some later occasions.[1]

In addition to these general tasks, there was the special
situation of the political poet. He had to keep in touch with
the most recent events, and therefore frequently added to his
text and made alterations up to the time of the performance.[2]
At the same time, there were particular dangers which a
political poet had to fear. Young Aristophanes had a taste
of them himself, when Kleon, a year after the punishment
of Mytilene, brought him before the council on a charge of
slandering the State in the presence of allies and other
foreigners. 'I do not say *the State*', he therefore emphasized in
the next year.[3] A year later he attacked Kleon in the strongest
and sharpest possible terms, with Kleon himself listening, no
doubt, from the front row, for he had the right of *prohedria*
since his success at Pylos the year before.[4] The same play, the
Knights, introduced the Demos, led by Kleon, as an old doddering blockhead. We are told that the Athenians would not
tolerate the deriding and slandering of the demos, but encouraged caricatures of individuals. The exact meaning of this
passage is much disputed and uncertain.[5] At any rate, it is

---

[1] Cf. A. Körte, *P.-W.* XI, 1330ff. In such a case, the 'teacher of the chorus'
was mentioned in the official records (ἐδίδασκε ὁ δεῖνα), while the poet's name
appears in the list of the victors which served mainly literary interest.

[2] Cf. A. Ruppel, *Konzeption und Ausführung der aristoph. Komödie*, Diss.
Giessen, 1913, *passim*.

[3] A.377ff, 502ff. — 515f.

[4] K.702, cf. 573ff.

[5] Ps.-Xen. II, 18. Cf. E. Kalinka, *Die pseudoxenophontische Schrift etc.* 7ff.
K. I. Gelzer, *Die Schrift vom Staate der Athener* (*Hermes, Einzelschr.* 3), 71f,
128f. The discussion is about the date and the nature of several 'laws' against
comedy. I cannot go into detail, but I wish to emphasize that Prof. Wade-Gery
has made a suggestion which may be the decisive step towards a solution of the
intricate question, namely that Ps.-Xen. II, 18 is not speaking of a law at all, but
simply defining actual practice. It is most remarkable that nobody (the present
writer included) realized before that the words of the text are not more than a
statement about general tendencies, a statement which was contradicted (perhaps
deliberately) by the *Knights*. Wade-Gery's view is more convincing, because
it is more comprehensive, than the opinion expressed by Kalinka and others
(cf. the discussion by Meder, 21ff), who take Ps.-Xenophon's statement to refer
only to Kleon's action after the performance of the *Babylonians*, 'ein einzelner
Fall, dessen typischer Charakter zu einem allgemeinen Urteil zu berechtigen
schien'. Both interpretations are in full harmony with what I say about the
relations between the poet and his audience. Ps.-Xenophon exemplifies once

important to note that the remarkable comic licence could have its limits.[1] It is somewhat surprising that Perikles seems to have been the first to introduce a kind of censorship; this happened during the dangerous revolt of Samos in 440, and the law remained in force for three years.[2] About the year 415, a similar attempt was made by one Syrakosios, though its operation is obscure.[3] On the other hand, Kleon's treatment of Aristophanes proves that a single citizen or member of the council had the means of bringing before the judges a comedian who is supposed to have offended public interests. Yet such incidents must not conceal the fact that what was really unique was not the occasional limitation and risk, but the unheard-of liberty of comedy. In no other place or age were men of all classes attacked and ridiculed in public and by name with such freedom as in Old Attic Comedy. The ultimate reason for this, apart from the magnanimity and the sense of humour which were inherent in the Attic character, was the fact that comedy was an internal affair of the sovereign people as a whole, and so there was complete *parrhesia*, freedom of speech. Kleon was therefore justified in calling attention, in his denunciation, to the presence of foreigners.

In a Greek Polis no citizen can be said to have been a private person; this is particularly obvious of the dramatic poet. He was a citizen who, together with a number of his fellow-citizens, presented a play to some thousands of people in the audience who also were for the most part citizens. Furthermore, in an *agon*, a contest with other poets in a single day's performance, he submitted himself to the judgment of his audience and a few specially chosen judges. In a preliminary ceremony, the so-called *proagon*, the chorus and the actors, the choregus and the poet had appeared on the stage of the Odeion; in this way, they were introduced to the people. Although our casual sources which refer to the *proagon* deal only with tragedy, it is possible that lyric choruses as well as

again the intense and active interest the spectators took in the plays. A similar view to Wade-Gery's is also expressed by H. Frisch, *The Constitution of the Athenians* (1942), 279.

[1] Cf. Körte, 1233ff, also the summary in Geissler, 17.
[2] Schol. A.67.
[3] Phryn. 26, cf. Eupolis 207. C. Jensen, *Abh. Preuss. Ak.* 1939, No. 14, 12f, finds an allusion to the law of Syrakosios (used by Kleophon) in Eupolis 40 P, 27ff.

comedies took part in it.[1] The relation of poet, chorus and actors to the audience was the same for all these kinds of poetry, but tragedy and in most cases also the choral lyric were too remote in their mythical themes to allow the situation to be expressed in words. It was the privilege of the comedian to make it clear that there were no barriers and no imaginary curtain between stage and audience. Citizens they were on both sides, united and linked together in space and spirit. Comedy is seen to be a social phenomenon, and so to demonstrate most plainly the social character of the Greek theatre.

The audience was the Athenian people, the same people who formed the assembly. There may have been a difference of theatrical technique and plot between the plays performed at the Dionysia and those at the Lenaea; but the audience will substantially have been the same.[1a] There were, at the Dionysia at least, foreigners in the audience, allies, ambassadors, and metics; but these few hundreds were unimportant, compared with the many thousands of Athenian citizens.[2] 'I don't fear

---

[1] Aristophanes wrote a comedy *Proagon* (frg. 461ff). The only other possible allusion in comedy is in A.9ff. In both cases it is a tragedy that is referred to. In general cf. E. Rohde, *Kleine Schriften*, II, 381ff, Haigh, 67. The whole thing was hardly more than an act of presentation and introduction, which included even the poet. Our main source (schol. Aeschin III, 67) speaks of an ἐπίδειξις. The scene in Plat. *Symp.* 194B does probably not refer to the *proagon* (P. W. Harsh, *Cl. Phil.* XLIV, 1949, 116f).

[1a] Cf. C. F. Russo, *Rendic. Acc. di Lincei*, (1956), 14ff.

[2] Boys, the citizens of the future, were naturally included in the audience (C.539, P.50, 766, Eupolis 244); cf. A. A. Bryant, *Boyhood and Youth in the Days of Aristophanes* (*Harvard Studies*, XVIII, 1907), 96ff. The question whether women were present at the performances of both tragedies and comedies is much disputed. The joke of P.966 does not prove anything. Plat. *Gorg.* 502d, where not only women, but also slaves are included, hints at a general ῥητορική of which tragedy is only part. Haigh, 323ff, by collecting all the available material, tries hard to prove the presence of women, and so does Kitto, *The Greeks, 233* — unsuccessfully, as I feel. The contrary cannot be finally proved either, but the long address to all sorts of spectators (P.50ff) lends at least some support to this view: the slave wants to tell the story to boys and lads and men, also to the great and greatest men; there is no mention of women, though it may be that it would have spoiled the intention to enumerate men 'in an ascending scale of manliness'. Other passages of comedy, however, strongly suggest that only men were in the theatre (P.965, B.793ff, L.1044,Th.395ff, E.165ff, 435ff, 1144ff). However, even if this view be right, as I believe, the whole question must not be regarded from a moralistic point of view. There was no prudishness in Athens, at any rate not before the Hellenistic

you', says Kleon to the sausage-seller and the knights, 'as long
as the council is alive, and the figure of Demos smiles, sitting on
the benches.'[1]   Kleon means the assembly and perhaps the
courts, but he hints at the audience.   Even if some people preferred, as they undoubtedly did, the sphere of politics, while
others found the excitements of tragedy and comedy more to
their liking, the general composition of assembly and theatre
was the same.   In many ways the playwright, in particular the
comedian, worked upon the minds of the people by means
similar to those used by the orator in the assembly.[2]

The gap between the play on the stage or in the orchestra
and the public is bridged by many utterances.   Each year,
there came 'to the art', that is to see the play, that multitude,
the number of which — like 'the sand of the sea' — is given as
'numberless myriads', or as 13,000; this, though not of course
exact, is not without significance.[3]   Tragedy and comedy were
the concern of the whole people, and part of their common experience.   Quite often the dialogue or the song of the chorus
alludes in some way to the audience who are thus drawn into
the action of the play.   Reference to outstanding examples will
make this clear.   Sometimes a situation is directly explained to
the audience to enable them to understand it; or 'a pert young
witling' will put questions with regard to the play which may
be answered by a neighbour; or the spectators are asked to
guess what they do not know, though they usually guess
wrong.[4]   Or on the other hand, the public is represented as the
cleverer party, as an 'assembly of all-wise old men', whose
judgment is decisive, who know better 'whilst all the chorus

Age, and I doubt whether Mme Staël was right when she thought that the
obscenity of Old Comedy was due to the fact that no women were in the audience
(cf. W. Süss, *Aristophanes u. die Nachwelt*, 100) [See Addendum, p. 418].

[1] K.395f.

[2] Much evidence for this — though not all valid — can be found in A. Burckhardt, *Spuren der athen. Volksrede in der alten Komödie*, Diss. Basel, 1924.

[3] Kratinos 23, Eupolis 286. — W.1010. Pl.1082f. Here I read (with Coulon,
after Rutherford and Willems): ὑπὸ μυρίων τε τῶνδε καὶ τρισχιλίων. The
MSS. have ἐτῶν τε (or γε). Neither ἐτῶν nor ἔτων makes sense. There is a
certain difficulty in reading 'by these ten thousand and by three thousand (more)'.
But is it too bold to assume that this is a facetious way of expressing the large
number — usually expressed by μύριοι alone — of those 'whose sport the old hag
has been'?   In W.1391 we have a similar use of two numbers forming a high
total.

[4] W.54ff, P.50ff, B.30, E.583. Plat. 167. — P.43ff. — W.71ff, 85.

PLATE II

a

b

c

COMIC CHORUSES

PLATE III

TYPES OF OLD COMEDY

stand like idiots by'.[1] Euripides can be blamed for dealing
with 'scenes of common life' which the audience knew
something about; a comedian would never be blamed for
this.[2]

The connection becomes even closer, when 'the house' is
given a part in the play.[3] They are told to sing hymns at some
good news from the stage, or an old hag complains that she is
being abused 'in front of so many men'.[4] 'You see', the chorus
asks the sausage-seller, 'those people on the benches? — I do —
You shall be overlord of all those people.'[5] When the goddess
of Peace appears, one can guess from the faces of the spectators
their different vocations — whether they have gained or lost by
the war.[6] But the goddess will not speak one word to the
audience; 'they have wronged her far too much for that', so
that Hermes addresses the people, communicating her questions and complaints.[7] The Just and the Unjust Logos wish
to fight their *agon* in front of the many spectators.[8] In another
contest one party is asked to gather all his rhetorical force and
to 'move the theatre'.[9]

It is, of course, a favourite joke to abuse the public, the 'sink
of spectators'.[10] As a rule this is done in so general a way (all
of them, for instance, are parricides and perjurers), that the
joke could only be laughed at, even if it was not particularly
funny.[11] Of an old hag we are told that she 'has been the sport
of these thirteen thousand'.[12] In a long list of more or less
deformed people the poet seems to be picking out individual
spectators.[13] Sometimes real criticism was pronounced. 'I
know these fellows, voting in hot haste, and straight ignoring
the decree they've passed.'[14] In their capacity as audience, the
people might be offered either criticism or flattery. The statement that the spectators detest hearing or seeing again what

---

[1] Plat. 90. — K.1210, F.1475, E.580ff. — A.440ff. It is mere nonsense that
the chorus of the *Acharnians* will not recognize Dikaiopolis, when he returns
disguised as a beggar. This seems to be a reference, once again, to Euripides'
Telephos.

[2] F.959ff.   [3] τὸ θέατρον, K.233.   [4] K.1316ff. — Pl.1061.
[5] K.163f.   [6] P.543ff.   [7] P.657ff, 664ff.
[8] C.889ff.   [9] adesp. 3 D.   [10] Kratinos 347.
[11] F.274ff; cf. C.1096ff, 1201ff, P.821ff, 877, F.783, E.440, Pl.98f.
[12] Pl.1082f. Cf. above, p. 28, note 3.
[13] Eupolis 276. I owe the explanation of this fragment to Mr. Edmonds.
[14] E.797f.

has been said or done before, and want the poet 'to make haste', is a criticism directed against some fellow-comedians rather than against the audience;[1] but when a young girl is fond of her singing, because it is amusing and pleasant, though the listeners are bored, then the hit is probably directed at them.[2] Kratinos shows a charming irony in the lines: 'Hail, ye throngs that laugh not at once, but the next day, the world's best judges of my art! Your mothers bore you to happiness as the thunder of the tiers.'[3] Another poet considers it shameful that the beauty of a play should be judged by the applause of the mob.[4] Pronouncements on the sagacity of the audience, who could be called insane and who, of course, were sagacious only as long as they applauded the poet,[5] culminate in the description of the 'clever spectator' as one who is 'over-subtle, on the look-out for sententious phrases', and as one who 'euripid-aristo-phanizes'.[6]

All this reappears in an even more striking, though often conventional, manner when the audience is accosted directly, which can equally happen in the course of the dialogue, in the *parabasis* or in a song of the chorus. Frequently the audience is exhorted to listen carefully.[7] The spectators are asked the most varied questions; for instance, whether they like the characters represented on the stage, whether they would share 'with the birds a life of pleasure', or whether they can produce for the slave who feeds the dung-beetle a nose with no nostrils.[8] The chorus exhorts the audience to cherish any poet who brings some new saying or device in his plays.[9] An invitation, though hardly a serious one, to participate in the common feast is a

---

[1] E.580ff.   [2] E.888f.

[3] Kratinos 323. The translation partly follows that of Norwood who, however, seems to be mistaken on two difficult points. I cannot discuss the fragment here at full length, nor do I claim that my translation does full justice to all its obscurities. I wish to add the prose translation of Mr. Edmonds which contains an interesting suggestion, as regards the personage addressed: 'Thou, tumult, that laughest at nothing and then after the event, soundest of all critics of our poetic art, thy mother bore thee happy, thou noise of the benches.'

[4] adesp. 518.

[5] K.228, 233, C.518ff, F.676ff, 1109ff. — Kratinos 329, W.1013.

[6] Kratinos 307.

[7] προσέχετε τὸν νοῦν: K.503, 1014, C.575, 1122, W.1015, B.688, Th.381, Kratinos 198, Pherekr. 79, Eupolis 37, etc.

[8] K.36ff; B.753f; P.20, also 150ff.

[9] W.1051ff.

favourite form of address to the audience.[1] An actor's mistake is mentioned with the remark 'if you still remember'.[2] There is a real unity between 'spectators and actors and choruses'.[3]

The most striking example of direct apostrophe of this type is the great speech of Dikaiopolis, in which he informs the people about the situation and at the same time criticizes them sharply.[4] Dikaiopolis, the Attic peasant, claims the right to criticize in this manner, 'although he is presenting a comedy; for even comedy can tell the truth'.[5] Here the poet is clearly speaking in his own character. Like the tragedian, Aristophanes regards himself as entitled to speak 'about the State' and to criticize. It is true that the passage which follows, in which he speaks of the causes of the war, is ridiculous and, to some extent, mere comic distortion; but that a serious attack on politics and serious criticism are intended is evident. In particular, the lightheartedness with which the Athenians seized every opportunity for going to war with Sparta was the subject of bitter irony.[6] On the other hand, Dikaiopolis had staked his head on his ability to convince the people of the justice of the cause of peace by telling them unpleasant truths.[7] When finally the warlike chorus is won over to the side of peace, the poet perhaps hoped that he had convinced the greater part of his audience as well.

Another special privilege of comedy is its ability to allude to current events. There was little point in introducing them except for the purpose of making in the end the audience think as well as laugh. The lament that it was beyond comedy to heal so old a disease of the Polis as the foolish passion for serving on juries shows that tasks of this kind were thought to be at least one of the final aims of the comic poets, even if their fulfilment was obviously beyond their power.[8] Comedy became a platform on which political men and events were not only derided, but also discussed.[9] No doubt, the 'rolling sea' of the audience took part in this debate by cheering and hissing, by laughing and interrupting, often indeed in a very rude

[1] P.1115, 1358f, E.1140ff.
[2] E.22.   [3] Th.391.   [4] A.496ff.
[5] A.499f: τὸ γὰρ δίκαιον οἶδε καὶ τρυγῳδία.
[6] A.541ff.   [7] A.317f.   [8] W.650f.
[9] Cf., e.g., Pherekr. 47. — This is something different from the view refuted p. 8, note 3.

manner.[1] The appeal of the comic poet to the people continually found new and surprising expression, but his jests
and his harshest satire sprang from a profound affection and
concern for their welfare.

An outward sign of Old Comedy, although one not altogether indispensable, is the *parabasis*, which had developed
from the original *komos* and had become the centre of the play.
The chorus 'came forward' or 'turned aside' — hence the name
parabasis[2] — and addressed the audience, usually in the name
of the poet. It is not our intention to discuss in detail the
various parts of comedy. To us each single comedy, like Old
Comedy as a whole, is a literary unit, even though composed
of the most different elements. The *parabasis*, however, deserves special mention, because it furnishes the clearest evidence for the relations between the poet and his public.

The *parabasis* is a rather complicated compound of various
sections, partly recitative and partly song. Within the lifetime
of Aristophanes it went through a process of gradual decay,
until it disappeared entirely. The problems of this development do not concern us;[3] but it is of fundamental importance
to realize that the 'anapaests' as well as the *epirrhema*, 'the core
of the *parabasis*', contain a direct address to the audience, in
which either the chorus or, through their voices, the poet
speaks to the people. The address is frequently introduced by
an exhortation to pay attention.[4] An early and also a rather late
play of Aristophanes lay the same stress on the idea which
underlies the *parabasis*. In the *Acharnians* the poet for the first
time speaks openly for himself.[5] He prides himself on having

[1] adesp. 864. — Cf. Haigh, 343f.
[2] A.629, K.508, P.735, Th.785.
[3] F. M. Cornford, *The Origin of Attic Comedy* (1914), 122ff, maintains that
the *parabasis* of the Lysistrate, which contains no anapaests and is divided between
two choruses, represents the original type. If so, it remains to explain why
Aristophanes neglected the original form in all his earlier plays. Actually the male
and the female choruses are the natural and necessary outcome of the plot, and
this is probably also the reason why there are no anapaests. It was not possible to
have a single chorus-leader speaking for the poet, at least not till after the reconciliation, by which time it would have been too late for the *parabasis*. We must,
however, recognize that, for whatever reason, the poet chose to keep entirely in
the background in this play. Also there are no allusions to the audience, with one
exception (1217ff), which is put in only to reduce the allusion *ad absurdum*.
[4] See above, p. 30, note 7.
[5] A.628ff.

saved the people from the deceptive orators, and on having helped them by his criticism. The man whom the chorus calls its teacher has indeed 'taught the things that are best'. He was 'the best of the poets', because he dared to speak what is just.[1] Again, the chorus of initiates in the *Frogs* begins its *parabasis* thus: 'Well does it suit the holy chorus to exhort the Polis and to teach it what is good.'[2] The poet is no longer mentioned; the chorus, as it were, has taken on a responsibility of its own. The form, and soon the contents as well, of comedy are becoming more and more impersonal.[3] The words of the *parabasis* do not always contain so serious an exhortation, nor are they invariably so irrelevant to the story of the play.[4] But it never varies in its essential function of giving expression to the unity of the people in both orchestra and auditorium, a unity in which the poet was certainly included.[5]

This unity is shown in still another way. In spite of everything that makes the comic no less than the tragic poet the 'teacher' of his audience and his people, he was, above all, a poet. His personal achievements as a poet are the outstanding theme of most of the parabases. The leader of the chorus sings the praise of the poet, which is thus self-praise. The poet 'has cheered you up and then sent you home'.[6] He even assures us that there has never been a better comedy than his. There is no need to call for Muses and Charites; they are always present when Aristophanes writes his plays — 'thus speaks the poet'.[7] The comedian's lot is not an easy one; the public is fickle, and the old poet is often hissed, though not always without justification.[8] To explain this, Aristophanes blames and attacks the older comedians. Such attacks upon

---

[1] A.658, 644.   [2] F.686.

[3] P. W. Harsh, *TAPA.* LXV (1934), 178ff, maintains that the *parabasis* was originally 'spoken in character' and only later became the mouthpiece of the poet. This is in conflict with the known history of the *parabasis* and the general development of comedy. Prof. Webster, in support of our view, suggests that ἀποδύντες in A.627, i.e. what the chorus did when embarking on the *parabasis*, may possibly mean 'taking off their masks', an action perhaps illustrated by a r.f. *Krater* in Heidelberg (*Ganymed*, 1949, 75, fig. 4).

[4] Cf., e.g., C.518ff, B.685ff, Th.785ff. Other examples from comic fragments are collected by M. Whittaker, *Cl. Q.* XXIX (1935), 188ff.

[5] Cf. K.507ff.   [6] adesp. 53.

[7] W.1046f. — frg. 334. For a somewhat different explanation of this fragment cf. Norwood, 252f.

[8] K.515ff, 520ff.

fellow-competitors, those 'vulgar people', are found fairly often,
and the discrimination of the audience is assessed according as
they like Aristophanes better than the other poets.[1] In the
main, Aristophanes claims over and over again, though certainly only with a limited justification, that his jokes are not so
stupid and coarse as those of others and that he does not try
to win the audience by throwing them figs and sweets.[2] Once
during a sacrifice corn is thrown to the spectators, but that is
done only to provide occasion for an obscene joke.[3] Aristophanes is proud of his great art, of his language and ideas, of
his jokes.[4] He demands the gratitude of his audience especially
for his unselfish political attacks: what an injustice was done,
for instance, by not giving the first prize to the poet of the
Clouds, who like Herakles tried to cleanse the State from all
evils![5]

The other poets, of course, repaid in like coin. 'Wake up,
spectators, and shake from your eyelids the nonsense of
ephemeral poets', are the words of Kratinos, who in his
Odyssēs declares that he has produced some new kind of stage
device. He derides a tragic poet Gnesippos whose chorus
'pulled out their songs' as slave-girls pull out the hairs of their
mistress (if that is the meaning of an obscure fragment).[7]
The chorus has 'to undertake and to dare everything', except
to use the melodies of certain other comedians.[8] The genuine
poet — possibly Kratinos — can claim 'to have got his art instead
of a wife';[9] his love belongs to his art, and the comedies he
writes are his legitimate offspring. Kratinos' last comedy, the
Wine-bottle (*Pytine*), was a magnificent effort of the old poet
against his detractors, especially Aristophanes, whose *Clouds*
he defeated on this occasion. The poet, who had been advised
by Aristophanes to sit as an honoured man among the spectators,[10] defended with the same vigour both his poetry and
his love of wine: 'wine's a swift steed to the bard of true wit;

---

[1] Competitors as ἄνδρες φορτικοί: C.524, cf. W.66. In general cf., e.g.,
A.1150ff, 1173. Discrimination of the audience: C.518ff, 560ff, W.1048ff.

[2] C.296, 537ff, W.58ff, P.734ff, 751ff, F.1ff, 12ff, Pl.797ff.

[3] P.962ff.

[4] P.748ff. In frg. 471 he claims similar standards in comparison with Euripides.

[5] W.1015ff, 1042ff, P.760ff.

[6] Kratinos 306, 145.   [7] Kratinos 256, cf. 15, 97.

[8] Kratinos 324.   [9] adesp. 498.   [10] K.536.

no water-drinker's work is worth a penny'.[1] Eupolis complained to the public that they preferred 'foreign poets', and
though the Greeks did not know the reproach of plagiarism,
Hermippos said that Phrynichos put other people's poetry in
his plays.[2] In a sense, the quarrels between the comedians are
more relevant to the discussion of purely literary matters,
which will be referred to later.[3] The same is true of the
innumerable attacks on Euripides. Occasionally, however,
something might be said against tragedy which reflected the
envy of a competitor:

> Truly to be clad in feather is the very best of things.
> Only fancy, dear spectators, had you each a brace of wings,
> Never need you, tired and hungry, at a tragic chorus stay,
> You would lightly, when it bored you, spread your wings
>   and fly away,
> Back returning, after luncheon, to enjoy our comic play.[4]

Naturally, every comedian aimed at displaying new and
original theatrical ideas, and their competition might be particularly concerned with the *agon* which played such an important part in almost every comedy.[5] The spirit of competition
indeed permeated the work of all the comic poets, culminating
in their *agon* for the prizes, for 'Nike, companion of the
choruses'.[6] The *agon* within the comedy and that between
certain poets are sometimes welded into one. The *Frogs* pro-

---

[1] Kratinos 181ff, 198, 199.

[2] Eupolis 357. Cf. above, p. 20, note 2. Eupolis and Aristophanes had been
friends at first, and some part of the *Knights* was written by Eupolis (78) —
Hermipp. 64.

[3] See ch. X.

[4] B.785ff. There were periods, then, when comedies had no special reserved
days, but were performed after the tragic trilogies. It might, in fact, have been
'shortly after noon' (B.1499) when the performance was coming to its end.
The exact extent of this arrangement is, however, unknown, and as long as
five poets competed (and not three, as at least during the Peloponnesian War),
comedy probably had a day of its own. Xen. *oik.* 3, 7 refers to people getting up
early in the morning to see a comedy. Generally, cf. Haigh, 23ff, Flickinger,
199, 363, Schneider, *P.-W.* III A, 498, 503, 508.

[5] frg. 528-9. Cf. J. Duchemin, *L' ΑΓῶΝ dans la tragédie grecque* (1945).
The book contains a short chapter (p. 31ff) on the ἀγών in Old Comedy.

[6] K.589: χορικῶν ἑταίρα. I take χορικῶν as neuter, including everything
which relates to the performance. I do not think there is any allusion in this phrase
to the oligarchic ἑταιρίαι.

vide the outstanding example, the *agon* between Aischylos and
Euripides before Dionysos.[1] It is significant for the wide scope
of this kind of competition that Euripides reproaches Aischylos
with having deceived the spectators after they had been made
stupid by Phrynichos.[2]

While it was important in the competition of the plays to
win the manifest applause of the masses, the decision was made
by the judges who were a few specially elected citizens, real
'auditors for the accounts of the choruses going out of office'.[3]
Individual judges might have been bribed or might have some
personal link with one of the poets or might be singled out for
an appeal.[4] The judges who at the *Choes* or Pitcher-feast were
to give the skin of wine to Dikaiopolis as a reward for the best
drinker, were at the same time the judges of the play.[5] The
choruses of the *Clouds* and the *Birds* promise the judges the
finest rewards if they are victorious, and threaten the worst if
they are not.[6] 'The judges I warn not to break their oath nor
to judge unjustly; else, by the god of friendship, the poet will
say other and far more slanderous things against you.'[7] The
oath of the chorus of the birds becomes strongest when they
swear by the wish to win 'by the vote of every judge and every
spectator'.[8] Only those of the audience 'who are well disposed',
and those judges 'who look not otherwards', are invited to the
feast; if the wise men among the judges will judge the poet
according to his wisdom, and those who like a good laugh
according to his jests, he will get every vote.[9]

It is possible, as we have said, to regard as an almost inevitable result of the *agon* of the comedies the extravagant
self-praise of the poets which we might otherwise feel to be
overdone, the crude attacks on rival competitors, the flatteries
addressed to the judges. But all these features appear only
because of the people's liking for such personal and literary
references, and the people's insistence on their inclusion. This
liking and insistence, however, are nothing but specific expressions of the general interest of the people, their interest in
the play, in the poet, in the *agon* of the poets as well as of the
actors. Although we are told that a good breakfast and drink

---

[1] F.830ff. Other examples: Kratinos' *Archilochoi*, Pherekr. 94, Plat. 128.
[2] F.909f.   [3] Eupolis 223.   [4] Personal link: Lysias IV, 3.
[5] A.1224.   [6] C.1115ff, B.1101ff.   [7] Pherekr. 96.
[8] B.445ff.   [9] E.1140ff, 1154ff.

were the usual preparation of the spectators, no time was too
early, no distance too great, to prevent punctual arrival at the
theatre.[1]   The poet was one of the people, the theatre was an
affair of theirs, and there was food for their natural delight in
every kind of *agon*.[2]   The theatre was the Polis.[3]

3. REALITY IN COMEDY

What we have learned about poet and audience gives us also
the ultimate reason for our assumption that comedy pictures
reality, the real pulsating body of life. We return to, and shall
try to develop, what has already been said in the introduction.
Tragedy, using mythological themes only, could rely on the
audience's having a general knowledge of the story. Comedy
lacking this aid was in need of some analogous starting-point.
Moreover, the tragic style provided a medium of immediate
impact by its very language, while the comedians had to find
a form of speech near to everyday talk and yet to be spoken
within the same theatrical setting as that of tragedy.[4]   The
difficulty affected the plot and the *dramatis personae*, as an early
writer of Middle Comedy declared.[5]   It was a particular
grievance that the comedians were unable to make use of a
deus ex machina. But the main trouble was the lack of any
common basis of understanding. The average spectator of
comedy, as of tragedy, must have familiar ground to stand on,
before he could follow the daring flight into the unfamiliar
and unreal. The poet had consciously to satisfy this need on
the part of the public; at the same time, he had to depict unconsciously or take for granted the facts of everyday life as
they were and as he and his audience knew them. The fact
that comedy was, as we have seen, in more than one aspect a
social phenomenon, made the unconscious representation of
reality a necessary feature and caused it to achieve a range and
strength unknown to any other kind of literature.

This necessity is one of the factors which determined the
nature of comedy. Old Comedy astonishes us, at a first glance,

---

[1] Pherekr. 95 (text corrupt and obscure), 194. — Xen. *oik.* 3, 7, 9.

[2] Cf. my *Ost und West*, ch. IV.   [3] Cf. K.1316ff.

[4] It seems doubtful whether Krates in an obscure fragment (24) actually
complained of such a predicament; but the different explanation by R. Goossens,
Rev. ét. anc. XLII (1940) (*Mélanges Radet*), 157, is also not convincing. As to
the general difficulty of writing and producing a comedy, see K.515ff.

[5] Antiphanes 191.

by its mixture of extreme reality and extreme unreality, by 'the romantic dissonance between real life and the fantasy of fairy-tale'.[1] The two ingredients cannot be separated. If we look at the clay figures representing types of comedy (Plates I, III, XIV), we realize how everyday reality is merged in the absurdity of mask, padding and phallos.[2] The plays reflect the same kind of mixture. The private treaty of Dikaiopolis in the *Acharnians* is grotesque and impossible, but it has its setting among entirely real persons and events. Trygaios in the *Peace*, riding on a beetle, brings the goddess of Peace from heaven, where he has dug her up; but he himself does not belong to a fabulous world, he is a simple *pater familias* and owner of a vineyard. It is the same with the sudden appearance of the chorus in heaven, when neither the poet nor the audience know by what miracle they have been transported thither. The city of the birds is indeed incarnate unreality, but the human beings who meet there are as natural and real as the walls which are built with stones and mortar. The manner in which the women in the *Lysistrate* put an end to war, though their plans are ingenious in conception and execution, or the government of women in the *Ekklesiazousai*, though much less ingenious — all this is grotesque and unimaginable. But how much there is of human reality, of psychological truth, of the mediocrity of the *petit bourgeois*![3] In each of the extant plays we find, even down to the smallest detail, the same mixture of reality and unreality.

It is hard to define the limits of the unreal and the supra-real within the plays. They are by no means confined to the non-human beings, gods, animals, forces of nature and the like. The limits of reality, however, are clear, just because it is reality. They are given by the everyday life of the Athenian

[1] F. Leo, *Geschichte der röm. Literatur*, I, 98.

[2] Much of our archaeological evidence refers to Middle Comedy. In general it is true to say that the cruder and courser the features, the closer is the figure to Old Comedy. Cf. the illuminating paper by T. B. L. Webster, *Cl. Q*. XLII (1948), 15ff.

[3] I shall speak repeatedly of the Athenian *petits bourgeois*, and I wish to apologize for using an expression which belongs to modern times. I have found no other word equally fitting. Those of my critics who objected to my use of the expression and also of 'middle-classes' were unfortunately unable to propose any alternatives. I shall do my best to explain and define the social meaning of both expressions.

citizens, which provides the poet with place and time and people, with their thoughts and feelings, their daily needs, and the events of social existence.

It is perhaps the greatest secret of the poet's art that he has contrived to blend two such different and even conflicting atmospheres in one picture, which despite all its variety is homogeneous. Something of the secret of his art may be revealed to us when we examine the nature of some of the 'heroes' of the comedies, in whom unreal intentions and actions are combined with a real private existence. Unimportant and ordinary people turn the order of the world upside down. World-reformers such as Peithetairos and Praxagora aim, in their ingenious folly, at changing the political and social conditions in ways which are grotesquely Utopian. Similarly these conditions are reduced *ad absurdum* by exaggeration of their unsoundness. This is most admirably accomplished, for instance, by the sausage-seller in the *Knights*. It is to be supposed that the conditions which are to be changed are, according to the poet, bad and in desperate need of improvement. He does not, therefore, depict the conditions with an objective mind; they are not real, but the negative cause of imaginative dreams which were suggested by his wishes, and realized in the sphere of supra-reality.

That means that the conditions of Athenian life are described in comedy in two ways, now with intentional distortion *in deteriorem*, then again, and this to a large extent unconsciously, simply as the reflection of reality. In the distorted representation of real conditions and abuses we have, so it seems, the link joining and uniting the real and the unreal.

It remains, of course, a problem every time we use a passage from comedy how to determine where reality ends and caricature or fantasy begins. One essential point, frequently overlooked, is that the situation on the stage, which is naturally part of the plot, must not be used as evidence for historical facts. It is the situation behind the plot which counts, the conditions of life against which the events and characters of the stage stand out. Sometimes doubts remain. Any conclusion then must be based on the existence or the lack of logical coherence with the general background picture which we are trying to draw.

The assertion made before that the comic poet's distortion

of reality is the link joining together the real and the unreal
can perhaps help us to surmount one last difficulty, the problem
of 'types' in comedy.[1] Even those who know Old Comedy
only slightly will agree that the persons represented are not
individual beings, not 'characters'. They have much less indi-
viduality than the mythical men and women of tragedy who,
though with little justification, have been denied that quality.
Citizen and slave, sophist and peasant, man and woman, mor-
tals and gods, rich and poor, young and old: all these can be
types in comedy, depicted or caricatured in mere outlines.[2]
Even historical persons suffer this fate, for example Kleon as
the Paphlagonian in the *Knights*, or Sokrates in the *Clouds*, or
Euripides in the *Thesmophoriozousai*. The type, once fixed,
needed little change or improvement. There was no need to
create it anew; it existed and had early become a permanent
factor in comedy. This applies even to such specialized types
as the rude doorkeeper, or the slave who carries his master's
baggage (see Plate XIV*b*).[3]

The complete range of types was not crystallized till the
time of Menander. But already in the first comedy of Aristophanes, the *Daitalēs*, two pairs of types appear: the good and
the bad son, and (as later in the *Clouds*) the conservative father
and his modern-minded son.[4] This shows that not only single
persons, but also pairs or, less commonly, social groups could
become typical, and so lead to the creation of stock motifs and
scenes. Moreover, the use of types is closely connected with
the limitations imposed by the number of masks available.[5]

While it is legitimate to make clear the links which con-

[1] Terracotta statuettes, representing types of comedy: M. Bieber, *The History of
the Greek and Roman Theatre* (1939), fig. 95ff. Archaeological evidence also
confirms the existence of Middle Comedy and its types: Bieber, fig. 122ff.

[2] See Plates I, III, XIV. — Cf. the excellent paper by K. Reinhardt, *Aristophanes und Athen. Europ. Revue* XIV (1938), 754ff. — An example of a mono-
graph on one of the comic types is H. G. Oeri, *Der Typ der komischen Alten in
d. griech. Komödie* (Basle, 1948).

[3] P.180ff, F.464ff. — F.12ff, frg. 323; cf. Xen. *mem.* III, 13, 6.

[4] Cf. F. Wehrli, *Motivstudien zur griech. Komödie*, 49 and elsewhere, who
should be consulted also for what follows. His conclusions about Aristophanes,
however, go too far. Cf. also W. Süss, *Gnomon* XIII (1937), 602.

[5] Cf. F. M. Cornford, *The Origin of Attic Comedy*, ch. VIII; but this argument
must not be over-emphasized, as it was quite common for new and original masks
to be used in comedy (cf. T. B. L. Webster, *Bull. of the John Rylands Libr.*
XXXII 1949, 3ff).

nected the New Comedy with its predecessors, the fundamental difference must not be overlooked. So far as our problem is concerned, it seems to me to rest on two main facts. First, the 'type' in Old Comedy and that in New Comedy are not identical. Menander draws in detail the character and psychology of his persons, although from a general and social point of view they are continually recurring types. Aristophanes pays no attention to psychology, but cares only for action and situation. What matters to him are the changing functions determined by the permanent general characteristics of the type.

This implies also the second fundamental difference, that of the world of the play. Menander, ingeniously and with many variations, involves his typical persons and motifs in a plot which again is typical. In spite of all their realism and psychological truth, they stand, so to speak, in a world outside time and space, which knows only seduced girls and frivolous youths, crafty slaves, depraved procurers, stupid fathers and so on, a world in which the only problems are those of love and money. It is true that the events and situations could have occurred, for they are quite natural and human; but what is represented is not simply a purely private sphere, it is, as it were, separated from the rest of the world by a screen of glass, through which only occasional glimpses are granted of the conditions and facts of real life. No doubt, New Comedy is an important source for the historical reconstruction of social life, partly because of its general, entirely unpolitical character, and partly because of its use of proverbs, its general statements, its occasional allusions to individual facts. New Comedy represents a certain spirit, a special state of mind, and it was performed before an audience which must have agreed with this state of mind. Behind New Comedy lay, we may say, what has been said to lie also behind the art of Praxiteles (though he lived about half a century before Menander): 'an intelligent life, quiet-tempered, fond of pleasure and tasteful in its pleasures, taking things lightly, or as lightly as one can'.[1] If this mirrors the spirit of New Comedy, it can be recognized in the characters as well as in the social circumstances represented on the stage; but they had to a large extent become conventional. Poetry in Menander's time, though it certainly represented the spirit of the age, had ceased to be an expression of

[1] J. D. Beazley, *Cambr. Anc. Hist.* VI, 537.

public life. So far as private life is concerned, it is simply a misinterpretation to regard the problems and events on the stage as something which mattered in real life. Life in New Comedy, though it apes life, was shut off from reality.[1]

In the plays of Old Comedy both men and action are often, as we have already emphasized, impossible in detail, they are unreal or supra-real, but the ground they stand on, or rather have arisen from, is the reality of political and social life. There is a telling story reported in the two anonymous *Lives* of Aristophanes that the tyrant Dionysios wanted to know all about the *politeia* of Athens, that is to say, its people and its institutions, and that Plato sent him the plays of Aristophanes. Old Comedy, in spite of its farcical conventions and gross caricature, pulsates with the spirit of the age in which it was written, and at the same time it is inspired by the problems of that Athens which lived through the Peloponnesian War and its aftermath. Behind type and convention stands not only the genius of the poet whose work appeals to mankind, but also an age and a place the like of which has not been seen again.

---

[1] I agree in its main points with Prof. Gomme's characterization of Menander (249ff), but I consider it insufficient to say: 'He, if you will, fails to give them (i.e. his characters) a satisfactory living background.' There was no failure, but a different intention. Körte, *Die Menschen Menanders (Berichte d. Sächs. Akad.* 89, 1937, Heft 3), describes this world of Menander's as one 'without patriotism, religion, duties, and labour', 'a society, on the whole, neither pleasant nor interesting'. Körte is convinced that this society actually existed. And so are others. I do not believe in the reality of that life and that society. It may be a little difficult to realize the conventions and the unreality of a realistic theatre, but we have a specimen today: the films, which are accordingly easy to understand everywhere and always — just as Menander was. W. S. Ferguson, in the brilliant chapter on Athenian society in his *Hellenistic Athens*, makes large use of New Comedy as a source (73ff). However, he remarks: 'We cannot use the data of the New Comedy to reconstruct more than the life with which it deals, the border life in which *monde* and *demi-monde* met, the life in public which was not political or commercial. The real private life of most citizens was closed to the drama' (77). I very much wonder whether this border life was not chiefly a poetic invention. 'The kind of plot . . . is altogether misinterpreted when it is construed so simply that rape, seduction etc. were of everyday occurrence in Athenian society. They could happen, since otherwise the New Comedy would not have been a mirror of life at all' (91). Exactly: if it was not a true mirror of life (and are we justified in *a priori* taking it as this?), those events usually did not happen.

CHAPTER II

THE COMEDIES

EACH of the comedies is a curious compound of very incongruous elements, of traditional forms of cult and religious festival on the one hand, and on the other of dialogue scenes which, being theatrical in a narrower sense, are dramatic and full of action. The whole, however, which emerges, has far less unity than tragedy, which developed on somewhat similar lines. The history of the development of the various parts of comedy, whether it is a matter of proof or conjecture, is irrelevant to our discussion. Aesthetic evaluation of the whole is also out of place. What matters to us is this: each play of Old Comedy is a loose structure in which much is incorporated for pure fun, the derision of well-known persons or farcical situations from which the last ounce of absurdity is extracted. Yet in this richness and variety a certain coherence can be detected. This is supplied partly by the idea and tendency of the play, partly by the general atmosphere, that is to say, by social circumstances and problems, but not by the events of the plot, which frequently lacks any proper coherence. There must be a trunk for the creepers to cling to. *Fabula docet*, not, it is true, as the close unity and architecture of tragedy does, but by way of a general picture. On closer inspection there is revealed no scarlet thread running through the incidents of the plot, but the observer becomes aware of a multicoloured fabric into which the comic play is worked.

Thus it cannot be our task to tell the story of each play. The exact order of scenes is of no great importance for our subject, neither is the loose manner of composition, for here comic and conscious invention naturally predominates. It is, however, necessary to inquire how, if at all, reality is reflected in the simple narrative sequence, and how far an understanding of the political and social situation can be gained from the narrative. Any single comedy, if treated as a whole, may disclose something that cannot be gathered from a mosaic of innumerable quotations from the whole field of comedy.

Let us then examine the plays one by one.[1] For this purpose we are, of course, practically confined to the works of
Aristophanes. That the story of a play cannot be satisfactorily
reconstructed from the extant fragments alone, is illustrated,
for instance, by the *Daitalēs* of Aristophanes.[2] The fragments
suggest that the conservative father and the good son are to
some extent duplicates, though they can hardly have been so
in fact. A similar uncertainty about plot and story prevails
with regard to other plays which have not survived, except
perhaps the *Dionysalexandros* of Kratinos and the *Demoi* of
Eupolis. The *Demoi* we shall discuss later. Kratinos' play is a
parody of myths and gods with a political background. We
know the main features of the play from a payprus which contains a short résumé of its contents, a *hypothesis*.[3] It does
not provide anything that I can see of value for our present
purpose. Apart from these two plays, we have nothing but
fragments to go on, useful only if the words and phrases in
themselves suggest certain conclusions quite apart from any
context in which they may have occurred.

Of the *Babylonians*, produced in 426, we know at least for
certain that in this play the young Aristophanes dealt with
the policy of democratic Athens, in particular the policy of
Kleon, and that it exposed its character in the presence of
strangers and allies.[4] One result of the performance was the
prosecution of the poet by the statesman. This is probably the
chief reason why, apart from the general and, indeed, all-impor-

---

[1] This whole chapter owes much to Croiset. His book is not yet obsolete,
though he thinks too much in terms of fixed political parties. His opinion that
comedy is the expression of the fight of rural democracy against an urban oligarchy
is entirely erroneous; cf. Gomme, *Cl. Rev.* 52 (1938), 98f. Good accounts and
discussions of the plots are to be found in Murray and Nicosia (and, in fact, in
several other books). The most extensive discussion of all comedies, whether
extant or not, as well as of much of the modern literature on the subject, can be
found in Schmid.

[2] An attempt to reconstruct this play, as far as it is possible, was made by
A. Rostagni, *Riv. di filol.* LIII (1925), 174ff.

[3] Pap. Oxyr. IV, 69ff = p. 31 D. — Cf. G. Méautis, *Rev. ét. anc.* 36 (1934),
462ff. J. Th. M. F. Pieters, *Cratinus* (1946), ch. VII.

[4] G. Norwood, *Cl. Phil.* XXV (1930), 1ff, has tried to show how little foundation there is for the general opinion that the allies were represented as branded
slaves from the mill of Demos. His own reconstruction, however, is itself not
very convincing. V. Frey (see p. 8, note 3), 133f, explains the plot as a double
betrayal of the Athenian people — by Kleon and by the allies!

tant question of peace, the questions of domestic and empire
policy hardly recur at all in the *Acharnians*, of the next year.
Aristophanes was by then more cautious. It is known, moreover, that the *Acharnians* was performed at the Lenaia, when no
allies were in the theatre.

Nevertheless the poet does not conceal his political ani-
mosities. In a play of which the whole trend is governed by
his passionate longing for peace, he is bound to find himself
up against Kleon, the champion of a warlike policy. But
Kleon himself is not represented, and there are few personal
attacks on him. Yet there is a subtle motive — it is more than
a clever device — in the allocation of the roles of the advocates
of peace and war respectively to Dikaiopolis, the 'just citizen',
and to the charcoal-burners and vine-dressers of Acharnai, that
is to say, of both views to members of the same stratum of
society, the rural middle-class. We may disregard Lamachos,
the regular soldier, all brawn and no brains, gallant, but almost
devoid of political and social significance. The Acharnians,
however, the clumsy, honest *Marathonomachai* — we know them
to be rough and wild from another comedy also[1] — hate Sparta,
though it is true that they hate Kleon even more. They intend
to fight the war through to absolute victory. It is certain that
at the time no small part of the people was full of patriotism
and the spirit of self-sacrifice. The war was continued not
merely because a bellicose party in power wanted it. A fact
emerges which hostile tradition tends to obscure: Kleon did
not stand alone, he was not simply a tyrannical demagogue,
but was supported by a large part of the people, consisting
mainly (as might be expected), though not exclusively, of the
townsfolk from whose ranks he himself had risen. On this
point Aristophanes supplies indirect but unimpeachable evidence. With great skill he makes a round-about attack at
the point where the enemy's lines are weakest. When he made
his Acharnians change from war-mongers into promoters of
peace, he probably cherished some hope of undermining the
desire to prolong the war, a desire which was certainly still
alive, even among the rural population. What he tries to show
is that the feelings of the Acharnians are justified from their
point of view, but that they feel as they do only because they have
been the victims of deliberate deceit. By this means he was

[1] adesp. 75.

sure of influencing his audience more strongly than if he
had shown every warlike feeling to be contemptible in itself.
Furthermore, he laid the responsibility for the war not on
Sparta but on Perikles and his Megarian Decree — surely an
astonishing line to take at that particular moment.[1] He depicts
Polemos, War, as one of those dissipated rich young men at
whom he so often aims his shafts. We need not doubt that,
when the chorus joined in Dikaiopolis' hymn of peace, many
of the listeners were of one mind with them, although (or should
we say, because?) in the play every attitude which was not
wholeheartedly in favour of peace had been condemned and
mere comfort and enjoyment had been extolled. Perhaps the
award of the first prize to this play expressed not only artistic
appreciation, but also the widespread longing for peace which
found itself in agreement with the poet's own desire.

Dikaiopolis begins his private conclusion of peace with a
sacrifice to Dionysos, the patron of both festival and comedy.
Here he is appealed to, above all, as protector of the rural
Dionysia and defender of peace; Dikaiopolis is, in fact, pretending to be back on his farm.[2] The sacrifice is accompanied
by the hymn to Phales or Phallos, the symbol of the fertility
of men as well as of animals and plants, the symbol of Dionysos,
and in particular the symbol of sexual love. This sacrifice of
thanksgiving is intended to illustrate the fact that peace will
restore the pleasant features of country life; it therefore reproduces the traditional forms of the rural Dionysia. At the same
time, it is the entirely personal and private peace of the little
vine-dresser Dikaiopolis in which he forbids any others to
participate. Unlike what we shall find in the later comedy
which is given the title *Peace*, this peace is not to be thought
of as a political affair, as something concerning all Greeks.
There is nothing heroic about it; its chief result is the restoration of trade and marketing and so of an easier daily life. A
peace of this kind corresponds exactly to the kind of war
depicted in the play. Naturally enough, since it is a comedy, it
does not resound with the great and tragic events of recent
years, the plague, the punishment of Mytilene, the heroic
resistance and final fall of Plataiai, or the horrible civil war in
Kerkyra. Dikaiopolis complains of the destruction of vines,

[1] A.515ff.
[2] Cf. A. W. Pickard-Cambridge, *The Theatre of Dionysus in Athens* (1946), 60.

the difficulties of trade, the scarcity of some foodstuffs. Can we doubt that Aristophanes gives us a true picture of the thoughts and feelings of the ordinary citizen? Here are the authentic tones of the 'small man', speaking to us plainly and honestly. The transformation of the bellicose, heroic ex-servicemen into enthusiastic followers of Dikaiopolis and his pleasure-seeking private peace is a reproduction of actual psychological possibilities, almost free from caricature.

Thus it is possible to see in the story of the *Acharnians* a victory of individualism and materialism, of private prosperity and economic welfare, over general idealism, over State and politics. What happens in the sphere of a comic and Utopian idyll is not merely a private action of Dikaiopolis, and therefore not only the fulfilment of a personal wish of the poet's. We learn the attitude of one section of the community, a section which was certainly considerable in numbers. The response to the poet's appeal for peace, which came very near high treason, was loud and immediate. We need not wonder at this: no amount of political energy or readiness to face hardship and sacrifice could rob the Athenians of the hope — should we say, the dream? — of a peaceful and prosperous life of their own.

The *Knights*, it will be remembered, is written round one central theme: the Paphlagonian slave, who is all-powerful in the house of Demos and who in fact represents Kleon, is re-placed in his master's favour by the sausage-seller, who suc-ceeds by being even more shameless, more obsequious, more boastful than his rival. The grotesque and unedifying *agon* between two rascals may appear to be little more than broad farce, but there are various indications that it has a deeper meaning, which is not, however, free from inconsistencies. First of all, the master for whose favour the two rogues com-pete, the idle old fool, represents the demos of Athens. The victorious sausage-seller succeeds in rejuvenating him and thus brings back to life the glorious Athenian people of the days of Miltiades and Aristeides. In this last part of the play, the sausage-seller, now called Agorakritos, that is 'approved by' or 'chosen from the market', has become an actual reformer.

Secondly, to our surprise, the chorus of knights, the noble youth of Athens,[1] sides unconditionally with the sausage-

---

[1] What such a chorus looked like on the stage, may be gathered from an earlier vase painting (Plate II*b*), depicting probably some kind of κῶμος.

seller, even when he surpasses himself in impudence and vulgarity. This association is, on social grounds, very strange indeed, and it can only be explained by a common hostility to Kleon. We must beware, however, of too hastily drawing conclusions about actual conditions. It is to be noticed, too, that this play, the fiercest attack ever launched in public against a leading statesman, came out in the spring of 424 (and won the first prize). It was therefore written not long after Kleon's policy had been justified by his brilliant success at Pylos. Finally, in this play the poet remains faithful to the ideal of the *Acharnians*. The last scene of the *Knights*, a scene of serene gaiety, reaches its climax when Demos, always described as a townsman, receives from the hands of Agorakritos the peace-treaty, in the form of a beautiful maiden with whom Demos can now retire 'to the country'.

If we regard, as we are certainly entitled to do, the last part of the play as definitely bringing out its inner meaning, then what Aristophanes desired above all was to put an end to the corruption of political methods. The methods in question are those ascribed to Kleon, and even more strongly, to the sausage-seller in the earlier scenes. This implies that they were used by men who belonged to the middle and lower classes of the townsfolk. Opposed to them we find the aristocratic chorus, and the spirit of pre-Periclean Athens which is conjured up in the final scenes. However, apart from a few perfunctory allusions, mainly in the Paphlagonian's boasts about Pylos, the poet does not mention the war in which Athens was then engaged, a war in which the prospects of the Athenians seemed good enough to justify in some measure Kleon's brutal and bellicose policy. Once more we see comedy emancipating itself from the general patriotic attitude, though apparently there are inconsistencies. In the revived Athens the people will vote money for ships rather than for fees, the threat of cutting off the imports of corn will fail to have any effect, the oarsmen's pay will be guaranteed, the corrupt intrigues to avoid active service will be stopped: all this means a strengthening of the external power of Athens. The real aim of Aristophanes is always to fight corruption, not to hamper Athenian might.

The corruption, however, which is, so it seems, a feature of all long wars and not especially associated with any particular political system, is the result of unrestrained egotism in economic and political life. As is shown by all the known facts of the history of the time as well as by comedy, the blame lay mainly with the town-dwellers. The Paphlagonian and the sausage-seller belong to the same social sphere, though on slightly different levels. Kleon is degraded, though at the same time comically put in his proper place in society, by the punishment which makes him a sausage-seller and compels him to sell his wares at the gate where only the scum of the people loiters. What matters to us is not the opinion of Aristophanes expressed in this extravagantly distorted form, but the fact that one section of the people strong in numbers, and even stronger politically, could not only see economic conditions as the basis for a peaceful existence on a small scale (as the petty farmer typified by Dikaiopolis had done), but could also look at them with an eye to increasing its own profit and power.

In contrasting this new kind of citizen with the older type, men of high morals and ready for any sacrifice, Aristophanes shows an understanding and offers an interpretation of the tendencies of his age. In the days of Perikles, and more intensely during the great war, a change began to take place which gave to economic factors an ever-increasing importance in the life and thought of the Polis. This tendency was strongly combated by the poet, who was, of course, the mouthpiece of an opinion widely held at the time. There were kindred spirits among great and small citizens alike, both in town and country. He stood not only for the supremacy of politics as such, which had been taken for granted in earlier times, but also for the supremacy of a new type of politics, conforming to a universal moral ideal rather than merely serving the brutally won advantage of the moment. The age of moral and political philosophy lay ahead. These ideas explain why Aristophanes could aim such vigorous attacks against the victor of Pylos and yet remain a good Athenian.

We must therefore refrain (as many scholars have failed to do) from calling the knights of the chorus oligarchs. Their point of view is the same as the poet's, and as we have said, there is no reason to conclude from their alliance with the sausage-seller more than that they were hostile to Kleon. This can almost be regarded as axiomatic: Aristophanes had indeed already emphasized it clearly enough in the much-discussed opening verses of the *Acharnians*. That the poet and the knights have been brought together by a common hatred of the all-powerful demagogue, is expressly stated by the chorus in the *parabasis*.[1] The knights belonged to the noble youth, they were 'gallant men', true *kaloikagathoi*.[2] But to the same social class belonged also the dissipated rich young men, educated in the new manner, whom the poet attacks so often and so passionately, and against whose spirit his next play was partially to be directed. In view of this it can hardly be maintained that Aristophanes allied himself with the opinions of a whole social group or the programme of a political party. He was not committed to a hostile attitude to democracy.

This will be confirmed by a closer examination of the picture of society as painted in the *Knights*. Noblemen and peasants found a common bond in their hostility to the demagogues, to their bellicose policy and to their desire for political power and the realization of their economic aims. Opposed to this partly aristocratic and partly rural group, which was united by political rather than social affinities, stood a group of middle-class townsfolk of which the internal structure was determined by the relative degrees of wealth or poverty of its members, who ranged from the small pedlar to the owner of a large workshop. In spite of its diversity, this group formed a social and psychological unit. It was, above all, the different situation created by the war which distinguished the two groups; 'the farmers and the rich' were the chief sufferers, while the townsmen felt little of the devastation and the misery of war.[3] However, it will become clear in the course of our investigations that the small farmers found their place within the structure of society by the side of the traders and craftsmen rather than of the noble knights. Their union with the rich and noble was, after all, only a temporary combination, mainly a fighting alliance against war-policy and democratic corruption. The contrast between the two groups of the *Knights*, which is perhaps the most conspicuous of all the contrasts in comedy, has also its political, social and professional features, but it is primarily a matter of morals, it is a contrast of moral aims.

The success of the *Knights* was followed by the failure of the *Clouds*. In its original form, produced in 423, Aristophanes seems to have overestimated the intelligence of the audience:

---

[1] K.507ff.   [2] Cf. ch. IV.
[3] Ps.-Xen. II, 14.

the play was probably above their heads.[1] The revised edition, which cannot be much later, was widely read, but never performed on the stage. In this two points are stressed: the underlying principle is made clear (the *agon* of the Just and the Unjust Logos), and a firm line of action is taken, expressed in burlesque by the burning of the 'thinking-house'.[2] No great difference is supposed to exist between the two versions; at any rate, there was no fundamental change. The denunciation of Sokrates, at first only humorous, afterwards sharper, was of course an expression of the struggle against the sophists and their modern education; but it falls far short of the violence of the attacks on Kleon. One obvious reason for this is that even in Athens a much smaller part of the population was interested in the things of the mind and in culture than in politics.

We may, however, take it as evidence of the deeper insight of Aristophanes, deeper than that of audience and judges, that he realized that this problem had an importance for the people as a whole. When looking for men educated in the old and in the new way, he took representatives of two generations, but also — though they were father and son — of different social classes. The old peasant Strepsiades, it will be remembered, had married into the aristocracy. Originally an honest and dignified, though narrow-minded countryman, he has been driven out of his proper course by his marriage, and is now fighting without scruple against the economic ruin that threatens him through the debts of his wife and son. Probably such marriages were not unknown, though it may be that Aristophanes invented the situation in order to be able to make the farmer's son, Pheidippides, representative of the noble and prodigal *jeunesse dorée*. Perhaps the poet preferred the young man, whose sophistic education had turned him from a reckless ne'er-do-well into a complete scoundrel, not to be a knight, even if he tried to win their favour.[3] Anyhow he is not one of those who, a short time before, had appeared as the allies of the poet, though the knights, too, are as mad on horses as Pheidippides, and some of them are educated in the new manner. It is, of course, difficult to say how far the peculiar social setting of the two principal figures is due to the desire for a particular comic effect.

[1] Cf. C.520ff.   [2] Cf. Murray, 87f.   [3] C.119f.

Yet we may be certain that Aristophanes' attitude, which, in spite of its conservatism, is never narrow, and not even uniformly conservative, reflects a somewhat complicated situation in society. Distinctions of class, profession and education were becoming very much less clear. The poet, who had called on the young aristocrats to fight against the demagogue, realized that they were in greater danger than anyone else from the activities of the sophists. The sentence on Sokrates is carried out by the farmer, who in this case represents also the older generation. In the last scene he is no longer stupid and clumsy, but appears as the honest and upright guardian of the good cause. Aristophanes seems to have been quite unaware of the fact that Sokrates with his basic demand for expert knowledge would have been his best ally against the demagogues.[1]

The really comic figure of the play is, of course, not Sokrates but Strepsiades. His utter narrow-mindedness forms a companion picture to the complete baseness of the sausage-seller, and like him, he ends up as a victor and a just judge. It is not so easy to find a parallel between Sokrates and the Paphlagonian, except in so far as the demagogic methods of the latter and the former's dialectical tricks are both means of deceiving the people, the only difference being that Sokrates acts from folly rather than from self-interest. The sophistic distortion of truth as taught by Sokrates is used by Strepsiades merely to repudiate his debts. But it might have helped someone else to become a demagogue, and the completely corrupt Pheidippides, who thrashes his father and threatens to beat his mother, is also a product of the new type of education. This education is therefore a menace to the whole people. The fight against the originators of the theory of private and public egotism takes its place beside the fight against self-seeking rulers and demagogues. The Sokrates of the *Clouds*, who at the most takes a cloak from his pupil and in spite of all his teaching remains poor and wretched, does not illustrate the economic thought so characteristic of the time. But his irreligious and opportunist materialism appears as another outstanding phenomenon of the great spiritual and psychological transformation which was a feature of the age.

The *Wasps* (spring 422) continued the attack on Kleon.

[1] In ch. X we shall try to give a more substantial answer to the question why Aristophanes depicted Sokrates in the way he did.

That is stated explicitly in the names of the two chief figures:
Philokleon, the 'Kleon-lover', with his passion for the law-
courts, and Bdelykleon, his son, the 'Kleon-hater'. In contrast
with the *Knights*, Kleon does not appear in person on the stage.
The attack on demagogic democracy is directed against one
of its prominent institutions, the popular courts. It is essential
for us to bear in mind that neither the courts as such nor democracy are the real objects of attack. No reforms are advo-
cated. Aristophanes merely endeavours to show how the
people's courts and the people are being debased to the level
of tools in the hands of a few self-seeking demagogues. The
father is taught the lesson by the son, and with the father the
chorus of his fellow-jurors.[1] The poet's attitude has remained
fundamentally unchanged.

In this, as in most of Aristophanes' plays, the contrast between the generations is a dominating feature. What is surprising is the complete financial dependence of the father on
his son. The former is poor, the latter apparently quite well
off. Perhaps the old man handed over his house to the son,
but it is more than that. The natural order of things is inverted,
the old man waiting for the death of the younger one, which
would enable him to manumit the flute-girl and make her his
concubine, the son looking after his father because he is 'the
only one he has', and this one is still too young to manage his
own property.[2] Thus the unnatural economic situation is only
part of the general fun and likewise not to be taken seriously,
while, on the other hand, the comic situation requires the old
man to be poor if he is to be a typical juryman. This is made
clear by the members of the chorus, whose children are more or
less starving. Nor is the inversion of the generations purely
arbitrary. The chorus of heliasts composed entirely of old men

---

[1] I have used the words 'jurors' or 'jurymen' for the members of the popular
courts. It is the normal way of translating ἡλιασταί. But they were also δικα-
σταί, and 'judges' — or perhaps 'sworn judges', though this is rather clumsy — is
an equally justifiable translation. Yet the word 'judges' normally implies the conception of an individual, professionally learned in the law, perhaps even a State
official; it therefore seems more misleading than the name of 'jurors'. In a way,
Mr. Cronin is right in saying that the dicasts were both judges and jurors (J. F.
Cronin, *The Athenian Juror and his Oath*, Diss. Chicago, 1936); cf. also my
review of G. M. Calhoun, *Introduction to Greek Legal Science* in *JHS*. LXIII
(1943), 127.

[2] W.1354ff.

reproduces, though in exaggerated form, a factor of the social conditions of the time. Younger men were serving as soldiers or employed where workmen had grown scarce because of the war. Amongst those who prized the three obols of the juror's pay, the old men, no longer fit for work, were the most likely to be available for the bench. They were a miserable, discontented set, and their sentences were influenced in a high degree by their many grudges and pressing poverty. They were old men, singing the songs of their youth, and so far as Aristophanes' description holds good, there was no malice in them; else they would not admit their mistakes so readily in face of Bdelykleon's arguments. But they succumb to the allurement of listening to denunciations of rich people, and of enjoying their own power in dealing with them. The crazy passion for judging, which is ridiculed, though not unkindly, in the play, was a dangerous political instrument in the hands of the rulers; as a feature of mass-psychology it was as easy to understand as it was difficult to eradicate.

For this there is an obvious reason: the individual heliast does not care much for justice, but he does care for his own advantage. Bdelykleon's arguments, which convince the chorus and his father and are intended to convince the audience as well, never once raise the question of the miscarriage of justice; his sole object is to prove that it is not the jurors who profit by their judgments. With a pleasant audacity the poet once more holds up a mirror to the people, and these obvious things were what the audience could most easily understand and appreciate. Only a keen observer might detect behind this screen the fighter for right, and perceive that the fight against demagogues and cheating jurymen was at the same time a fight for the independence of the law-courts and for just verdicts.

This play suggests that Aristophanes had formed a low, indeed a pessimistic, estimate of the ordinary citizen. But his pessimism is confined here to the heliasts, and the verdict in the end refers indirectly to the institution. At any rate, when the chorus, and finally even the stubborn Philokleon, are converted by Bdelykleon's arguments, the other and more optimistic side of the picture appears: better conditions are both desired and possible. There Aristophanes' faith in his people breaks through, faith not in their political greatness, but in their natural, joyful humanity. The war is still raging, a new

campaign in Thrace is imminent, in assembly and law-courts
sycophants and demagogues reign supreme — but the comedy
ends in burlesque and obscene revelling, with the grim old
juryman turned into a young ne'er-do-well. If everything is
taken into account, there is more in this than the traditional
end of a comedy, the *gamos*, the final sexual union. With the
end of the play all the earlier bitterness disappears, and the
ultimate meaning of the whole play, and indeed of all of
Aristophanes' comedies, is revealed, the portrayal of the fickle
yet lovable Athenian people.

Kleon was dead and peace near, when Aristophanes wrote
the comedy which takes its title from the goal for which he had
striven so long: 'Eirene', *Peace*. The winning of the peace was
the theme of the play. Trygaios, the bold rider on the dung-
beetle, who brings down Peace from Heaven, is, as his name
shows, a vine-dresser and farmer like Dikaiopolis. The members of the chorus, however, though rustic too, and apparently
thought of as representing all the cities of Greece, are not the
bellicose Acharnians, but more or less eager helpers in the
cause of peace.[1] Only interpreters of oracles and armourers,
that is to say war-profiteers, are still dissatisfied at the idea of
peace. Their struggle is the half-hearted rearguard fight of the
war-party, which had lost its leader Kleon; across their stubborn
will events move on.

The *Peace* has generally been classed as one of Aristophanes'
weakest comedies. Yet the first scenes are admirable, only the
second part is lacking in action and spice. But it must not be
thought that the poetic skill of Aristophanes has failed him.
The fault lies rather with the subject. The struggle for peace
was over, it remained only to acknowledge and enjoy it: *komos*
and *gamos* were enough by themselves. It is significant that in
the second part, after peace has actually arrived, Eirene does
not appear again. The plot in fact was exhausted. As deputies,
so to speak, for Eirene there appear Opora, fruit and harvest,
and Theoria, personifying the sacred embassy and holy festival.

[1] There is some inconsistency in the composition of the chorus, as sometimes
all Greeks, sometimes only the Athenians, appear to be meant. Some scholars
have sought to trace in this remains of the two different texts which are known to
have existed. Cf. Norwood, 232f. Another solution of the problem, involving
the introduction of 'supers' representing different States, is discussed by Pickard-
Cambridge, *Theatre of Dionysus*, 62, 1. I personally do not think that the inconsistency goes beyond the limits of the comedian's poetical licence. Cf. also p. 90.

These allegorical figures are presented as very realistic hetaerae. The vine-dresser Trygaios marries Opora in order to beget young vines.[1] Theoria is brought to the council which in time of peace had sent the *theoroi* to Delphi and Delos. Thus peace is realized in what seemed to the poet, and to the majority of the people, its most important aspect: as the necessary condition for the farmer's tranquil work and for the religious obligations and festivals which were part of the normal life of Greece.

There are two interesting points to notice about this, one positive, the other negative. There was no 'patriotic' rejoicing at a peace which maintained the greatness and power of Athens, the real cause of the war. Instead we see a manifest desire to celebrate the Panhellenic importance of the peace, the salvation and rescue of all Greeks. This gives us the true political measure of the play. The attitude is one that is easily understood, since dualism in Greece had culminated in war and severed most Panhellenic ties. For the individual man, and in a sense for the individual State, peace was still identified, as it was in the *Acharnians*, with the ideal of a quiet existence, an ideal almost out of touch with politics. Ten terrible years of war had gone by, yet men were still clinging blindly to the hope that in the end those years would have left no mark, that life could simply continue where its pleasant and prosperous course had been interrupted in 432. Nor did the politicians think otherwise when they attempted in the peace of Nikias to restore the *status quo*. In this self-deception of leaders and led is to be found the ultimate reason why the peace of 421 was no real and lasting peace.

From the seven years which followed no comedies of Aristophanes survive. Those were the years of half-peace and renewed war, the years also of the struggles and preparations for the Sicilian expedition. To the author of the *Peace* who maintained the ideal of an idyllic and care-free life, those years must have been a series of disappointments and sorrows. He even ceased to attack in any elaborate way his old enemies, the demagogues. He certainly hated men like Hyperbolos as much as he had hated Kleon, and he must have felt very uneasy about Alkibiades. But he left that field to other comedians, whom he had previously blamed for attacking the contemptible Hyperbolos, while he fought against the formidable Kleon.[2]

[1] P.706ff.   [2] C.549ff.

Now, for several years he wrote plays of a more conventional character, such as mythological parodies. This kind of escapism, however, could not satisfy him, and he soon found new and different ways. A generation later, Sokrates' great disciple fled from mean and corrupt reality into the Polis of 'placelessness': Utopia. So, too, the *Birds* of Aristophanes, however it may be interpreted in relation to contemporary events, is an escape from reality into the least material of all regions, the air, the realm of the birds, and at the same time the realm of pure poetry.[1] Hence, to discover what is relevant to the inner meaning of this comedy two questions must be discussed: why the two Athenian citizens who are the principal figures in the plot have left their home, and what sort of superiority the new Birds' City has over the earthly Polis.

Of the two Athenians the one, Euelpides, 'the man of good hope', is a typical good-natured citizen.[2] His only part in the play is to act as interlocutor to the ingenious creator of Cloudcuckooborough, whose name and character we may assume to have been 'the persuasive friend' (Peithetairos) rather than 'the reliable friend' (Pisthetairos).[2a] Though both are 'citizens among citizens' and respectable men of mature age, they have left Athens not because of any hatred of it, but because they are completely disgusted with the prevailing mania for litigation.[3] It appears, however, to be a case of putting *pars pro toto*. The two men are in search of a *polis apragmon*, a city where one can stretch one's limbs on soft cushions and live one's own quiet and private life.[4] The emigrants wish to be free of their debts; but their chief concern is to find a place free of politics where food and love are of paramount importance. They have had enough of the endless difficulties, of the troubles and violence of life at Athens, dominated by politics. Their desire, then, is

[1] I cannot share the opinion which regards the *Birds* as wholly fairy-tale, although a bird's chorus was nothing new (see Plate II*c*).

[2] Croiset has rightly compared Thuc. I, 70, 3, where the Corinthians characterize the Athenians *inter alia* as ἐν τοῖς δεινοῖς εὐέλπιδες. Even closer to the *Birds* is Thuc. VI, 24, the description of the reasons which moved the people in favour of the Sicilian expedition; there we read (§3) of the younger men εὐέλπιδες ὄντες σωθήσεσθαι. This 'unreflecting confidence' in some bold design appears again as typically Athenian in Thuc. IV, 10, 1.

[2a] Possibly Pisthetairos had something to do with the part played at the time by the *Hetairiai* (cf. F. Sartori, *Le eterie nella vita politica* etc. (1957), 101f.

[3] B.40f.   [4] B.121f.

not to escape from democracy, and their adherence to tribe and clan does not involve any oligarchic or even conservative tendency.[1] Euelpides denies explicitly that he is looking for an aristocratic State.[2] They are not anxious to avoid war and danger, they do not even mention them. Nor are they fleeing from the irreligion of the new age: there is no allusion to the Hermocopids or the profanation of the mysteries. Yet, all these troubles derive from the same world from which they try to escape, the restless and joyless, even malignant, atmosphere of the Athenian law-courts and Athenian politics. Aristophanes' old ideal of peace has not changed, but there seems now no chance left of realizing it on earth. The result, born of a general sense of estrangement from the State, is the flight of the two old men, and therefore of the poet.

Of course, like will stick to like, and the Athenian to politics. The escape from the State is succeeded by the foundation of a new State. The goal, the achievement of non-political life, is to be approached only by the path of true politics. When the new Polis is built in imagination, Euelpides thinks of nothing beyond the money he will be able to make out of it; Peithetairos, however, stands above this level which we can easily believe to be the general and natural level of the Athenian middle-class. Peithetairos is a born leader. He continues a tradition which, in Aristophanes' plays, has hardly any connection with the real statesmen of the past (it is otherwise, as we shall see, with Eupolis), and which has certainly no representative in the poet's time, a tradition which perhaps goes only back to Agorakritos in the last scenes of the *Knights*. It is a type of leadership which could hardly be found outside comedy, and which the poet could not have created without himself being guided by the spirit of sophistic individualism, and without doing a certain injustice at least to the politicians of the 'good old times'. Peithetairos is rewarded by receiving as his prize Basileia, the daughter of Zeus and embodiment of all political virtue.[3] She does not make an ordinary monarch out of the cunning bourgeois. In a fairy-tale myth (similar to the rejuvenation of Demos by Agorakritos) the marriage

---

[1] ἡμεῖς δὲ φυλῇ καὶ γένει τιμώμενοι, B.33.   [2] B.125f.

[3] B.1538ff. I do not propose to discuss the various, partly rather wild, attempts at explaining the meaning of this allegorical figure. I do not think we can, or in fact need, go beyond what is said in the text, and below on p. 348.

crowns the picture of an ascent that is tied to no reality, and gives to the ruler the full dignity and grace, the *charisma*, that is the right of his position.

Yet in spite of its fabulous character the 'ideal Polis', this fantasy-city Cloudcuckooborough, shows some connection with reality — at least negatively, in the nature of the people driven away from it by Peithetairos. First come persons who usually appeared when a new Athenian colony was to be founded, a priest and a poet, that is to say, a beggar-priest and an opportunist poet, followed by an oracle-monger and the mathematician Meton, here a town-planning architect, likewise a quack and an impostor. After Meton comes an 'inspector' (one of the officials elected by lot) and a 'decree-seller'. The priest and poet, Peithetairos dismisses with words, to the poet he even gives some clothes: the others, however, he drives from the stage with whips, convinced that all those who try to make money as sophists or by profiting from, and corrupting, politics are impostors. This impression is confirmed by a second scene which shows the would-be members of the new city. The first to appear is one of those unpleasant youths who beat their fathers and drain their resources. Peithetairos makes a soldier of him, that is to say, turns him into a useful citizen. On the other hand, the well-known poet Kinesias is treated like the sycophant and whipped. The principle underlying this representation of the founder of a State as one who is always ready to use the lash is moral, not political. It is exemplified again in the fact that democracy is not renounced in Cloudcuckooborough, nor are democratic institutions; only those who make a selfish profit out of them are repudiated. The inclusion of Meton amongst the impostors is, of course, to be attributed to the same attitude of mind in the poet which made him depict Sokrates as a mere sophist and an observer of the stars. Although Aristophanes' chief aim was to make fun of anyone who in one way or another was different from the average, it is hardly rash to conclude from his emphasis on the money point that to him intellectual pursuits were as wicked a source of economic gain as politics. The greater his contempt for sophists and sycophants, the more fervently must he have believed in the worth of those who earned their living as farmers, craftsmen, or merchants. He does not name them here, but together with the defenders of the State (who of course come first) they are its true pillars. Significantly enough, Peithetairos sends his *alter ego*, his comrade Euelpides, to take part in the building of the wall, and to supervise workmen and guards. Disinterested service to the community and a life spent in real work, those are the forces that maintain the State.

The *Demoi* of Eupolis, the last and, according to ancient opinion, the best work written by this poet, was probably produced in the spring of 412. The plot can be partly reconstructed, since the fragments have been supplemented by a number of papyri.[1] It is significant that Eupolis conjures back to life the great statesmen of Athens, from Solon to Perikles, to help the State in the hard times after the collapse of the Sicilian expedition. The reason for this is, of course, that there seemed to be nobody amongst those in power at the moment capable of dealing with the situation. Previously, in his *Baptai*, Eupolis had also attacked Alkibiades. While Aristophanes flees from his own time and State and takes refuge in Cloudcuckooborough, or in the fantasy of the women's struggle for peace, or in the world of literature as in the *Thesmophoriazousai*, while, in short, his attitude is fundamentally non-political, we find in Eupolis an active, though moderate, political conservatism more pronounced than that exhibited by Aristophanes even in his younger days. Not long after, Eupolis seems to have vindicated his resolute political attitude and his unquestioning love of Athens by dying in battle.

A peculiar part is assigned in the *Demoi* to Myronides,[2]

---

[1] A full reconstruction is impossible, as the widely different attempts show. After C. Jensen, *Hermes* LI (1916), 321ff, and A. Körte, *Ber. Sächs. Akad.* 71 (1919), cf. W. Schmid, *Philol.* 93 (1938), 413ff, D. L. Page, *Greek Literary Papyri*, I, no. 40, and (on the ground of a new reading) J. M. Edmonds, *Mnemosyne* VIII (1939), 1ff, *Fragm. of Attic Com.* I 978ff. Mr. Edmonds offers, in spite of a few errors and bold conjectures, an improved text and a general reconstruction which is as ingenious as it is daring. I, however, keep to what is reasonably certain, from which I omit the alleged plea for the return of Alkibiades. — Jensen has dealt again with the fragments, though only with the *parabasis*, in *Abhandlungen Preuss. Akad.* 1939, no. 14, a paper which I was able to use for this second edition. Against his date of 411 see below, p. 153, n. 7.

[2] Cf. my article in *P.-W.*, Suppl. VII. I was able to test Edmonds's new reading of 40 P, 53f in the original photographs. Though it is not quite certain, it eliminates, in my view, Jensen's reading which implied that Myronides had six years of political leadership.

who was never a ruling politician but appears as a representative of former times. Here he guides the dead statesmen up to Athens. His very character is a return to the past, recalling the *Marathonomaches* type. He is shown as an honest, courageous, public-spirited citizen who, however, seems to represent an ideal of the past rather than one which is likely to be realized in the future. Eupolis hurls violent attacks against the *strategoi* and politicians of the day. The statesmen of the past, Aristeides first, Perikles last, and in between probably Solon and Miltiades, give their advice to the people which are represented by the demes. The whole is a purely political comedy with a social background provided by the chorus. The deme, which Kleisthenes had made the smallest political unit in the State, was for the citizen (we shall confirm this later from the evidence of comedy) his 'home, sweet home'. He was attached to it by strong local and sentimental associations. The demes form the chorus of Eupolis' play. They represent the whole body of the narrow-minded and insignificant population of town and countryside, who in their close attachment to the land and to their neighbours were the very basis of the State.

In spite of its remoteness from reality, or perhaps because of this conscious remoteness, Aristophanes' 'escapism' in the *Lysistrate* (411 b.c.) testifies to his high courage and humanity. At a moment when Athens was making heroic and successful efforts to avoid final defeat, when every word of peace must have seemed weakness, this play of peace was boldest defeatism. The poet avoids committing himself in the party-struggle, he is even somewhat antagonistic to the rising oligarchs. He shows this in the ridiculous character of the *proboulos*, and in the personal attacks, which are directed against Peisandros, the 'coming man'. But he seems not to have fully realized the dangers of an oligarchic revolution, or if he did he was not sufficiently interested in the domestic issues. The only real issue to him was to end the war. Aristophanes makes the women attain by methods only too feminine a truly Panhellenic peace, marked by a general reconciliation.[1] The fight for peace becomes possible only when the Spartan woman supports Lysistrate's proposal that the women shall deny their husbands the pleasures of love; the rest of the women do not feel strong enough. This plot provides ample scope for some of the best

[1] This is Διαλλαγή who appears in person (L.1114ff).

fun the poet ever wrote, but it is at the same time one of the
rare occasions when Aristophanes looks beyond the confines of
his own Polis: here he is, like many of the sophists, a champion
of Panhellenic unity.[1]

The comedy can be called Utopian not only because of the
part played by women, but also because of its conciliatory Panhellenic trend, which was indeed Utopian at such a time. It is
a conception of Utopia in which solemn, almost tragic, strains
continually make themselves heard through the light-hearted
burlesque. The idea of a Panhellenic peace is proclaimed by a
woman — her very name, 'she who disbands the army', shows
what she stands for—and so the war ends. The role of the woman
is in itself enough to introduce into the idea an element of
warm and uncorrupt humanity. Even the comedy of some of
the scenes, loose and often obscene, draws some of its life from
the same source. The ideal of a peaceful and carefree existence
is set up as the vital principle and basis of life as a whole.

Though we do not know what place was assigned to the
play in the competition, the Athenian people, at any rate, stand
out in an exceptionally brilliant light, if words and thoughts
such as those in the *Lysistrate* could be said and thought at a
time of overwhelming danger, of great military and financial
efforts, of grave political troubles. The poet displayed a fine
courage. A few years earlier, when Athens was intoxicated
with power and imperialist ambition, this play could hardly
have been written and would not have been produced. By 411
the desire for peace was undoubtedly very much stronger, but
that it was voiced in such a sublime way, and with such complete justice to the enemy, is a particularly striking testimony
to the character of the Athenian people.[2]

The *Thesmophoriazousai* (411) and the *Frogs* (405) are both
concerned with literature, especially with the work of Euripides, though there are fundamental differences between them.
It is no mere coincidence of survival which brings them together, since except for the *Triphales* (probably an attack on
Alkibiades) and the first *Ploutos*, all the plays of Aristophanes

---

[1] Cf. W. M. Hugill, *Panhellenism in Aristophanes* (1936).

[2] Whether, and to what extent, it is permissible to draw conclusions from the
Lysistrate as to the mentality and education of Athenian women is another
question which can only be discussed if other sources are taken into account as
well (cf. ch. VIII).

during this period, so far as their names are known, appear to
deal with literary questions. This can be said with least cer-
tainty of the *Women under Canvas*, a play about women, in
which apparently literary matters are touched on.[1] It is certainly true of the *Phoinissai*, the *Gerytades* and a second play
with the title *Thesmophoriazousai*. At such a time of hardship
for Athens, both poet and audience were capable of taking an
active interest in literary questions. Undoubtedly this is significant; but we must not forget that Greek literature, and Attic
tragedy in particular, was neither seriously nor in caricature a
matter of pure art, not *l'art pour l'art*. It was never considered
or judged on aesthetic grounds alone. On the contrary, its
roots lay deep in the soil of political and social life; there too
lay its purpose and function.

The *Thesmophoriazousai* is a good illustration of this, in that
Euripides is persecuted by the women simply as a woman-
hater. We almost get the impression that Aristophanes was
at pains to avoid depicting the effects of the new education
which was introduced into the world of the theatre by Euripides. It can even be maintained of this play that the women
fare a good deal worse at the author's hands than the tragedian,
whose immense popularity is attested by various parodies and
numerous quotations. The most noteworthy feature, however,
of the play is the setting — the festival of the Thesmophoria,
to which only women were admitted — not so much for its own
sake as because it is held up to ridicule. Yet there is nothing
new in this, except that it is not here a case of exposing to
ridicule individual gods or oracles or sacrifices, but one of the
most sacred of the Athenian festivals, which is revealed,
certainly far beyond reality, in its only too human atmosphere.

It is a long step from the *Thesmophoriazousai* to the *Frogs*.
I do not refer to the artistic value of the plays, for both rank
as masterpieces. But what is important to notice is that in the
Frogs problems of literature are associated with the grave political and intellectual situation of the time. In a sense, though
with far greater detachment than previously, the poet returns
to the urgent issues which were menacing the State. Aristophanes takes from Eupolis the motif of fetching the dead from
Hades, and transfers it, as he did in the *Gerytades*, to the tragic

[1] Σκηνὰς καταλαμβάνουσαι. The meaning of the title is disputed; cf. below,
p. 201, n 6.

poets.[1] As Eupolis brings statesmen, so Aristophanes summons poets, to save the State. Both comedians also allude to
the part played by Alkibiades, which is a further link between
the two plays. Aristophanes, at the moment of the State's
imminent collapse, when, now under the leadership of the
lyremaker Kleophon, it was about to waste the fruits of the
victory of Arginusae, summons the great tragedians to an *agon*
before Dionysos. He is an extremely ridiculous, yet extremely
Athenian, Dionysos; and the *agon* is also Athenian, even if it
is ridiculous and a travesty of the real thing. Aischylos wins
his victory over Euripides not by greater wisdom or art —
Euripides' words and advice are often clever and simple, while
Aischylos is obscure — but by an almost arbitrary decision.
Euripides is treated with much more fairness than usual.
Athens still stood under the impression of his and Sophokles'
death the year before, and Aristophanes was not likely to forget that Sophokles had dressed his chorus in mourning when
Euripides had died. The fun of the *agon* is concerned with
Aischylos no less than with Euripides. The real issue is politics rather than poetry: was the State to be ruled by clever
reasoning or by the moral standards and religious traditions
of the past?[2] Aischylos must be victorious, in order that he,
the representative of the great times of old, and not Euripides,
the exponent of the modern spirit, may be sent to Athens
by the ruler of the nether world, 'to save our Polis'.[3]

As we have already indicated, this *agon* is based on the idea
that the poet has a moral task, moral implying also political:
'because we make the men in the cities better'.[4] Euripides is
pledged to a belief in this task no less than Aischylos (and
Aristophanes). But not till the time of Aristophanes could it
be presented as a conscious aim. It was only when the sophists
made education an end in itself and their teaching had spread,
that the fundamental question of the *Frogs* became possible.
For they lifted the idea of general education clear of the self-
contained, unconscious atmosphere of the earlier Polis-com-
munity, turning it into a programme of deliberate education

---

[1] *Gerytades*, frg. 149. The appearance in the upper world of the chthonic
Πλοῦτοι in Kratinos' comedy of that name (160ff) is something quite different
from the return of human beings from Hades (against Schmid, 81).

[2] Cf. J. T. Sheppard, *JHS.* XXX (1910), 249ff.

[3] F.1501.   [4] F.1009f.

and instruction. Of course, Aristophanes did not consider the task of Aischylos in the light of the educational work of the sophists; he thought of it rather as a complete contrast to it. Again, as so frequently, he preaches a return to the standards of the *Marathonomachai* and their vigorous simplicity: therefore Aischylos had to win. The education he desires is not that of a cultured governing class, based on politics and fundamentally intellectual, but the education of a public-spirited people, still based on politics, but fundamentally moral and religious. Aischylos' epitaph shows that according to common opinion even the greatest poet fulfilled his real task not as a poet, but as a soldier and citizen. It was, on the one hand, a feature of tragedy that its poets aimed at proclaiming or even discussing the fundamental truths of human life and divine nature. The tragedian was always also a preacher. No generation, on the other hand, earlier than that of Aristophanes would have thought of making the poet a teacher, consciously chosen and consciously carrying out his task. Much more clearly than Eupolis, who only summoned the better statesmen of old to help their successors, Aristophanes in spite of his retrospective attitude appears as a child of his age — an age whose character was largely determined by the work of the sophists.

According to ancient tradition, which originates in Dikaiarchos, the *Frogs* was performed a second time, 'because of the *parabasis* which is contained therein'. Possibly there is a mistake in the tradition here, and we should read *katabasis*, that is the descent of Dionysos into Hades, a series of amusing and clever scenes.[1] Certainly the superb fooling of Dionysos-Xanthos and Xanthos-Dionysos was received with particular enthusiasm. Nevertheless the *parabasis* is noteworthy, not least for our purpose, though it is hardly the principal reason for the comedy's effectiveness.[2]

After a *captatio benevolentiae*, addressed to the 'audience in which thousands of clever men are sitting', the 'holy chorus' claims for itself the right, conceded later in the play to the tragic poets, 'of advising and teaching things useful to the State'. The gist of this teaching is that all citizens are to be recognized as possessing full and equal rights, even if they have taken part in the machinations of the oligarchs. This

[1] This is an ingenious, though perhaps superfluous, conjecture of Weil's.
[2] F.675ff.

demand is not made for the sake of the oligarchs, but to restore the unity and concord among the citizens. At the same time the *kaloikagathoi* are compared to the good coins of old, which have gone out of circulation because the new bad coins are preferred. There is no question of setting up party-rule by oligarchs. They are introduced, as in earlier plays, to point a contrast with the ruling democrats, whose partiality and egotism are the real object of attack.

Aristophanes' point of view has remained the same; but, as was stated above, there is an important difference between this later period and the years immediately preceding. The point of view has been, as it were, revitalized. During the internal struggles of 411 and the years which followed, the voice of the poet had been subdued; but now, in view of the new dangers of 405 and the ruinous folly of the demagogues, he could hope to find a response to his demand for reconciliation and concord. Aristophanes wrote this play, which was so successful in both its comic and its serious aspects, in the same winter in which the demos condemned the unhappy victors of Arginusae. One can imagine the strength of the group that hated the radical democracy. The poet's demands for concilia-tion therefore had not only a political but also a social signifi-cance. We cannot assess the relative strength of the different groups and classes of the people with such exactness as to ascertain, for example, whether or no a majority had been overwhelmed by the demagogues and the general hysteria. But it may be assumed that a large proportion even of the town population rejected the methods without rejecting the principle of democracy. It needed the tyranny of the Thirty to make democracy — for the time being under the leadership of a true man of the people and not of mere demagogues and orators — popular once more, and even to prove that it was inevitable.

What we have called Aristophanes' 'escape' was, no doubt, prompted by his personality, though not entirely so. There was, as with any great man, that mysterious 'sympathy' and interplay between the life of the individual and that of the community.[1] In this case the idea of flight from politics and

[1] This 'sympathy', it will be remembered, is stressed in J. Burckhardt's *Weltgeschichtliche Betrachtungen* — now in English translation under the title *Reflections on History* (1943).

actual events was inherent both in the development of comedy and in the general development of the age; but it was influenced and carried several stages further by the mind and outlook of the greatest of the comic poets.

The two surviving plays of Aristophanes' last period, the *Ekklesiazousai* and the *Ploutos*, are sometimes bracketed with the *Wasps* as 'social' comedies; but while in the *Wasps* real social conditions are depicted and criticized, the poet in these later plays gives expression to, and elaborates his longing for, a complete change in social conditions, for an ideal society. The *Birds* was a political Utopia, its theme a new and 'decent' State; the two late works are social Utopias. The *Ekklesiazousai* shows communism in practice; its farcical possibilities are fully exploited, while the serious implications are not worked out. The *Ploutos* is the fairy-tale of Wealth coming to good men; here, from the beginning, the poet takes his stand outside reality.

The communism of the *Ekklesiazousai* is partly pure fun, but it is also meant to be taken seriously. The end of the play, with its appeal to both the wise and the laughing, gives explicit proof of this.[1] Of course, when the magnificent spread at the public dinner is announced and, at the same time, the citizens are warned to bring with them their own little bit of soup, the whole scheme is reduced *ad absurdum*. We are right, however (though the point has been disputed), to connect some of the ideas in the play with serious philosophical thought, though there is hardly any direct reference in Aristophanes to Plato's *Republic*.[2] The comic poet used and ridiculed certain ideas current in his own time — not only the fairy-tale of a fool's paradise. He was quite entitled to select as most useful for his purpose some features of communism which need not have been important in theory. Communist theories and Utopias

[1] E.1155f.
[2] Gilbert Murray, *Greek Studies* (1946), 36ff (cf. already his *Aristophanes*, 186ff), assumes 'that Plato occasionally gave readings to a select body of friends', or 'merely gave lectures in the school', and that Aristophanes either heard these himself or used notes from one of Plato's disciples. I doubt that the comedian took as his model such an esoteric example. There will have been others who drew pictures of a communist Utopia. Similarities, on the other hand (such as E.635ff with Plat. *Rep.* V, 461 D) do not necessarily prove direct allusion nor, if we assume such an allusion, do they establish Plato's priority. For a recent discussion cf. Schmid, 216ff.

were undoubtedly in fashion, and the fact need not surprise us. They originated in that 'escapism' which is not peculiar to Aristophanes, but characteristic of his age as a whole. They mark, at the same time, a definite transition from purely political to social-economic thought. This movement, which was part of a general change, was given a turn in exactly the opposite direction by Plato, when he restricted the communist ideal to the 'guardians', and so directed it away from the politics of the day and from the economic desires of the lower classes towards absolute politics, that is to say, towards a union of politics and ethics.

In the *Ekklesiazousai* the communist programme forms the theme of the second part of the play. It is worked out in relation to money and love, and concerns itself equally with these two subjects. It tries to describe a system by which the ordinary citizens enjoy their life, while the State pays and the slaves do the work. Only the humorous and grotesque elements are prominent, and this part of the play has no organic connection with the first part, where the theme is government by women. This is after all only a natural outcome of the hitherto conspicuously bad government by men; something new must be tried. For the comedian this was a fitting and fertile subject; it can hardly be taken as a genuine argument in favour of the emancipation of women. The actual serious background and some of the worst faults in the State are revealed in the defence of feminine government made by the women's leader Praxagora, that is she 'who is active in the market'.[1] Old grievances are pressing again, stirred up by the developments since 403, that is to say, since the restoration of democracy, and some of them have even become worse: bad politicians, the draining of the State's resources by the payments for the ecclesia and army, an uncertain foreign policy, corrupt financial administration, a chronic desire for change. Of all this the women will be the natural enemies, not least so because as mothers they have to protect their sons.

Not without strong words, though without the passion of earlier years, the poet again states the demand he has repeated so often for the purge of the State. Yet we must not overlook the fact that his points are put forward in the form of a theoretical programme rather than in terms of practical politics and

---

[1] E.173ff.

individual effort. The poet has grown old, but the times too
have changed.

A particular political and social programme, whether serious
or comic, is perhaps not so interesting as the reaction to it, and
that also is shown in this play. We must look for it not so
much in the applause of the other women, or in the amusing
exchange of question and answer between Praxagora and her
husband, but in one scene which has a peculiar charm of its
own: two citizens, one decent and willing, the other a sceptical
egoist, voice their reactions to the decree which demands that
all property shall be handed over to the State.[1] The scene is
not only extremely comic, it also reveals the whole psychology
of the people. Two strongly contrasted types are depicted, the
public-spirited, law-abiding, essentially democratic citizen,
and the self-seeking opportunist for whom democracy is
merely the means to his own advantage. Sketched in a few
lines we have the *Zoon politikon* and the *Zoon oikonomikon*, the
political and the economic type of man. The short and ingenious scene, which ends without making clear which is the
'wiser' type (we should ourselves be inclined to say the opportunist), gives a picture not only of the actual conditions and
possibilities of the time, but also of the eternal struggle that
endangers liberty and social equality.

The same subject is dealt with in the last of the surviving
comedies. In the *Ploutos* the poet turns his back on the political world, which gave the *Ekklesiazousai* at least its basic
situation. The extant play was probably not only a recast of
a much earlier comedy of the same title, performed in 408,
but completely re-written. In its form and in the types of
character as well as the non-political setting, the *Ploutos* marks
the beginning of Middle Comedy; and this change of outward
and inward form is to be attributed not to the weakness of ad-
vancing age, but to the triumph of the spirit over this weakness. It is noteworthy that in the following centuries the
Ploutos was one of the most widely read comedies and kept its
place even beside Menander. Fighting passion, creative intui-
tion, spirited wit, may have grown scarce and weak; but the
fact that Aristophanes was himself capable of leading the way
from Old Comedy to a new literary form, adapting himself
in his latest works to the changed times and even giving

[1] E.730ff.

an impetus to those times, is no small proof of his genius.[1]

The economic situation of Athens in 388 was one of deep depression. The peasants suffered most from the general pauperization. The impoverished farmer class is represented both by the leading figure Chremylos and by the chorus. The plot is chiefly concerned with the restoration of his sight to the blind god of Wealth, who therefore ceases to favour with his presence rascals and impostors, and visits good people only. This is clearly pure fairy-tale. We are in fairy-land, though in the sad fairy-land of poverty. The story realizes an ideal which is not, as before, that of modest bourgeois enjoyment. It stands simply and unequivocally for Money, Property, Wealth. Because the story deals with honest and moderate men, this new life of wealth keeps within modest limits, but it has lost most of its poetry, lightheartedness and mirth. It is governed by stark economic facts.

The explanation is that the Attic peasants, the small farmers whom Aristophanes has described again and again, now occupy a social and economic position different from and inferior to that of earlier times. The tale of Ploutos is based on the existence of radical poverty, so radical as to be necessarily hateful to the poor man who refuses to listen to the arguments of Poverty, even when they are just. He has abandoned all hope of driving out poverty by 'work and thrift'. Only the 'good luck' of a fairy-tale can help him. Trade and craftsmanship are hardly mentioned in the play, yet we know that at the time they were entering on a new and prosperous phase. The contrast with the desperate situation of the country people must have been all the greater. Economically and psychologically the peasants were undergoing a process which, without too much fear of using a false modernism, we may well call the growth of a rural proletariate.

Ploutos' recovery of his sight has various results. The sycophant becomes a pauper because there are no more lawsuits; we must assume that money was essential for going to

---

[1] We might easily think that the mythological parodies of Aristophanes (*Kokalos, Aiolosikon*) which continued an earlier tradition, did not attain the same importance in the development of literature as the type of comedy of which the *Ploutos* is the earliest example; but we learn to our surprise that ancient scholars talked in similar terms of the *Kokalos*. In the *Life* of Aristophanes we are practically told that in that play he anticipated Menander!

law, and that good and honest people — who are now the rich —
did not go to law. The rich old hag is in danger of losing her
lover — that is quite in order; we are less satisfied that the
young ne'er-do-well who had been dependent on her should
be among the enriched, but the just order of things is restored
by his inability to get rid of the woman. All this is a rather
feeble and lifeless repetition of the closing scenes of the
Ekklesiazousai. But mark the effect on the gods: pious people
are now rich, they no longer need the gods or bring them
sacrifices, so the gods are starving. The logical result of this
remarkable piece of reasoning is that the starving wretch
Hermes and the unemployed priest of Zeus have to enter the
service of Ploutos. However, when Zeus, who made Ploutos
blind, is said to have profited by his blindness, the joke ceases
to be harmless and becomes very bitter. The gods are acces-
sories in the unjust and miserable state of the world. We have
previously noted a famine on Olympus in the *Birds*, but in that
case it was an amusing war-measure necessitated by particular
and fanciful circumstances and leading to a happy ending.
The second famine also arises out of circumstances, but they
are the outcome of real human misery, and it is a social grievance that finds its expression in the conception of the starving
gods. Revolutionary ferment had begun amongst the lower
classes, and religion no longer had the power to arrest it.

The conversation with the sycophant makes clear another
important point. He is one of those men whose sole activity is
the wresting of some personal advantage from politics and
law-suits. He refuses every kind of work, whether as peasant
or trader or artisan. No distinction is made as to the social
standing of the various professions which all of them involve
manual labour. This implies, as it were, the existence of a
psychological 'labour front', a collective consciousness among
labourers, by which they recognize each other's equal rights.
Though at first distress was greatest among the agricultural
population, the accumulation of great wealth in trade and business had led to the emergence of a poor class among the urban
working class as well. These 'proletarians' among the townsfolk were to prove of vital importance in changing social and
political conditions.

Thus the last play of Aristophanes is of special interest for
us. It has taken us beyond the general view formed from an

examination of the earlier works. It shows us the completion of the great change which we have so often noted in its earlier stages, the change from a political to an economic outlook, from the political consciousness of a citizen to the economic purpose of an individual human being. We must not forget that this change was closely linked with the individualization of life and mind which is typical of the period. Social life became private life, the patriotism of the citizens became the egotism of class-conscious individuals. The new factors which appear in the *Ploutos* confirm our conviction that there is a fundamental unity throughout the varied aspects of the change. In the following chapters our task will be to demonstrate the unity of the whole by examining the social, economic, and spiritual aspects of the various spheres in which it displayed itself.

CHAPTER III

THE FARMERS

I

ON innumerable occasions we find the comic poets describing peasants and farmers, praising, or slightly ridiculing, their life and work, and emphasizing their importance to people and State. In consequence, the reader receives a general impression, the truth of which must be discussed. No doubt, Aristophanes was, so to speak, in love with those modest and industrious small farmers and vine-dressers who formed a large part of the Attic population. The question is whether that liking was more than personal, more than a view based chiefly on a private, primarily ethical, bias. It is true that many of the phrases in which the hard-working peasants are contrasted with the idlers, sycophants and snobs of the town are the expression of such a personal opinion; but to recognize this fact is not enough. Who were the peasants who play such a large part in comedy? To find an answer in comedy, an answer which is neither tendentious nor distorted, it will not suffice to regard figures such as Dikaiopolis or Trygaios as typical representatives of their fellow peasants as a whole. The importance of these 'heroes' of the comedies is, at any rate, exceptional. Whether they are typical in other respects, is a question which can only be answered after considering the arguments which will form the subject of this chapter.

We begin with the economic basis of farming, the cultivation of the soil. 'The earth bears everything and takes it back.'[1] The first fact which emerges is that the cultivation of vine, olive and fig tree predominated, and that corn-growing was much less important. Ever since the days of Solon, Attic agriculture had been undergoing a process of transformation which had led to this result, which is confirmed by the evidence of comedy. It is interesting to hear a farmer say almost the opposite of what we in our northern climate should expect a peasant to say: 'I had sold my grapes, and, with my mouth full

[1] Eur. *frg.* 195.

of coppers, I went off to buy flour in the market.'[1] A fragment
which runs: 'One man gathers grapes, the other picks olives',
is probably meant to describe the two chief kinds of crop.[2]
Similarly grapes and figs are mentioned together.[3] The vines
were either supported by stakes or grew between, and climbed
up, the olive trees or fig trees.[4] Thus the owner of even a small
estate was able to cultivate all the chief fruits of the country
within a small space. We realize that they all grew together
when we hear, for instance, that the slave who has stolen some
grapes is led to the olives in order to be flogged.[5] The stump
of an olive tree could be an obstacle to the growing of vines.[6]
Old and young vines, young fig-tree shoots and olives grew
next to each other.[7] For work among the olives, figs and
vines there were special words which can be paraphrased, but
not translated.[8] Wine, figs (either fresh or dried) and olives
represent, together with myrtles and fragrant violets, the
established natural life of the country.[9] The cultivation of
these three fruits, above all of the vine, needed great and
intensive care, and the character of the Attic peasant, who
himself worked and cultivated his soil, was strongly influenced
by this fact. The goddess of Peace is called 'giver of grapes',
and she has another name which is also applied to the peasant
himself: 'vine-loving'.[10]

The three fruits, of course, were not the only food; but
besides bread and fish (and a little meat), they provided the
staple diet. The main point, shown by the words already
quoted of the peasant in the market,[11] is that the average farmer
grew no corn, or, at any rate, less than he needed for himself.
It is estimated that Attica produced herself about a quarter of
the grain she consumed.[12] Much corn came from Euboia, and

---

[1] E.817ff. For his way of carrying money see below, p. 226.
[2] frg. 15 D = adesp. 437. Olive-gatherers: Plate V*a*.
[3] P.634.   [4] A.986, Pherekr. 109.   [5] W.449f.
[6] Lysias VII, 14.   [7] A.995ff, cf. frg. 374.
[8] Words such as ἐλαΐʒειν (frg. 119), οἰναρίʒειν (P.1147), συκάʒιν and
τρυγᾶν (B.1698f), ἀποσυκάʒειν (K.259, Ameips. 33), also the composite
word ἀμπελουργεῖν (frg. 43 D). Of course, there is also σκάπτειν τοὺς
ἀμπέλους (adesp. 674).
[9] ἡ δίαιτα παλαιά, P.572, cf. P.557ff, 571ff, 596ff, 1159ff, 1248f, frg.
586-7, 729, adesp. 766.
[10] P.520, cf. frg. 294, 6. — P.308, adesp. 918.   [11] E.817ff.
[12] Glotz, 258.

after the occupation of Dekeleia this amounted to more than what Attica supplied.[1] There was, of course, some corn-growing, chiefly of barley, in the fertile plains, and elsewhere either in small fields or in the space between the rows of fruit trees or vines.[2] Trygaios, who is a vine-dresser, prays to the gods that they may give to the Greeks (that is to say, not only to the Athenians, but perhaps also to some corn-growing districts like Boeotia or Thessaly) wealth such as barley, wine, figs and children.[3] The farmer had not much to do after sowing time, when the ground was too wet for working in the vineyard.[4] 'I know', says a peasant, 'how to tend goats, how to dig, to plough and to plant.'[5] Here we have the whole scope of farming, and 'ploughing' means corn-growing. Occasionally we hear of someone carrying sheaves, or of a boy being bound with a sheaf-band.[6] Phrynichos knows the song which people sang when winnowing the grain.[7] The tilling of the soil, which was necessary for corn-growing, was the hardest part of all the hard work of husbandry, especially in the Greek climate, where the farmer performed his work almost naked; the soil of Attica was, to a large extent, poor, stony and often still uncultivated.[8] Deforestation was far advanced; yet, charcoal-burning, as the *Acharnians* shows, was still being practised and important.[9] Swelling land which could be graphically described as 'the buttocks of the field' was rare, in spite of the famous phrase of 'rich Athens', or the beautiful patriotic outburst of Aristophanes: 'O beloved city of Kekrops, native-born Attica, hail, thou rich soil, udder of the good land!'[10] When Wealth comes, says someone to Poverty, we shall have no further need 'of thy ploughmen or yoke-makers, thy sickle-makers or blacksmiths, of

[1] W.715f, Thuc. VIII, 96, 2.   [2] P.568, frg. 120.
[3] P.1320ff.   [4] P.1140ff.
[5] Eupolis 13.

[6] frg. 42 D, though ἀμιλλοφόρος may also be the epithet of a god. — Kallias 3 D.

[7] Phryn. 14.   [8] L.1173. — Kratinos 26 D, adesp. 380.

[9] In Euripides' *Herakles* (240f) Lykos orders wood to be brought to Thebes from Helikon and Parnassos. The reason why he sends so far is the tyrant's boastfulness rather than real necessity.

[10] Archipp. 7 D. — λιπαραὶ Ἀθῆναι, A.639f, C.300, B.826. λιπαρός means oily, sleek, then comfortable, rich, fruitful. The famous phrase, first known from Pindar (*I*. 2, 20, *frg.* 83) has nothing to do with the greasy brilliance of sardines, but refers to the fertile plain round the city and its silvery olive groves. Cf. also Eur. *Tro.* 801ff, *Iph. T.* 1130f. — Quotation by Aristophanes: frg. 110.

sowing or fencing the fields'.[1] Here again, the activities named
refer to the tilling of the soil, and it was only in the dreamland
of fairy-tale that ample crops would grow without hard labour.

When ploughing and tilling the peasant used oxen or cows.
The name and cult of one of the oldest Athenian families, the
Bouzygai, symbolized this, especially in the plain of Athens.
Various breeds of cattle were known in Attica.[2] 'The ox in
the stable' was a proverbial phrase for some useless person.[3] In
the early morning the poor peasant drives out his oxen to sow
his fields.[4] The farmer who looks forward to peace and work,
remembers above all his yoke of oxen. This 'yoke of two oxen'
was a fixed and much-used expression, and represented the
usual modest number of cattle the farmer owned (see Plate
IV *a*, *b*).[5] Euelpides was the owner of a 'puny pair', a two-oxen
man.[6] A peasant from the mountainous district of Phyle,
where ploughing and tilling were especially hard, has lost his
two oxen and with them the support of his farm.[7] We never
hear of larger numbers of cattle, although they must have
existed; the property of a rich man could be described as fields,
sheep and goats and cattle.[8]

The peasant, who did some corn-growing, needed his two
oxen. Milk and cheese, however, were usually taken from
goats and sheep, not from cows, and the farmer from the
Mycenaean mountains — where, as on those of Attica, few
cattle could be kept — is expressly called 'milk-drinking'.[9] It
can be said as a general rule that cattle were of little importance
in the holding of the average farmer.[10] 'Ox-loosing time' as an
hour of the day was certainly a Homeric reminiscence rather
than a practical expression of time used in Attica, and in

---

[1] Pherekr. 130.
[2] Eupolis 49 speaks of καινόν τι φῖτυ τῶν βοῶν.
[3] Kratinos 32.　　　　[4] Eur. *El*. 78f.
[5] ζεῦγος βοιδαρίων, or similar, frg. 82, 109, 387, Alkaios 14. ζεῦγος or ζυγόν
therefore can take simply the meaning of a 'pair', e.g., of horses (Isokr. XVI,
Andok. IV, 26) or even of human beings like the brothers Agamemnon and Menelaos (Eur. *Hel*. 392); exceptions are ζεῦγος τρίδουλον (frg. 576) and ζεῦγος
τριπάρθενον (Eur. *frg*. 357).
[6] B.582, 585.　　　　[7] A.1022ff.
[8] Eupolis 153.　　　　[9] Eur. *El*. 169f.
[10] It is, however, an exaggeration to say that 'in historical times ... cattle
became more or less the sacred animals of the temples, bred for sacrifice' (Michell,
60). Cattle, of course, as well as pigs and lambs were often used for sacrifices
(cf. P.925ff).

PLATE IV

a

b

c

AGRICULTURE

PLATE V

a

b

c

AGRICULTURE

general one expects to find that in a country where the cultivation of fruit trees and vines predominated, the usual domestic
animals were donkeys, mules and goats.[1] It is still the same in
many parts of Greece today. The comedians, too, mention the
donkeys, the animal most frequent in Greek proverbs, and the
sheep and goats of Attica.[2] Attic sheep and wool were highly
valued. Pigs, too, were common.[3] It was known to be most
lucrative to kill a pig: 'its meat is delicious, and nothing in a
pig is lost except the bristles, the mud and the squeal'.[4] The
mule is mentioned occasionally.[5] More frequently we hear
about horses; they were mainly used for aristocratic sport, and
we may assume that the horses of the State cavalry came from
native stock. Horse-breeding was practised, for instance, in
the plain of Marathon, but, as a rule, horses came from abroad.[6]
Horses and, even more, cattle needed green food, and that was
scarce in Attica.[7] It is clear why stock-farming could never be
undertaken except on a small scale.

A great deal of rural work consisted in market-gardening
by the country people and especially by the yeomen burgesses
who lived in the town or nearby and brought their produce to
market. Most of the gardens were situated outside the walls;
later Epicurus' garden was said to be the first inside the town,
but this statement is an exaggeration.[8] Gardening on a somewhat larger scale is revealed by the comic writers' knowledge
of a great number of different vegetables. An abundance of
flowers and fruit grew well in the mild climate and were available for a longer season than elsewhere; 'no one any longer
knows what season of the year it is', though this was largely due

[1] βουλυτός (sc. καιρός): B.1500. In general, cf. V. Hehn, *Kulturpflanzen u.
Haustiere* (1894⁶), 130. There was a saying 'If you can't drive an ox, drive an
ass' (adesp. 543), though often the latter was much more difficult. The meaning
of the proverb is, if you cannot afford a good help, you must be content with a
bad and cheaper one. See also Plate IV for the various animals in agriculture.
[2] A great deal of the psychology of the Attic donkey is implied in the saying
which indicates fatalistic resignation: ὄνος ὕεται, 'the donkey lets the rain soak
him' (Kratinos 52, Kephisodoros 1). — Evidence of comedy: C.71f, W.170,
1310 (κλητήρ = the 'brayer'; cf. 189), B.714, Pl.292ff, 820, Eupolis 14, etc.
[3] See, e.g., W.844, P.24, 926f, L.1073, Pl.820, 1106, frg. 258, Kratinos·3,
148, 312, Pherekr. 44, 102, Eupolis 453, Phryn. 43, Plat. 110, 111, 211,
Strattis 58, Nikochares 17. Cf. also Plate V*b*.
[4] Plat. 28.   [5] F.290.
[6] Strattis 52. — Kratinos 346. — frg. 41-2; cf. p. 138f.
[7] frg. 798.   [8] Against Pliny, *n.h.* XIX, 50f, cf., e.g., Isaios V, 11.

to the extension of trade.[1] The saying: 'You are not yet on the
celery and rue' was used to mean: 'You are scarcely at the edge
of a thing', for these plants formed the borders in gardens.[2]
Further allusions to the products of the vegetable garden are
made, when a stye on the eyelid is compared with a pumpkin,
or when Odysseus is said to have bought in Samos a seed-
cucumber.[3] Bees and poultry were included in this kind of
farming.[4] People were naturally proud of hens who laid well,
and seem to have believed that it was possible to force them to
lay 'wind-eggs'.[5] Geese and pigeons apparently were usually
imported from Boeotia.[6] The frequent combination of agriculture and gardening is shown in a lively fashion by the proverb 'A pig among roses.'[7] It had the same meaning as our
'A bull in a china-shop'; the Athenian expression, however, is
not taken as it were from a story, but from the possibilities of
everyday life.

The picture of husbandry and gardening gains in vividness
when seen in its dependence on nature.[8] The farmer loved all
the seasons, each of which had its beauty, its pleasures and
its advantages;[9] but they could also do much harm. 'The
fruits are spoiled by hoar-frost, and I give my sweat to the
winds':[10] the picture is harsh; it may be an allusion to some

---

[1] frg. 569, Kratinos 98; cf. P.577. Some scholars have drawn the conclusion
— as far as I can see, from frg. 569 only — that in Athens violets were grown by
forcing during the winter (cf. Heichelheim, 387). But the climate of Attica
itself sufficed. Th. v. Heldrich (in A. Mommsen, *Griechische Jahreszeiten*, Heft
5, 1877, 592) assures us that violets (*viola odorata*) blossomed from the beginning
of November until April, or, according to the diagram, p. 484, from the beginning of December until the middle of May. At any rate, there is nothing special
about these violets. The conditions are similar for other plants mentioned in frg.
569, e.g. the late pumpkins or the early carrots (Heldrich 585ff, 590ff). Xenophon (*Poroi*, 1, 3) sums up the climatic effects: πάντα ἐνταῦθα πρωιαίτατα
μὲν ἄρχεται, ὀψιαίτατα δὲ λήγει.

[2] W.480.   [3] C.327, Kratinos 136; cf. also K.630f.

[4] W.366. — frg. 18, Plat. 209, Strattis 58; cf. B.500.

[5] Theop. 9. — frg. 185-6, Plat. 19-20. A wind-egg is an 'unfertilized egg
incapable of producing chicken' (*C.O.D.*). Pliny, *n.h.* X, 166 describes such
sterile eggs as much less pleasant than normal eggs. It is possible that in the
passages mentioned the ὠὸν ὑπηνέμιον is supposed to be an egg produced
without impregnation, such as that of Νύξ in B.695. On the other hand, adesp.
5 D = 44 P, 9f, seems definite about the wind-eggs: νεοτ[τί' οὐκ ἔνι].

[6] A.878, P.1004.   [7] Krates 4.   [8] Cf. Xen. *oik.* 5, 18.

[9] P.1127ff, 1140ff, 1159ff, cf. 1168: ᾽Ὧραι φίλαι.

[10] adesp. 381.

mountain district of Attica. The winds certainly made the
peasant's work very hard, especially the growing of corn; this
is perhaps confirmed by the saying 'to till the winds' as a proverbial phrase for useless toil.[1] The blessings of rain and wind
as well as the damage they cause are frequently mentioned.[2]
In general, the farmers' labours were heavy. 'No idle man,
however much he may talk of the gods, can gather a livelihood
without toil', says the hard-working peasant in Euripides.[3]
The soil on the hills was poor, although the Attic mountains
were not so inaccessible as, for example, Mount Taygetos, and
it was thought better to live in a remote place among the rocks
than to have unkind neighbours in the plain.[4] We hear too
of the fear of wild animals, such as the wolf carrying off sheep
and goats.[5] The dependence of human beings on nature is
expressed in a general sense, when the birds, who are specially
important to the peasant, as, for instance, in heralding the
seasons, promise reward or punishment to mankind.[6] Either
they will kill all the animals that harm the plants, such as
locusts, ants and wasps, or the sparrows will devour the seeds
of grain, and the ravens will pluck out the eyes of the ploughing
oxen and the grazing sheep. As a rule, the Attic farmer did
not try very hard to force more than its natural yield from the
soil. He had his busy times, but a passage already quoted
proves that there were intervals.[7] Farming was largely a
seasonal occupation in Attica, and in winter after the olive
harvest, as at midsummer, there was very little work.[8] It
might happen that the value of an estate was doubled by
intensive labour, but that was exceptional, and it would be

---

[1] ἀνέμους γεωργεῖν, adesp. 840. Wade-Gery has suggested (cf. also Liddell
and Scott, s.v. ἄνεμος) that the phrase is of the same kind as 'to plough the sands'
or 'to fight the air'. That is quite possible; but even so it remains significant. The
expression 'to till the winds' seems to lack that force of sensual perception which
is so strong in the Greek language — unless the struggle with the winds was, in
fact, part of a peasant's real experience.

[2] e.g., W.264f, P.1140ff.

[3] Eur. *El.* 80f, cf. 71ff. This seems a slightly more realistic, though less pious,
view than that expressed in a simile questioning the axiom that the χρηστός
remains a χρηστός also in misfortune (Eur. *Hek.* 592ff): 'Is it not strange that
bad soil which is blessed by the gods with a good season bears ample crops, while
good soil failing to get what it needs gives bad fruit?'

[4] Taygetos, L.117f. — adesp. 380.   [5] W.952, Eupolis 1.

[6] B.709ff. — B.578ff, 587ff.   [7] P.1140ff.

[8] Cf. W. S. Ferguson, *Amer. Hist. Rev.* XLV (1940), 276.

wrong to regard as a usual feature the gradual intensification
of the methods of farming.[1]

Whether he grew more corn or gave the greater part of his
time to market-gardening, whether he cultivated chiefly vines
and olives which certainly paid best, or earned his living mainly
by charcoal-burning[2] — the Attic farmer, as far as we know
him and his rather primitive methods and modest aims, was
as much a *petit bourgeois* as was the tradesman or craftsman
with whom we shall deal in a later chapter. We shall also see
that the vocations overlapped. The ideal of the small holder
as of every *petit bourgeois* was for the most part the peaceful
and care-free enjoyment of simple pleasures, of food and drink
and love. Aristophanes again and again gives expression to
such hopes.[3] This is, on the whole, a realistic picture, although
in comedy such longings may sometimes be idealized, or at
least have a touch of unreality. In war-time many peasants
reached the depth of poverty and misery like the man who asks
Dikaiopolis for a small share in his peace,[4] while in general it
is true that modest and scanty conditions, and modest and
simple men, were characteristic features of rural life.

On the other hand, the fact that almost all these small people
kept at least one or two slaves bears witness to a certain *bourgeois*
standard of life. There is very little evidence indeed for slave
labour in the fields, except on comparatively large estates; and
they were not frequent. Still, one slave girl at least, chiefly
employed in the house, can in general be regarded as a minimum.[5] There were also free workmen who worked for a wage
as seasonal workers, for example as olive-gatherers,[6] although
we do not know how many of the olive-orchards were so large
that their owners could not do without paid workers during the
harvest. The 'diggers, donkey-drivers and mower-women'
who are mentioned together may have been day-labourers of
this type, and a poor cottage will be the home of such 'a delver

---

[1] Value doubled: Isaios IX, 28; as exceptional: Xen. *oik.* 1, 4; 20, 23. See A.
Jardé, *Les céréales dans l'antiquité grecque*, 190ff.

[2] This type is, of course, best known from the chorus of the *Acharnians.* Cf.
also Philyll. 14, Eur. *frg.* 283.

[3] A.271ff, 665ff, C.408ff, P.571ff, 591ff, 1130ff, 1140ff, 1159ff, 1318ff,
Pl.253f, frg. 109, 387, 16 D.

[4] A.1018ff.

[5] See ch. VII, esp. pp. 166, 182.

[6] W.712; cf. Lysias VII, 17.

or herdsman'.[1] We know almost nothing about the extent to which the individual farmer enjoyed social and economic security, but during the fifth century his position was not too bad. When someone spoke of 'measuring the land',[2] the peasant did not think of big estates to be divided into allotments, but rather of cleruchies, or colonies of Athenian citizens abroad, which, from the point of social economy, were attempts not so much to improve the conditions of Attic peasants as to provide with land the surplus of Athenian citizens, and thus to relieve the overpopulated town. The Attic farmers were not much affected by such measures, at least those of them who remained at home. There was, in fact, a process of gradual deterioration, largely by the war, and the clear evidence of the last plays of Aristophanes is the best illustration of the change from earlier conditions, and shows the direction of the development. In the *Ekklesiazousai* and the *Ploutos* we find the situation of the peasants very much deteriorated. Then, and not until then, they were on their way to becoming something that could almost be called 'proletarians'.

As late as the *Ekklesiazousai*, in the 'nineties of the fourth century, it is said that naval expenditure is good for the poor, but not 'for the rich and the farmers'.[3] Only the poor townsman is called a poor man, just as he was a generation earlier.[4] The peasant, however, is not described as wealthy, but as naturally averse from naval service. So we cannot draw a definite conclusion from that statement. In the same comedy the dramatic contrast between rich and poor forms the very basis of the communist programme.[5] One man has extensive

---

[1] Archipp. 44, Eur. *El.* 252.   [2] C.203ff.
[3] E.197f.   [4] Ps.-Xen. II, 14. Cf. above p. 50.
[5] E.590ff. — I speak of communism in Greek political theory, although I know that it was very different from what is called so today, especially because it was a communism of 'citizens', not of 'men'. In Greece, the communist ideal was not concerned with the whole population nor indeed with the 'proletariate', but only with a citizen class living on public means. They existed by the labour of another class or classes, either enslaved or at least dependent and without full political rights. This system could be called communism, because in the Greek city to own slaves or even to employ workmen was more or less the same as to own any other kind of property. It is unnecessary to introduce a new word 'Koinonism' (O. Erb, *Schmollers Jahrbuch*, 62, 1938, 277ff), which must first be explained, and in fact means just the same in Greek as communism in Latin. Books like the well-known one of Poehlmann (*Geschichte der sozialen Frage and des Sozialismus in der antiken Welt*, in the first edition: *Geschichte des antiken*

landed property, the other not enough for his grave. One has
many slaves, the other not even one; the communist ideal, in
this case, does not abolish slavery, as slaves are needed for the
common agricultural work.[1] In those years the number of
comparatively large estates must have slowly increased. Their
owners were the 'gentlemen-farmers' for whom Xenophon
wrote his *Oikonomikos*. In the *Ploutos* the social tension has
further increased, and we find an almost revolutionary atmosphere. The peasants of this play are a poor, hard-working
class, the community of those without bread, or those who like
to chew the roots of thyme growing by the wayside, a habit
which indicates a very simple and frugal life, or even severe
poverty.[2] To them the miracle of the coming of Wealth meant
the true and only release from their misery.

2

Among the social and economic contrasts in the life of the
farmers, that between town and country was the most obvious.
No doubt the evidence of comedy on this question is rather
one-sided. To arrive at the true facts, we must first ask if
townsfolk and countryfolk were as rigidly separated as many
quotations seem to prove.

It need hardly be specially emphasized that town and
country depended on each other, and that both of them, 'town-
and country-folk', suffered alike in war.[3] A living proof of the

Sozialismus und Kommunismus) show that there is a danger in using these words,
but I think it is not difficult to avoid this danger. In fact, there was in the ancient
world neither socialism nor communism in the modern sense of the words.

[1] E.651.

[2] Pl.219, 253f, 282.

[3] P.918ff. In these lines Trygaios, who has brought Peace from Heaven, puts
before the chorus the claim of having been πολλῶν ὑμῖν ἄξιος. He does this in
semi-official language, as though he were proclaiming an honorary decree.
Thus he calls himself by his official name: Τρυγαῖος ᾿Αθμονεύς (or ᾿Αθμονεύς,
cf. also P.190). He then proceeds to mention those who have benefited when he
put an end to Hyperbolos' policy: τὸν δημότην ὅμιλον καὶ τὸν γεωργικὸν
λεών. Usually ὁ δημότης is the demesman; but I cannot agree that this is so in
this passage. It would mean that Trygaios is referring to his fellow demesmen,
and that they are again the 'rustic people' of the next line. It makes far better sense
if he is describing two different, and even contrasting, groups of the population, and
not merely using a *hendiadys*. The chorus consists of all sorts of men (cf. P.296ff
and above, p. 55, n 1), not of Trygaios' fellow demesmen only. He does not
boast merely of the liberation of his deme, but of Athens — town and country.

connection of both sections of the populace were, for instance, the artisans who were glad when, after the war, they could sell their wares 'to the country'.[1] Kleon is said to have sold bad leather to the peasants.[2] On the other hand, the farmers naturally tried to sell their vegetables, poultry and other products in the town market (see Plates IV*c*, V*b*).[3] Especially on festival days a great number of peasants used to come to town, and some used to stay with friends.[4]

However, the relation between town and country involves more than the plain fact of mutual economic dependence. The barriers between them were not nearly so high as some scholars seem to believe. It was altogether exceptional when during the rule of the Thirty some people were expelled from the town, but apparently lived in the country without difficulty; this could occur only at that time, when the populace was profoundly divided.[5] At other times town and country were very closely connected. One who as a boy had been a poor shepherd might later become a demagogue, and one who was educated in town as the son of wealthy parents might cultivate his estate when he had grown up.[6] The chorus of the *Clouds* tries to get the judges on its side; as clouds can do nothing except send rain, it is natural that they should address those to whom the rain brought benefit or damage, the farmers.[7] Their fallow land, their crops and vineyards and olives, even the home-made tiles are threatened if the vote of the judges is given against the poet. This speech would be entirely meaningless if the people addressed did not feel themselves concerned. We are entitled to assume that a large part of the audience had a hand in farming.

Even more distinctly than in the theatre we recognize in the assembly the rural part of the town population, or to put it more accurately, the inseparability of the two spheres. Clearly the men who often arrived in the assembly at the last moment, dusty and smelling of garlic, were peasants.[8] The men 'from

---

The δημότης ὅμιλος is the urban δῆμος; but **οἱ δημόται** are often simply 'the people'. A similar use of δημότις can be found in L.333; cf. also Eur. *Alk.* 1057, *Hik.* 895, *Ion* 625f, *frg.* 362, 25, perhaps *frg.* 227. See also Her. II, 172, 5, V, 11, 2.

[1] P.1198ff.   [2] K.316f.   [3] frg. 569.
[4] Alkaios 19. — Lysias, *frg.* 23, 4. Cf. also Eur. *Or.* 866.
[5] Lysias XXXI, 8.   [6] Ps.-Lysias XX, 11f, 33f.
[7] C.1115ff, cf. also 264f.   [8] E.290ff.

the fields', though a minority, voted against the motion to give the rule to women.[1] The assembly was composed of both townsmen and countrymen, but the former were in the majority, and when they were absent, the assembly more or less ceased to function; in later years they only turned up regularly after the fees had been raised to three obols.[2] Nevertheless, when the voters who had elected bad officials are cursed, the words of the curse are: 'neither shall their cattle produce offspring, nor their soil bear crops'.[3] This, again, would be nonsense if the majority of the people in the *ekklesia* were only townsfolk, as is generally believed. They were peasants as well.

Other sources tell us, for instance, that the wealthy citizen used to own not only a house in town, but also houses in the country, which were either let or administered as an estate by a paid steward.[4] It was possible even, though probably not before a rather late date, for an *oikos* to be distributed over the territories of more than one State.[5] Less wealthy people also lived in town, but cultivated their holdings and kept there various kinds of property, especially agricultural tools.[6] Strepsiades asks pardon for his kicking at the door, because he lives 'far off in the country';[7] in fact, he lived in town as a yeoman burgess, but his original home was in the country. Others lived so near — Trygaios, for example, whose vineyard was at Athmonia, about six miles out of town[8] — that they might easily turn up at the pnyx or in the theatre or even unexpectedly in their own house; but they might also be so late that they would find no supper ready any longer.[9] Euelpides, invited for the so-called *dekate*, the name-day feast of a boy, 'first drank in town', then slept and went back to Halimus; on his way home (about four miles) he was robbed of his coat.[10] It is difficult to say whether he belonged to town or country, and it seems almost impossible to draw a sharp line of demarcation between the two sections of the people.

The rural outlook also predominated in the town. The

---

[1] E.280f, 432ff.   [2] E.299ff.

[3] Eupolis 40 P, 31f.   [4] Xen. *oik.* 1, 4.   [5] Xen. *oik.* 1, 5.

[6] P.1318; cf. *IG.* I², 325ff. (*Syll.*³, 96ff, Tod, 79f), Thuc. II, 5, 4f (this reference is to Plataiai); 13, 1; 65, 2, Lysias I, 11, 13, 20, 22, Isaios V, 22, VIII, 35, XI, 41f, 44.

[7] C.138.   [8] P.190, 919.   [9] Lysias I, 11, 22.   [10] B.494ff.

chorus-leader of the *Wasps*, a townsman if ever there was one, thinks only of the effect on the fruit, when rainy weather comes.[1] The average town household at least owned poultry, and other birds, which might be kept in special cages, also a donkey, goats and other animals.[2] The baker Nausikydes possessed pigs and even cattle.[3] People who could not bear the crowing of the cock were clearly townsfolk.[4] It is significant, too, that we occasionally come across comparisons or metaphors from country life, such as a modern townsman would hardly understand, and certainly not use.[5]

In the first years of the great war the farmers who were crowded together between the Long Walls naturally longed to get back to their fields.[6] 'Now let us leave the town for the country; it is high time we were taking our ease there after a bath in the bronze tub.'[7] Many, however, had settled in town. There were intermarriages like that of Strepsiades.[8] The question arises whether we have here the signs of an actual migration from country to town, which Aristotle believed to have occurred as early as the 'sixties of the fifth century.[9] It may be taken as significant that the owners or tenants of some estates or farms changed more than once within a comparatively short time;[10] but it is impossible to give definite figures for those who left the country for good. Sometimes comic characters give utterance to bitter remarks about people who wanted easier work or a fine style of living. 'He may well become refined, as he lives in town.'[11] 'The countryman standing at the perfume shop'[12] was a proverbial saying. By and by, it seems, people left the country and went to town. There were enough honest professions besides toilsome 'digging'.[13] In the comic ideal of women's communism the slaves were to cultivate the fields.[14] It is advisable, however, to take into account the tendencies and sympathies of the comic poets, and not to overestimate such remarks. There was no real migration from country to town, no *Landflucht*, simply because the majority of the townspeople still had their farms or at least their gardens

---

[1] W.264f.   [2] C.4, frg. 18, 405, 441. — W.170.
[3] Xen. *mem.* II, 7, 6.   [4] Kratinos 311.
[5] e.g., K.1344, W.1306, P.24, frg. 731.
[6] K.805ff is one of several passages confirming this.
[7] frg. 107.   [8] C.46ff.   [9] *Ath. pol.* 24, 1.
[10] Lysias VII, 4, 9.   [11] Alkaios 26.   [12] Eupolis 209.
[13] B.1432ff.   [14] E.651, cf. above, p. 82.

which were economically important.¹ The process of man's
alienation from the soil was still in its beginnings, and the
evidence from comedy in general does not disprove the view
that in the last part of the fifth century not more than a quarter
of the Athenian citizens was without landed property.² Beyond
doubt, Athens and Attica were a State and a country with a
large class of small farmers.

In spite of all these facts, there was an undeniable cleavage
between townsfolk and countryfolk. The peasants would
incline to pride themselves on rarely going to town and knowing little of the evil things going on there.³ A peasant, wearing
perhaps his warm cap, the rural *kynē*, attracted attention in
town.⁴ Someone who seems to have come to town, along with
a very typical peasant, was asked: 'Are you going to bring to
town this "rest-harrow"', this weed from the countryside?⁵
There actually was an opposition between town and country,
caused chiefly by differences of social position and intellectual
level. Here we must be specially careful not to take as valid
evidence what is tendentious or satiric in comedy. Aristophanes frequently gives idealized pictures of a delightful
bucolic life, and, on the other hand, dwells on and exaggerates
the wickedness of town life.⁶ But even in such one-sided pictures, when he jokes, for instance, about the differences of
language and behaviour, the poet has to keep close enough to
real facts in order to be understood and to evoke the right kind
of laughter. Euripides was abused because of his 'agrarian'
mother.⁷ It was indeed a clever touch to make Strepsiades
stress the difference of smell between himself and his wife;
he had the peasant's inferiority complex.⁸ The word *asteios*,
which indicated the townsman, became an expression for a
'fine man', and 'urban' meant something like 'refined' or
comme il faut.⁹ At the same time the word *agroikos* developed

---

¹ Also Francotte, II, 320, believes that Aristotle's words on migration to town
should not be taken too literally.
² Francotte, II, 336. Heichelheim, 388, based on Lysias XXXIV.
³ Eur. *El.* 298f, *Or.* 917ff.
⁴ C.268.   ⁵ adesp. 438.
⁶ Some examples for the former: A.32ff, K.805ff, P.529ff, 569f, frg. 387; for
the latter: A.836ff, 978ff, K.384f.
⁷ F.840.   ⁸ C.49ff, cf. 1457.
⁹ F.5, 901, 906, Pl.1150, Alkaios 26.

from meaning a peasant to meaning a bucolic and uneducated
man, even a 'barbarian', or a man 'making rude jokes, and
telling idle tales in a stupid fashion, relevant to nothing'.[1] The
god who took no notice of the fact that in his temple someone
loudly broke wind was called a true peasant.[2] Demos himself,
when finally dealing with the demagogues, will be on their
trail as a 'fierce *agroikos*'; he will be a peasant again then, but
he will also be rough and rude.[3] Under the influence of the
sophists, town language, above all among the younger generation, became both refined and affected.[4] When speaking in
public, the peasant had to face the arrogance of the townspeople, and the point is specially stressed when he did not
speak like a rustic.[5] If a man found it difficult to proceed in
his speech, he sometimes used the proverbial phrase of an ox
standing on his tongue — a bold allusion to a countryman's
inhibitions.[6] It was possible to distinguish three sorts of Attic
pronunciation: 'the midway speech of the Polis, the town-
speech which had a flavour of effeminacy, and the rugged
speech with a flavour of the country'.[7] It is understandable
that as a rule the farmer did not like to speak in town before
the public, and that the educated townsman did not care for
country people, nor they for the man 'who had tramped the
town and had the knack of words'.[8] 'If you search a bit, you
will find in the country the anti-heliast's seedling', but those
who always go to the courts and make speeches before the
juries no longer care for rural life and least of all for its hard
labour.[9] There is no trace in comedy of the attitude well
known from many ancient writers,[10] when the peasant is contrasted with every other kind of manual worker, when he alone
is not a despised *banausos*. This is a very remarkable fact in

---

[1] K.41, C.492, 628f, 646, 655, W.1320f. Cf. also Eur. *Rhes.* 266, 271.

[2] Pl.705.   [3] K.808.   [4] frg. 198.

[5] adesp. 627, 694. Cf. also E.241ff.

[6] Strattis 67, cf. Aisch. *Ag.* 36, Theognis 815. None of these passages can
vindicate the explanation that the phrase indicates a silence caused by bribery
(a coin showing the picture of a bull?).

[7] frg. 685. This fragment, in spite of the differentiation it makes, seems to
give proof of the unity of town and country; each had an accent of its own, but
at the same time there was a way of speech common to the whole of the Polis.

[8] Eur. *Bakch.* 717 (transl. by Verrall). Cf. also *Or.* 902ff, *Iph. T.* 275.

[9] B.109ff. — adesp. 382. — B.1432ff, Pl.903, frg. 221.

[10] Cf., e.g., Xen. *Oik.*, ch. 4 and 5.

view of the general partiality of the comedians in favour of the peasants.

The passages mentioned prove that the deeper reason for the opposition between town and country, which developed in spite of their close connection, was based on actual differences in social and economic conditions. The 'most pleasant country life',[1] which is so often described in its modest happiness and care-free peace, was, at the same time, hard and dirty and poor. The idealization of a peaceful and sensual life is not the romantic glorification of bucolic existence as with Theokritos; that was unknown to the earlier Greeks. Even the comedians of the fifth century, though they praised to the utmost the peasant's life, did not deny its hardships and difficulties. You must be content with porridge and olives.[2] If you get into debt, the demarchos as a bailiff 'bites you from the mattress'.[3] The farmer, on the whole, still adhered to the old *oikos*-economy, and he hated all trade where he was always cheated.[4] Here older and modern forms of economy met, and they could not easily work together. The peasant also felt himself somewhat harshly treated by the State, worse, at any rate, than the townsman, for instance, when he was called up for active service; townspeople always found a trick to get out of it.[5] 'What in town seems golden, becomes lead again in the country', runs a saying.[6] Often the peasants had the feeling that they fought or suffered for a cause unknown to them; 'there is a lot we don't know'.[7] The poor husbandman, even if by chance he was not ignorant, could not be concerned with public affairs, because he had to work so hard.[8] Undoubtedly the farmers had to suffer more than anybody else during the Spartan invasions. When they were forced to settle inside the walls, it was as if each of them 'had left his own Polis'.[9] The country people longed to leave the safety of the town and return to

---

[1] C.43.   [2] K.806.

[3] C.37. It is a bug which actually bites Strepsiades ἐκ τῶν στρωμάτων. This, that the bug drove him from the mattress, is the point of comparison for him when he calls the bug δήμαρχός τις, a bailiff who turns a debtor out of his house.

[4] A.32ff, K.316f, frg. 387. That is right, however, in principle only. Cf. P.563, where the farmer wants to go home to the country, 'after having bought a good portion of salt fish'. He could not live without the market in town.

[5] P.1179ff.   [6] Kratinos 318.   [7] P.618.

[8] Eur. *Hik.* 420ff: ἔργων ὕπο οὐκ ἂν δύναιτο πρὸς τὰ κοιν' ἀποβλέπειν.

[9] Thuc. II, 16, 2; cf. 14, 2.

their homes, though they had lost a great deal of their property, while the townsfolk 'lived without fear'.[1] On the other hand, the people left behind in the country suffered even more, and after the occupation of Dekeleia, Eupolis could say that 'those inside the Long Walls' had a much better breakfast than the demes in the country.[2] Even in Sparta, it is said, it was the peasants and not the 'big people' who suffered in war, though we may wonder to whom the poet here refers — certainly not to the helots who cultivated the fields of the Spartiates, perhaps to the perioeci, and even other Peloponnesians, who had suffered from Athenian raids.[3]

These varied references show that the ordinary Attic farmer had very little money (see the inscription, Plate Vc), though he needed it for buying seeds, manure and even food, and, after the invasions, for restoring his farm; but that (at least before 404) he was not wholly impoverished, and had just enough to live on. The modesty or even meanness of rural life was not caused by the accumulation of land in the hands of a few. There were some wealthy men whose estates were cultivated by slaves or tenants; but the large estates, in fact never very large, were not of decisive economic importance. The characteristic feature of Attic agriculture was a far-going partition of the soil rather than the reverse. The small peasant, though not oppressed by big landowners, was oppressed by poverty and the growing difficulty of living on the yield of his piece of land. The population, on the whole, was growing, and so were the people's economic demands. In an ever-increasing degree the economic life of Attica was shifting to the town where political and social life had always been concentrated. The soil was too scanty and too poor, and there was no important intensification in farming methods; so that among the farmers poverty increased steadily, and the social and intellectual level sank.

---

[1] Longing for the country, e.g., A.201f, K.1394, P.551ff, 569f. — Ps.-Xen II, 14: ὁ δὲ δῆμος ... ἀδεῶς 3ῇ. Wade-Gery, *JHS.* LII (1932), 213, traces the reasons for this alienation of town and country back to 447, i.e. to the loss of the Athenian land empire; 'henceforth hoplites and farmers count little, sailors and cockneys much'.

[2] A.1022ff. — Eupolis 40 P, 12ff, cf. Thuc. VII, 27.

[3] P.622ff.

3

Aristophanes describes the farmers as the part of the population that wanted peace. Whether he praised the farmers
because he himself wanted peace, or whether he longed for
peace because he took it as the means of salvation for the
peasants and therefore also for the State — this is an academic
question, not easy and perhaps not important to answer. But
his opinion must have been sound, else he would not have
repeated the same idea over and over again. A yearning for
peace was deep in the farmer's heart. Hatred of the Spartans,
who had ruined the land, was of course very strong;[1] but, as
we have seen, the poet converted the vindictive Acharnians
and most likely made a deep impression on a large number of
his audience. The peasant who wanted nothing but his peaceful work was willing to pay heavily even to be spared office,
that is to say, his duty in war-time, as the context shows.[2]
The facts are symbolized in *Georgia*, that is 'Farming', the
personification of all agriculture, who was all in one: 'nurse,
stewardess, helper, guardian, daughter, sister, of Peace'.[3] The
chorus of the peasants cheered the goddess of Peace, for they
had always desired and awaited her coming.[4] Although all
Greeks, of every occupation, were called on to dig up the
goddess, the poet is fully justified in making the peasants,
and the Attic peasants alone, actually achieve the task.[5]

'The farmers accomplish the work, no one else'; they are
the 'wisest peasants'.[6] Not only the peace, but all matters of
State are here in the poet's mind. His view, however, is partial
and cannot be simply accepted. No longer did the State
exist by its agriculture. Among the things the old poets taught
mankind farming was the only economic subject; but it had
ceased to be this in real life, and it is the old and old-fashioned
Aischylos who speaks as if it still were so.[7] Aristophanes, as is
well known, cherished the old traditions, which in fact were
and are characteristic of the rural life of every people in every
age. The peasants had their old songs and their old festivals.[8]
Their customs and manners were somewhat primitive, little
altered since the days of Paris, when princes tended the cattle

---

[1] A.509ff, frg. 108.   [2] frg. 100; in general cf., e.g., A.1021, P.569f.
[3] frg. 294.   [4] P.586ff.   [5] P.296ff. — 508ff.
[6] P.511, 603.   [7] F.1032ff.   [8] C.984ff, E.277ff.

and the same shears were used for sheep and shepherd.[1] The comic poets praise the conservatism of the country people who for the most part had always lived in the country.[2] No doubt this conservatism was of great and special value in times when changes and reforms were far too frequent, in times of a radicalism impatient of restraint. On the other hand, such people lagged behind the times, and this is most clearly revealed by their lack of any productive idea.

Already the events of the first years of war showed plainly how independent of her agriculture Athens had become. For several years a considerable part of the population lived inside the walls of town and harbour. The men had taken with them their wives and children, their household goods and even the wood from their houses, and had sent off their cattle to the islands.[3] A State with such a population is not an agrarian State. The political attitude of a city like Akanthos was determined 'by anxiety for the crops';[4] with Athens it was otherwise. State and town, though they had not yet lost their agrarian features, were in fact dependent on the sea. 'Most of you earn your living from the sea', a Peloponnesian envoy said later to the Athenians.[5]

The first decisive weakening of Athens was caused not by the Spartan invaders who devastated Attica, but by the plague which decimated the people. The State as well as the farmers made a surprisingly quick recovery during the following years, but never again could the peasants argue that their work was indispensable. There ran a proverb which referred to the prospects of the crops, that the farmer was not rich before the next year. A comedian modified the phrase and said that the farmer was 'not useful before the next year, as first of all he was getting away from hunger'.[6] He probably meant by this rather obscure sentence that the farmer, who was himself starving, was not able to abolish the misery and want of the time. The conditions of real life seem to be reflected when the three vocations of peasant, merchant and artisan, all of them equally 'virtuous and patriotic', are opposed to the activities of the mischief-making sycophant.[7] It is hardly a coincidence that the two last quotations are of the fourth cen-

[1] Kratinos 37.   [2] Cf. Thuc. II, 14, 2.   [3] Thuc. II, 14, 1.
[4] Thuc. IV, 88, 1.   [5] Xen. hell. VII, 1, 4.
[6] Theop. 1 D.   [7] Pl.899ff.

tury. Other sources, such as speeches and inscriptions, show that the predominant importance of agriculture was not seriously doubted before the end of the period of Old Comedy. It was about the same time that the theoretical discussion and glorification of farming began.[1]

Among many features and variations three facts seem to stand out. First, the ordinary, that is the small, Attic farmer was a *petit bourgeois*, but on the way to becoming a proletarian. Secondly, there was a growing opposition between town and country, though as yet there was no distinct line of demarcation between the two sections of the population. Finally, the economic importance of agriculture to the State was gradually declining. All these three facts were closely connected, and they do not conflict with the further fact that wine and, to an even greater extent, oil were important articles of export.

The farmer who after the conclusion of peace would, once again, set to work without grumbling and rebuild his house was economically on the down grade, in spite of his moderate wants and modest life.[2] We may now ask again how Dikaiopolis, Trygaios and similar figures of comedy fit into the general picture. They were 'heroes', and were therefore given a certain style, a unique mixture of real genius and comic folly. Nevertheless, they were peasants, and, as far as their sociological aspect is concerned, typical peasants. It is not their way of life, but the importance they are given in comedy, that is 'unhistorical'. It is both strange and significant that Aristophanes, in spite of his affection for them, says on the whole less about the social situation of peasants than of tradesmen and craftsmen. Behind Dikaiopolis and his private peace, behind Trygaios who brought about general peace, behind Chremes who introduced wealth to good people, there was a section of the population which in spite of its large numbers had neither the economic nor the social nor, least of all, the political power to influence developments in a decisive way. Some scholars believe Athens, at the end of the fifth century, to have been still an agrarian State, because there were no industrial magnates and big business men, or because the merchants and artisans were largely foreigners. We shall deal later with these points, but we may here anticipate and say that this view, even

[1] Cf. Xen. *oik.*, esp 6, 8; 16, 1.
[2] Allusions to the farmers doing their building themselves: C.1126f, frg. 402ff.

PLATE VI

a

b

ARISTOCRATIC YOUTHS

PLATE VII

a

b

MEN AND BOYS

if not altogether mistaken, is certainly misleading. It is true that the land belonged to Attic citizens only — a very important fact. But the attempts made once more to link citizenship exclusively with the ownership of landed property failed from the beginning.[1] The occupation of Dekeleia was ultimately a very severe blow to agriculture.[2] There still remained a large number of small estates: fields, orchards and gardens, but on the whole (and this is decisive) agriculture was not self-sufficient. The peasants were almost as much a consuming as a producing part of the people, and, as we have said before, Athens could exist without farmers better than she could without imports.

This, however, is not the last word to be said on the importance of Attic farmers. An adequate judgment can only be formed by looking at future developments. Undoubtedly the existence of Attic agriculture was almost decisive for the economic stability of the succeeding centuries. It remains true that the birds, by killing the peasants' enemies in field and garden, saved mankind as a whole.[3] What then was there to counterbalance the impoverishment of the peasants? For this impoverishment was a fact, and one which is confirmed by the large number of ward-stones found in Attica, which prove that during the fourth century the small farmers ran more and more into debt, and were frequently forced to give up their farms.[4] Small estates were bought up — at low prices, of course — by the owners of larger estates, and often sold again; land became a subject of speculation.[5] The later development is characterized partly by the growing migration to town which presently relieved the country of the poorest and least efficient farmers. On the other hand, it may be surmised from theoretical treatises on agriculture that the methods of exploiting the soil were improved and intensified.[6] There must have been, however, another decisive reason for the survival of Attic husbandry. In my belief it was that the Attic farmer, with his grapes and olives, his figs and honey, worked, to some extent,

[1] Cf. Lysias XXXIV.   [2] Thuc. VII, 27, 3ff.   [3] B.1058ff.
[4] *IG.* II², 2684ff. On the meaning of the ὅροι cf. M. I. Finley, *Studies in Land and Credit in Ancient Athens* (1951); V. A. Fine, *Horoi (Hesperia,* Suppl. IX, 1951).   [5] Xen. *oik.* 20, 22ff, cf. Lysias VII, 4.
[6] This is confirmed by the *Hellenica Oxyrhynchia* (XII, 5) which belongs to the sixties' of the fourth century. In general, cf. G. Glotz, *Histoire grecque,* III, 9ff.

for export. Agriculture, improved by specialization and by
certain, though late and modest, attempts of intensification, and
thus enabled to survive periods of reduced trade and export,
was on the whole saved by trade. The main producers for
export were, of course, the larger estates, but it must have been
useful and even essential for the small farmer, that, poor as he
was, he could always make some money from part of his produce. In consequence Attic agriculture did not perish during
the Hellenistic Age; it even experienced a kind of revival
during the second century B.C.[1] Although Athens lost her
pre-eminence as a centre of trade and industry, she lived on,
though enfeebled, for two reasons: because of the Peiraeus
where corn was always imported, even when later the harbour
was no longer a centre of international commerce, and because
of Attic agriculture which even attained a new degree of
prosperity.

---

[1] W. S. Ferguson, *Hellenistic Athens*, 207, 231f, emphasizes the new and
considerable importance of the rural part of Attica, the 'Mesogaia', in the
second century B.C.

CHAPTER IV

THE UPPER CLASSES

ARISTOPHANES twice made an attack on Kleon the main theme of a comedy — in the *Babylonians*, the play which resulted in his prosecution by the statesman, and in the *Knights*, the chorus of which is formed by noble youths from whose ranks the Athenian cavalry, the 'thousand brave men', was recruited.[1] These knights were primarily a military body; but they were more. In so far as their name of *hippeis* covered the second Solonian class, it was more or less obsolete; but they certainly formed part of the upper classes, who liked to be called the 'fine and brave men', the *kaloikagathoi*. Aristophanes occasionally makes a distinction between the two names.[2] This shows that not all the *kaloikagathoi* were *hippeis*, but it is quite certain that all the *hippeis* were *kaloikagathoi*.[3] It was rather a bold action on the part of the poet — for which, indeed, he apologizes[4] — to introduce them as a chorus. We have seen before, and we can confirm it by a curious indication in the *Acharnians*,[5] that the situation can be adequately explained by the fact that the knights, like the poet, were violently hostile to Kleon and to the *poneroi*, the 'bad men', the members of the commercial middle-classes who had gained power chiefly through and with the rise of Kleon.[6] Kratinos is supposed to have called the *poneroi* 'hares', and the reason given for this is that the 'urban hare' as contrasted with the 'rural hare' is not only a coward but also poisonous.[7] Unless we assume that the

---

[1] K.731 (οἱ νεανίσκοι, cf. Thuc. VIII, 92, 6), 225.   [2] K.225ff.

[3] Cf. Gomme, *Comm. on Thuc.* I, 15f: 'officers and men were alike gentlemen'.

[4] K.507ff.

[5] A.5ff. The story of the five talents which the knights had forced Kleon to 'cough up' is very obscure. I do not see how the knights could in real life compel him to do anything of the kind. So it may be a reference to a comedy (cf. Starkie, in his edition of the *Acharnians*, p. 241ff), though I must admit that this is rather a surprising idea, since the *Knights* was performed a year after the lines were spoken. There seems actually to be another reference to the future play in A.300f.

[6] K.185f, 223ff, 510f; cf. also A.300f.

[7] Kratinos 16 D.

Greeks had a completely fantastic view of the nature of the innocent rabbit, we must conclude that the poisonous hares were, in fact, the urban middle and lower classes. In the opinion of their enemies, they have come 'from the market' and have been brought up there, or even worse, they have come from 'near the gates of the town'.[1] The sausage-seller prides himself on his being a 'bad man', and on being able to prove his origin from 'bad men', and so did others in real life.[2]

That pride is the comic and grotesque counterpart to the intransigent pride of the aristocrats, which could be regarded as justifiable or simply ridiculous, whichever way one looked at it.[3] The nobleman might stress the fact that he was going to Kolonos, the hill 'of the knights', not to the market-hill, the Kolonos Agoraios, which was also called 'the hired Kolonos', since it was the place where hired labourers gathered.[4] Nothing more outraged Andokides, who was of a noble family, than the news that during his exile Kleophon, the lyre-maker and politician, had lived in his house.[5]

Aristocratic pride is, first of all and in its most legitimate form, pride in a high personal tradition. All the old families believed in their descent from the gods, but along with tradition there was certainly much vain boasting and sheer humbug.[6] It counted much to be able to point to ancestors who had served the State well without gaining any advantage for themselves, and also, of course, to one's own exploits in war.[7] This sort of pride frequently showed itself in court, but often deteriorated into a mere enumeration not only of the naval battles one had taken part in, but, in the main, of material benefits to the State, such as the undertaking of choregies, trierarchies and the payment of war-taxes.[8] The same elementary kind of aristocratic feeling can be traced in comedy, and we find very little of that interest in the nature of 'true' nobility, that of character rather than of birth, or still less of wealth, which we find in Euripides.[9]

[1] K.181, 218, 293, 333, 634ff, 1258. — 1245ff, 1398.
[2] K.336f. — Plat. 219.   [3] Cf. Th.329f, F.22.
[4] Kratinos 263, Pherekr. 134, adesp. 35 D; cf. schol. B.997.–On the Κολωνὸς μίσθιος, as a kind of Labour Exchange, see A.Fuks, *Eranos* XLIX (1951), 171ff.
[5] Andok. I, 146.   [6] A.47ff.   [7] K.565ff, 595ff.
[8] Cf., e.g., Lysias XVIII, 7, XIX, 29, 57, XXI, 2ff, XXV, 12, Isokr. XVIII, 58ff, XIX, 36.
[9] Examples of such arguments abound in Euripides' plays and fragments, and need not be collected. Some are given below, p. 98, n 3.

The noble class longed for a life like that of their ancestors, in which, without interference or annoyance, they could wear their hair long and have their bodies oiled and scraped.[1] To wear one's hair long was, in fact, the chief symbol of aristocracy, and there were still quite a few who did so (see Plate VIa).[2] We see the noble youth endeavouring to keep up the aristocratic style of living, which in those democratic times was becoming very unpopular. Thucydides tell us that 'a short time ago' at least the older men among the nobles wore linen chitons and 'buns' of hair pinned with golden 'cicadas'.[3] In comedy it is said that the nobleman wears rings; the old man has in his hair those golden grasshoppers, and the young people, both boys and girls, like to wear fine clothes and golden trinkets.[4] We may assume, at least for the time of the Peloponnesian War, that the harmless and simple-minded vanity of this aristocratic ideal is exaggerated. But it is far more than a mere caricature. Otherwise we should have to assume that a vase-painting like that on Plate VIa, which represents the noble youth of an earlier generation, was intended to give an exaggerated and comic picture, which it certainly was not. The dandies of the late fifth century cherished an ideal which at the time of their grandfathers had been the normal fashion for noble youths. On a higher social level it corresponds to the day-dreams in which Dikaiopolis and other farmer-heroes of comedy enjoy the pleasures of rural life. The similarity which there is between the two in spite of the obvious social differences, has a basis of historical truth, and also bears witness to the importance which form and style in living had for the *kaloikagathoi*.

In the pamphlet of the Pseudo-Xenophon the two social strata are contrasted with each other under various names and from every point of view — their political, their social and economic outlooks as well as their military importance and their education. We cannot deal with all the various epithets which simply indicate the writer's wish to emphasize, indeed to over-

[1] K.578ff, 1121.

[2] C.14, W.466, L.561, adesp. 12-14; cf. C.1101, B.911. Thus κομάω can gain the meaning of 'giving oneself airs': C.545, W.1317, Pl.170, 572.

[3] Thuc. I, 6, 3; cf. Gomme, I, 101f, who adduces a long list of vase-paintings to illustrate the κρωβύλος and the τέττιγες.

[4] E.632. — K.1331, C.984f. — L.1189ff.

emphasize, the contrast between the two classes. The poet
has something of the same purpose when he occasionally compares them with the good old and the bad new coins.[1] Noble
origin is like the strong and clear stamp of a coin, we read in
tragedy.[2] The advantages of noble birth and upbringing are
a favourite theme in tragedy, though their greater fate may also
cause greater suffering to noblemen than is given to the
'numberless'.[3] All this reflects the heroic and aristocratic
world of myth, but frequently becomes mixed up with the
moralism of the fifth century, which suspects that the coin of
noble origin may be false.[4] In the social scale of fifth-century
Athens, there still was a nobility of birth, contrasted with the
non-noble sections of the populace. We may permit ourselves
to call them the nobles and the commons; though there is a
false and modern flavour in that antithesis, it may perhaps do
more justice to the true historical character of Athenian society
than the half-political, half-moralistic language of some of our
sources.[5] It is easy to see that the difference between nobles
and commons was not, or at any rate was no longer, a question
of origin only. The *lekythion*, or oil-flask, which Dionysos
advises Euripides to buy for one obol, was a *kaloskagathos*, a
true aristocrat among its kind. Its price was probably the
normal one; if anything, it was a little higher than usual, as
even decorated pottery was very cheap;[6] but it was the
important part that Aischylos caused the flask to play which
made it a 'noble'. The farmer Strepsiades has a son who
is called a *kaloskagathos*, and not only because his mother belonged to an ancient and noble family.[7] Clearly the men 'of the
great families, the foremost in wealth and birth', formed the
main part of the upper class.[8] But the opposition of the two
classes is to some extent also based on the antagonism of two
generations. The younger men in particular were active in the
clubs and in politics in general.[9] Other references make it
clear that even more factors play their part; we must realize

---

[1] F.717ff.   [2] Eur. *Hek.* 379f.

[3] Cf., e.g., Eur. *Andr.* 768, *Herakl.* 297ff. — *Hel.* 1678f.   *Phoin.* 1623f.

[4] Eur. *El.* 550, cf. 558f, 572.

[5] Cf., e.g., the χρηστός and the πονηρός, K.1278ff.

[6] F. 1234ff. Cf. D. A. Amyx, *Univ. of California Publications in Class.
Archaeol.* I (1941), 190.

[7] C.797.   [8] Eupolis 117, 5.

[9] K.852ff, W.342ff, 887ff. Cf. below, p. 110.

that the social differences between nobles and commons were complex indeed.

A man is a noble — or should we say: a gentleman? — because of the way and style of his life. Strepsiades would have called Sokrates and his friends and pupils, of whom he as yet knows nothing, *kaloikagathoi*, whereas Pheidippides, knowing them to be charlatans, 'palefaced and barefoot vagabonds', regards them as *poneroi*.[1] He himself is a noble in his luxurious style of living. He has 'galloping consumption'; that means, he keeps expensive riding and racing horses, wanting to drive, like his ancestor, in purple garments from a victory at the games to the Acropolis.[2] Moreover he wastes his father's money in a life of leisure and physical vanity, in bathing, oiling and anointing his body, and tending his hair.[3] It was the fashion to admire a man who is 'youthful' or 'dashing', both in his appearance and in his actions.[4] This is the life for which the knights of the chorus are longing, and — despite all exaggeration — we may take those features as symbolic of the general aspect of aristocratic education and life.[5] Similarly, peasant-like manners were not confined to peasants, but often meant simply the reverse of good manners.[6]

The noble was instructed and trained in the palaestra, in sports, dancing and music; these were the usual forms of education in earlier times.[7] The gymnastic and musical education, with its emphasis on the 'agonal' feelings, was the inevitable accompaniment of nobility. It might easily replace political ambitions or, on the other hand, all feeling of responsibility for, and solidarity with, one's fellow citizens.[8] We learn that the gymnasium in the grove of Akademos was a favoured place,[9] and it was hardly a mere coincidence that later this place was to become so famous as the original home of the education of mankind. There were, however,

---

[1] C.101f.   [2] C.243. — 69f.   [3] C.835ff.
[4] K.611, W.1204f, 1307, 1362: νεανικός.
[5] K.578ff.   [6] Cf. above, p. 86f.
[7] F.729; cf. also, e.g., Eur. *Troad.* 833f, *Phoin.* 368.
[8] Cf. Eur. *Hipp.* 1013ff. It is only natural that a young man of such upbringing should have been unable and also unwilling 'to speak to the masses, but better in addressing a few of his comrades' (*Hipp.* 986ff). They 'who give themselves airs' resent it when they are beaten in an argument by inferior people (Eur. *Androm.* 189ff).
[9] C.1005, Eupolis 32. (? Ἑκάδημος).

many gymnasia, and there were competitions between them.[1]

The son's fancy for horses drove the rustic father to despair, but we see the same thing in quite a different aspect in the chorus of the *Knights*. When they invoke Poseidon Hippios, the patron of all kinds of racing, of horses as well as of triremes, and when they praise the efficiency and courage of their horses, we get the impression of gallant youths, and we may remember Hippolytos' love for his horses, or the noble beauty of the young men in some vase-paintings (see Plates VI*b*, VII*b*), or of those who rode in the procession of the Panathenaia as they appear on the Parthenon frieze.[2] This last comparison is not incidental; we learn that the ancestors of the knights were men 'worthy of this country and the *peplos*',[3] and it is well known that presenting the *peplos* to the goddess was actually the object of that procession.

Let us not forget them when we proceed to examine a phenomenon which reveals a somewhat unpleasant side of that youth. The outstanding quality which characterized the nobleman was, according to the view of comedy, the practice of paederasty. The allusions and innuendoes about this practice are legion, for it is one of the most favoured (and most exaggerated) themes of comedy. Everyone who as a noble wore his hair long was a paederast.[4] As a lover of Demos the sausage-seller felt like one of the nobles.[5] Love between man and boy was one of the essential features of the great past; it belonged to the *archaia*, and was closely connected with the whole atmosphere of the palaestra.[6] There were, of course, very different types of paederasty, from romantic love and fashionable 'liaisons' down to pure venality. There is little in common between the blushing boys of Plato's dialogues, and the world of unnatural lust and vice which the comedians depict. They sneer at the members of the aristocratic circles as paederasts, and it made no great difference whether their names were mentioned or they were merely but sufficiently characterized. Even the Thracian king was in love with the

[1] W.526f, 531ff.

[2] K.551ff, 595ff; cf. C.83. Neil, on K.551, well remarks that 'here it is natural that the horse comes before the ship'. — Eur. *Hipp.* 1240, 1356.

[3] K.566.   [4] adesp. 12-14.

[5] K.732ff, cf. 1341ff, also 1162f with Neil's comment.

[6] K.1385, 1387. — W.1025f, P.762f.

Athenians and behaved like them when he wrote on the wall: 'The Athenians are beautiful.'[1] The love-inscriptions which could once be found scrawled on Athenian walls and doors[2] have disappeared, but we still have many on vases (see Plates VI*b*, VIII*a*). The boys could be seen 'swathing themselves in bright cloaks and chewing the mastic smelling of perfume', loitering in the market and flirting with the men; afterwards the 'heartless charm of youthful beauty' mocked and laughed at them.[3] The boys and youths were often jealous of one another, and they could be extremely coarse.[4] Old Demos was scolded by the sausage-seller for behaving like those boys in preferring middle-class people as lovers to noblemen.[5] However, after he had just claimed himself to be Demos' lover like 'many noblemen', it seems preposterous to accept this as a true characterization of the boys in general. Naturally, it was frequently important that the lover was wealthy and generous. The comedians tell us, as the vases do (see Plate VII*a*), that the beloved boys, 'smooth as an eel, with golden ringlets', were given hares and birds as presents.[6] Noble boys were bitterly scorned, for though they might not take money and therefore were not simply male prostitutes, they took horses and hounds, which was not much better.[7] Sometimes boys did, in fact, take money and could even be cheated out of it.[8]

---

[1] Ἀθηναῖοι καλοί, A.144.   [2] W.97ff.

[3] adesp. 338. — Phryn. 3. This last fragment is very obscure indeed. I admit that I am not certain either what the κέντρον ἐν τοῖς δακτύλοις is, or what the βάθρα mean. Mr. Edmonds, in explaining the fragment, understands the 'sting in the fingers' as referring to the applause in the theatre or at the Odeion where the *proagon* took place (about the latter see above, p. 27, n. 1). But are the βάθρα the seats in the theatre? Was clapping the usual form of applause? I am not sure whether this is the meaning of κρότος χειρῶν in F.157. And are the people referred to part of the audience, or even, as Kaibel thought, other comedians? I believe they must be some of the boy-minions. However, I should like to quote Edmonds's very charming translation of the relevant lines:

> And there's no one so sweet
> when at market we meet;
> but once at the benches they sit,
> they mangle and rend
> their yesterday's friend
> with sniggering whispers of wit.

[4] Cf. Lysias, *frg.* 17.   [5] K.735, 737f.   [6] P.11, frg. 218. — B.707.
[7] Pl. 153ff.   [8] F.148; cf. Lysias III, 22, 25f.

More than one house was ruined economically by paederasty.[1]

Undoubtedly the middle-class man who had gained wealth followed the custom of the nobles in this as in other ways although he would be more inclined to be ashamed of it.[2] It remained a characteristic privilege of the upper class. The gentleman, the *gennadas*, was generally characterized by his inclination to drinking and sexual pleasures;[3] but boys were a far more frequent object of his love than women. Even if we allow, as we must, that comedy generally over-emphasizes the importance of paederasty as of all sexual matters, the part which it played in the life of the upper class was highly significant and important.

There were other characteristic features also. In general, the nobles paid much attention to their manners and bearing. It could be regarded as the duty of a nobleman to save his face and not to show his feelings in front of the people.[4] In the *Birds* Poseidon, the special god of the knights, adopted a very distinguished manner, and was horrified at the barbarian god because he wore his coat in the wrong way.[5] We have already mentioned the old-fashioned style of appearance which the nobles preferred. Some of them, from affectation, wore the simplest clothes; they were the *lakonizontes*, people who imitated the manners of Sparta, *the* anti-democratic State.[6] They, of course, also followed Laconian habits as paederasts.[7]

Hunting was one of the enjoyments of the young noble countryman.[8] But a larger part of the social life of the nobles was devoted to singing and drinking. This general impression gained from comedy is confirmed by a great number of vase-paintings. Although this sort of life was not confined to the noblemen, they again were the only social class for which it was typical. 'The shadows are seven feet long; the company of friends calls me to dinner.'[9] The meal and the drinking party were usually distinct affairs.[10] Sometimes small boys accompanied their fathers in order to sing during the dinner,[11] and they

[1] Isaios X, 25; cf. Xen. *mem.* I, 3, 11, *oik.* 2, 7.
[2] Cf. Lysias III.   [3] F.739f: πίνειν καὶ βίνειν.
[4] Eur. *Iph. A.* 446ff.   [5] B.1567ff.
[6] W.474f., B.1281f., Plat. 124.   [7] frg. 338.
[8] K.1382; cf. Eur. *Hik.* 881ff, *Her.* 860, *Iph. T.* 709, and, of course, the *Hippolytos.*
[9] frg. 675 (the meaning is clear, though the text seems slightly corrupt).
[10] P.770.   [11] P.1265ff, 1290, 1295, E.678f; cf. B.131, L.1067.

would naturally afterwards go home. Most of the guests attended both dinner and symposium. Boys, women, the game of kottabos, good food, drinking and laughing, these were the pleasures of contemporary youth.[1] To be a 'lover of drink' is called the 'disease of honest people'.[2] The drinking parties sometimes lasted through the whole night, and even if you felt out of sorts in the early morning, you continued to drink.[3] War himself is depicted as one of the dissolute youths who sing and drink.[4]

The drinking parties, the symposia, one of which forms part of a comedy and is vividly described by the serving slaves, began with a libation of unmixed wine to the 'Good Daemon', and that libation could be made an excuse for drinking pure wine at other times.[5] Later the men used to propound riddles or tell each other fables and jokes.[6] Conversation, however, played a smaller part than drinking and music. The men drank wine, often by order of the 'president', the *symposiarchos*, and played kottabos, the famous and favourite game of throwing heel-taps into a metal basin; there were prizes for the best thrower, and it was usual to invoke Dionysos or, instead of the god, a beloved boy.[7] There was no drinking without singing, and little singing without the flute-girls to accompany it (see Plates VIII*b*, XV*a*).[8] They or the attendant boys were also expected to offer help when the drinkers were sick. Pheidippides refuses to sing or to play the lyre.[9] He does what he has learned from his master Sokrates, and we can be sure that Sokrates indeed preferred a good conversation to all the other entertainments; Xenophon's, and to some extent even Plato's, *Symposion*, however untypical of a normal party, were typical of the kind favoured by Sokrates. Otherwise drinking-songs or *skolia* were sung, each of the party in turn taking up the song.[10] The best known of the *skolia* was 'the Harmodios', the famous song about the tyrannicides; it was accepted by Kleon him-

---

[1] C.1073, P.339ff.

[2] W.79f; τῶν χρηστῶν may possibly here mean the upper classes.

[3] frg. 13.   [4] A.978ff.

[5] Plat. 69. — K.85, Theop. 40-1.   [6] W.21ff, 1258ff.

[7] Eupolis 147. — A.525, C.1073, P.343, 1244, Hermipp. 47, Eupolis 86, adesp. 586. — Kratinos 116, Kallias 9, Kephisodor. 5. — frg. 152, Kratinos 273.

[8] Cf., e.g., A.752, W.1219, 1368f.   [9] C.1358f.

[10] W.1222ff, 1242ff, L.1236f, frg. 706, Theop. 64.

self, the chief enemy of the nobles, because it had become a kind of anthem of Athenian democracy.[1] The youths generally preferred modern songs, and the great lyric poets of the seventh and sixth centuries were, it is said, more or less forgotten.[2]

Certain social formalities and customs were observed at the symposia, and it was difficult for an ordinary citizen like Philokleon to conform to them. Water and towel to wash the hands were usually offered before and after the meal.[3] It was shocking to burst into a symposium 'in the Mykonian way', that is, probably, unannounced or uninvited.[4] On the whole, however, there was an increasing tendency to coarseness. The old songs were largely replaced by lighter entertainments, by flute girls, dancers and acrobats (see Plates VIII, IX).[5] Xenophon describes these half sportive, half erotic performances of girls and boys, and we know them also from vase-paintings. A fragment of the comic poet Platon apparently refers to the luxury of modern symposia; the people 'lie on couches with ivory feet, covered with purple coverlets and robes from Sardes'.[6] In considering such descriptions we must remember that it has been customary in all ages to exhort younger people to live the simple life of their ancestors; even the comic writer Chionides, who is said to have lived in the age of the Persian War, reminded an effeminate youth of the example of those soldiers who 'sleep on mats'.[7]

It is, however, neither mere fancy nor the usual grumbling of older people, when the comic poets again and again deride the idling of the *jeunesse dorée* who from dawn on loitered in the market place, standing near the perfume stalls and making affected speeches, or prattling stupidly about fragrant flowers.[8] These are the youths who had a warm bath early in the morning, and were drunk before the market was full.[9] Her-mippos says the 'good man' must not get drunk nor indulge

[1] A.980, 1093, W.1224ff, cf. L.632ff. On the originally aristocratic nature of the *skolia* see my *Aspects of the Ancient World*, 89, P.-W., Suppl. VII, 294, *Historia* I, 530ff, *Wiener Studien* LXIX (1956), 59ff.

[2] C.1356ff, frg. 223, Eupolis 139.   [3] W.1216f, B.463f, frg. 502.

[4] adesp. 439. — frg. 272, 483. This is regarded as typical of having an easy life: οὐ γὰρ ἄκανθαι. But it certainly was not good manners. Cf. Herbst, *P.-W.* XVI, 1031f.   [5] adesp. 680.

[6] Xen. *Symp.* 2. — Plat. 208, cf. already Kratinos 301.   [7] Chionides 1.

[8] ἀγοράσαι, K.1373, 1375ff, adesp. 42 D. — Pherekr. 2.

[9] Pherekr. 2; 29.

in warm baths; his purpose is to point out the contrast with
the dissipated and degenerate *kaloskagathos*.[1] Such a type
is often exemplified in a certain Kleisthenes, whereas the
young Alkibiades was attacked far less frequently, if not by
all the comic writers, certainly by Aristophanes, who occasionally alluded only to his 'lisp' or to his use of the modern
manner of speech; once, however, he is depicted as the leader
of the dissolute younger generation.[2] He was the most
prominent representative of aristocratic youth, both in good
and in bad qualities.[3] 'Their life is nothing but headache, bathing, pure wine, chamber-pot, idleness, and drinking.'[4] The son
in the *Daitales* who was given a modern education was
ignorant of everything except 'drinking, bad singing,
Syracusan cooking, Sybaritic luxuries and Chian wine from
Laconian cups'.[5] Many of these youths and men, among them
especially the poet Agathon, were sneered at, not only as
dissolute, but as effeminate. Agathon, according to comedy,
always carried with him his shaving-utensils, not only to get
rid of all traces of the male beard, but to shave as women do.[6]
The 'Weaklings' (*Malthakoi*, as already a comedy of Kratinos
was called) decked themselves with the most elegant flowers,
wore coats of Persian wool which were much warmer than the
ordinary coats, and even wore 'white felt slippers on their feet'.[7]
But when the poet blamed the young men for wearing the
himation instead of going naked or wearing only the *chiton*, he
diverged, as the vases show, from the normal Athenian custom
and was pleading for the Laconian fashion.[8] On the whole the
average youth, who enjoyed his life and did not wish for anything better, was 'a little weakling', like the young man so
described by an old hag, half in love and half in contempt.[9]
Many of the young men were also accused of having provided
for themselves lucrative and safe posts in war-time, and
Aristophanes even maintains that young men educated by the
sophists and without the training of the palaestra were filling

[1] Hermipp. 76, cf. also frg. 237.
[2] Alkibiades: Pherekr. 155, Eupolis 158, adesp. 3-5. His lisp and manner of
speech: W.44ff, frg. 198, 6; his leadership: A.716.
[3] Cf., e.g., Thuc. VI, 15, 3, Lysias XIV, 25ff, *frg.* 30, Isokr. XVI, 25, 31.
[4] adesp. 375.   [5] frg. 216.   [6] Th.218ff. — E.65f.
[7] Kratinos 98. — W.1151ff. — Kratinos 100; cf. K.889, Hermipp. 47, 4,
Lysipp. 2.
[8] C.965, 987. See Plates VIIa, Xb.   [9] E.1058.

the ranks of the new class of 'small clerks and beggarly charlatans'.[1]

Nobility and wealth were often connected; for, on the whole, the nobles still represented the landed gentry of old.[2] Nevertheless they were not the rich. The prologue of Euripides' *Stheneboia*, quoted in the *Frogs*, begins with the commonplace that nobody is lucky in every way: 'one man is of noble birth, but lacks money'.[3] In the *Phoenician Women* Euripides expressly tells us that noble birth 'does not feed a man'. 'A nobleman who is poor is nothing.'[4] The impoverishment of part of the nobles is confirmed by their very way of living. Though many of them squandered their hereditary property, there were others who had little to squander. We cannot say whether the noblemen from Karystos mentioned by Aristophanes were entertained by aristocrats, though their connection with the oligarchs as recorded by Thucydides makes that likely; their feast, at any rate, was ridiculed as consisting of some of the popular pea-soup and the remains of a sacrificial sucking-pig.[5] This was certainly not a luxurious dinner, for pea-soup was the favourite dish of the glutton Herakles, who always cared more for substance and quantity than for quality.[6] One of the knights and swaggering officers went shopping in the market on horseback to 'buy a pease-pudding, stowing it in his helmet'.[7] In a later chapter we shall deal with the importance of money and wealth for the whole of Athenian life, and for the individual Athenian in general; but we must mention here the changed aspects of the wealth of the upper classes. The habits of noble youths (horses and boys) were very expensive. Apart from the traditional connection between aristocracy and inherited wealth, there were no doubt a certain number of well-to-do and even rich people in Athens, and it is almost certain that not only most of the nobles and the upper class in general were rich, but also the majority of the higher State-officials and even many members of the Boule.[8] The evidence of the official inscriptions is confirmed by the evidence of the

---

[1] A.600ff. — F.1083ff.
[2] Cf., e.g., Eupolis 117, 5; Isokr. XVI, 25, 31, XIX, 7, 36.
[3] Euripides 16 P, 1ff = *frg.* 661, F.1217f.
[4] Eur. *Phoin.* 404f, 442.
[5] L.1059ff. — Thuc. VIII, 69, 3.   [6] F.62f.   [7] L.559ff.
[8] Cf. W.1171. — J. Sundwall, *Epigraphische Beiträge* (*Klio*, Beiheft IV).

love-inscriptions on vases.¹ Many of the *kaloi* became archons or strategoi, all of them became 'good men'. Good men were brave men, and thus served their Polis,² but they did this not only as hoplites or strategoi, also as magistrates, as councillors, as citizens in general. Here we touch on the very nature of those who claimed to be the 'fine and brave' (or whatever English words we like to use for the not translatable *kaloi-kagathoi*). When we realize that the boy was *kalos*, i.e. beautiful, and the man *agathos*, i.e. a good citizen, in particular as a soldier, we seem to be approaching an explanation of the obscure expression *kaloskagathos*.³ The word had been used to characterize the aristocracy and its members, but eventually it came to indicate some special qualities which might be ascribed to that class but were not confined to it. The *kaloikagathoi* were said to be the real and true 'men', the 'good men'.⁴ They had been fine boys, they now were fine, brave, worthy and dignified men. In recognizing that style in living is the outstanding quality of the *kaloskagathos* we combine the two meanings of the *kalos* and the *agathos*. *Kalokagathia*, when it became a sort of personal virtue, was no longer confined to the old social sense, but it was still used of the upper classes alone.⁵

Its meaning was therefore somewhat ambiguous, for it referred to an upper class which was no longer simply the aristocracy. This becomes particularly clear when we think of the highest office in the State. The social change here is

---

¹ Cf., in spite of their obvious insufficiency and incorrectness, the valuable suggestions in D. M. Robinson and E. J. Fluck, *A Study of the Greek Love-Names* (1937), esp. 47f, 66ff. See also above, p. 101. For a full list of love-names by rf. painters see J. D. Beazley, *Attic Red-Figure Vase-Painters*, App. III, pp. 912ff.

² A.696.

³ ἀγαθὸς πολίτης, K.944. In introducing the two age groups of boy and man as an additional element of the composed expression καλὸς κἀγαθός we go beyond the explanation formulated, e.g. by H.-I. Marrou in his valuable book *Histoire de l'éducation dans l'antiquité* (1948), 77ff, as the union of 'l'aspect moral et l'aspect physique'. Nor does it seem adequate to base this double aspect on 'sport' alone.

⁴ K.179, 333, 392, 1255, W.1185, 1256, Cf. J. Jüthner, *Charisteria f. Rzach* (1930), 101f.

⁵ This is perhaps the case of the man who in Eupolis' *Demoi* (109) claimed to have a γυνὴ καλή τε κἀγαθή who had loved him from a girl (cf. Eur. *Iph. A.* 750). It is, however, also possible that a second Strepsiades is speaking, as probably also in another fragment (Kantharos 5) which emphasizes the woman's Athenian origin: γυναῖκ' Ἀθηναίαν καλήν τε κἀγαθήν.

described, though also strongly exaggerated, by Eupolis: 'in previous times, the strategoi were taken from the highest families, now they come from the scum of the people'.[1] We know that many noble or at least wealthy men were among the strategoi, and that fairly often there was a certain heritage in office from father to son. A sort of military aristocracy still held the *strategia* and other higher military posts throughout the fourth century.[2] But there were many 'new' families, and moreover, ever since Kleon had been strategos in the years 425-422, there had been signs of a gradual invasion by the middle and lower classes.

Although examples of these facts are given as early as the *Knights*, it is obvious that there was more change and development during the succeeding years. The chorus of the *Knights*, though they sneered at the Demos for being fooled by the demagogues, yet hailed the regenerated Demos as 'King of the Hellenes' who was 'worthy of the State and the trophy of the plain of Marathon'.[3] The knights were not the representatives of an oligarchy, which actually grew in strength during the following decades, an oligarchy filled with hatred, and eager to fight democracy, regardless of the fact that the war might be lost and the empire destroyed. Although Aristophanes had every reason not to bring before the public such an attitude if it existed, the mere fact that the poet gave the nobles such an important part in the play, and the way he describes them, prove that at that time the people did not regard them as the sworn enemies of democracy.[4]

The aristocracy became poorer, and in other classes wealth had increased so as to reach upper-class standards. Some rich men were accepted by the aristocrats among their own ranks, and Nikias even became to some extent their political leader. In the oligarchic revolution of 411 citizenship was not to be restricted to the owners of landed property or of other great wealth, nor to the 'Eupatridai', but was to include all people of hoplite census. The rule of the upper classes was, in fact,

[1] Eupolis 117 (in the *Demoi* of 412).
[2] Cf. Sundwall, *l.c.*, 27ff. Beloch, *Griech. Gesch.* II, 2, 260ff.
[3] K.1111ff. — 1333f.
[4] Cf. the more general remarks on the patriotism of oligarchs by Gomme in a paper on *The Old Oligarch* (*Harvard Studies, Vol. for Ferguson*, 238ff). In later years the νεανίσκοι, as a sort of stormtroopers, played a sinister part in the service of the oligarchs or the Thirty (Thuc. VIII, 69, 4. Xen. *hell.* II, 3, 23).

PLATE VIII

a

b

WINE AND MUSIC

PLATE IX

a

b

DANCING GIRLS

neither pure plutocracy nor pure oligarchy. It included a larger part of the people, and it opposed, at least theoretically, the democratic leaders and some of the democratic institutions rather than the demos.

Without dwelling on the composition of the upper classes, the comic poets saw the change of attitude, especially in the younger generation. Euripides is accused of having made the citizens 'market-walkers'.[1] In earlier times the young man went to the gymnasium or went hunting, now he frequents the agora and concerns himself with *psephismata*, the decrees accepted in the assembly of the people.[2] In adapting the proverb 'Don't give a knife to a child', Eupolis gives a warning against handing over the State to a child.[3] Miltiades and Perikles, who in the same comedy of Eupolis, the *Demoi*, had come to life again, took charge of the State: 'nor let us suffer the rule and the sway of peevish minions who trail high offices like a flaunting robe'.[4] In spite of his origin one of these young men was also the demagogue who had only recently been admitted as a citizen, and who is said to have his friends among the 'lazy profligates', or to be one of them himself, and not a man of dignity.[5] 'They are not happy, unless they carry baskets full of verdicts and heaps of decrees!'[6] It has been proved from the inscriptions that most of the speakers in the assembly, and the movers of public decrees also, belonged to wealthy families.[7]

In his famous description of the age Thucydides mentions the fact that relationship was pushed aside by the *hetairia*, the party club.[8] We may assume that the youths of Bdelykleon's drinking

---

[1] ἀγοραῖοι, F.1015.

[2] K.1373, 1382f, C.991, and elsewhere.

[3] Eupolis 121.   [4] Eupolis 100.

[5] Eupolis 40 P, 24. It depends on the restoration of the missing end of the line whether the upstart himself or his friends belong to the ἀπράγμονες πόρνοι, translated by Page as 'non-political pansies'. Jensen, *Abh. Preuss. Ak.* 1939, no. 14,8ff, following A. Mayer, *Berl. Phil. Wochenschr.* 1912, 832, takes them as 'Prostituierte niederen Ranges' and contrasts them with the noble σεμνοί. But ἀπράγμων is not a contrast to σεμνός, although it is here a word of blame. Eupolis seems to be at variance with the condemnation of πολυπραγμοσύνη, so well known from Aristophanes and other sources, though the issue is not quite so simple. I have dealt with these questions in my article on *Polypragmosyne* (*JHS*. LXVII, 1947, 46ff).

[6] frg. 217.   [7] Sundwall, *l.c.*, 62ff.   [8] Thuc. III, 82, 6.

party, 'Phrynichos' gang', were a sort of informal *hetairia*.[1]
Frequently groups of young noblemen joined company without
any thought of politics. The 'young comrades' of Hippolytos
in Euripides' play are of that kind; their aims are not political
power, but a victory in one of the Panhellenic festivals and,
being second in the State, to live on good terms with the 'best
men'.[2] Perhaps it is the same kind of people whom Euripides
describes as the young men eager to win glory in just and
righteous warfare.[3] But as early as 424 the nobles were censured for being conspirators.[4] The expression 'conspirators'
is, in fact, the word normally used in comedy for the members
of the oligarchic clubs.[5] Almost all the passages in which the
'conspirators' are mentioned, testify — although with comic
exaggeration — to the widespread fear that the clubs would
one day try to overthrow democracy, in particular with the
help of oligarchs from other States.[6] To democracy the policy
of these clubs or *hetairiai* meant the same as tyranny, and somebody 'riding' (the word is used in an obscene sense) was
obviously aiming at a sort of 'Hippias' tyranny'.[7] Impoverished
nobles were the natural supporters of a tyrant, aiming at civil
strife and at plundering those who by steady industry had
gained wealth.[8] The fact that they had become involved in
everyday politics, secretly or openly, in *hetairiai* or in the

---

[1] W.1302. It seems much more probable that the Phrynichos mentioned here
was the oligarchic leader of later years than the dancer of v. 1490 — unless Andok.
I, 47 (Φρύνιχος ὁ ὀρχησάμενος, altered by A. Wilhelm into Ὀρχησαμένου)
proves that the dancer is a comic invention to fit in with the name of Phrynichos'
father.

[2] Eur. *Hipp.* 1098, 1179ff. — 1013ff.

[3] Eur. *Hik.* 232f.   [4] K.257.

[5] συνωμόται, K.257, 452, 475f, 628, 862, W.345, 483, 488, 507, 953. In
general, cf. G. M. Calhoun, *Athenian Clubs in Politics and Litigation* (1913).

[6] That is why Ps.-Xen. II, 15 states that the Athenians would get rid of this
fear if they lived on an island. Cf. also L.577f, words spoken on the stage a few
weeks before the outbreak of revolution in 411, and very similar to those of Thuc.
VIII, 54, 4, when he describes the activities of the συνωμοσίαι at that very
moment.

[7] W.501f.

[8] Eur. *Her.* 588ff. Wilamowitz, comparing Plato, *Rep.* VIII, 555 D, takes
this interesting and realistic passage as a picture of something that could happen
in an oligarchy only. But Euripides describes Lykos' rule, i.e. the rise of a tyrant
in a mythical monarchy, and if he is alluding to contemporary conditions, as he
undoubtedly is, he is thinking of those people whose political intrigues eventually
led to the oligarchic revolutions of 411 and 404.

assembly, was one of the reasons why the nobles, and especially the noble youth, were no longer what they had been.

The nobles had either given way to the commons or had become degenerate. The picture thus drawn is no doubt inconsistent. That may, to some extent, be explained by the peculiar attitude of comedy. Aristophanes had no definite political bias.[1] To the conservatism of most of the comic poets the miseducated or the dissolute aristocrats of their day were just as intolerable as the democratic demagogues. The same kind of view prevailed in religious matters. The pious Nikias who worshipped the old images of gods caused the poet's mockery no less than his colleague who denied all gods.[2] The wise Aischylos knew — and this was, as may be supposed, Aristophanes' own point of view — that 'neither frieze nor woollen tunics', neither commons nor nobles, would save the State.[3] Party spirit grew sometimes stronger than the attachment of either side to their Polis, but the lack of loyalty was much more manifest among oligarchs than among democrats.[4]

In general, a certain tendency on the part of the comedians to hark back to the good old times can easily be recognized. If we try to grasp the truth which underlies idealization and caricature, we find as the essential, both in its good and bad aspects, the aristocratic mode of life, which in the last decades of the fifth century underwent a critical change. This was caused partly by the new education with which we shall deal in a later chapter, and partly by the social change in politics. It was a crisis from which there was no return. For a long time the Athenian aristocracy had been, politically, socially and intellectually, the ruling class, also in the democratic State. Gradually they lost their position and the upper classes changed in character. Much more fatal than the partial intrusion by the more wealthy among the middle classes was the change the nobility underwent in itself. This was even more devastating in its effect than the war casualties which had fallen most heavily on the upper classes. The nobles were rapidly moving towards self-destruction.

---

[1] Cf. Gomme, *Cl. Rev.* LII (1938), 97ff, and above, p. 8f.
[2] K.30ff.   [3] F.1458ff.
[4] These facts are at the bottom of a denunciation of Greek lack of 'patriotism' in general — rather overdone, I feel — by N. M. Pusey, *Alcibiades and the* φιλόπολι. *Harvard Studies in Cl. Phil.* LI (1940), 215ff.

We learn next to nothing from comedy about the women of the upper classes. This may only confirm that they lived a life remote from public affairs and social events; but their moral standards were probably on the decline, and it is perhaps not without significance that Euripides' Phaidra charges women from noble families with having introduced adultery.[1]

At the time of the performance of the *Knights*, the old aristocratic ideal was still fully alive, but the threatening signs of change were also visible. Twenty years later the process was more or less complete. The attempts to restore, once again, the political rule of the upper classes, though, as we have seen, this did not mean merely that of the nobles, continued the decline of the aristocracy. The revolution of the Four Hundred in 411, and even more the rule of the Thirty in 403, failed, not so much because of the resistance of the democrats as through the weakness and corruption of the oligarchs. The *kaloikagathoi*, represented by the tyranny of unscrupulous and individualistic 'supermen' like Kritias, using the knights as their main military weapon, were a bitter caricature indeed,[2] and opposition, though powerless, arose among their own followers.

The political leaders and events finally crushed the fading ideal of aristocracy. The name of *kaloikagathoi* entirely lost its social meaning, it was no longer descriptive even of a general upper class, and became a merely individual and moral title.[3] This was part of a general development, in the course of which, for instance, the name of the Hellenes became an expression of the standard of personal education. People who aimed at 'being called' *kaloikagathoi* had to excel in several good qualities, which, of course, were not only those of an honest and pedantic *pater familias* and farmer, as they are in Xenophon's description.[4] The result of the process was clear enough. In the fourth century, there were still some prominent individual aristocrats in Athens, there were theories and ideas of truly aristocratic life and mind, but there was no longer an aristocracy worthy of the name.

---

[1] Eur. *Hipp.* 407ff. In general, see ch. VIII.

[2] Xen. *hell.* II, 3, 12ff, 38; 4, 6f, 24.

[3] Xen. *mem.* I, 1, 16; 2, 17; *symp.* 3, 4; 9, 1, Antiphon I, 14, and elsewhere.

[4] Xen. *oik.* 6, 12ff. Jüthner, *l.c.*, 102ff, deals at length with the various meanings of the word and their changes.

CHAPTER V

TRADERS AND CRAFTSMEN

It is perhaps our chief task, when explaining the structure of Athenian social life, to discover the occupations followed by those members of the population who were not peasants. They were the majority, though perhaps not of the citizens, certainly of the townsfolk who were the most influential section of the people. The sources, especially of the fourth century, make it clear that they were engaged in trade, or in some form of industry or manufacture. It is of great importance for our purposes to discover the meaning, in fifth-century Athens, of those two terms, traders and craftsmen, and to understand the social position of the two classes.

I

Modern research on Attic trade has rightly taken as its starting-point the Greek words for the 'merchant'. The chief words which occur are *kapelos*, retailer, *emporos*, trader, and *naukleros*, shipowner.[1] But in dealing with these expressions, nearly all scholars assume too readily the accuracy of interpretation of the many different words, given by philosophers like Aristotle, or even by late scholia and lexica.[2] It has therefore been justly emphasized that wide divergences can be found, even in the same author, in the use of the terms mentioned above, as indicating various kinds of trade.[3] The whole question is well worth consideration, and we can find in comedy confirmation that *kapelos* and *emporos* at least were two

---

[1] H. Knorringa, *Emporos*. Cf. Ehrenberg, *DLZ.* 1927, 1308ff. Oertel, *Gnomon* VI (1930), 35ff. Most important: Hasebroek, 1ff; cf., on the German original, Oertel, *DLZ.* 1928, 1618ff. Salin, *Ztschr. f. d. gesamte Staatswiss.* 89 (1930), 353ff.

[2] e.g., Aristotle, *pol.* 1258b, 20ff. Moreover, it is very doubtful whether special names like αὐτοπώλης, παλιγκάπηλος, μεταβολεύς covered real occupations, and were used in daily life. I shall have to speak later of the παλιγκάπηλος.

[3] Finkelstein, *Cl. Phil.* XXX (1935), 320ff.

forms of trade which differed in nature and importance.[1]

The *kapelos*, a word very often used in its feminine form,[2] was the local retail-trader, from whom one could buy many and miscellaneous things, even torches and weapons;[3] but, above all, he or she was a wine-seller and the keeper of an inn or public house.[4] It is significant that the word which expressed the pouring of wine into cups gradually acquired the meaning of general retailing.[5] Apparently more women than men were engaged in this occupation. Thus the rhetorical question is asked: what can the *kapelos* buy from the *kapelis* except wine?[6] The hosts or hostesses of public houses were well-known people, especially to women who, again and again, are depicted in comedy as drunkards. Of the many women who appear at the women's assembly only the wife of the *kapelos* is called by the name of her husband's occupation.[7] The *kapeleion* was the 'pub', the door of which could be compared to an eyelid, because it was constantly opening and shutting.[8]

The *kapelos* was on the whole looked down on. Dishonesty was the characteristic feature of the 'mind of a *kapelos*', and to translate this phrase by 'a shopkeeper's outlook' would be to give it too favourable an interpretation; it simply meant the desire and ability to cheat.[9] The women who sold bread were another typical example of the profession, notorious for their powers of invective and abuse; like all hucksters, they were low people who might easily receive harsh treatment.[10] The 'egg-and-seed-and-potherb-market-girls' and 'garlic-selling-barmaid-bakehouse-girls' were true *dames des halles*.[11] When a

[1] The suggestion of one of my reviewers that the mere translation of ἔμπορος and κάπηλος as given by Liddell and Scott reveals all that I have tried to illuminate with regard to the two professions from the evidence of comedy, hardly needs refutation. It has, in fact, been rejected beforehand by the extensive discussion on the social implications of the two words, that has been going on for years among a number of scholars.

[2] ἡ καπηλίς. *Kapelides* was also the title of a comedy (Theopomp. 24ff).

[3] C.614, P.447; cf. Lysias I, 24.

[4] L.466, Th.347, 737, Pl.435, 1120. πανδοκεύτρια (hostess) is only another word for καπηλίς: F.114, 549ff, Pl.426, Eupolis 9.

[5] κοτυλίζειν: frg. 683, Pherekr. 168. Cf. Heichelheim, 345.

[6] adesp. 567.   [7] E.49.   [8] L.427, adesp. 493.

[9] κάπηλον φρόνημα, adesp. 867. Cf. also the proverbial phrase οὐδεὶς ἐν τοῦ καπήλου νοῦς in Plat.1174, 3f; the text here follows Edmond's reading.

[10] W.1388ff, L.560ff.   [11] L.457f.

woman shouted at somebody, she was like an inn-keeper or
pease-pudding-seller.[1] And an old woman who used 'make-up'
looked 'like a *kapelis*', that is, in professional style,[2] probably
not because of her attractive shop-front, but because she belonged to the world of the innkeeper or retailer: a wine-shop
was often a brothel. It was a frequently repeated insult to refer
directly or indirectly to Euripides' mother as a greengrocer,
or to that of Kleophon as a fishmonger; Euripides himself was
called a chervil-seller.[3] A man who got his nickname from
owning a stall or a tent, and who in fact was a very low fellow,
was probably some sort of *kapelos*.[4] Therefore the sausage-
seller at first asked himself modestly enough, how he 'could
become a man', meaning 'a good man', a gentleman; for his
stall was not even in the market, but at the gate.[5] This implied a still lower and more disreputable standing, probably
because there were no fixed stalls there. Later, after his success
in the contest with the Paphlagonian, he gradually became 'a
man', even felt himself one of the nobles, and sneered at the
lamp-sellers, shoe-makers, cobblers and leather-sellers, that is
to say, men such as Hyperbolos and Kleon.[6] All these
references are evidence of the low and despised position of
the retail trade.

The *emporos*, on the other hand, was an important and
respected man, and at the same time his work was profitable.[7]
A man who gave himself the airs of a 'big *emporos*' was a
boastful fellow and his wealth a sham,[8] though these words
confirm the fact that, in public opinion, *emporia* and wealth
went hand in hand. The chief difference between *emporia* and

---

[1] Pl.426f.

[2] καπηλικῶς, Pl.1063; cf. K.492 (παιδοτριβικῶς), and the parallels
mentioned by Neil.

[3] A.478, K.19, Th. 387, F.840; cf. adesp. 16. — Plat. 56. — adesp. 2 D.

[4] Isokr. XVII, 33. Πυθόδωρος ὁ σκηνίτης καλούμενος, probably because he
owned a tent or stall instead of a shop. Cf. *IG.* II², 1672, 13, 15, 171 (*Syll.*²,
587); also VII¹, 2712, 72.

[5] K.179; 1245ff.   [6] K.333, 392, 1255. — 738ff.

[7] P.296, B.594, 717f, Pl.520f, 904; cf. Xen. *mem.* III, 4, 2. Is it because of
the different estimation of καπηλία and ἐμπορία that Theseus in Euripides'
Hippolytos charges his son with some sort of καπηλεύειν (953 — whatever the
corrupt line may mean), but speaks of Phaidra as κακὴν ἔμπορον βίου (964)?

[8] Eupolis 122. I believe that Eupolis used μεγαλέμπορος in this sense, and
not merely as 'wholesale merchant' (Liddell and Scott), — if he used it at all, since
we cannot say which words in schol. B.822 actually go back to Eupolis.

kapelia, however, did not lie in the difference between wealth and poverty, but in the type of trade which the words denote.[1] It is significant that the *emporos* was a trader who was not confined to his own particular locality. The word *emporos* originally signified a man who went as a passenger on another man's ship. This, of course, usually meant not a tourist, but a trader who took his goods with him and sold them at various ports. Thus the *emporos* was the overseas trader, and ultimately *emporia* implied all trade abroad both by land and sea. Therefore goods from Boeotia and Megara were called 'goods of *emporia*'.[2] Goods from Euboia were as a rule sent by land along the Oropos road; but the occupation of Dekeleia made necessary the detour round Attica by sea.[3] Land-trade, on the whole, however, was exceptional, and generally *emporia* meant sea-trade, as we should expect from the geographical situation of Greece, and of Athens in particular.[4] So it can be said of some cargo-ships that they accompanied the Sicilian expedition 'because of *emporia*', although they only went for retail trade with the troops.[5]

In many cases the *emporos*, as the original meaning of the word implies, was not the owner of the ship on which he carried his goods. The shipowner was the *naukleros*.[6] But the

---

[1] Cf. schol. Pl.1155.

[2] A.974. — Finkelstein, 336, 66 believes the 'wholesale dealer' to have been a small retailer in winter, and then to have dealt with agrarian products from Boeotia and Megara. By this explanation, however, he restricts, in a way similar to that of the scholars opposed by him, a certain idea, in this case that of the *emporos*, to limits far too narrow. Besides, none of our sources gives any ground for this view, and there is no reason why the Boeotians and Megarians should not have brought their goods to Athens in all seasons.

[3] Thuc. VII, 28, 1. Westlake, *Cl. Rev.* LXII (1948), 2ff, has shown that the common interpretation of that passage is mistaken. The increased expenditure, of which Thucydides speaks, does not refer to the costs of transport by sea, but to those generally incurred by the necessity of compensating for the loss of Attic production. Thus we need no longer try to support the surprising 'fact' of the higher costs of the sea route by the regulations in *IG.* I², 40, 19ff, which, though reducing in certain cases the fees for ferrying across the Euripus, have really nothing to do with the trade from Euboia to Athens (cf. Ziebarth, 123).

[4] A *poros* therefore could not be imagined except at sea (P.124f, F.1465, Kratinos 206).

[5] Thuc. VI, 44, 1, cf. 36, 5. Such ἔμποροι in the train of an army became more and more numerous and usual; they could be called an ἀγοραῖος ὄχλος (Xen. *hell.* I, 6, 37, VI, 2, 23). Cf. H. Schaefer, *Museum Helveticum* VI (1949), 52.

[6] Thus Charon's ferrying could be called ναυκληρία (Eur. *Alk.* 258).

distinction, clear as it seems, does not always hold good.
Although in exceptional cases, as we have said, the *emporos*
was also a land-trader, in fact both *naukleros* and *emporos*
together represented sea-trade.[1] Especially since every corn-
ship had to call at the Peiraeus, it had become impossible to
distinguish one from the other.[2] In a famous fragment of
Hermippos, Dionysos is called a *naukleros* who brings all the
products of the world to Athens.[3] In another fragment we are
told that the tomb of Themistokles could be seen by the
emporoi when entering harbour and leaving it.[4] In another
source, the *emporoi* and 'those who enter harbour' are the same
people, the wholesale corn-traders, and there were *emporoi*
who sailed round the Peloponnesos.[5] There was no clear distinction between *emporos* and *naukleros*, and the actual usage
implies that the words were interchangeable.[6] Many a *naukleros*, who sailed with his own cargo, sold and bought goods;[7]
many an *emporos* used to hire a ship and sail from port to port.
Andokides, as he himself tells us, was *naukleros* and *emporos* in
one.[8] Both shipowner and trader ran the risk of losing either
ship or cargo or both.[9] It is confirmed from other sources that
there was only a small number of people who used one or more
ships of their own for trading, unless they took up a loan, or
were engaged only in the carrying-trade.[10] All sea-trade was as
yet on a small scale. In general, when a man had enough
money, he did not sail himself, nor did he let his ships sail,

---

[1] Cf., e.g., Xen. *Poroi* 3, 4f.   [2] Glotz, 184.

[3] Hermipp. 63. Only a knowledge of the lost play would tell us how Dionysos
came to be a shipowner; there may be some recollection of the story of the god
and the sailors. It is hardly probable that the fragment alluded to 'a captain
Dionysos' (Ziebarth). Dionysos as the name of a man is very rare indeed.

[4] Plat. 183.

[5] Lysias XXII, 17, 21. — Thuc. II, 67, 4.

[6] We have, it is true, two inscriptions of the time, dealing with (perhaps even
a sort of guild of) ναύκληροι (*IG.* I², 127, 128). Unfortunately they are badly
damaged, and in both places where ναύκληροι are mentioned it is possible that
ἔμποροι, too, were referred to (127, 33; 128,3 f); cf. already Ziebarth, 138.

[7] αὐτόφορτος, Kratinos 248. — Xen. *oik.* 8, 12.

[8] Andokides I, 137. — Heichelheim, 335, speaks of the mutual economic
approach of *naukleria* and *emporia*. I should think a growing distinction is more
probable, considering the increasing specialization of the time, and the growing
importance of bottomry.

[9] B.593ff, 598, 711, Pl.1179, adesp. 377; cf. Eur. *frg.* 417.

[10] Its existence is proved by Heichelheim, 337f, against Hasebroek.

but lent money to the *emporoi*. It is not accidental that the comic poets do not distinguish the *naukleros* from the *emporos*, and indeed scarcely mention him.[1]

The idea of sea-trade was even more familiar to the average man than that of agricultural life. Nautical metaphors and similes abound in comedy as well as, for instance, in Euripides.[2] The huge beetle in the *Peace* could be compared to the men coiling ropes into ships.[3] There was a saying which meant that nothing can be done beyond a man's power: 'Let not the cargo be larger than the ship.'[4] Of a man unable to stand an ordeal, it is said that he 'cannot keep his head above the bilge-water', and a clever man could be called one 'who has sailed over the seas', who knows 'how to shift to the comfortable side of the boat'.[5] Or if one wished to indicate the moment when the greatest care was wanted, one could say: 'into the harbour'.[6] Sea-trade, supported by the political power of Athens, and reaching 'from the Black Sea to Sardinia', was the cause of special pride.[7] Athenian ships and *emporia* were found as far as Caria in the East and Carthage in the West.[8] These geographical claims were hardly exaggerated, and the pride based upon them implied that the profession of the *emporos* enjoyed general and high esteem. The freedom of the sea and of international trade seemed entirely indispensable for peace and prosperity. That is why the consequences of the Megarian Decree were so disastrous to everyone concerned.[9] That too is the reason for such internal measures in Athens as the practice of hearing the lawsuits of the *emporoi* in winter, when sea-traffic was almost impossible.[10] It is also from such presuppositions, that we are to understand the fantastic announcement of Prometheus, the deserter from Olympus, that Zeus is

---

[1] Perhaps it is a further proof of the vagueness of the word *naukleros* that it could also be used to indicate the owners of lodging-houses (Sannyrion 6; cf. Isaios VI, 19). Boisacq, *Dict. étymol.* 658 apparently supposes that both meanings derive from *naukraros*.

[2] Examples from Euripides: *Hipp.* 1221f, *Hek.* 1081f, *Androm.* 554f, 854f, *Herakleid.* 427ff, *Her.* 631, 1094, 1424, *Tro.* 538f, 688ff, *Iph. T.* 1133ff, *Or.* 706f, 727f, *Kykl.* 505, *frg.* 306, 417, 793.

[3] P.36f.   [4] adesp. 512.

[5] P.17. — F.533ff, cf. also 999ff, 1220f, E.1091, 1105ff.

[6] frg. 85.   [7] W.700.   [8] K.169ff.

[9] A.532ff, P.608ff. Cf. below, ch. XII, pp. 328ff.

[10] E.1027, Pl.904, frg. 904(?); cf. Andok. I, 137, Lysias, XVII, 5.

subjected to threats by the barbarian gods, because he did not
keep open the trading places.[1]

Aristophanes seems to criticize the *emporos* only once, in the
Ploutos, at a time when social tension had greatly increased.
He then speaks of the 'insatiable Thessalian slave-dealers'
who took great risks for the sake of gain.[2] No doubt such men
represented a type that to some extent cut across the usual
pattern of *emporia*, and therefore caused resentment. It is for
this reason, and not because he was engaged in a special kind
of local trade, that even the slave-dealer could be called a
kapelos.[3] Otherwise there is no sign of criticism of the
emporoi, and the question how the *emporos* has made his money
is never asked. It seems to have been the general opinion,
needing no explanation, that it was not the *emporos*, but the
toll-gatherer, who made illegal gains from sea-trade.[4] To carry
contraband, and thus to break the customs laws, was a heavy
crime, and one with which again the toll-gatherer is charged,
not the merchant or shipowner.[5]

Their way of making money, however, certainly helped to
give rise to feeling against the *kapeloi*. Again and again, the
comic writers allude to the insidious machinations of the flour-
dealers, the innkeepers, the bird-sellers, the wool-merchants,
or the fishmongers — all of them *kapeloi*.[6] A lame *kapelos* got
the nickname 'partridge', because of the tricks this bird is said
to play in order to lead the hunters away from its nest.[7] A
comic writer also called a man a racketeer when he forced up
prices 'like Achilles' with Priam.[8] It goes without saying that
war-profiteers were most unpopular, so that spear-makers or
dealers in arms are regarded as deserving very heavy punishment, no less than ambitious generals, runaway slaves and

[1] B.1520ff.   [2] Pl.520t.
[3] ἀνδραποδοκάπηλος ὁ νῦν λεγόμενος σωματέμπορος (Isaios in Harpokr.,
s.v.).
[4] K.248.   [5] F.361ff.
[6] K.1009, C.639f, E.422ff, frg. 465. — E.153ff, Pl.435f. — B.1079ff,
adesp. 934. — F.1386f. — frg. 387, 7ff, Plat. 29, Archipp. 25. If the word
ἀλφιτάμοιβοι (E.422ff) is really to be interpreted on these lines, it must have
meant tradesmen who gave flour to the peasants in exchange for their products
(cf. E.817ff). But this I doubt. I should rather believe the word to be a comic
perversion of ἀλφιτοπώλης or ἀλφιτοποιός, suggesting that the flour was exchanged, i.e. that they gave bad flour instead of good; they were 'flour-swindlers'.
[7] B.1292f, cf. 767f.   [8] Phryn. 52.

other profiteers and advocates of war.[1] To the same class
belonged Kleon, the leather-seller, who is said to have sold
bad shoe-leather,[2] or Hyperbolos, the lamp-maker, who made
a fortune 'by evil doing', that is to say by cheating; the
scholiast explains that he used lead instead of bronze.[3] Dieitrephes also, who became *phylarchos* and *hipparchos* and a
powerful man, had grown rich by selling wicker flasks, and
by following crooked paths.[4] How differently the comic poets
judged *emporoi* and *kapeloi* is obvious. We shall see later how
far this difference was justified. Clearly one reason why in
comedy more attention is paid to the *kapeloi* was that their
methods of trading touched the people much more directly.

2

Modern historians usually think of the leading politicians
after Perikles, of Kleon, Hyperbolos and their like, as big
manufacturers or at least as owners of an artisan's business on
a large scale, that is to say only as producers. In comedy they
are placed on the same level as retailers and hucksters. Even
the cattle-dealer Lysikles, Perikles' friend who after his death
married Aspasia, was called a 'sheep-retailer', a vocation which
certainly did not exist.[5] All this is, no doubt, comic distortion
and exaggeration. It is, however, a historical fact that these
leading politicians belonged to the middle-class of business men.
They gradually displaced the aristocratic leaders, the men
'from the great houses'.[6] Their appearance in political life
was quite new when the earlier plays of Aristophanes were
written; so it seemed worth while to attack the upstarts. Apparently, it made no great difference to him whether they were
industrial townspeople or of agrarian origin. Eukrates returned
from politics 'to his bran', a phrase, however, which may imply
trade as well as agriculture.[7] Men who in earlier times would
have been refused appointment as wine inspectors (certainly a
public office) were now generals.[8] All this caricature, as always,
must have contained a certain amount of truth; above all it

---

[1] P.441ff.   [2] P.270, 648, adesp. 61; cf. K.852. — K.316f.
[3] C.1065f. The scholiast's explanation is doubtful; perhaps Aristophanes
simply alluded to political corruption. Cf. the evidence below, p. 125.
[4] B.798ff; cf. Thuc. VII, 29, 1, VIII, 64, 2.
[5] προβατοκάπηλος, adesp. 62.
[6] Eupolis 117, 4f.   [7] K.254; cf. frg. 696.   [8] Eupolis 205.

symbolizes the social facts which lay behind it. We must ask ourselves what position in the social scale was held by the group or class, represented by Kleon and Hyperbolos as its leading men.

It is, perhaps, surprising that it is just these men who are deliberately characterized as tradesmen, as 'sellers of something'. A well-known list mentions as rulers of the State one after another: the oakum-seller (Eukrates), the sheep-seller (Lysikles), and the leather-seller (Kleon).[1] From such words there emerges an independent word 'seller' or 'monger', which, indeed, was as impossible a Greek form as it is unusual in English. It was a joke, but a significant one, and a similar word seems, in fact, to have been in use.[2] It was Aristophanes' intention to suggest a certain degradation in the occupation. Nevertheless, it is important that, as far as such men are concerned, stress is laid not on their being producers, but on their activities in buying and selling.[3]

The case of the leading politicians is not isolated. The comedians refer to many vocations which got their names in the same way, many of which were used in the feminine form. There were several 'something-sellers' already mentioned, such as the famous sausage-seller, the bread- and flour-sellers, the greengrocers, the wool-sellers, the pease-pudding-sellers, and the fishmongers.[4] Others were the honey-seller, the pig-seller, the bird-seller, called a board-seller because the birds were

---

[1] K.129ff. — Kleon was also called βυρσοδέψης and βυρσοπώλης (K.44, 136), and the Athens of his time therefore Byrsa (frg. 292). Probably this was a joke meant to allude to Kleon as well as to Carthage, which once bore this name. She played at that time a part in some of the political plans of Athens. It would be the oldest Greek testimony, hitherto overlooked, to that name; it belongs to the *Dramata*, probably of about 426 (cf. Geissler, 33). This would confirm the view that the restriction of the name to the acropolis of Carthage was of later date; cf. O. Meltzer, *Geschichte d. Karthager*, II, 192f, 534ff, St. Gsell, *Hist. anc. de l'Afrique du Nord*, I, 377.

[2] The 'seller' would be πώλης. Hermipp. 93 perhaps has πωλητήρ, while the πωλητής was an official.

[3] It is significant that Nikias does not appear on the same level. Although he seems not to have belonged to an aristocratic family, and his great wealth came from the ownership of mines, he was not a 'seller'. This seems to show that he did not belong to the same class as the others (against A. B. West, *Cl. Phil.* XIX, 1924, 137); see also above, p. 108.

[4] W.1388ff, F.858; cf. E.686; title of comedy: Hermipp. 8ff. — L.457f, Th.387. — F.1386. — Pl.427. — frg. 387, 10, Pherekr. 64,5.

put upon a board, and the cheese-seller who, with his scales, was the very type of retailer.[1] Furthermore, we hear of cake-sellers, drug-sellers, sellers of purgatives, incense or myrrh, crests, figs, books, garlic, poultry, sacred bands, needles and coal.[2] By way of a supplement to all these specialists was the business of the 'general dealers' who sold all kinds of small goods; they were a type of huckster or pedlar, perhaps identical with the re-retailers.[3] The people of Aigina, who were a sort of inter-Hellenic retailers, were called 'general dealers'.[4]

Once again, the true facts of economic life are both exaggerated and confirmed in comedy. Possibly specialization did not go quite so far as is suggested by the professions mentioned; even in a few of those passages the same person sells more than one commodity. Some doubt may be justified about the comic medley in such a list as that given by Nikophon, one of the later poets of Old Comedy: 'Sellers of sardines, coal, figs, leather, flour, small spoons, books, sieves, cakes, and seeds',[5] though most of these occupations are also mentioned elsewhere. The same sense of comic distortion is shown when Amphiaraos is called a drug-seller, or the mother of the mythical hero Meleager is said to have in her house the box of a Megarian drug-seller, or the Delphic Apollo is called a laurel-seller.[6] One of the parasites, expelled from Cloud-cuckooborough, was even a seller of public decrees.[7] The 'theatre-seller' probably corresponded to no real occupation;

---

[1] K.853. — A.818, frg. 578. — B.13f. — K.854, F.1369; cf. adesp. 722.

[2] frg. 256, 265. — C.766, Ameips. 27. — frg. 265. — E.841, frg. 807, 821ff, Pherekr. 64, 1, Theop. 1, 16, adesp. 372, 951. — frg. 812. — Pherekr. 4. — Aristom. 9, Theop. 77. — Kratinos 48, Hermipp. 13. — Phryn. 13. — Eupolis 243. — Pl.175. — Philyll. 14.

[3] παντοπῶλαι, Archipp. 31. — παλιγκάπηλοι, Pl.1156. See also Plate IIIb.

[4] Schol. Pind. O. 8, 29.   [5] Nikophon 19.

[6] frg. 28, Theop. 2, frg. 764.

[7] B.1035ff. C. N. Jackson has dealt with the decree-seller (*Harvard Stud. in Cl. Phil.* XXX, 1919, 89ff). He explains him as one of the professional and corrupt politicians who might 'move, alter and misinterpret laws for the benefit of particular clients', unlawfully appropriate public property, etc. I do not think Mr. Jackson has proved his case. The scene in the *Birds* shows that the ψηφισματοπώλης does nothing but provide texts for all sorts of decrees. It is just possible that a man might earn his living by helping ordinary citizens when they wished to move a bill. But it is more likely that Aristophanes invented the character to make fun of the Athenian love of decree-making. The man does, however, allude to certain well-known Athenian decrees; cf. below, p. 159, n. 10, and *A.T.L.* III, 146, n. 32.

but he may have been a man who early in the day bought up
good seats in the theatre and afterwards re-sold them.[1] Actually, it does not matter whether every something-seller of
comedy had his counterpart in reality. Specialization in trade
clearly existed.

The long list drawn from comedy can easily be extended
from other sources, but they add nothing of importance.[2]
The fact that all the names of these different occupations are
formed in the same way, all with the suffix '-seller', proves that
buying and selling played a large part in the economic life of
the people, and that usually the producer and the seller were
the same person.[3] It is important to assess the social circumstances of this type of trader. We must assume that not all
those something-sellers were in quite the same stage of economic development. The perfume-seller and -producer, for
instance, was clearly distinguished from the *kapelos* who was
said to be on a lower level.[4] We must ask what exactly were
the activities of all these men and women selling things.
Above all, we shall have to find out whether they sold their
products only to the consumer, or whether there was, at least
in some branches, what has been called 'a well-developed class
of intermediate traders', a 'pre-seller', for instance, or a re-
retailer.[5] This latter name was given as a comic title of honour
to the god of tradesmen, Hermes Empolaios, but also to the
Phoenician merchant who 'gave with one hand and took with
the other'.[6] He, however, was a sea-trader, an *emporos*, according to the Greek terminology, though only an intermediary
one.

We begin with the interpretation of a scene, in which the
salesman is apparently not the producer, the scene in which
the various merchants of arms allege that they have been
reduced to bankruptcy by the peacemaker Trygaios.[7] The
several branches of this kind of trade are specifically distinguished, probably not because the poet wished to represent

[1] frg. 562.
[2] Cf. the enumeration in Heichelheim, 346, 1042.
[3] Cf. Plates Vc, X.   [4] Lysias, frg. 38, 5.
[5] Hasebroek, *Staat u. Handel*, 5. Here I quote the German original, as the
translation of the sentence concerned in the English edition is not quite exact.
προπώλης, frg. 707. For the παλιγκάπηλος see the following sentence in
the text.
[6] Pl. 1155f, cf. A.816 — adesp. 397.   [7] P.1210ff.

real facts, but only to show the great number of war-profiteers. Elsewhere, however, one man is declared to be both a 'lyre-turner' and a 'shield-maker', and a corslet-maker is also mentioned by Xenophon, a spear-maker by Euripides.[1] In that scene we are told of the makers (or sellers) of crests, spears, corslets, trumpets and helmets.[2] The spokesman for all these was a merchant of arms. He was not, as the manuscripts indicate, the same as the maker of crests; for this man as well as the spear-maker is mentioned by the speaker himself.[3] He was, as also the list of the *dramatis personae* in the codices puts it, a 'retailer of arms', a *kapelos* like the retailer of shields.[4] He himself had spent a great deal on corslet, trumpet and helmet.[5] Therefore he asks back from Trygaios at least the money they have cost.[6] He says that both his craft and his livelihood have vanished with the peace, but the expressions he uses, which are applied also to the makers of crests and spears, do not disprove that he was a merchant rather than an artisan.[7] Can we assume, however, that all the manufacturers of arms had some sort of organization for selling their products? I do not think we are justified in taking the poet literally on this point, especially as the wording of the dialogues implies craftsmen who act on their own, and in another scene no difference is made between the spear-maker and the shield-retailer, who are anxious to market their wares.[8] I am convinced that all these specialized armourers themselves sold their own goods. The form of the scene is clearly determined by the dramaturgic necessity of having a single spokesman. From the economic aspect it is an entirely unreal picture, and it would be wrong to draw general conclusions from this scene, or to press the wording unduly.[9]

[1] B.491, Xen. *mem.* III, 10, 9, Eur. *Ba.* 1208.

[2] P.1211, 1213, 1258, cf. 447, 549, 1224, 1240, 1255.

[3] P.1213, cf. 545.   [4] P.1209, cf. 447.

[5] P.1224, 1241, 1251.   [6] ἰσωνία, P.1227.

[7] ἀπώλεσάς μου τὴν τέχνην καὶ τὸν βίον, P.1212. Cf. the τέχνη of the man who sells onions (Pl.160, 167).

[8] P.447ff.

[9] It is also not quite certain whether hoe- and sickle-maker on the one hand, sword- and spear-maker on the other, represented quite distinct occupations (P.547ff). Perhaps the contrast was meant only to demonstrate the contrary economic effects of war and peace. However, the sickle-maker in P.1197ff must be taken into account.

PLATE X

a

b

TRADERS AND CRAFTSMEN

PLATE XI

a

b

WOMEN WORKERS

When the most important occupations are mentioned together in comedy, it is usual to distinguish between merchant and craftsman.[1] But the greengrocer is included among various craftsmen, cobbler, smith and carpenter, all of them representing a certain craft.[2] In the list of townspeople who have to get up early because of their work, some craftsmen are mentioned as well as the flour-seller.[3] We find the coal-seller in the company of the confectioner, the gardener and the barber.[4] In war-time, unrest in the town was caused partly by military measures, partly by the special intensity of economic life, by the extra work to be done by craftsmen, merchants and ship-builders.[5] All these references show clearly that there was no strict line of demarcation between handicraft and retail trade. The *ergasterion*, the workshop, was nearly always the shop or place of sale as well.

The implication of comedy is quite clear; it even proves something incidentally, something which will be confirmed when we look for other types of craft mentioned in comedy. Hyperbolos is said to sell his lamps in *skaphai*.[6] The word is ambiguous; it may mean 'ships', and the conclusion has been drawn that he sold his goods as an *emporos*, sailing from place to place, probably on his own ship.[7] But we cannot argue positively from so weak a basis, for *skaphe* may just as well, and more often does, mean a tray or bowl; so the whole phrase will be nothing but a pun. It is more likely that the comedian wished to depict Hyperbolos, who could be called a lamp-seller as well as a lamp-maker, as a *kapelos* who made and sold lamps,[8] even displaying them like a huckster on a tray which possibly had a boat-like appearance. Retailers of a similar kind were certainly the producers of the common clay lamps, the sale of which was widespread in the market.[9] Even Hyperbolos, who is said by another source to have made metal lamps, was sometimes simply called a 'potter'.[10]

The same connection between production and direct sale to the consumer is shown when Kleon sells his bad leather not to a shoemaker, but to a peasant.[11] The myrrh-maker was the myrrh-seller as well, and the *jeunesse dorée* loitering about in

---

[1] P.296ff, cf. Pl.904f.   [2] τέχνη, Pl.160ff.   [3] B.489ff.
[4] Philyll. 14.   [5] A.544ff.   [6] K.1315.   [7] Hasebroek, 14; Heichelheim, 324.
[8] K.739, P.690.   [9] Hermipp. 28, Plat. 190, also Kratinos 196.
[10] Schol. C.1065. — Eupolis 21 D, schol. K.1304.   [11] K.316f.

the myrrh-market certainly wasted their time at the spot where
the perfumes were both produced and sold.[1] It was the same
at the barber's and saddler's.[2] The circumstances are not very
different from those of all small independent craftsmen
throughout the ages, who sell the goods they themselves produce in their workshops.[3] Such a type is the bronze-founder
who has plenty of identical or similar statues in his workshop.[4]
From the smith's, who is elsewhere depicted as toiling away in
smoke and heat, one might buy a mascot, probably a clay
figure, which he had hung over his furnace.[5] The fuller sold
warm coats.[6] The soldier's widow who plaited wreaths for
religious worship and drinking-parties alike had to sell them
herself in the market.[7] In the monody in which Aischylos
derides the realism of Euripides, even a woman rich enough
to own several slave-girls goes herself to the market to sell
what she has spun.[8] Thus even what the housewife had formerly
produced for the use of her own household only, was drawn
into the process of general trade.[9]

The breadshop was at the same time the bakery where the
baking-pans stood, where the making or turning of the loaves
was done, and where, perhaps, the slaves, kneading the
dough, wore round their necks the *pausikape*, a big collar to
prevent them from putting anything in their mouths.[10] Lazy
and sensual Dionysos regarded the breadshop as one of the
necessary incidents of a journey, like the road, the spring, the
inn and the brothel.[11] Most likely it was in a bakery that
people got the toasted bread and pancakes which 'hiss when
honey is dripped on them.'[12] Frequently in comedy women
are mentioned who went round selling bread. But this does
not disprove that there were also bakers' shops. The woman

---

[1] Lysias, frg. 38, 2, 5. — K.1375ff, Pherekr. 2, 64, Eupolis 209.
[2] Lysias XXIV, 20.   [3] See Plate X*b*.   [4] Lysias, frg. 32.
[5] frg. 592. — adesp. 443. It is, however, unlikely that a smith was normally
prepared to sell his Hephaistos or whatever deity he had hung up; this is no
ordinary case of buying and selling, but as we do not know the context, we
cannot say what it really meant.
[6] E.415ff.   [7] Th.446ff.   [8] F.1346ff.
[9] Wade-Gery reminds me of *Il.* XII, 433ff. But the γυνὴ χερνῆτις ἀληθής
who works for the 'scanty pittance' of her children certainly belongs to different
social conditions.
[10] frg. 1, 125, 155. — frg. 313, 748, Phryn. 27. See Plate XI*b*. — frg. 301-2.
[11] F.112ff.   [12] Magnes 1, Kratinos 125.

who is called a bread-seller and, at the same time, owned a big
and heavy *holmos*, a kneading-trough, was both baker and
dealer in bread.[1]   Other women were more or less vagrant
saleswomen, and represented some sort of small intermediate
trade; but as they sold the bread baked in pans while it was
still hot, they also took part, to some extent, in the process of
production.[2]

Spinning and weaving was the work of women and girls at
home, and was provided for even in the communist State.[3]
The difficult process of cleaning the wool was also often the
housewife's business, for unfulled wool was sometimes used.[4]
But there was also the wool-seller who often sold his goods
when still wet and so heavier.[5] This use of women's labour,
the work of those 'who spin with their hands the softest thread',[6]
was a relic from the self-contained economy of the *oikos*.
Although the material was, as a rule, handed over for further
treatment to skilled workmen and to specialized makers of
various kinds of garments,[7] belief in the so-called process of
'industrialization' is a modern error, as far as this and other
branches of production are concerned; though the fact that
part of the women's home-production was sold in the market
makes it clear that even in this most persistent branch of
home-industry the days of *oikos*-economy were past and
gone.

The potters, who contributed particularly to the glory of
Athens, even down to the time of Aristophanes which saw in
general a decline in vase-painting, were both producers and
retailers of their wares.[8] They 'turned the potter's clay', producing their pottery 'at home'.[9] The vases were made by both
potter and painter in the same workshop; sometimes the same

---

[1] W.238. I wonder whether the ὅλμος in the house of Bdelykleon (W.201)
was a kneading-trough, or rather some sort of mortar, such as L. R. Palmer,
Eranos XLIV (1946), 54f, has found as the type used in the simile *Il.* XI,
147, and indicated in Hesiod, *Erga* 423.

[2] frg. 125.   [3] L.735ff, Th.821ff, Hermipp. 2. — E.654.

[4] L.574ff, E.215ff. — Plat. 18 D. See Plate XI*a*.   [5] F.1386f.

[6] Eupolis 319.   [7] Pl.513. — *Xen. mem.* II, 7,6.

[8] This is indicated by E.1f, 252, frg. 469. — Athena was the patron of the
potters and appears in some of the pictures of a potter's shop. It is for
this reason that Peithetairos and Euelpides could protect themselves with pottery
against Athena's bird, the owl (B.358).

[9] Sannyrion 4, Phryn. 15. See Plate XII*a*.

man 'made' and 'painted' a vase.[1] In many workshops a number of men and boys, sometimes even a woman, were engaged as potters and painters. It could happen, though comparatively rarely in the manufacture of ordinary ware, that two men shared in the painting. Some of the painters worked for different potters. Many of them specialized in certain types or a certain technique, and we may assume that some of the potters did so as well.[2] 'Potters' wealth' meant uncertain property, an allusion, of course, to the fragile earthenware which the potter kept in store, and tried to sell to customer or *emporos*.[3]

Many artisans' shops will have been as small and modest as the 'art' of the invalid who fought for the small public allowance of one obol a day, because, as he said, he could not afford a workman, which apparently means a slave.[4] Probably an example of such a small workshop, in which the artisan worked alone, was the *ergasterion* from which the sausage-seller, when a boy, stole a saucepan from the fire.[5] It is certainly worth noticing that in comedy, though slaves are mentioned so frequently, we never hear of them as industrial workers in a large business. The only occasional exception are the mine-workers; but even in the mines of Laureion the individual owner had an *ergasterion* and a small *metallon*, a little mine, of his own.[6] Furthermore, in the communist State of the future, depicted in the *Ekklesiazousai*, there is no provision for industrial pur-

[1] The main evidence comes from the signatures on many vases (εποιεσεν, εγραφσεν); it is confirmed by some vase-paintings. Cf., e.g., G. Richter, *The Craft of Athenian Pottery*, fig. 58, 66. A full discussion, on which the following sentences in my text are based, is now found in J. D. Beazley, *Potter and Painter in Ancient Athens* (*Proceedings of the Brit. Academy*, XXX).

[2] Painter of λήκυθοι: E.996. Beazley, 42, calls for a full study from the point of view of the potters.

[3] adesp. 749. Cf. Cloché 50. The purchaser at the potter's — it was the potter, not the painter, who owned the shop — was the consumer, as far as local sale was concerned. The trader came into operation for the big overseas business; there were probably also foreign purchasers. The general statement of Rumpf(*Gnomon*, 1938, 450) that only the trader bought at the potter's shop must be limited in that sense.

[4] Lysias XXIV, 6, 19f.

[5] K.744f. The translation in the Collection Budé: '*en flânant au sortir de ma boutique*', is hardly right, as the sausage-seller will not have owned an *ergasterion*; ἀπ' ἐργαστηρίου depends on ὑφειλόμην.

[6] *IG.* II², 1582ff, Isaios III, 22.

suits. These are partly *argumenta ex silentio*, and contradictory
evidence must be noted. Many rich men 'owned' artisans, just
as they owned land or houses; they were the proprietors of a
workshop run by slaves.[1] But in spite of some exceptions, the
negative evidence of comedy must be considered as proving
that the average business was a small concern, and that there
were few larger ones.[2]

There were other trades in which we are certainly justified
in assuming that the 'master' — who, though he might have
apprentices,[3] was very different from the master-craftsman of
medieval and modern times — sold his products directly to
the consumer, as, for instance, the mask-maker who sold to the
theatre-people, the sickle-maker who sold to the farmers,
the amulet-seller who sold to the general public.[4] The bath-
man, whose vocation was disreputable, made and sold bad
soap.[5] The craftsman normally needed no middleman in
order to sell his products. Besides usual and necessary vocations such as those of the barber and the shoemaker, the smith
and the cartwright, who often lived together in certain streets,
and all had their pride in their crafts, there were also some
specialized *technitai*, the ring-maker, for instance, the theatre-
mechanic, or the man who made yokes for cattle.[6] Neither
their pride nor their specialization was an obstacle to their
selling without middlemen. Even collective labour such as
shipbuilding, the noise of which could be heard far away, was
carried on by individual craftsmen.[7] Otherwise Aristophanes
would not have depicted the poetry of Agathon as a sort of
shipbuilding, and the official regulations applying to individual
shipbuilders or rather carpenters confirm the fact.[8] But, of
course, shipbuilding, on the other hand, was like all building,
also team-work, and the 'architect' was the foreman in a more

[1] Xen. *mem*. III, 11, 4.

[2] I wonder whether the φαυλουργοί (frg. 882) were slaves in a workshop, or
unsatisfactory free artisans.

[3] Xen. *mem*. IV, 4, 5.   [4] K.232, P.1202, Pl.883f.   [5] F.708ff.

[6] L.407, Nikoch. 9; cf. the τέκτων, χαλκεύς, σκυτεύς as the main trades in
Xen. *mem*. 1, 2, 37; 4, 2, 22, 4, 5, and the metaphorical allusions to these
professions in K.461ff. — Pherekr. 207, Philyll. 15. — frg. 188, adesp. 98. —
frg. 449.

[7] B.1154ff. — Pl.513; cf. Eur. *Kykl*. 460, *frg*. 988.

[8] Th.52ff. — *IG*. I², 74, II², 1604ff. It has been calculated that within 52
years 183 ships were built by 59 different shipbuilders (Glotz, 268).

general sense.¹ Here again, the normal business was on a small scale, the *cheirotechnes* poor and without capital, often even without a house of his own and living in hired rooms.² In times of war at least, workmen might even go to another city to help in some urgent building work.³ Such conditions brought artisan and tradesman close together. Usually they were one and the same person, and if not, at least they stood on the same social level.

Even the peasant, the Attic as well as the Boeotian or Megarian peasant, sold his products himself in the market of Athens, and afterwards made his own small purchases.⁴ The vine-dresser naturally sold to the consumer or to the inn-keeper. Frequently he may have sold his wine straight from the press, just as the olives, or the oil produced from them, were sold either on the spot in the olive-orchard or in the market.⁵ Cattle were often sold direct to the household; therefore the *mageiros* was both cook and butcher, and he had to know how to detect possible diseases in the cattle.⁶ For the poorer towns-people, however, there must have been some retail trade in meat. The greengrocers, usually women, as a rule sold the products of their own garden and fields; it is said as a joke that Euripides grew up 'among the herbs of the field', as if his mother did not even sell garden products.⁷ A peasant or a gardener coming to town may have sold some of his neigh-bour's fruit as well, but that did not make any essential difference in the nature of this kind of trade which was every-where on a small scale, and consisted in the producer selling his own products.

Not quite the same is true of the fish-trade.⁸ It can be shown by a very large number of passages from comedy that fish was,

---

¹ P.305. Cf. the combination of specialization and team-work in the Erech-theion inscriptions (*IG.* I², 373-4).

² Pl.533f, 615ff. — Xen. *symp.* 4, 4.   ³ Thuc. IV, 69, 2, V, 82, 6.

⁴ W.169f, E.817ff. — A.719ff, 818, 900.   ⁵ Cloché, 81ff.

⁶ A.1015, P.1017f. — K.375f. — Ramalho, *Emerita* XVIII (1950), 35ff (cf. also *Humanitas* IV (1952)) makes it clear that the female butcher and the female fishmonger in Pherekr. 64 are creations of comedy without any parallel in real life.

⁷ W.497f, Th.387. — Th.456.

⁸ Cf. Bohlen, *Die Bedeutung der Fischerei für die antike Wirtschaft.* Diss. Hamburg, 1937.

next to bread, the chief food of the town population.[1] 'To be
nourished by white-coloured sprats' was a characteristic of the
Athenian, and only barbarians were called 'fishless'.[2] In a
successful comedy the chorus composed of fishes fought the
Athenians in order not to be eaten up.[3] The wish uttered by
Deukalion's wife after the deluge: 'Never again offer fish to
me, even if I ask for it',[4] was a good joke because, if expressed
in earnest, it would have been incomprehensible to any
Athenian. It was a vital matter to Athens that a certain kind of
small fish, which came mostly from Phaleron, should be cheap.[5]
These as well as sprats were the most popular dish, while the
dearer fish were left to buyers of a higher social standing and
smelled of 'tyranny'.[6] Some kind of a mixture of sea food,
something like *frutti di mare*, made a cheap dish, while the
cuttlefish was a modest delicacy.[7]

Obviously the Athenian market needed a large daily supply
of fish, and it was therefore impossible for the Attic fishermen
alone to satisfy it with their catch. There were traders who
bought fish from fishermen all round the shores of Attica, and
brought it to the market. Salted fish, too, frequently appeared
in the market, a common but little-esteemed food, not sold by
the same people and at the same places as fresh fish.[8] These
dried salt fish naturally needed some time for their preparation
between being caught and sold, and frequently they came from
distant seas.[9] People complained that fresh fish also were often
several days old.[10] The fish-market probably opened every day,
and one might go there to change a drachma into small coin.[11]
Fishing was a vocation which, apart from a boat and the necessary tools such as a net and a three-pronged spear,[12] required so
much time and hard work, that the fishermen from the more

[1] e.g., K.283, Pl.894, frg. 475, Kratinos 147, 161, Krates 17, Eupolis 38,
Hegemon 1.

[2] frg. 137. — frg. 564-5; cf. Eur. *frg.* 366.

[3] Archipp. 14ff.   [4] Pherekr. 120.

[5] They were the ἀφύαι. K.645, 671f, B.76, frg. 506-7, and elsewhere.

[6] Sprats (μεμβράδες or βεμβράδες): W.493ff, frg. 137, Eupolis 28, Phryn. 50,
Plat. 123, Aristonym. 2, 3, Aristomenes 7. — frg. 52. — W.493ff, cf. Kratinos
303, 1 Mazon.

[7] frg. 247. — K.929.   [8] W.491f, frg. 200, 686 — K.1247.

[9] Kratinos 40, Eupolis 186.   [10] frg. 387, 8f.

[11] W.788f. Or does this only occur, because the man gave to the teller of the
story, instead of the three obols he owed, three fish-scales?

[12] Epilykos 1 D.

distant coastal villages, or even from the Peiraeus, only went to market occasionally, as a rule when they wanted to buy for themselves. On such occasions they brought their catch with them, and one might easily happen to meet them selling their fish *en route*.[1] Fishermen are also depicted thus on Attic vases (see Plate XII*b*, *c*).[2] The catching of certain fish required special skill and organization; there were, for instance, official tunny-watchers.[3] With freshwater fish matters were different. The Boeotian eels, in Athens a highly esteemed delicacy, were brought to market by the fishermen themselves.[4]

Quite a number of people were engaged in overseas trade. There must have been a proper organization in a few branches, in the buying and selling, for instance, of pottery and oil;[5] but an official arrangement was made only for the corn-trade which more than anything else was of vital importance to Athens.[6] Here we need not concern ourselves with the various laws on this matter, but it is important to know that the corn-traders, the *sitopolai*, who, surprisingly enough, are never mentioned in comedy, formed an organized group, superintended by special officials, the *sitophylakes*. These traders bought the corn from the *emporoi* who could be called real 'corn-lovers', and between the two groups bitter economic quarrels occurred.[7] It is significant of the organization of the corn-traders that they arranged for a common price-policy such as we cannot suppose to have existed in any other branch of trade. To prevent speculation no *sitopoles* was allowed to buy up more than fifty 'baskets' of grain.[8] In the speech of Lysias just referred to the corn-traders are described as swindlers and extortioners. It seems almost certain that the impression given by that speech is misleading, and that, on the whole, they were quite honest merchants. At any rate, they formed a unique and most important group of middlemen.

[1] Plat. 29.

[2] Cf. also, e.g., H. Schaal, *Vom Tauschhandel zum Welthandel*, pl. 21. Cloché, pl. XXXVI, XXXVIII, 2.

[3] K.313; cf. for other areas Strabo V, 223, 225, XVIII, 834.

[4] A.880ff, 962, K.864ff, L.36, 700ff, frg. 363-4, 499, (?), Strattis 44.

[5] New and striking evidence of the size and importance of the trade in Attic pottery is given by the excavations at Al-Mina; cf. L. Woolley, *JHS.* 58 (1938), 1ff, 133ff.

[6] Cf. Heichelheim, *P.-W.* Suppl. VI, 833ff.

[7] Xen. *oik.* 20, 27. — Lysias XXII.

[8] Lysias XXII, 5. For the φορμός of wheat cf. also Th.813.

We see that there were intermediary traders, but only in some cases, and even then mostly of limited importance.[1] In general, it remains true that producer and salesman were one and the same person. Because of this, the market became the centre of both trade and craftsmanship, and therefore the place where one could hope to find every sort of work.[2] This co-ordination between production and sale, both of which were types of business on a purely monetary basis, made the market an organized unit, where a widely specialized trade found safe and convenient accommodation. State officials such as the *agoranomoi* had the power of suppressing all disturbances and safeguarding honest trade.[3] On the other hand, everybody knew where to go in order to get what he wanted, even though this might mean only gossip.[4] The hall where flour was sold was one of the chief places in the market because of the importance of that trade.[5] The same observations are valid for the various quarters of the market as for the occupations referred to above: the comedians exaggerate the specialization, but it existed nevertheless. Eupolis mentions stalls with garlic, onions, incense, perfume, frippery and books.[6] Of course, garlic and onions are hardly likely to have been sold at different stalls, but on the whole the specialization and distribution was as Eupolis implies. Differing in its production and goods, each part of the market, each little street in the neighbourhood, had its own character, and we may include here the tanners' quarter which, because of its bad smell, was situated outside the town, and also the brothel streets, which were not confined to the market district.[7] Perhaps the 'packed body' of traders in leather, honey and cheese, who were said to be Kleon's chief supporters, had their stalls near the flour market; they would

---

[1] Cf., e.g., Francotte, I, 299: '*Dans une société où l'industrie n'a pas dépassé le métier, le producteur et le consommateur sont déjà distincts; mais ils ne sont pas encore séparés par de nombreux intermédiaires comme dans les sociétés plus avancées.*'

[2] Ameips. 1. Because of the business character of the normal *agora*, we find sometimes a second (or rather first) market place, an ἀγορὰ ἐλευθέρα, as the true centre of an ideal city, where no buying and selling was allowed (Xen. *Kyrop.* I, 2, 3, Aristotle, *pol.* 1331 a, 30ff).

[3] A.723, 824f, 968, W.1406ff.   [4] Xen. *oik.* 8, 22, Lysias XXIV, 20.

[5] E.686. — K.857.   [6] Eupolis 304. Cf. also Pherekr. 186.

[7] A.724 and schol. — K.137 and schol., 857, 1375, W.789, P.165, B.13, L.407, 557f, Th.448, F.1068, E.302, Pl.338, frg. 299. Kratinos 196. Cf. also Lysias XXIII, 6.

thus easily be able to stop the sale of flour.[1] Some retailers, whose shops were not specialized, were apparently to be found in various quarters of the town.[2]

To a large extent intellectual output followed the same economic tendencies as retail trade. To Aristophanes medical treatment, it is true, was not a *techne* in the ordinary sense, but something that was taught to mankind by true poets in the same way as morality, honour and bravery, or, on the other hand, farming.[3] He loathed the various 'sophists', the prophets, physicians, thinkers, rhapsodes, astronomers and others, because all these specialists earned money by their art.[4] Without accepting the comic poet's view of them we can discover their economic standing. Among the hateful individuals who rushed into the newly founded Cloudcuckooborough were several of this kind, for example the poet and chorus-trainer Kinesias, who was famous among the tribes.[5] It shows a peculiar inconsequence on the part of the poet that he derides another chorus-trainer, Kallimachos, as well as the painter Pauson, merely because of their poverty.[6] The physicians in particular had the reputation of running after money.[7] Euripides describes his treatment of tragedy as if it were his patient: the doctor, by a special therapy, first causes the patient to lose flesh, and afterwards puts him on a special diet, the object, of course, being to keep him under treatment as long as possible.[8] It is easily understood that people did not hurry to call in the doctor, and when a woman suffered from stomach-ache, her husband simply mixed some powder to relieve her.[9] But if the patient died, the doctor ran the risk of being accused of carelessness.[10]

The members of the various intellectual professions — including, perhaps, the 'writer of books' — were more or less *kapeloi*.[11] There were some 'honest vocations', which Aristophanes approves of, besides his favourite, agriculture, and we

---

[1] K.852ff, 857.   [2] Lysias, frg. 38, 3.   [3] F.1032ff.
[4] C.331ff, W.52 and elsewhere.
[5] B.1403f.
[6] E.809. — A.854, Th.949, Pl.602. The part which Pauson plays in the obscure lines of Eupolis 40 P, 5ff, remains unexplained, also in Jensen's treatment (*Abh. Preuss. Ak.* 1939, no. 14, 6).
[7] B.584, Pl.407f.   [8] F.939ff.   [9] Th.483ff.
[10] Antiphon, *tetral.* III, 2.
[11] The βιβλιαγράφος (*sic*, Kratinos 249) was a scribe rather than an author.

know that he was thinking of the *emporos* and the *technites*.[1] As we have seen, the latter were chiefly tradesmen. Economically they were interested in sale as much as in production. Little wonder that intellectual *techne* took the same line.

Such specialization in production and trade, far-reaching as it was, was possible only in a place where trade was extensive. Each single shop was small, but there were many of them, and so the business of the town as a whole was on a large scale. Production and sale were mostly combined, and as yet somewhat primitive. The workmen and retailers themselves were of a type similar to that of the average farmer. They were small people of the lower middle-class, *petit bourgeois* like all the others. In many cases the workshop or shop was probably hereditary; but we hear of a cutler who was the son of a cook or butcher.[2]

On the other hand, the intensity of economic life brought about a strong improvement in the methods of production. In the most varied branches of craftsmanship there arose the specialist and expert, a type which was to gain fundamental importance in the philosophy of Sokrates and Plato, but could do so only because he had gained importance in life. Economically this was of great consequence, and the predominance of Athenian craftsmanship and its extremely high artistic standard was partly due to the improvement in production. Improved quality, however, did not necessarily imply increased quantity. Production remained, on the whole, on a small scale, and when people became rich by bread-making or by manufacturing *chlamydes* or *chlanides* or *exomides* (all different sorts of clothes), it did not mean that they owned factories.[3] The smallness of each shop is confirmed even by that passage of Xenophon (a *locus classicus* for the 'industrialization' of Greece), and also by various passages in comedy; for nobody who learns that 'the majority of the Megarians lived on making *exomides*' can believe that the bulk of Megarian citizens (not slaves) worked in large mills.[4] There was no industry whatsoever — only craftsmanship. In spite of a few timid beginnings, the step from specialization to mechanization of labour was never taken,

---

[1] B.1432ff. — P.296ff, Pl.902ff. Cf., in general, above p. 85.
[2] B.440f, frg. 394. For the hereditary character of specialized crafts cf. A. Zimmern, *Solon and Croesus* (1928), 156.
[3] Xen. *mem.* II, 7, 6.   [4] A.519, P.1002. — Xen., *l.c.*

the expert never became a factory-worker, and specialization did not imply organized division of labour in large-scale production.[1] The whole process of intensification, however, did take place and was closely connected with the fact that a hitherto unknown economic spirit was growing and spreading among a great part of the population. Those small people, including the farmers, represented a uniform social type, and it was they who carried on production and retail trade.

3

We know that the *emporos* played a great part in trade and industrial production. The question arises what position he held in social and economic life. To answer this question we must distinguish between home production and import, and discover the importance to Athens of import and export, both the concern of the *emporos*. Here, too, the evidence of comedy throws much light on the situation.

It is significant of the conditions in Athens during the first years of the Peloponnesian War that at that time goods, formerly supplied by the Attic countryside, became scarce and expensive. For the country was then devastated, and, to a large extent, abandoned by the peasants. Many of the necessities of daily life could not easily be supplied by sea-trade. Thus the farmer, accustomed to produce such things himself, had to buy, and certainly not at a cheap price, for instance coal, which in normal times was supplied by the charcoal-burners of the mountain demes near the town.[2] Vinegar, formerly extracted from the cheaper sorts of Attic wine, and even oil were scarce.[3] There are many complaints about the lack of oil, which was necessary both for cooking and for anointing the body.[4] Wine was one of the most important products of the country, although many better sorts were imported from various places abroad.[5] The Attic farmer produced honey and figs, Attic sheep provided wool, and during the war woollen clothes were

---

[1] In Prof. Michell's book the chapter on industry deals exclusively with the various kinds of crafts.

[2] Cf. the *Acharnians*, also Philyll. 14, Eur. *frg.* 283.

[3] A.34f.   [4] C.55f, W.251ff, Plat. 190.

[5] Attic wine: A.183, P.557, 596, 612, frg. 579. — Import from Chios, Thasos, Pramnos, etc.: K.107, P.1162, L.196, E.1119, 1139, Pl.1021, frg. 317, 350, 531, 579. Kratinos 135, 370, Hermipp. 82, Eupolis 253, Phryn. 65, Strattis 61, Philyll. 24, Epilykos 6, adesp. 1278.

as scarce as shoe-leather, which was produced from the hides and skins of Attic cattle and goats.[1] Clay for pottery was found in Attic soil, silver and lead in the mines of Laureion, and salt came from the sea, but not, it seems, in sufficient quantity, since the Megarians used to bring it to the Athenian market, along with certain kinds of vegetables, pigs and hares.[2] This import was on rather a small scale, and when it was stopped, only 'trifles which we also have in our own country' were affected.[3] The various delicacies from Boeotia were also of little general importance.[4] Only oversea goods really counted as imports.

In the attempt to discover what these were, it would be a mistake to take as reliable proof of the place of origin all the apparent indications of provenance.[5] 'Persian bird' was the name of the ordinary Greek cock, and the *Persikai*, a certain kind of elegant ladies' shoe, were made by Greek shoemakers.[6] So, too, the Laconian shoes mentioned frequently as usually worn by most Athenians and perhaps similar to the so-called *Amyklades*, from Laconian Amyklai, were men's shoes, shaped in the fashion of Spartan shoes, but certainly made at Athens.[7] We may assume that the description 'made in Athens' was also correct for a kind of women's shoe called Argive.[8] I doubt whether the Laconian and Chian cups, or the elaborate keys, called Laconians, actually came from Sparta or Chios.[9] The Amorgan chitons had once, perhaps, been the fashion in the island of Amorgos, or they were called after a certain plant; but for a long time past they had come to mean some kind of transparent clothes made by Athenian women.[10] Equally the

---

[1] P.252ff. — W.297ff, P.558, 597, 628f. — L.574ff, F.1386. — K.870, 881f.

[2] A.901f, cf. schol. L.2. — E.814. — A.520ff, 760, P.999ff.

[3] σμικρὰ κἀπιχώρια, A.523.

[4] A.873ff, K.479f, P.1003ff; cf. also W.508ff. Boeotian eels: see above, p. 132.

[5] The collections of Knorringa are insufficient and misleading in this as in other respects.

[6] B.485, 707. — C.151, L.229f, Th.734, E.319.

[7] W.1158ff, Th.142, 423, E.74, 269, 345, 508, 542. — frg. 44 D, Phryn. 5 D; cf. Hesych, s.v. It is perhaps worth mentioning that Knorringa, 57f, has concluded that about 400 B.C. Sparta was noted for the export of shoes!

[8] Eupolis 266.

[9] frg. 216, Hermipp. 55. — Th.423. Frequently such a name indicated the origin of the shape only of a vase; cf. A. Rumpf, *Chalkid. Vasen*, 45; cf. 123.

[10] L.150, 735ff, Kratinos 96, Eupolis 241. — Amorgan origin: schol. L.150. — Transparent clothes: Poll. VII, 74. — The same is probably to be said of the

names of various kinds of food do not reveal their provenance.
'Large dirty loaves of bread' were called 'Kilikian'; neither did
Laconian figs come from Sparta nor Kydonian apples, that is
quinces, from Crete.¹ Certainly, Sicilian cheese, though it was
'Sicily's pride', was not always made there; in the same way
not all of our Swiss or Dutch cheese comes from Switzerland
or Holland. It seems certain that the Sicilian cheese which the
dog stole from the kitchen was freshly made.²

However, it is true that Athens received goods from almost
all parts of the producing world.³ Among the products, the
import of which was of general importance, Aristophanes mentions silphium, which was a favourite spice; Kleon's order to
lower its price was very popular.⁴ Similarly the import of
salted fish was essential for the poorer people.⁵ Other articles
imported in peace-time, besides the various sorts of food from
Megara and Boeotia, were, wine and fish of better quality,
scallops from Mytilene, almonds from Naxos, Milesian,
Phrygian or Persian, also Sicilian or Cyprian wool, covers and
curtains, the wood (or cones?) of the cedar, used in sacrifices,
Egyptian ointments, Rhodian perfume, *olisboi* from Miletus,
purple dye from Sardes, beans from Lemnos(?).⁶ Foreign
slaves also had to be imported; the Thessalian *emporoi* dealing
in slaves have already been mentioned.⁷ Horses of well-known
breed, such as the luxurious nobles demanded, were the
Boukephaloi which came from Thessaly, and there were others
the provenance of which was indicated by a branded initial.⁸

'Egyptian' linen clothes (Poll. VII, 71) ἡμιτύβιον (Pl.729) and ἡμιφωσώνιον
(frg. 784) or φώσων (Kratinos 250), and of some other articles of dress which
were called Cretan or Syrian, Thessalian or Laconian (Th.730, Kratinos 207,
Eupolis 311, Lysipp. 2, Theop. 10). Or is one to imagine the Athena of Pheidias
who had 'Tyrrhenian' sandals (Kratinos 131) as wearing imported shoes?

¹ Plat. 86. — frg. 108, Kantharos 6.
² adesp. 786. — W.837f, cf. 924, adesp. 880.
³ frg. 569, Hermipp. 63, Ps.-Xen. II, 7, Thuc. II, 38, 2.
⁴ K.894f, B.533f, Pl.924f. — See Plate Xa.   ⁵ See p. 131, 9.
⁶ Wine: see p. 136, n. 5. Fish: K.361, frg. 363-4, Theop. 51. Scallops: Philyll.
13. Almonds: Eupolis 253, Phryn. 68. Wool, covers, etc.: W.1137, B.493,
L.729, F.542, 938, frg. 611, adesp. 534; cf. also the 'barbarian', i.e. oriental:
tapestries in Eur. *Ion* 1159. Cedar: adesp. 34. Ointments: frg. 206. Perfume,
L.944. ὄλισβοι: L.109f. (though that may be a joke). Purple: A.112,
P.1174. Beans: frg. 356.   ⁷ Pl.520ff.
⁸ C.15ff. — frg. 41. — There were the κοππατίαι (C.23, 438, frg. 42),
which were considered Corinthian because of the ϙ, and the σαμφόραι (K.602,

Thus most of the horses came from abroad, and the saying
'What kind of horses?' was used when some strange matter
was discussed.[1] Dogs and cattle came from the Molossians,
and he-goats from Cilicia, but that probably indicated the
breed rather than their immediate provenance.[2] When vases
of alabaster were used for ointment, either the vase or the
material was imported. The word *alabastros* was often used for
clay-vases of the shape originally made in alabaster, but a
'box for *alabastroi*' contained probably the real thing; there
were other domestic utensils of more elaborate manufacture
which came to Athens from abroad.[3] Also the material for all
the statues and other objects in bronze was not to be found in
Attica. The rope which marked off the assembly was dyed
with ruddle; this was chiefly needed for ship-painting, and
came from 'ruddle-mines' in several places such as Keos,
which in the middle of the fourth century renewed an earlier
agreement with Athens about the supply of ruddle.[4] Gold and
ivory for temples and statues, jewellery and plate, naturally,
were of foreign origin.[5] When Peithetairos complains of the
cost of building temples, he mentions marble and gold, in
order to indicate how cheap it would be to worship birds on
trees and in groves; it is significant perhaps of the general
economic outlook that he finds the cost too high, but makes
no distinction between Attic marble and foreign gold.[6]

All these passages give instances of the many and varied
imports which reached Athens from everywhere inside and
even outside the Mediterranean world. The most famous
description of the great variety of imported goods is given in
the long fragment of Hermippos already mentioned.[7] Import
was in the hands of both foreign and Athenian *emporoi*, and
their chief business was to provide Athens with the necessary
wheat, partly bought by the State for public distribution or

C.122, 1298). Prof. J. L. Myres, *Cl. Rev.* 47 (1933), 124, and 53 (1939), 9,
gives some ingenious arguments to prove that those initials were of Egyptian and
Phoenician origin, and meant Egyptian or Phoenician breed. On coins the Corinthian Pegasos sometimes has the ϙ on his hind-quarters (*BMC. Corinth*, nos. 162,
167).
[1] Metagenes 7.   [2] Th.416f, adesp. 18, 696. — adesp. 806.
[3] frg. 548. — Pherekr. 85, Eupolis 58.
[4] A.22, E.378. — Ameips. 15. — *IG.* II², 1128, 9ff (Tod, 162).
[5] Cf., e.g., Theop. 25.   [6] B.612f.
[7] Hermipp. 63; see pp. 117, n. 3; 138, n. 3.

cheap sale. Aristophanes shows the need to many citizens of
these grain-distributions, and in court they were used to exert
pressure on the judges.[1] Much corn came from the Black Sea
or Egypt, some also from Sicily, but Euboia was no less important.[2] In times of emergency, of course, this import was even
more urgent. Thus the chorus of the cargo-ships in the *Hol-
kades*, performed in 423 B.C., boasts of all their transport to
Athens. Besides other foodstuffs, all kinds of grain, flour and
bread are especially mentioned.[3] The *emporoi*, who carried on
the work, were Athenians, and it was only to Athenian *emporoi*
that the Bosporanian kings gave permission to export corn
from their country.[4]

The great quantity of imports brought to Athens was paid
for chiefly by the Attic silver money from the mines at Laureion.
Its high quality caused it to be the most widespread currency
even outside the Greek world. 'The men carrying that money
carried good trade.'[5] The fact that Athenian silver coinage
reached all parts of the world is perhaps indicated by a comic
invention when Theseus is said to have changed Charon's fee
into the typically Athenian 'two obols'.[6] Besides, there was
the tribute of the allies, and the Peiraeus and its trade. Political power forced all grain ships of empire States to put in
there, even in transit, and to bring two-thirds of their cargo to
Athens;[7] this law, introduced probably during the Peloponnesian War, provided Athens with the necessary corn as well
as large harbour-dues. Aristophanes probably exaggerates the
total of the Athenian revenues when in 422 he says they were
about 2000 talents, but at any rate they were very high during
the first part of the Peloponnesian War.[8] Export trade, too,
was on a considerable scale. 'Sprats and clay', which means
fish and pottery, were important articles of export, and pottery
included the contents of the vases: wine and, even more, oil.[9]
Pottery was, however, an article of export in itself, a product
of Athenian art, like metal shields and other fine work. During

---

[1] K.1101, 1359f.
[2] W.715ff; cf. Thuc. VII, 28, 1, VIII, 1, 3; 4, 1; 95, 2; 96, 1f.
[3] frg. 412-22.   [4] Isokr. XVII, 57.
[5] F.721ff. — Xen. *Poroi* 3, 2.
[6] F.140ff. — For the general use of Athenian coins, cf. Gomme, 46f.
[7] Aristotle, *Ath. pol.* 51, 4.   [8] W.656ff, cf. Xen. *anab.* VII, 1, 27.
[9] A.901f.

the war it was quite a common allegation against a man that he had exported as contraband various material needed to equip ships.[1] In peace-time, therefore, those things formed part of the regular export trade, as well as wool and occasionally marble. On the whole, Athenian export trade included both agrarian and industrial products, and it is hardly possible to decide which predominated. On the Corinthian pinakes of the sixth century the chief economic activities depicted are mining of ore, making of pottery and sea trade (see Plate XIII).[2] We must add agriculture (which in Corinth was comparatively neglected) in order to form a true picture of Athenian economic conditions in the fifth century.

Harbour dues on imports and exports amounted to a large sum.[3] They must have been a considerable burden on the *emporoi*, and the collectors of customs duties were much disliked, as we have seen, both at the Peiraeus and at the Bosporus where they collected the tithes.[4] We do not know the exact ratio of export, import and transit duties, but doubtless those on imports were the highest. The balance of trade was certainly not favourable according to the modern view of trade policy. Athens felt this, when the tribute was no longer paid and the mines at Laureion, especially during the Dekeleian War, had a lower output; but she never aimed at economic self-sufficiency, and neither in peace nor in war did the idea ever occur to the Athenians of protecting Attic production against imports from abroad. If, as has recently been emphasized, the State did not encourage trade, it certainly was still less likely to restrict it in favour of Attic products. We have said before that, despite the lack of government measures, trade even supported agriculture. There were two chief motives in public economy, as it had been conceived for some

---

[1] K.278f, F.362ff. ἐξάγειν ταῖσι Πελοποννησίων τριήρεσι ζωμεύματα, thus Kleon reproaches the sausage-seller. The 'soups' are, of course, a joke appropriate to the opponent, ζωμεύματα replacing ζυγώματα (van Leeuwen).

[2] Cf. *Antike Denkmäler*, I, II. It is, however, possible that the scene in Plate XIII*a* depicts the digging of clay and not the mining of ore.

[3] It seems possible that there were duties on ships and passengers as well as on goods, ἐλλιμένια (cf. Eupolis 48) καὶ ἐμπορικά (Poll. VIII, 132); on the other hand, we do not know of any other duty levied at the Peiraeus except the ἑκατοστή (Ps.-Xen. I, 17) which later became a πεντηκοστή (Andok. I, 133). Cf. Boeckh, I, 388ff. Andreades, 138, 5; 296, 5.

[4] Cf. frg. 455.

time past: one, to give the people all it needed, chiefly food, and the other, to gain by harbour dues public revenues as large as possible. What we are told sometimes about all the allies, namely that they could not exist without imports and exports,[1] was even truer for the State that ruled the sea and had the widest political and economic power of control.

We learn from our survey that corn, wine, silphium, certain articles of luxury, fish and slaves were the chief Athenian imports.[2] The list could be enlarged from other sources, but its character would be unaltered. Only some important raw materials should be added, such as timber and other wood, iron and bronze.[3] The so-called 'industrial' production certainly supplied a large part of the export trade. It is nevertheless clear that the extent and intensity of Attic trade did not depend on the extent and intensity of 'industry'. Mass production was out of the question, because the requisite conditions of either production or sale did not exist. On the other hand, the smallness of the average workshop did not by any means prevent the general importance of trade.

The goods mentioned were dealt with by various people, some of whom dealt with their production or import, others with the sale to the consumers. Here we can speak of intermediary trade. The fishmonger made his purchases partly from the Attic fishermen, partly from the *emporoi*. The wine-seller was, in most cases, identical with the innkeeper; he bought Attic wine from the vine-dresser, imported wine from the *emporos*. Some of the articles of luxury and some delicacies may have been sold by the *kapelos*. In corn and flour, provided it was not taken over by the State, there doubtless existed intermediate trade between peasant or miller on the one hand, and baker or consumer on the other. The conditions of the slave trade were somewhat exceptional; certainly the *emporos* who traded in slaves not only brought them into the country, but sold them himself in the market. Timber and metals too may often have been sold directly by the *emporos* to the craftsman.

Taking all these facts together, we may say that some of the

---

[1] Ps.-Xen. II, 3.

[2] I do not think the characterization by Michell, 234, is to the point. He minimizes the importance of Athenian trade by regarding many of the imported goods as occasional curiosities only.

[3] W.301, Xen. *hell.* VI, 1, 11, Ps.-Xen. II, 11.

emporoi sold to re-sellers. The so-called *deigma*, the bazaar
building in the Peiraeus, apparently served this purpose.
Here, during the *coup de main* of Teleutias in 387 B.C., some
emporoi and *naukleroi* were taken prisoner.[1] Here the *emporoi*
exhibited specimens of their goods while the cargo was still on
board the ship; most of the purchasers were retailers or State
officials. Aristophanes compares the *deigma* with the *heliaia*,
the 'bazaar of legal judgments'.[2]

It is clear that these *emporoi*, as compared with the *kapeloi*,
were wholesale traders. But it would be a mistake to assume
that all *emporoi* sold through middlemen. Almost all business,
even overseas trade, was still on a comparatively small scale, and
most of the *emporoi* sailed from port to port, selling their goods
themselves. To repeat it once more: the outstanding difference
between *kapelia* and *emporia* was that between home and
foreign trade, but there was no real social gap between them.[3]
Translations such as 'wholesale merchant' for *emporos*, 'ship-
ping-magnate' (*Reeder*) for *naukleros*, 'grocer' (*Krämer*) for
kapelos, are not only misleading because of their modern
flavour; more than that, they hide the fact that there existed a
single middle class, which we may divide into a higher and a
lower section, but which nevertheless formed a social unit. It
included not only the tradesmen, but craftsmen and farmers
as well.[4] Even the distinction between these groups was not
absolute. The Attic farmer, it is true, did not normally go to
sea in order to sell his wine and oil, as two centuries earlier
Sappho's brother had done; but it is by no means impossible
that occasionally the owner of a larger estate or workshop went
on board a ship and sold his goods himself. There is no
evidence for this, but even without this supposed mixture of
vocations, all of them, the *emporoi* and *kapeloi*, the craftsmen
and farmers, belonged to the same class.

Rich and poor, of course, formed something like two camps,
no less in life than in comedy, and there was a wide difference
of opinion concerning the two groups. Nevertheless, there
was no 'class-struggle'; not all the wealthy outside the nobility

---

[1] Xen. *hell.* V, 1, 21; in Lysias, *frg.* 17, 6, the δεῖγμα is described as the
place where a great many citizens and foreigners meet.
[2] K.979.
[3] On this point I believe Hasebroek is entirely right.
[4] Cf. Xen. *mem.* III, 7, 6, and above, pp. 80 ,92f.

actually belonged to the upper class.[1] No suggestion is made of economic groups fighting each other, not even when, for whatever ridiculous reasons, the wealthy man was suspected of political intrigues and of aspiring to tyranny;[2] the reason was the distrust in which democracy held the traditional alliance of wealth and oligarchic policy. All economic differences were still subordinate to the political unity of democratic citizenship. Only in Aristophanes' *Ploutos* of 388 B.C. (and the late date is significant) do we find the poor waging war against the rich in full consciousness and with real hatred.[3] Here we have clear evidence of a change in the social climate.

The difference, however, in social rank between *emporos* and *kapelos* is a fact, though it was hardly so general or so strict as the comic poets seem to indicate. An important psychological factor was, as we have emphasized before, that the ordinary citizen was in much closer touch with the *kapelos* than with the *emporos*; but the whole system of retail trade in market and streets was, in fact, looked upon with suspicion and as disreputable, even though we cannot altogether trust the evidence of comedy.[4] On the other hand, it has rightly been emphasized how much sea-trade and banking, which were linked by the frequent use of loans, were based on the principles of honesty and good faith.[5] From Solon's time more and more nobles had become *emporoi*, and some of the middle-class *emporoi* had found their way into the upper class. A *kapelos*, even if he did not 'stand behind the counter' any longer, or work in his own workshop, would never be called a *kaloskagathos*. It is, however, equally mistaken to assume that every owner of an *ergasterion* or every workman was more or less looked down upon. The distinction between 'banausic' professions and those carried on by 'liberally educated people', which was inherited from the period of aristocracy, had more importance in literature than in real life. Although it later became a general feature, in classical

[1] Class-struggle: see, e.g., Murray, 70.
[2] W.493ff.
[3] Cf. Pl.535ff, 594ff. See p. 69ff.
[4] This evidence is ample and well known. Cf., e.g., A.836ff, K.181, 333, 634ff, 1245ff, 1373, 1398ff, C.991, frg. 387, 471, also Eur. *frg.* 1114.
[5] Cf. Calhoun, *passim.* — So much the more unfair (to put it mildly) was the action of the trustee who shared the risk of seaborne trade with his nephews and grandsons, but kept the lucky gain for himself (Lysias XXXII, 25).

times it concerned a small upper class rather than the people as a whole.[1]

The sycophant despises trade and craftsmanship as well as agriculture.[2] But this should not be taken as proof of a general contempt for manual labour; it proves, indeed, the far-reaching equality which in the eyes of the public existed among all who earned their living by the work of their hands. The exceptional position of agriculture, largely due to the greater independence of the peasant, was also an inheritance from earlier aristocratic times, kept alive in later ages chiefly by literature. In spite of the social and political differences which, as we have seen, existed between the farmers and the townsfolk, the economic situation brought them together on more or less the same level. These facts are, perhaps, the final reason for believing in the unity of the social class formed by the preponderant part of the citizen body, farmers, tradesmen and artisans, and chiefly characterized by the sale of goods which they produced themselves, or by overseas trade. We have stressed the middle-class character of these men, but we must emphasize that there was among the citizens a class, or at least the remains of a class, above them, and none below. For the dregs of the populace, even the paid day-labourers, were — at least before the general impoverishment after the war — not so numerous that they could be counted as a distinct class.[3] We have mentioned the poor, and we shall do so again; but it would distort the facts if we regarded them as a class by themselves. We may call the body of *petit bourgeois* the 'second estate' which, like the third estate of the French Revolution, was a unit in spite of all its differences in wealth and education; economically they were men, great and small, who lived on their earnings, not on property.[4] The advocate Robespierre

[1] For that distinction cf., e.g., Xen. *mem.* II, 7, 4. *oik.* 4, 2f. In general see Bolkestein, 191ff, and above p. 85ff.

[2] Pl.901ff.

[3] This seems perhaps a sweeping statement, and I admit that it is open to misunderstanding. It is always a matter of personal opinion where to draw the line between the poorer people among the lower middle-class and 'the poor' as a kind of proletariate. I believe that it is misleading to speak of a proletariate in fifth-century Athens. But as there is no statistic evidence, full proof seems impossible either way. I try to justify my view not only in the following sentences, but also in various passages throughout the book, especially in chapter IX.

[4] I have been reminded by one reviewer that 'earnings' could derive from

and *les dames des halles* stood at the extreme opposite ends, but they were of the same class. A deep social truth lies behind the juxtaposition on the same social level of the two scoundrels, the Paphlagonian who represented Kleon, and the sausage-seller who defeated him.[1]

investment as well as from wages. That, of course, is true. But the 'investment' of the shopkeeper or even the *emporos*, who usually had hardly any working capital, was something fundamentally different from the investment of the few 'men of property' who owned estates or ships or mines. The shopkeeper and his like belonged to the same social class as the wage-earner.

[1] The class I have tried to describe under the catchword of *petits bourgeois* developed into the dominating *bourgeoisie* of the Hellenistic Age, which has been pictured in Rostovtzeff's work. See below, p. 371f.

CHAPTER VI

CITIZENS AND FOREIGNERS

HERMES was the god of trade. In comedy he is called Empolaios, 'engaged in traffic and commerce', and Agoraios, 'belonging to the market'.[1] He was, above all, the god of small
tradesmen and hucksters, and so is derided as a 're-retailer'.[2]
As Dolios and Strophaios a deceitful and shifty god, he was the
patron of all dubious methods of business.[3] He was, however,
more than the god of trade. We shall not take into account
all his functions, important as they were: some of them are also
mentioned in comedy; he is the god of herds and flocks, the
doorkeeper, the god who shows the way, or the god of games.[4]
The part, however, which he plays in the *Peace* is of immediate
relevance to our questions. The god from whom the chorus
asks help is a god of peace, humane and bountiful, and when
directing 'like a good craftsman' the work of excavating the
goddess of Peace, he is thought of as the god of craftsmanship.[5]
The unity of the two sides of business life, which we have
discussed in the preceding chapter, is personified in Hermes.

This god of the small tradesman and craftsman became the
mouthpiece of a non-political material outlook. Hermes proclaims the eudaemonist idea of *ubi bene ibi patria*: 'A man's
home is wherever he gets on.'[6] Such sayings were not infrequent at that time.[7] No doubt this outlook was largely the
result of trading by sea, which brought experience of many
countries, of the manners and life of the 'natives'.[8] Equally
strong, however, was the influence of a general change in the
minds of many who directly or indirectly heard of views
refuting the claims of the State against the individual, and pro-

[1] A.816, Pl.1155. — K.297.   [2] παλιγκάπηλος, Pl.1156.
[3] Th.1202, Pl.1157; cf. F.1141ff. — Pl.1154, frg. 860; cf. P.421ff.
[4] Th.977, F.1141ff, Pl.1154, 1159ff.
[5] P.389ff. — δημιουργικῶς, P.429.   [6] Pl.1151.
[7] frg. 58 D, Lysias XXXI, 6, Eur. *frg.* 777, and elsewhere. In the same
spirit of unpatriotic materialism the famous heroic line of Homer (*Il.* XII, 243)
was modified to 'one omen is best, to fight for one's dinner' (Metagenes 18).
[8] ἐπιχώριοι, F.461.

claiming materialist well-being as the only real goal. The firm close texture of the Polis was becoming looser, its narrowness widening and many a man who found a new country to settle in could, like Herodotos, be called either after it or after his native town.[1] Sometimes he became homesick, and longed for his *patris*, but these feelings were a personal and sentimental affection rather than due to any political connection.[2]

We must bear these facts in mind when we now turn to the important question, which we have occasionally referred to already, the question of the economic status of 'political man'. We must discover first the part played in economic life, especially in trade and craftsmanship, by the citizens of the Polis on the one hand, and by foreigners and non-citizens on the other.

We have seen that the leading statesmen after Perikles were 'traders', 'something-sellers'.[3] It is certain that comedy exaggerated, and included in this description, without distinction, men who had workshops which employed a number of slaves as well as retailers and hucksters. The real Kleon was so different from the sausage-seller who in comedy became his successor that the fun almost misses its point, and even the Paphlagonian was a drastic distortion of the real man. But apart from the moral distinction which is here irrelevant, we saw that they belonged, more or less, to the same social class. The real distinction between the two groups is not that they followed different vocations, but the simple difference of wealth and poverty. Hyperbolos owed his wealth to his lamps, Dieitrephes to his flasks,[4] and it goes without saying that to such men wealth gave an opportunity of intense political activity, whereas the small poor craftsmen had little time to spare for it. In spite, however, of a different standard of life, they were men of the same social and economic nature. They were chiefly engaged in the sale of their own products. Craftsmen and traders formed the majority of the townsfolk, and therefore the 'Man in the Street' as well as the political leader liked to use technical terms from their common activity in

---

[1] Eupolis 280.

[2] adesp. 379, 431. — Expressions of love for one's native land are frequent in tragedy. Apart from the various praises of Athens cf., e.g., Eur. *Med.* 643ff, 846ff, *frg.* 6.

[3] K.129ff; see above, p. 120f.   [4] K.1315, B.798ff.

order to give a more impressive stamp to his speeches. The
Paphlagonian and the sausage-seller take expressions from the
joiner's or the blacksmith's work.[1] They do not use the terms
of their own professions; the poet does not want to characterize
the individual speaker, but reflects a general way of speaking.

All these men, whether rich or poor, were Athenian citizens.
One of the fragments probably describes the artisans as such.[2]
The sycophant, doubtless a citizen, refuses to be a farmer,
tradesman or craftsman; this shows that it was usual for
citizens to be engaged in these occupations.[3] For this reason
the *prostates*, he who not only led, but represented the people,
and therefore 'tramples down the council and trims the
generals', is said to be master of market, harbours and pnyx.[4]
If we interpret this passage aright — and we shall return to it —
it refutes the view of those historians who over-estimate the
part played in economic life by non-citizens. The Athenian
citizens ruled in ekklesia *and* trade, and no less in the harbour
than in the market, that is to say, no less in *emporia* than in
kapelia.

The sovereign people in the assembly was a chance selection
from the whole citizen body, and therefore always (except in
comedy when women invaded the assembly) of like nature and
composition. It was the type of *petit bourgeois* whom we have
recognized as peasant, tradesman or artisan, that predominated in the assembly. Sokrates significantly remarks that the
assembly was composed of the various artisans, of peasants,
merchants and retailers.[5] The social position of Sokrates himself whose father was a stone-dresser, and the sociological
character of his thinking and teaching, cannot be understood

[1] Cf., e.g., K.462f, 468f.

[2] τῶν πολιτῶν ἄνδρας ὑμῖν δημιουργοὺς ἀποφανῶ, adesp. 38. Not
knowing the context, we cannot be certain about the meaning of the fragment,
but I see no reason why the *demiourgoi* should be poets 'who make the citizens
better' (as in F.1009f), and not ordinary artisans (as, e.g., in the discussion on
the divine demiurge in Plato, *Rep.* X, 597f). — I do not know whether the actor
Oiagros and the flute-player, who performed their art before the judges in order
to express gratitude for their acquittal (W.579ff), were citizens.

[3] Pl.899ff. The sycophant occasionally does 'feign to be an *emporos*', but not
in order to be exempt from military service or payment of taxes. That is a wrong
explanation of the scholiast (Pl.904). He does so in order to avoid a legal action
or at least to postpone it until the winter (cf. p. 118). This happens also in Lysias
XVII, 5: ἔμποροι φάσκοντες εἶναι.

[4] K.165f.   [5] Xen. *mem.* III, 7, 6.

unless we see him for what he was, 'a man of the people' who drew ethical and logical conclusions from his surroundings. It was not Sokrates but the aristocrat Plato who in founding a new State based his social philosophy on contempt for the *banausos*, the manual worker.

It is, however, beyond dispute that many crafts and trades, *emporia* as well as *kapelia*, were carried on by foreigners, mostly by the resident metics. Among the retailers, for instance, there were many foreign women. We do not know how many of the female inn-keepers, huckstresses and hetaerae mentioned in comedy were foreigners; some probably were, though the hetaerae were usually slaves. Other sources, as for instance the well-known building-accounts of the Erechtheion, show that sometimes foreigners formed a larger or smaller majority among the craftsmen.[1] But the modern view that practically all trade, banking and craftsmanship were in the hands of metics is false at least for our period, and the identification of the metic and the *banausos* has rightly been challenged.[2]

Wealthy foreigners, Greeks and non-Greeks, many of them resident, were not infrequently seen in Athens, and many a metic owned a number of houses and slaves and plenty of cash, paying large sums in taxes and even taking on liturgies.[3] Like Lysias they might put money, soldiers and weapons at the disposal of the democrats who were led by Thrasyboulos.[4] Aristophanes speaks of the Phrygian *nouveau riche*; he may have been a metic or some other kind of foreigner, perhaps one of the enfranchised slaves.[5] They too quite frequently became rich and acquired the status of metics; Xenophon speaks of 'Lydians, Phrygians, Syrians, and other barbarians from every country, who formed a large section of the metics.'[6]

---

[1] *IG.* I² 372ff, especially 374, II, 5ff. — For potters ánd vase-painters cf. G. Richter, *The Craft of Athenian Pottery*, 98ff (though not entirely convincing), also Beazley, *Potter and Painter*, 21ff. There can be no doubt that most of the potters were Athenians.

[2] Cf. Hommel, *P.-W.* XV, 1433ff, 1449ff, with ample indications of modern literature.

[3] ἐπίδημοι ξένοι, frg. 543 (in Meineke's and Kaibel's reading). — Lysias XII, 8, 10f, 18, 20.

[4] Lysias, *frg.* 1, 165.   [5] W.1309.

[6] Aristomenes 16, cf. Isaios, *frg.* 8. — Xen. *Poroi* 2, 3. — Theagenes, according to schol. B.822, was περαΐτης. If this means 'a man from Peraia' (Liddell and Scott), the boastful fellow, whom the people called 'Smoke', was a Syrian.

Another Phrygian is said to have succeeded even in getting into an old Attic family, a *genos*.[1] Someone blackmailed a rich foreigner out of his money.[2] The Thirty even planned to have thirty metics put to death, simply in order to confiscate their property; the demos, on the other hand, enjoyed the 'petty suit' against a metic.[3] Among those who 'filled their belly by means of their tongue', the well-paid teachers of rhetoric, there were foreigners, although we need not believe Aristophanes when he calls them barbarians.[4] Gorgias and Philippos, both mentioned in that passage, were certainly Greeks, but at least Gorgias was not a metic. Paapis, whose cups Hyperbolos was said to have stolen, was, as his name shows, an Egyptian, probably a trader.[5] Other Egyptians known to us by name are Hermias and Deinias; they were hellenized and perhaps metics, the former a fraudulent fishmonger, the latter a perfume-seller or perfume-lover.[6]   There were numerous Egyptians in Athens; they were conspicuous by their dark colouring, and a comic writer said: 'If the sun burns you, it will turn you into an Egyptian.'[7]

These last references have brought us to the smaller and poorer people among the foreigners whom we also meet in comedy. The two hostesses, at whose inns Herakles put up in Hades, were metics.[8] A woman who sold sacred bands was a Thracian; the same was true, according to comedy, of the mother of Kleophon.[9] She and possibly Hyperbolos' mother

---

[1] B.762f.   [2] Eupolis 40 P, 65ff.

[3] Xen. *hell*. II, 3, 21; 40. — K.347.

[4] B.1694ff. It was probably on account of the new-fangled artificiality of their language that they could be regarded as people who did not ἑλληνίζειν. Cf. H. E. Stier, *Grundlagen u. Sinn d. griech. Geschichte* (1945), 84.

[5] Leukon 1.   [6] Archipp. 25, Strattis 33.

[7] frg. 569, 15. — adesp. 9.

[8] F.549ff. They want (F.569ff) to call up Kleon and Hyperbolos. Gilbert Murray, 44 (cf. already Croiset, 245), concluded from this that Kleon was regarded as a protector of the poor; Hyperbolos is not mentioned. I cannot accept this conclusion. The two persons were not only women, but metics. The *prostates* was the usual patron whom every metic needed in court, and whom, of course, he paid. It is, however, not likely that the two demagogues in real life ever pleaded for metics. In the *Frogs* it is simply a joke based on the double meaning of the word *prostates*, which makes the *prostates*, leader of the State, *prostates*, patron of metics. The same play on words occurs in P.684, when the demos is abused because οὕτω πονηρὸν προστάτην ἐπεγράψατο, where Hyperbolos is meant.

[9] Eupolis 243. — Plat. 60, cf. Archipp. 27.

were ridiculed because of their bad Greek.[1]   A drug-seller would come from Megara, while, on the other hand, Asiatic women had the reputation of being experts in love-potions.[2] In many cases, foreigners who were not legally metics were resident in Attica.[3] Among the lower classes were non-citizens of all sorts. One of them, unless this is comic fiction, was a certain Nikias, father of Hagnon and grandfather of the famous Theramenes; he is said to have been a hired carrier of burdens, and his son (if the reading is right) 'did not know his own deme'.[4] He belonged to the same profession as those 'carriers' — probably sailors from merchant ships — of whom we are told that they spent their money on sleeping with flute-girls and other hetaerae.[5] In Athens, and even more in the Peiraeus, there was a strange mixture of language and dialect, of clothes and ways of life.[6]

It was the large number of foreigners which won the Athenians high praise for their *philoxenia*, and the ancient custom still prevailed of honouring a foreigner who had been a guest-friend from one's father's time.[7] There were, however, other voices as well. We may doubt whether it is possible to take the verdicts of Euripides' *Ion*, necessary as they are for the plot, as reflections of a real hostility on Athens' part against aliens.[8] Yet the matter had its two aspects, and the demos did not always feel very friendly to foreigners; still less did the government of the Thirty.[9] Some of the non-Greeks, for instance the Lydians, Egyptians and Carians, or the Phoenicians, had a proverbially bad reputation.[10] In the community planned in the *Ekklesiazousai* agriculture and making of clothes had their place, but there is no mention of other essential industry, and none of metics or foreigners.[11] The whole plan is so incomplete and sketchy that it is better not to draw any conclusion *ex silentio*, but the women's government attacked the hetaerae

---

[1] Cf. Hermipp. 11-12 (?)   [2] Theopomp. 2. — Eur. *Andr.* 155ff, 205.
[3] Thuc. VI, 30, 2.
[4] Kratinos 38 P, 30; cf. Xen. *hell.* II, 3, 30. About the evidence from Kratinos' *Ploutoi* for Hagnon cf. *AJP.* LXVI (1945), 120, note 23.
[5] ἄνδρες φορτηγοί, Metag. 4, Aristag. 2.   [6] Ps.-Xen. II, 8.
[7] Kratinos 17 D; cf. also the description of Kimon as ἀνὴρ θεῖος καὶ φιλοξενώτατος (Kratinos 1).
[8] Eur. *Ion* 589ff, 721ff.   [9] Phryn. 58. — Lysias XII, 4f.
[10] adesp. 387, 397; cf. also Eur. *Or.* 1111ff, 1369ff, 1483ff.
[11] E.651ff.

and slave-girls for fear of sexual competition, and many of them must have been foreigners.[1] The joke takes for granted an unfriendly attitude of citizen towards non-citizen, but this can hardly have arisen from general rivalry in business.

The comedians, although they sometimes derided foreigners who pushed their way into citizenship,[2] generally favoured the metics, at least the Greek metics, and supported their attempts, which undoubtedly were very vigorous, to become as like citizens as possible. The subject was taken up and developed by Xenophon, although he objected to non-Greek soldiers, many of them metics, in the ranks of the Athenian army.[3] The presence of a large number of resident aliens naturally caused difficulties and misgivings. It was widely felt that it was the duty of a metic to comply with the life of the city and not to interfere with politics, though if necessary to fight and even to die for the Polis.[4] On the other hand, foreigners were excluded from the distributions of corn.[5] The comic poets chiefly pleaded for equality of treatment and position between citizens and metics. As flour and bran are needed to make good bread, so citizens and metics are needed for the State. Friendliness to foreigners as well as to fellow-citizens will be rewarded even in Hades.[6] Eupolis attacked Peisandros because he did not allow a foreign friend to share his meal.[7] Peasants and traders, artists and craftsmen, metics and foreigners, and the *nesiotai*, the allies from the islands, were

---

[1] E.718ff.   [2] B.32, Kratinos 38 P, b.   [3] Xen. *Poroi* 2, 2f.
[4] Cf. Eur. *Med.* 222, *Hik.* 888ff, *Herakleid.* 503ff.   [5] W.716ff.

[6] A.507f. — F.454ff. There seems to be here a reflection of the ethics taught in the Eleusinian mysteries into which also non-citizens were frequently initiated (cf. Eur. *Hik.* 173).

[7] Eupolis 40 P, I a. Peisandros appears in comedy as a big and greedy fellow (Hermipp. 9, Eupolis 182, Phryn. 20, Plat. 95), but that does not help very much to explain the context. However, I do not follow Mr. Edmonds, *Mnemosyne* VIII (1939), 1, in altering the text of the papyrus. To make sense of it, we may compare Lysias, frg. 1, 168. But the real meaning cannot be determined. Jensen, *Abh. Preuss. Akad.* (1939), no. 14, 4f, thinks that the passage refers to Peisandros' change of party. He builds up his theory very ingeniously, but it seems pressing our incidental evidence too hard when he bases his view mainly on one inscription (*Syll.*[3] 92) in which a Peisandros (there were two according to Eupolis 182) moves the προξενία for Lykon, an Achaean shipowner. Why, in general, should the oligarch be less friendly to foreigners than the radical democrat? The opposite would be more likely. There is, at any rate, insufficient evidence for dating the performance of the *Demoi* a year later than usual (i.e. spring 411).

called on to unite in the common task of bringing in the peace.[1] No conspirators or place-hunters might share in the citizenship (it was the year of the oligarchic revolution), but metics, well-disposed foreigners and citizens who had lost their rights because of debts to the State, were to be admitted.[2] The chorus of the *Frogs* demanded that citizens should not be done out of their rights, while slaves who had fought in the naval battle of Arginusae were made 'masters'; all who fought together should be made 'kinsmen and citizens with full rights', and this included metics and foreigners.[3]

We see that the comedians opposed the policy of restricting the conferment of citizenship, a policy which democracy upheld though it did not strictly enforce it.[4] We may suppose that this attitude towards metics and other foreigners was shared by many people. At any rate, the importance of 'Athena's foster-children' to the State and in life in general is confirmed, and there is no doubt that most of these foreigners, who had settled down in Attica for good, felt entirely Athenian. Some of them received citizenship, for instance Chairephilos, a big merchant in salted fish, who lived about 350 B.C.[5] This was not a frequent practice, although in Athens immigration was never made difficult by 'seal and signet' (in modern terms: passport and visa), as was the case in the city of the birds.[6] It is, however, important to note that such a possibility existed, though it was not common Athenian practice, and, we may think, this is true of Cloudcuckooborough also; for, as the song of the chorus goes on to say, no other place is so pleasant for metics to live in.[7] To become a metic was in itself a goal to be coveted, and a reason for foreign traders to bring corn to Athens.[8] It is a mistake to picture the majority of metics and foreigners who earned their living by trade and craft as men

[1] P.296ff.
[2] L.576ff. Cf. Schulthess, *P.-W.* XVIII, 627ff, Wilamowitz, 51f.
[3] F.693f, 700ff.   [4] Cf. Andokides II, 23.
[5] See Kirchner, *Prosopogr. Attica*, 15187.
[6] B.1212ff. The two Greek words are σφραγίς and σύμβολον, and the meaning of both seems more or less the same. Certainly σύμβολον is here not a written document, since the bird-official is supposed to 'affix' it; it has to be fixed to such a document like a σφραγίς (cf. also B.559f). Cf. also *ATL*. II, 50 to T 164, D 7, 15.'
[7] B.1313ff, 1318ff.
[8] Lysias VI, 49.

wandering from town to town.[1] There was a certain contempt for barbarians among the Athenians, and even pride among the Attic-born towards foreigners from other Greek countries.[2] Poseidon's disgust at the way the Triballian god wore his coat may have been more than a mere joke.[3] But there was no striking difference between the citizens and the Greek metics, whether rich or poor.

Many of the paid workmen who had to be punctual at their working-place, and therefore were under strict control, were citizens.[4] There were probably citizens even among the wine-bearers, although they were generally slaves.[5] On the other hand, citizens as well as metics owned slaves, and their wives walked through the streets, followed by one or more slave-girls.[6] Citizens and metics were lessees of the mines at Laureion, and both made up the crowds in the *deigma*, the bazaar in the Peiraeus.[7] Evidence from comedy adds to the knowledge we possess from other sources, especially from the honorary decree for those who fought at Phyle, by which citizenship was granted to several metics who were either specialized tradesmen and craftsmen, or even farmers and market gardeners, or day-labourers.[8]

It was usual also for the metics to take part in worship and festivals, though they were sometimes segregated from the citizens.[9] They were, in fact, more highly esteemed in public opinion than the allies who had to work hard to win the good-will of the citizens, and were treated as subjects rather than as allies.[10] The metics loved Athens as their new fatherland, the allies from 'the thousand cities paying tribute'[11] certainly did not.

Whenever the Athenians thought of the allies, that is to say, of their empire, their predominant idea, according to comedy, was to get as much money out of them as possible, and the demagogues were not so much blamed for exploiting the allies

---

[1] Here and later in this chapter I give and controvert the views expressed by Hasebroek.

[2] Eupolis 71.   [3] B.1567.

[4] adesp. 35 D. These are the often mentioned μισθωτοί.

[5] frg. 299, 45 D.

[6] *IG.* I², 329 (*Syll.*³ 96, Tod, 79). — K.448f, B.69ff, Th.279ff.

[7] *IG.* II², 1582ff, Xen. *Poroi* 4, 12. — Lysias, *frg.* 17, 6.

[8] *IG.* II², 10 (*Syll.*³ 120, Tod, 100).

[9] *IG.* I², 84, 25; cf. Eur. *El.* 795.   [10] W.675ff.   [11] W.707.

as they were accused of pocketing most of the money themselves and robbing the ordinary citizens of their share.[1] Sometimes we are told of 'foreigners' who were exploited, like those
'fruit-bearers' whom Kleon had milked, or those who came to
town through the gates and there met Kleon, now degraded
to the position of a sausage-seller.[2] We may regard these
foreigners in the main as allies.[3] Some of the devices by which
the allies are supposed to be cheated are obvious comic invention, others may have been used; but even from comedy it
becomes clear that the rule over the 'cities' or 'islands' did not
mean continuous exploitation, though the importance of the
tribute is beyond doubt. Aristophanes seems to indicate that
Athenian embassies went out whenever there was delay in
payment by the allies.[4] This payment was an official transac-
tion, and the State and the city of Athens were its chief gainers.
From Perikles' time the latter fact became the main point in
the oligarchic opposition, and it is this that lies behind the
distortion of the comedians.[5] Normally the cities sent their
tribute by delegates, but frequently during the war 'the silver-
collecting ships' went round the allied States.[6] Old men were
proud to remember the days of their youth when the treasure
of the Confederacy was brought from Delos to Athens.[7] The
allies, on the other hand, tried to make use of the plight of
Athens during the war, in order to free themselves from the
heaviest of their burdens.[8] Compared with the *phoroi*, the
tributes of the allies, all the other revenues, whether legal or
not, which the Athenians might gain from the empire, seemed
petty advantages.[9] It is, on the other hand, a mistake to think
too exclusively of the *phoros* as an important instrument of

[1] K.312f, 326, 801f, 832ff, 930ff, 1034, 1408, W.666ff, 673ff, 707ff, P.45ff,
639ff, B.1021ff, 1035ff, 1422ff, 1453ff, Ps.-Xen. I, 14ff.

[2] K.326, 1408; cf. P.46ff. It is significant that Euripides coined the word
ξεναπάτης (*frg.* 667).

[3] Cf. A.503. Gilbert Murray, *Greek Studies*, 60, maintains that Aristophanes
in the *Knights* 'is always indirectly championing the cause of the subject allies,
but that he never mentions them by name till the last line of the play'. He calls
them ξένοι there — in fact, in the last word of the play — but he had spoken of
ξένοι, πόλεις or νῆσοι before (see the passages cited in note 1).

[4] A.192f.   [5] Cf. Plut. *Per.* 12.

[6] A.643. — K.1070f, Thuc. II, 69, 1, III, 19, IV, 50, 1; 75, 1.

[7] W.1098ff.

[8] P.619ff, cf. Thuc. I, 122, 1.

[9] Cf. the lists, W.656ff, Ps.-Xen. I, 16ff.

PLATE XII

a

b   *c*

VASE PAINTERS AND FISHERMEN

PLATE XIII

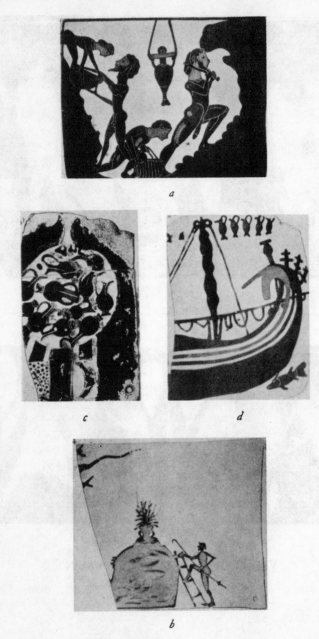

a

c   *d*

b

MINING, POTTERY, SEA TRADE

politics, which in its changes would always reflect changes in
political relations.[1]

The empire was, above all, an expression of power, a fact
realized even by the comedians. The chorus announces to the
sausage-seller that he will become 'the greatest of the Hellenes',
to administer the whole State and 'to rule the allies, a trident
in his hand'; in the end, it is Demos again who is 'the monarch
of Greece as well as of this land'.[2] The rule of Athens reached
from the Black Sea to Sardinia, and countless cities paid tribute
to her.[3] We do not know what Pherekrates meant by turning
the official formula of the Athenian confederacy into the
feminine;[4] the comedy in which this is done was called *The
Old Women*, and it may have depicted a women's revolt similar
to that in the *Lysistrate*. At any rate, a foreigner was insulted
when called a glutton 'for pay', which makes it likely that he
was no metic.[5] Friend and foe alike, Perikles himself before
all others, realized that Athenian rule was, and had to be,
absolute — a *tyrannis*, its guiding principle being the advantage
of the ruling city.[6] Kleon is always on the look-out for revolts
of the allies.[7] The claims of Athens, based on her former deeds,
in particular the liberation of the eastern Greeks from Persian
rule, would hardly suffice to justify that tyranny in the eyes
of its victims, and a man like Alkibiades therefore preached
the advantages common to Athens and her allies.[8] Aristophanes too fought for the weal of both the city and the allies,
but that meant chiefly to fight against the demagogues.[9] What
really mattered — as, for instance, the economic unity of the
empire, expressed in its uniform weights, measures and
coinage — was only cause for a joke.[10] The unification of law

---

[1] Cf. H. Schaefer, *Hermes* LXXIV (1939), 225ff.

[2] K.838f, 1330.   [3] W.700, 707.

[4] αἱ Ἀθηναῖαι καὶ αἱ ξύμμαχοι, Pherekr. 34.   [5] Pherekr. 32.

[6] K.1111ff, Eupolis 217 (?), cf. Thuc. I, 122, 3; 124, 3, II, 63, 2, III, 37, 2,
VI, 85, 1; cf. V, 84ff.

[7] K.237f, 361.   [8] Thuc. VI, 18, 4.   [9] K.1319, P.759ff, 935f.

[10] B.1035ff. This refers to a colony, but is essentially true for the allied cities
as well. The speaker is a ψηφισματοπώλης (see above, p. 122, n. 7), but I do not
believe that he pronounced a ψήφισμα by which the μέτρα καὶ σταθμοὶ καὶ
ψηφίσματα of Cloudcuckooborough were to be equal to those of another fancy
city. This incongruous combination is nonsense without being funny. Bergk's
emendation νομίσμασι for ψηφίσμασι seems obvious; the error was easy enough
in view of the speaker's profession. The right word is fully confirmed by the
well-known Athenian decree, Tod, 67 (now best in ATL. 579, I, 69, II, D 14).

and the centralization of jurisdiction, with all the inconveniences necessarily connected with them, were naturally
regarded by the allies as a burden, the more since the evils of
the popular courts, of sycophantism and corruption, were
equally inflicted upon them.[1] It must have been a much
resented blow to the autonomy of the allied States when the
Athenians decreed that, if an Athenian citizen was killed in
allied territory, the city itself concerned had to pay the heavy
fine of five talents.[2] The chief trouble was that everything was
dominated by political issues, and that Athens—naturally enough
—wherever and whenever it was possible, supported the local
democrats against their oligarchic opponents.[3] The rule of the
Athenians and their treatment of the allies was truly tyrannical
and frequently no longer bound by normal moral standards.[4]

Several comedians, for instance Eupolis and Philyllios,
wrote plays in which 'the Cities' formed the chorus.[5] In
Eupolis' play one of the allied cities spoke like a slave who
wanted another master: 'when I suffer such misery, am I not
even to beg to be sold once more?'[6] An Athenian leering at
one of the girls who represented the allied towns, was told to
take himself off to a colony.[7] That is significant. Citizens
wanting to make money, and usually making it, out of the
allies were advised by the poet to go to one of the colonies.
The colony of Brea, for instance, was founded in order to give
the poorer classes of citizens economic relief.[8] The story of
Cloudcuckooborough, in particular the appearances of *episkopos*, decree-seller and sycophant, points to the fact that the
colonies, even if they were not cleruchies of Athenian citizens,
remained under the sway of the Athenian demos and suffered
from the same evils which the comedians found in the democratic, or rather demagogic, rule both at home and within the
empire.[9] There was no remedy against the subject status of
the allies. It happened only late and in a few exceptional cases

---

[1] K.326, P.639ff, B.1422ff, 1453ff, cf. W.577.

[2] P.169ff. The allusion in these lines has been explained by P. Roussel, *Rev. ét.
anc.* XXXV (1933), 385 (cf. *Mélanges Glotz*, II, 817, 1 and 3) and by R. Meiggs,
Cl. Rev. LXIII (1949), 9ff.

[3] A.462, P.639f, Ps.-Xen. I, 14.

[4] Eupolis 217.   [5] Eupolis 205ff, Philyll. 10ff.

[6] Eupolis 225.   [7] Eupolis 206.   [8] *IG*. I², 45 (Tod, 44, *Syll.*³ 67).

[9] B.1021ff, 1033f, 1035ff, 1422ff, 1453ff. About the mutual approach of the
different types of colonies cf. my *Aspects of the Ancient World*, 119ff, 128ff.

like that of Chios that the Athenians genuinely acknowledged
and rewarded the loyalty of an ally.¹ It is significant for the
decay of the empire, and for the hatred which had accumulated
against Athens, that Lysistrate in her striking call for unity
speaks of metics and 'if there is any friendly foreigner' — that
is, so it seems, to say, individual men or women only; she also
speaks of colonies, but does not mention the allies at all.² That
was in 411 B.C. When at last everything had gone and Sparta
ruled the seas, the comedian Platon wrote a comedy *Hellas or
The Islands* — as far as we can see from the few fragments
extant, a pathetic obituary on the empire, in which Poseidon
threatened Sparta to destroy her supremacy of the seas, if she
did not willingly give it up; and Greece lamented that she
herself had become blind and weak.³

The allies, apart from official embassies, did not come into
direct contact with the Athenian people. That is probably the
reason why they did not appear as individuals on the comic
stage, while men from neighbouring countries such as Megara
and Boeotia did. There could be only a chorus of personified
allied cities. Nevertheless, the relations between the citizens
and the allies are, as we have seen, clearly reflected in comedy.

To return to the mixed crowd in Athens, we must emphasize
once more the part played by the citizens in the economic life
of the city. We shall thus more easily discover to what extent
the various types of foreigner were important. It is obvious
that in comedy none of the leading characters were metics or
foreigners. Peasant or townsmen, rich or poor, all were citizens.
Not only Trygaios was a 'worthy citizen'.⁴ The poor wood-
worker Lamios, called 'the saw' or 'the axe', would hardly have
been mentioned in such a way, if he was not a citizen.⁵ It has
often been pointed out that the potters must have been citizens
from early times, for a district of the town, the Kerameikos,
was called after them.⁶

¹ B.879f, Eupolis 232.
² L.576ff. I read in 580 (with Boissonade and Coulon) κεῖ τις ξένος ἢ
(instead of ἢ) φίλος ὑμῖν. It is just possible, but not likely, that Lysistrate here
proposed to do what the Athenians did only in 405-4, when they granted
citizenship to the Samians 'as far as they were on the side of the Athenian people'
(*Syll.*³ 116, Tod, 96).
³ Plat. 24, 1D.   ⁴ P.910.   ⁵ adesp. 823-4.
⁶ Cf. already Blümner, *Gewerbl. Tätigkeit*, 66, 1. Büchsenschütz, *Hauptstätten
des Gewerbefleisses*, 13. Cf. above, p. 127f.

There was no rule against bringing metics on the stage. In fact, they appear frequently, though usually in subordinate parts. At least three of the comic poets, Krates, Pherekrates and Platon, wrote comedies with the title *The Metics*; but we do not know how important the part of the chorus was in these plays.[1] If the metics had been so prominent in economic life as most modern scholars believe, it would be impossible that nearly all the tradesmen and merchants and artisans in comedy are citizens. Having an audience of citizens, or even of citizens and metics together, the poets no doubt usually preferred to present citizens, but they could not regularly depict general conditions which were contrary to the real facts.[2]

Aristophanes could represent citizens even as slaves, but that was a kind of 'mask', a fiction easily dropped.[3] Moreover, some of the politicians were attacked and insulted by the suggestion that they were foreigners or even foreign slaves.[4] Hyperbolos as a Lydian or Phrygian is a barbarian slave who cannot speak correct Attic; Kleophon was sometimes called a Thracian slave, sometimes — which was obviously closer to the facts — the son of a Thracian mother.[5] The strategos Diopeithes is called 'Cretan, barely Attic', and a certain demagogue is said to have had no *phrateres* even the day before, and to be unable to speak Attic.[6] When Aristophanes complains most violently of the political leaders of the day, they are called rascals, animals, aliens, all in one.[7] There was, however, little danger that foreigners who had recently become citizens might succeed in becoming leaders of the people. In most cases this was pure invention and comic distortion; on another occasion Hyperbolos, for instance, was called 'a sour citizen'.[8] Also the blear-eyed Archedemos, one of the best-known demagogues of

[1] Krates 22, Pherekr. 112, Plat. 77f.

[2] There was a common audience of citizens and metics, though not of allies, at the Lenaia (A.507f).

[3] K.1ff, 44. — K.319ff.

[4] Even in tragedy a violent speaker in the assembly at Argos can be described as Ἀργεῖος οὐκ Ἀργεῖος (Eur. *Or.* 902ff). He spoke in favour of Tyndareus' charge against Orestes and is therefore called ἠναγκασμένος, which may mean 'forced upon the people' or 'suborned by Tyndareus' (thus Grube, 389).

[5] Plat. 170, Polyzel. 5. — B.1244, Plat. 166, 187; cf. Andokides, *frg.* 5. — Plat. 168. — Kleophon: schol. F.679, 681 (cf. Plat. 60), Aischines II, 76. — Eur. *Or.* 903 (see last note) is, according to the scholion, a reference to Kleophon. Cf. Jensen, *Abh. Preuss. Ak.* 1939, no. 14, 9.

[6] Plat. 31. — Eupolis 40 P, 21ff.   [7] F.730ff.   [8] K.1304.

about 400 B.C., was no foreigner, as the scholiast maintains.[1] He was not a *phrater*, not a member of a phratry, and therefore probably a bastard or the son of an alien mother.[2] Politics remained the domain of citizens, not only legally (that goes without saying) but also socially.

No doubt many of the citizens who appear in comedy were of the type which, in order to make a few obols, was eager to serve on the juries and subsequently to get into the assembly. Many of them, the 'many of the obol', depended on this money, as on their days of official duty they could not earn a living for their family.[3] It must have been worse during the war, when many of the peasants lived in town, with no earnings and no work. Although there were also in the courts and the assembly well-to-do people who might perhaps give the three obols as pocket-money to their children,[4] the majority of those who drew this money were poor men. This fact is well known and needs no long argument to prove it, but most of the people were able to divide their time between business and politics, and the jurymen, who sometimes sat for weeks in court from morning to evening, were mostly old men.

These arguments, both positive and negative, suggest that a large and, for the most part, uniform section of the population was made up of both citizens and metics. Leaving aside the question of political rights and taking into account only the social and economic conditions, we may say that both together formed a higher and lower middle-class of the type we have tried to define in discussing the citizens only. There was no division of labour between citizen and metic, in the sense that service of the State and agriculture were for the citizen, trade and handicrafts for the metic. We have seen that some metics were even farmers and market gardeners. On the other hand, even in vocations where metics formed the majority, they were never so predominant that their position could be considered analogous to that of the citizens in agriculture. It is still more incorrect to speak of a 'deep social gap' between citizens and

---

[1] F.588. — Schol. F.416f.

[2] F.418. — B.1649ff, especially 1669. Cf. Radermacher, 204; Latte, *P.-W.* XVII, 1069ff.

[3] οἱ πολλοὶ τοὐβελοῦ, K.945. Or does it mean 'the many *for* an obol'? Cf. below, p. 230, n. 2. — W.300ff, E.460ff.

[4] W.606ff.

metics, for both, whether rich or poor, were on roughly the same social level, and actually formed one and the same social body. The unity of the *bourgeois* class must be extended to include the metics.

It is therefore obvious that the number of metics was not so large as is often supposed. Otherwise the opposition against them would have been stronger, and the poets would not have pleaded that they be treated like citizens. The widespread idea that the citizens formed an exclusive social group, rigidly separated from metics and foreigners, is not defensible. Melas the Egyptian was the good friend of a citizen from boyhood up, and we certainly do not get the impression that his case was exceptional, though later the friendship broke down on account of money matters.[1] Marriage with foreigners, on the other hand, whether of men or women, was rare after Perikles in 451 had introduced his citizenship law which barred the way to political rights to the sons of mixed marriages. It is with true Athenian feeling that Theseus in Euripides' *Hiketides* blames Adrastos for having given girls of his city to foreigners.[2]

The barrier of political privilege was high, but social life flowed over it. This is shown not only by the fact that non-citizens had won, in some degree, a position of social equality, but also by the fact that the activities of the citizens were not exclusively political. From the middle-class came most of the political leaders after Perikles as well as some of the State-officials, but the class which earned its living by trade and craft was also largely composed of citizens. Manual labour was not looked down on, though of course those who worked as workmen, paid by, and dependent on, a master, were not very highly esteemed.[3] In the assembly and the courts there were only citizens, but many of these citizens were also workers. This is the true meaning of the statement that the demos was lord of the market, of the harbours and of the pnyx.[4]

A further question relates to the economic importance of

[1] Isaios V, 7f, 40.

[2] Eur. *Hik.* 135, 219ff. Cf. also Ion's amazement that Kreusa had actually married a foreigner (*Ion* 293).

[3] Cf. Isaios V, 39: τοὺς δὲ περιεώρα τοὺς μισθωτοὺς ἰόντας δι᾿ ἔνδειαν τῶν ἐπιτηδείων.

[4] K.165f.

the metics and their effect on the economic position of the
citizens. This question is hard to answer because of the
poverty of evidence. Undoubtedly, however, trade and craft
needed the metics and had needed them ever since Solon had
favoured their settlement, and increasingly with the growing
demands of an always extending civilization.[1] That is to say,
neither trade nor manufacture would have flourished as they
did without the help of the metics. And the facts we have
enumerated show that, at the same time, there was no economic
jealousy between citizens and metics, except when the metics
usurped rights reserved for the citizens, for instance participa-
tion in the distributions of corn. On the whole, the metics
helped to create the prosperity of State and people, but in the
long run they might easily oust the citizens economically, since
the latter were frequently engaged in political duties. A man
who now and then closed his shop in order to attend the assembly or courts would certainly lose customers to the man whose
shop was always open. This is perhaps the chief reason for the
increasing and in some respects undue share which the metics
took in Athenian business life during the fourth century.[2]

The relations between citizens and metics involved only one
side, though the most important one, of the question of
foreigners in Athens. We have referred to the other foreigners
who though not few in number never came to form a unit.
Many of them remained in Attica only for a short time; others
settled there more or less permanently, but even then did not
form a social group of their own. Their common origin made
them associate in small circles and special cults, but they
remained individuals.[3] If economically important, they tried
to acquire the status of metics. Apart from them, there were the
slaves. We must consider, in the next chapter, to what degree
the economic role of both citizens and foreigners was influenced
by slave-labour.

There remains, however, one more question, based not on
social or economic, but on ethnical difference, the question of
Greek and non-Greek. To comedy the barbarians were little

---

[1] Cf. Plut. *Sol*. 24, 4; Aristotle, *pol*. 1275b, 36f; Ps.-Xen. I, 12.

[2] But the opinion about the general and overwhelming economic superiority
of the metics, and about the citizens 'forming a gigantic Civil Service' (Michell,
127), is mistaken both for the fifth and the fourth centuries.

[3] Cf. Pherekr. 11 (a rather obscure fragment), Archipp. 54.

more than material for many good-natured jokes. The great
number of passages about barbarians, some of which are given
above, prove that there were many non-Greek elements among
the population, especially among the poorer people. Even in
relation to the barbarians, the Athenian generally felt less of a
Greek than an inhabitant of Attica and an Athenian citizen.
There is no parallel to the scene when Philokleon, maltreated
by barbarian slaves, complains that they are 'barbarous men',
not that they are slaves.[1] The old form of antagonism to the
barbarians still survived, chiefly based on the nature of the
Polis; but as conditions developed socially and economically,
this antagonism became less strong and less conspicuous.
The value of Greek education overshadowed that of Greek
origin; the barbarian was the uneducated.[2] At the beginning
of this chapter we spoke of the first signs of a somewhat
'cosmopolitan' attitude. It is clear from comedy that first of
all for social but partly also for ethnical reasons, the substance
of the Polis, the self-contained citizen-body, became slack and
relaxed. This gradual internal disintegration of the Polis went
hand in hand with a deeper realization of the unity of mankind.
Athenian social life had a considerable influence on intellectual
development, and in the days of the sophists the foundations
were laid of those general conceptions of the relations between
man and man which prevailed during the Hellenistic Age.

[1] W.439.
[2] C.492. — It is well known that in many tragedies the relations between
Greeks and barbarians are of fundamental importance. Euripides in particular
discusses the question (and often it is a real discussion) from every possible point
of view. While he frequently treats 'barbarian' as a synonym to 'foreign' or even
to 'savage', and some of his characters as, e.g., Iason and Pentheus, maintain the
traditional Greek arrogance and exclusiveness, there are clear signs of a far more
generous and also more profound view — undoubtedly shared by the poet — which
finds the decisive criterion in the standards of civilized humanity. Cf., e.g.,
Andr. 243f, 261, *Iph. T.* 660, *Iph. A.* 558ff, *Ba.* 483f, and whole plays such as
Alexandros and the *Trojan Women* (cf. B. Snell, *Euripides' Alexandros*, 68).

CHAPTER VII

THE SLAVES

FOR some time past it has been acknowledged that slavery was not such an important element in Greek economic life as was formerly believed. There were many free workmen who frequently had to work much harder than many a slave. Nevertheless, social life both in town and country was inconceivable without slaves, and the idea of an age without them was merely one of the favourite fairy-tale motives of comedy. Women might be pictured in a primitive early age as forced to grind their own corn, or a man as making the furniture and the crockery on the dinner table move and work by themselves.[1] A misanthropic hermit, of course, like Timon, had neither wife nor slaves.[2] The thought of a life without slaves was so preposterous that even the ideal communist society had to include them, at any rate as agricultural workers.[3] The gods themselves had servants who were slaves: Polemos, for instance, was accompanied by Kydoimos; War was the master, Uproar his slave.[4]

Slavery was recognized as a normal and natural institution. It is significant that several words for the slave could be used without distinction. Both male and female slave were an 'unfree body', *andrapoda*, 'human-footed stock', corresponding to the *tetrapoda*, the 'four-footed stock'.[5] The fellow belonging to the household, the boy or the little boy, the servant and attendant — they all had different names which meant the same thing;[6] only occasionally was the specific function of a slave stressed by the use of one of these words.[7]

Slaves then were found everywhere, even in places where

---

[1] Pherekr. 10. — Krates 14.   [2] Phryn. 18 (read ἄδουλον for ἄζυγον).
[3] E.651.
[4] P.255. Cf. also the slave-girls of Helios in Euripides' *Phaëthon* (H. v. Arnim, *Supplementum Euripideum*, 69f. = *frg.* 773).
[5] Pherekr. 8.D, 16 D.
[6] δοῦλος, οἰκέτης, παῖς, παιδίον, ὑπηρέτης, διάκονος, ἀκόλουθος.
[7] But often a non-slave would be called by one of those less definite words, such as οἰκέτης (cf. e.g., Isokr. XIX 25f.).

perhaps one would not expect them. Chremylos — both he
and his friends were poor and hard-working peasants — owned
several slaves.¹ The metic women who keep small public-
houses in Hades appear on the stage, each with her maid.²
The bird Tereus, much to the surprise of the two Athenians,
has a bird slave as attendant who had been his slave when both
were human beings.³ A Dionysiac festival, with tragedy and
music and songs, with bleating lambs and wine and maenads,
was not complete without a drunken slave-girl 'and other good
things'.⁴ The Greeks could not visualize a life without slaves,
and everybody, even the most wretched market-woman, is
proud of being free and not a slave.⁵ It was a serious reproach
to be told that one behaved 'in the most slavish manner'.⁶ The
idea that master and slave should change places, even only for
a short time (as happened in comedy), was just as unthinkable
as that there should be no slaves at all; Dionysos expresses
himself in very drastic terms on the subject.⁷

In trying to find out what was the function of this necessary
part of the population, we must first inquire into the number of
slaves.⁸ In comedy just as in other sources nothing definite or
direct is said about the question of how many slaves were kept
in a normal household, either in town or country. Wealthy
landowners such as Ischomachos in Xenophon's *Oikonomikos*
had a number of slaves working in the fields, even under the

---

¹ Pl.253ff. — 26, 228, 1105. We ought not to try to interpret these facts away
by assuming that Chremylos is just a comic character, and 'a trusted slave' like
Karion merely a comedy type (Sargent, 77f).

² F.569ff. Some scholars believe that there were not two hostesses, but only
one and her maid. For our purpose both views lead to the same result.

³ B.69ff.   ⁴ P.530ff, 537f.

⁵ L.379, 463f. The fate of those who once had been free and masters themselves, and then became slaves who bewailed their misery and were either pitied
or scorned by others, is a well-known theme in tragedy. Cf., e.g., Eur. *Hek.* 332f,
354ff, 397, 448f, *Andr.* 12f, 29ff, 136ff, *Tro.* 614f, *El.* 898f.

⁶ Kratinos 403, Eupolis 396, Theopomp. 87.

⁷ F.541ff.

⁸ Against the popular over-estimation of the numbers of slaves cf. the careful,
if too schematic, investigation by Miss Sargent. Written from a more general
point of view, but on similar lines, are the valuable contributions of W. L. Westermann, *P.-W.*, Suppl. VI, s.v. *Sklaverei*, and *Athenian Studies for Ferguson* (1940),
451ff. If I disagree with him on some points, I completely share his views on the
part played by slaves in Greek economic life in general. On some points of
dispute in the question of slave numbers, see A. W. Gomme, *JHS.* LXVI (1946),
127ff.

control of several overseers who were also slaves.[1] But it cannot have been exceptional for a household to have only a single slave, especially where the sons and daughters helped with the work. The position of a single slave is described in the phrase: 'One slave is the absolute master of the house', which, by exaggerating his indispensability, inverts the usual relationship of master and slave.[2] Everybody aspired to have his 'attendant', his own servant, and even revolutionary thought considered it as bad to have no slave as to have no land, if only enough for one's own grave.[3] It is important to note this, because there exists a view, drawn mainly from some lists of property in Isaios, that there were some owners of not inconsiderable property who kept no slaves.[4] In fact, this view is hardly right; even the small farmer had a slave or a maid, and it is pressing Euripides' realism too far, if the extreme poverty of Elektra's husband, necessary for the plot of the play, is taken at its face value and as evidence that Attic farmers often worked without a slave.[5] Only of an exiled man, impoverished and ill, is it said that he has lost his last slave, and the poor cripple, who chiefly lived on his public rent of one obol a day, complains that he has no slave to take care of him.[6]

---

[1] Xen. *oik.* 12ff.   [2] frg. 645b, Kock, III, p. 725. Cf. Pl. 1ff.

[3] E.590ff. We remember the same idea (no soil for one's own grave) in the speeches of Tiberius Gracchus (Plut. 9, 5). But he spoke of the impoverished Italian peasantry. At his time, and in Italy, the slaves represented a political and economic problem, because the *latifundia* were worked by slaves and because there was the danger of slave revolts; but the position of the slaves as an object of reform did not concern the Gracchi any more than the Athenians of the fifth century.

[4] Westermann, *P.-W.*, Suppl. VI, 911, *Athenian Studies for Ferguson*, 468f. I believe that the conclusion is not proved for any of the cases (II, 29, 35, XI, 42, 44), since, for some unknown reason, only houses, fields and ready money are mentioned, but no household goods, in which slaves were probably included. In VIII, 35, some slaves who were let out and three house-slaves, but also τὰ ἔπιπλα, the movables, are mentioned. The passages Isaios V, 22f, 29, VIII, 8, and Lysias XXXII, 5 seem to me irrelevant; the last mentioned contains only money legacies. I cannot explain why slaves were frequently left out; but cf. de Ste. Croix, *CR.* VII (1957), 56. That it was done, despite the fact that they belonged to the property in question, is confirmed by Isaios VI, 33, a passage in which some goats are valued 'together with the goatherd' — which is nearly the same as no mentioning of the man at all. Xen. *mem.* II, 3, 3 is too vague to prove anything in this matter.

[5] Eur. *El.* 71ff, 78ff, 303ff. The man is expressly called an αὐτουργός (cf. also Eur. *Or.* 920).   [6] Isokr. XIX, 25f. — Lysias XXIV, 6.

Thus it is clear that people who could not be called wealthy owned a few slaves. The jurors, whose fees were of some importance to them (if sometimes only as pocket-money for their daughters), might yet own a steward and several other slaves.[1] The woman who early in the morning herself brought her home-spun work to the market for sale nevertheless kept some maids.[2] The sausage-seller, when a boy, had stolen the meat from the hearth in the presence of the cooks; we do not know, however, in what kind of house this happened.[3] It goes without saying that Strepsiades, being the husband of a niece of Megakles, had several slaves.[4] But none of these references proves that large numbers of slaves were kept. From all our evidence it has been concluded that numbers varying from three to twelve were normal in most houses.[5] There was sometimes a larger number of slaves in workshops, but they are never mentioned in comedy. Lysias, in speaking of the 120 slaves owned by his father, who was an unusually rich metic, included in that number slaves both of the household and of the workshop.[6]

Generally speaking, slaves were acquired by purchase, though a slave in a temple may have been given as an offering to the god.[7] The chief market-day for slaves (and cattle) seems to have been the day of the new moon.[8] 'Who is the man selling the slaves?' someone shouts.[9] Slaves for sale frequently stood on a table, so that they could easily be seen by everybody.[10] Of course, the trader, the 'slave-dealer', tried to make the slaves look as healthy and strong as possible, like the bird-seller who manipulated his animals in various ways.[11]

[1] W.606ff.   [2] F.1346ff. Mistaken by Knorringa, *Emporos*, 53.
[3] K.418f. The plural of the μάγειροι is remarkable.   [4] C.5.
[5] Glotz, 200. It comes to slightly less when Gomme speaks of 'no more than one domestic servant per adult among the hoplite and richer classes, and very few among the thetes'. An average of three for a well-to-do household (Michell, 161) seems an equally low estimate; Miss Sargent's detailed and differentiated account of the slaves owned by members of the various social classes also tends to present very moderate numbers.
[6] Lysias XII, 19. There is no evidence, as far as I can see, which could justify the widely held view that the 120 were employed in the 'shield factory' alone.
[7] Eur. *Ion* 310.   [8] K.43f, W.170f.   [9] Hermipp. 50.   [10] frg. 874.
[11] B.1077ff. The slave-dealer was called ἀνδραποδιστής (Pl.521, cf. K.1030) or ἀνδραποδώνης (frg. 312), and there could be also an ἀνδραποδοκάπηλος (Isaios in Harpokr, s.v.); cf. above, p. 119, n. 3. Euripides makes the slave-dealer a ψυχαγωγός who is either a sorcerer or just a scoundrel (Eur. *frg.* 933).

The Thessalian traders had a special reputation for not being afraid of enslaving even free Greeks; this was a dangerous but lucrative business.[1] It was possible because, during the war and even more after the final decline of Athenian sea-power, piracy became, once again, more frequent.[2] There were also cases of children being kidnapped. Runaway slaves found a temporary, but often-used, asylum in the sanctuary of the *Semnai* or Eumenides, or particularly in the Theseion, where they had to offer themselves for re-sale.[3] Thus they avoided punishment, and the buyer got cheap goods. We are not told in comedy anything about the price of slaves, but we know that it varied very much.[4] Occasionally a slave whom the master, for some reason, wanted to be rid of would be offered for sale at any price.[5]

New-bought slaves, that is to say, slaves who had not been brought up in the house, were welcomed at the door like a newly wed couple, nuts and figs being thrown at them, a rite which was to make their work a blessing to the house.[6] Apart from them, there were slave-children, born or brought up in the house.[7] We do not hear of prisoners of war, but we know that many of the slaves, especially women and children, had lost their freedom in this way, and this happened also during the Peloponnesian War.[8] It is interesting to note that even in the fourth century a man could become enslaved through economic difficulties, 'because of a small sum'; as servitude for debts had been abolished in Athens as early as Solon, Karion, the slave concerned, must have been sold in his own country.[9] Financial

[1] Pl.520f.

[2] B.1427, Andok. I, 138, Xen. *hell.* II, 1, 30; cf. Plut. *Per.* 19, 1. H. A. Ormerod, *Piracy in the Ancient World*, 108ff. Ziebarth, 9ff.

[3] K.1312, Th.224, frg. 458-9, 567, Eupolis 225; in general cf. Eur. *Hik.* 268. See below, p. 188.

[4] Cf. Xen. *mem.* II, 5, 2.   [5] Eupolis 258.   [6] K.2, Pl.768f, cf. Theop. 14.

[7] Th.426, 564f. The word σηκίς (W.768), a rare expression used to indicate a female slave or a housekeeper, seems to have meant originally 'born in the house' (Poll. III, 76). It became a normal slave-name (Pherekr. 10). It is well known

[7] that slave children are of importance in some tragic plots (cf. Eur. *Andr.* 24f, 199f, 638, 942, *Ion* 1382f).

[8] Westermann, *op. cit.* 905. This was, of course, the most common feature in mythical stories and therefore in tragedy.

[9] Pl. 147f. The phrase μικρῶν ἕνεκα συμβολαίων δουλεύειν occurs at least twice in our sources (Lys. XII, 98, Isokr. XIV, 48), in both cases referring to places abroad. Apparently it was fairly common in Athens that slaves had suffered such a fate.

distress may have driven many a free man into slavery, just as the Megarian in the *Acharnians* is forced by hunger and poverty to sell his daughters into slavery.[1]

We do not know much of the relations between the slaves themselves. The two slaves of Demos, who feared the Paphlagonian, prove little, but there was, of course, in all households with a larger number of slaves, and in workshops also, a kind of hierarchy with at least one chief slave. Incidentally, the expression 'fellow slaves' had a double meaning: either slaves of the same master, or human beings in the same circumstances.[2] The two words used to indicate the different meanings reveal the two sides of the social position of slaves — their relations with their master and with their fellow slaves. From comedy we learn no more of solidarity among slaves than from other sources, although it must often have existed, at least among those belonging to the same household; nor do we get further evidence about the personal and family life of the slaves. To an enslaved Trojan princess it might seem the utmost disgrace to have to sleep with a slave, but in everyday life unions between male and female slaves must have been common, and a wise master would lock up at night the female slaves in the women's quarter in order to prevent undesirable intercourse.[3] If some of the slave-children were the master's bastards, most of them certainly were born from slave parents. However, all this was of little general interest to the audience in the theatre; to the public mind slaves really existed only in relation to their masters.

Even before Aristophanes the slave had been developed as a typical person in comedy, though the type is hardly to be considered as a true specimen of an actual slave. No doubt, the stage-figure had developed from reality, and this is true of tragedy as well as of comedy. The utterance, for example, of Phaidra's nurse: 'It is better to be sick than to tend the sick', is realistic, but at the same time typical.[4] The mere fact that the type was complete in its essential features at such an early date arouses suspicion. The insolent and lazy slave, foolish and cunning, who cried because he had been beaten, was

---

[1] A.812ff.

[2] Poll. *onom.* III, 82. σύνδουλοι: P.745, Theop. 32, 7, Eur. *Andr.* 64, *Ion* 1109; ὁμόδουλοι: Euthykl. 4, Eur. *Hek.* 60. Cf. also F.756.

[3] Eur. *Hek.* 365f. — Xen. *oik.* 9, 5.   [4] Eur. *Hipp.* 186.

almost a necessity for dramatic purposes; he was the buffoon
who could only rarely be found among the characters at
bourgeois level.[1] The Xanthias of the *Frogs* and the Karion
of the *Ploutos* are hardly characteristic specimens of the slaves
of their age. Among other reasons for this view it may be
emphasized that the comic type (this does not mean every
individual slave who played a part in comedy) was always a
Greek, while in real life many of the slaves, perhaps the
majority, were non-Greek. The right method of investigation
is, as always, to search for information in incidental evidence,
not in characters intentionally shaped by the poets.

The Paphlagonian Kleon, therefore, is not a good example
of a non-Greek slave. He is a Paphlagonian chiefly so that it
may be said of him by way of a pun: 'the man boils over', he
is 'bubbling up' like boiling pea-soup, he is boastful and bluster-
ing.[2] Moreover, his slavery is only fictitious, and before long
the Paphlagonian is called a citizen.[3] It would, however, have
been impossible to bring this figure on the stage unless, as we
know from all our evidence, the barbarian slave was quite common in Athens. There were, above all, Lydians and Phrygians.[4]
Manes — also the name of the bronze post of the kottabos
game: a 'dumb waiter', so to speak — and Mania were typical
slave-names of Phrygian origin; Manodoros was a Greek varia-
tion.[5] A maid called Syra had come from Syria, and Sikon
was a name derived perhaps from the original population of
Sicily.[6] An Arabian cithara-player was certainly a rarity,[7] while
Carians seem to have been fairly common. It was a good joke
to alter the well-known cry at the Anthesteria: 'Be off, you
Keres' (who were demons of death) into 'Be off, you Carians.'[8]
Egyptians are mentioned as brick-carriers and as doing other

---

[1] B.1328. — P.743ff.

[2] ἀνὴρ παφλάζει, K.919; cf. P.314, B.1243. — frg. 498, cf. Kratinos 206.

[3] K.335.

[4] W.433, 1309, B. 762, 1244, frg. 566, Plat. 170, Polyzel. 5; cf. Eur. *Alk.*
675f, *Or.* 1111ff.

[5] P.1146, B.523, 1311, 1329, L.908, 1211, Pherekr. 10. — Hermipp. 47,
Nikoch. 10. — Th.728, 739, 754, F.1345, Pherekr. 125. — B.657.

[6] P.1146. — E.867.

[7] Kantharos 1.

[8] θύραζε, κῆρες became θύραζε, Κᾶρες (adesp. 548, cf. B.764). This is disputed. Κᾶρες is taken as an ancient error or even as the original form. R.
Ganszyniec, *Eranos* XLV (1947), 100ff, explains it as referring to the slaves
present at the festival. Cf. now H. J. Rose, *Harv. Theol. Rev.* XLIII, 1950, 159.

heavy labour.[1] Slave-girls came frequently from Thrace; they are mentioned as housemaids and attendants, and as the servants of farmers.[2] Sometimes Thratta was used as a proper name. The name of Masynthias, too, is said to be of Thracian origin.[3] Among public slaves, the policeman was a Scythian, and therefore the female public servant in the *Lysistrate* is also Scythian.[4] Even in Hades the police-slaves have barbarian names.[5] Negro slaves, who later on became fashionable, are not mentioned in comedy.[6]

The names reflect the multicoloured picture of Attic slavery most clearly.[7] They include any number of variations, from the name of the great Phrygian king, Midas, to the flute-player Teredon, the 'wood-worm', and the 'rubbish-heap' Syrphax.[8] The comedians naturally favoured either typical or unusual names, and generally preferred not to use those which were also used for free people; it is unlikely that there were many of that kind. One slave-name was perhaps invented by a comic poet, that of Sosias; though at that time citizens also were occasionally so called, Sosias was later used exclusively and commonly for slaves.[9] Apart from origin, a physical or mental attribute, whether desired or actually existing, was often expressed by a slave's name. Hylas probably was expected to be as beautiful as the hero of this name, Parmenon was meant to be faithful and persevering and Pistos trustworthy, Spinther as quick as a 'flash', Chrysos had fair, and Xanthias (or in the

---

[1] B.1133f, F.1046. From a number of records we know in particular that in building-work citizens, metics and slaves took part without distinction (*IG.* I², 374, II, 5ff, II², 1672, 33). Aristophanes speaks only of the μισθωτοί (B.1152) or the φορτηγοί (frg. 886). It may be, however, that the Egyptians are mentioned only because of the pyramids, of which everybody had heard, and that they actually never worked in Greece.

[2] A.273, W.828, P.1138, Th.279f, 293f; cf. Antiphon V, 20.

[3] W.433.

[4] τοξότης, Th.1001ff. — L.184.

[5] F.608.

[6] The slave in Plate XIV*a* shows negro features, but has no dark skin, as that could not be represented on r.f. vases.

[7] Cf. Lambertz, *Griech. Sklavennamen*, Progr. Vienna, 1907.

[8] W.433. — Th.1175, cf. K.1308. — Plat. 160ff. If, however, someone called his slaves Mousaios and Hesiodos (Lysias, *frg.* 8), it must have been the caprice of a literary snob; it was certainly exceptional.

[9] W.136. I consider it most unlikely that in W.78 one of the spectators is meant by ὁδὶ ... Σωσίας, and not the slave of this name who stands on the stage.

PLATE XIV

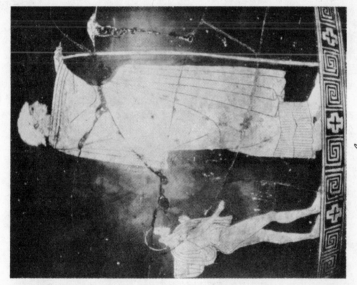

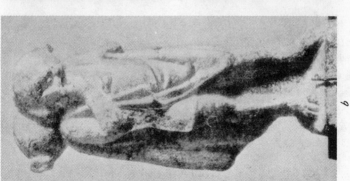

SLAVES

PLATE XV

a

b

c

HETAERAE

pet form: Xanthidion) red hair.[1] The last name was so frequent that it confirms the existence of a great number of
Thracian and Scythian slaves.[2]

The outlook of comedy is, as always, limited; but as to the
origin of slaves and the way they were acquired, no evidence
from other sources adds much to the picture. For instance, the
male and female slaves of the metic Kephisiodoros were offered
for sale, as we know from an inscription; they included
Thracians, Syrians, Carians, Illyrians, Scythians, Colchians,
Cappadocians and Lydians.[3] Probably the ratio of Greek to
non-Greek slaves, indicating a certain preponderance of non-
Greeks, is rightly reflected in comedy. The fact that so many
non-Greeks were among the slaves gave force to the assertion
that the Eastern peoples were naturally destined to be the
slaves of the Greeks. This view took its justification from
mythical events like the Trojan War, but dominated contemporary opinion, and was largely based on the assertion that in
the East all but the king were slaves.[4]

Comedy is also true to life in representing female slaves as
outnumbering the male slaves. They were in part servants of
the mistress, in part concubines of the master or, in general,
servants of Aphrodite.[5] The child of a maidservant, born in the
house, was sometimes put in the place of the child of the
mistress, a boy for instance in the place of a girl.[6] Naturally,
most of the work of the female slave was housework.[7] The
comedians sometimes refer to lazy or drunken slave-girls, or
to an allied city talking like an ill-treated maid.[8] We shall see
further on that these various features will fit into a general
picture.

Of male slaves we may first mention the public servants,
who formed a group of their own.[9] The *demios*, or executioner,

---

[1] K.67. — E.868. — Theop. 32, 8; *IG.* I², 329 (*Syll.*³ 96, Tod, 79), 9. —
W.1251 (where Wilamowitz, however, reads Κροῖσε instead of Χρυσέ). — A.243,
C.1485, W.1, 136, B.656, F. *passim* (Ξανθίδιον, F.582), Kephisod. 3.

[2] Kratinos 336.　　　　　[3] *IG.* I², 329 (Tod, 79).

[4] Cf., e.g., Eur. *Hek.* 479ff, *El.* 315f, *Hel.* 274ff, *Iph. A.* 1400f.

[5] L.328f, Th.279ff, F.569f, E.1113, 1126, Kratinos 256. — A.271ff, 812ff,
W.1351ff, F.519, E.721f, 1117.

[6] Th.564f.

[7] Krates 14, Phyrn. 2 D. Cf. below, p. 176.

[8] P.537, frg. 34 D, adesp. 590. — Eupolis 225.

[9] δημόσιοι (sc. δοῦλοι or ὑπηρέται) was their general title.

is mentioned once; otherwise we hear only, though a good deal, of the policemen.[1] It is uncertain whether the 'dung-gatherers' or 'scavengers' were slaves; they were perhaps private day-labourers, though they seem to have been those who had 'to besprinkle and to sweep again the market-place', work typical of private slaves in the house.[2] There is also no proof that the 'mortar-carriers', apparently the lowest class of men engaged in the building-trade, were slaves or even public slaves.[3] The beadles of the judges in the theatre were almost certainly officials, that is citizens.[4] It is surprising that the comic poets never mention any of the public slaves who worked in the courts and offices, for instance in the mint.[5] They were a group of real importance, 'the only non-elective and permanent Civil Service'.[6] From an inscription we learn that in Eleusis at the *Choes* such public slaves were entertained at the public expense with meat and wine; two of them were even initiated.[7] Occasionally, when the talk is of those who fought at Arginusae and subsequently received citizenship, slaves are mentioned as oarsmen serving in the fleet.[8] They may have been private slaves who could not join up without their masters' consent, but by serving in the fleet they served the State. Whatever

[1] δήμιος: E.79; cf. Lysias XIII, 56. He could also be called δημόκοινος (Antiphon I, 20, Isokr. XVII, 15).

[2] ἄνδρ:ς κοπρολόγοι: W.1184, P.9, frg. 662. O.Jacob, *Les esclaves publiques à Athènes*, 13ff, regards them as free labourers. — The line quoted is Pherekr. 5 D; for the same activity of private slaves, see p. 176, n. 12.

[3] E.309f, cf. B.1142. The phrase E.309f is, I believe, misunderstood by Francotte, I, 314. He assumes that here public slaves are concerned, and that the triobolon was a special form of payment ('*pas un salaire, mais une indemnité de nourriture*'). The πηλοφοροῦντες are simply a comparison intended to put to shame the citizens who filled the assembly once more since a fee of three obols had been introduced.

[4] They were the ῥαβδοῦχοι (P.734). Cf. Thuc. V, 50, 4.

[5] Andok. *frg.* 5 = schol. W. 1007. Here, Hyperbolos' father is described as a branded slave working in the ἀργυροκοπεῖον. The story is clearly made up, though it seems that such a thing could happen.

[6] Michell, 358. The clerks and minor officials mentioned in comedy seem all to have been citizens (K.1256 — although the speaker is one of the Paphlagonian's 'slaves' — F.1083ff, 1505f).

[7] The inscription (*IG.* II², 2, 1672 [*Syll.*² 587], 204, 206) is close enough to our period (329-328 B.C.) to be used as evidence for circumstances which were sacred and unlikely to be altered. Cf. also Ps.-Dem. LIX, 21 (about 340 B.C.).

[8] F.33, 190ff, 693ff, 700ff.

their status, the case was exceptional, and in general the fleet was manned by citizens of the lower classes.

None of the groups of public slaves mentioned gave much scope for fun; the Scythian archers who served as policemen emphatically did. They had come to Athens after the Persian War, about the middle of the century, when there were still citizens serving as archers in the army.[1] Apparently the Scythians were militarily organized in four *lochoi*, and possibly comprised altogether about 300 men.[2] It seems doubtful whether their chief weapon was the whip, which would correspond to the modern rubber truncheon; perhaps that is an invention of comedy.[3] At any rate, as their usual name of 'bow-men' shows, they carried the bow as well as spear and knife.[4] One of their main duties was to keep order in assembly and council; generally they acted as the servants of the prytaneis or other officials.[5] Their uncouth behaviour, their broken Greek and their alleged stupidity were open to derision, and so provided the poet with a useful and easy target for fun.[6] It is somewhat surprising that the Athenian State gave barbarian slaves executive powers over citizens; but the comedians hardly ever suggest any resentment on the citizens' part at the power of the Scythians. Only Lysistrate's feminine pride is outraged by the grip of a policeman who 'is a public slave'.[7] On one occasion, a person maltreated by a bowman merely arouses pity because of his age, and it is even probable that the 'bowman' here mentioned was an advocate alleged to be of Scythian origin.[8] The existence of these policemen was generally accepted without grumbling and without any feeling of humiliation; it is best, however, to assume that they did not use the whip. There was even less resentment against other public slaves who as a rule were Greeks and, being more or less well educated, dealt with important public matters.[9]

---

[1] Andok. III, 5. — *IG.* I², 44.

[2] L.451ff. — Andok. *l.c.* But there is also different evidence (cf. schol. A.54). The question of their number is obscure.

[3] Th.933, 1125, 1135.   [4] Th.1127, 1197, 1215.

[5] A.54ff, K.665, L.184, 433ff, E.142f, 258f. — Eupolis 258.

[6] L.424ff, Th.1001ff, 1082ff, 1176ff.   [7] L.436.

[8] A.706f. — 704f, 712. Similarly a citizen, as we have mentioned before, complains only of maltreatment by *barbarians*, though they were also slaves (W.439).

[9] Cf. Lysias XXX, 2ff.

Private slaves are mentioned in comedy much more frequently than public slaves, and domestic slaves play a very large part, as they certainly did in everyday life.[1] When someone knocked at the door, he expected a slave to open to him.[2] Steward, housekeeper and cook were slaves; they were found in houses where a larger number of slaves was kept, and a division of labour was therefore usual.[3] Frequently a slave, either man or woman, went shopping in the market.[4] The maids went to the spring and the wells for water.[5] Slaves of both sexes, who often had to be called in the morning by the mistress, cleaned the house and waited at meals.[6] It is perhaps a joke, or at least the exception rather than the usual custom, that the slave should offer his hair to the master to wipe his hands on after he had blown his nose, or that the drinkers should cry during a party: 'Boy, the chamber-pot!'[7] The flute-players, who played during dinner, often did not belong to the house, but were hired. Slave-girls ground the corn, but it was a punishment to be sent to the mill.[8] Slaves kneaded the dough, and perhaps wore the famous collar to prevent them from putting something in their mouths.[9] It probably often happened that a domestic slave stole some food; at any rate, this is a typical practice of the slave of comedy.[10] The general evidence of comedy as to the duties of slaves is supported by a number of passages in Euripides, in which the typical duties, especially of female slaves, are described; foremost among them are: sprinkling the floor and cleaning the house, grinding corn and making bread, and weaving cloth.[11]

[1] Aristotle declares that the holding of slaves serves πρᾶξις, which represents life, not ποίησις, which means production (*pol.* 1254a, 7f).

[2] F.37, cf. Pherekr. 86, also Eur. *Tro.* 492f. Aiakos (F.465), who opens the door for Dionysos-Herakles, is later not a slave (F.616f). Cf. Radermacher, 211. It is probably on account of this inconsistency that in our MSS. the person conversing with Xanthias (738ff) is sometimes called Aiakos and sometimes οἰκέτης Πλούτωνος.

[3] W.613. — Xen. *oik.* 9, 10ff. — K.418, Philyll. 10. In this fragment cook and flute-player seem to have the same social status. They may be hired men, but they are hardly free men. See Plates IIIa, XIVc.

[4] frg. 299, 503, Pherekr. 126; cf. Lysias I, 8.   [5] L.328ff.

[6] L.18 — Phryn. 2 D. — Krates 14, Pherekr. 184, Ameips. 2.

[7] K.910. — Eupolis 351, 5. [8] Pherekr. 10. — Lysias I, 18   [9] frg. 301-2.

[10] P.14, Pl.320, 1139f.

[11] Eur. *Hek.* 332f, *Andr.* 166f, *Tro.* 491ff, *Ba.* 514, *frg.* 773, 10ff; 12 P, 31ff. Ion (cf. *Ion* 102ff, 128ff, and elsewhere) is Apollo's slave; that probably means: no true slave at all (cf. Meunier, *L'antiquité class.* XXVII [1958], 451), but a private slave's duties could be very similar.

An important duty of slaves was to attend their masters in
the streets (see Plate XIV*a*) — with a lamp or torch, if dark-
ness had set in.[1] If the master had to be fetched from a dinner-
party, which might, but did not always, last far into the night,
it may have been a difficult and sometimes even dangerous
task to bring him safely home.[2] For in many cases the gentleman was drunk, and besides, the streets were apt to be unsafe
on a dark night.[3] When the young son went to the palaestra,
a slave, carrying his ball and strigil, accompanied him.[4] When
the mistress went for a walk, the maid carried behind her the
box, the contents of which — besides the cake for the sacrifice —
may have resembled those which nowadays a lady carries in
her handbag.[5] On longer journeys the slave had to carry the
luggage on a wooden bearing-pole on his shoulder (see Plate
XIV*b*).[6] When the journey led to Delphi — and it may well
have been the same at most of the other holy places — the
attendant slave shared the meat of the sacrifice and also wore
a wreath.[7] No doubt, the relations between master and domestic slave were often close and patriarchal.[8] More than that, a
slave-girl frequently made herself pretty so as to please her
master, and slaves sometimes slept with their mistress.[9]

As a rule, however, sexual relations between citizens and
slaves were confined to those between free men and slave
women and girls. Such relations were of great social importance, as we should naturally expect in an almost purely male
society, as that of the Greek cities was at that time. It is
significant of the current standard of morals that the adultery
of a wife, or of a man with a married woman, was heavily
punished, but otherwise the sexual life of the men was abso-
lutely free, as long as they did not try to make money by it.[10]

Sexual relations between the male members of a family and
the slave-girls were frequent.[11] Thus we find the grown-up
son falling in love with a young slave-girl.[12] There may have

---

[1] B.69ff, F.569ff, Pl.823. — Pherekr. 40; cf. C.614.
[2] frg. 464. — Pherekr. 6 D.   [3] Antiphon, *tetral.* I.
[4] frg. 139.   [5] κίστη, Th.279ff, 285.
[6] F.8, 12ff, 165ff, frg. 323, 559, 852, Xen. *mem.* III, 13, 6.
[7] Pl.21, 227f.
[8] Pl.1ff, frg. 645b. Ample evidence for this can be found in tragedy.
[9] E.1117. — Th.491, frg. 695, perhaps adesp. 5 D = 44 P, 18f.
[10] Punishment of adulterer: C.1083; see below, p. 196.
[11] Cf. also ch. VIII.   [12] frg. 9.

been occasional parallels to the many mythical stories in which a conquering hero takes an enslaved captive girl as his mistress. Quite another matter, though usually also slaves, were the professional hetaerae, 'mercenary women', 'common women'.[1] They were of very different origin, and included Greeks as well as barbarians. Besides Corinth and Megara, which are often mentioned, Lesbos seems to have been especially the home also of this kind of love.[2] The comedians in general exhibit a very low type of hetaera, and we may assume that the girl who was able to meet men on a high intellectual level, such as we hear of more frequently in the following centuries, as for instance Isokrates' friend Lagiska, was an exception in the days of Aspasia.[3] Flute-players, however, and dancers formed a large number of the hetaerae (see Plates IX, XV).[4] They might belong to a master who hired them out, lived on their earnings and often cruelly exploited them.[5] Other hetaerae had no special accomplishment; fond of dresses and perfumes, they lived on love and for love, protected by 'master, friend and lover'.[6] Some of them lived with their lovers, or even with two lovers.[7] It is not surprising that these girls, partly free women, but the great majority of them slaves, sometimes had sexual relations also with slaves.[8] Lysias tells us that many hetaerae gave up their profession when still very young; they were probably free women or manumitted slaves who had induced their lovers to marry them.[9] Many of the hetaerae lived alone, and were dependent on the business efficiency of procurers and, even more frequently, procuresses.[10] Some of them were very well known all over the town, and one man would ask another: 'Have you been spending the night at that impertinent strumpet's?'[11] Another could be admired for her beauty which

---

[1] Andokides IV, 14. — Phryn. 74. — πεȝαί, Eupolis 169, Plat. 155. Another expression is inexplicable: κασαλβάδες, frg. 478.

[2] Strattis 26. — Pherekr. 149.

[3] Lagiska: Strattis 3.

[4] W.1353, 1368, Plat. 155, Archipp. 27, Metag. 4, Aristagoras 2. — C.996f, F.514ff, Krates 27, Eupolis 77.

[5] Myrtilos 4, cf. Xen. *symp.*, *passim*.

[6] E.721, 1117. — Lysias, *frg.* 18.

[7] P.439f. — Lysias IV, 8.

[8] W.500, E.721.

[9] Lysias, *frg.* 44, Isaios III, 17.

[10] L.957f, Th.335ff, 1177ff, adesp. 8.

[11] K.765, W.1032, Th.98, 805, F.1328. — Eupolis 344.

would 'glow through her garment like a flame from a new lantern'.[1]

Many hetaerae lived in brothels.[2] The owner often had only two girls; in such a case it was possible to speak of his 'yoke', his pair, of cattle.[3] A drachme was apparently a small fee for a visit, but a stater, either a *didrachmon* or a *tetradrachmon*, rather much for 'medium' goods.[4] The brothel was a normal place of accommodation and rest, in town as well as on a journey.[5] Most frequently it was situated near the gates of the town or in the harbour-districts.[6] There visitors and hetaerae drank wine, played kottabos and the girls danced naked and clean-plucked.[7] There were 'falling-ripe' girls or half-children, 'firm as salted olives',[8] though there were others who retired only at a fairly advanced age.[9] It was also possible for a man, without any harm to his own status as a respected member of society, to send his concubine to a brothel.[10] The story of the girls of Aspasia, whose abduction was said to have been the cause of the war, implies that Perikles' mistress was a brothel-keeper.[11] That view is one of the coarse marks of disrespect shown by the comedians, but was perhaps shared by part of the people; Lysikles, who married Aspasia after Perikles' death, is mentioned in one breath with two well-known hetaerae.[12] Sometimes Herakles is depicted at a brothel as a guest who is finally turned out, and even Persephone had to provide him not only with plenty of food and drink, but also with girls.[13] The owners of the brothels who earned their living from the girls, or the hetaerae, if they lived by themselves, had to pay special taxes which were farmed out in the

---

[1] frg. 8. I retain Salmasius' correction of κενῷ into καινῷ, since an empty lantern does not make sense; in Pherekr. 40 we hear of a light put into a lantern. The woman wears an ἐξωμίς, normally a poor man's or slave's garment (see M. Bieber, *Griech. Kleidung*, p. 21 and pl. XXII, also below p. 184f), a short chiton which left one shoulder and part of the breast bare. Was it a somewhat daring costume suitable only for a hetaera?

[2] frg. 273, cf. P.849, Plat. 159, Isaios VI, 19f.

[3] adesp. 804, cf. P.842ff.   [4] Th. 1195. — Theop. 21.

[5] F.112f, Eupolis 40 P, 25. I confess, however, that I do not fully understand either the Greek or Page's translation of the latter passage.

[6] K.1398ff, adesp. 805. — P.165, Eupolis 48, Metag. 4, Aristag. 2.

[7] F.514ff, Krates 27, Plat. 46-7.   [8] frg. 141, adesp. 766.   [9] Isaios VI, 19.

[10] Antiphon I, 14. From §20 it is clear that she was a slave.

[11] A.524ff, cf. Eupolis 98.   [12] K.765.

[13] Plat. 46ff, 3 D. — F.504ff.

same way as other public resources; but this kind of business was, as we can easily understand, not highly esteemed.[1] Incidentally, a place with as bad a reputation as the brothel was the bath-house.[2]

It goes without saying that sexuality is unduly prominent in comedy; but public opinion was agreed that sexual intercourse with hetaerae was entirely natural and beyond moral criticism. The moral judgment of paederasty and its treatment in comedy are different. Probably even here the comic attitude followed a feeling held by many of the people. Paederasty may sometimes be depicted as a sort of last resort.[3] But, in general, it was the privilege of the rich youth; at any rate, it meant exclusively a relationship with free and noble boys.[4] No slave is ever mentioned as the object of homosexual love, though boys as well as girls could be flute-players and acrobats.[5] All the persons attacked in comedy for paederasty belong to the upper classes;[6] but paederasty as practised in Sparta, shared by all Spartiates, that is to say the whole of Spartan society, and considered a necessary part of its organization, was a thing unknown and foreign. The Spartan ambassador, who calls Lysistrate Lysistratos, makes some insinuations not appropriate to her as a woman, but in accordance with the notorious Spartan practice of paederasty.[7]

Thus slaves played an essential but limited part in the sexual life of the Athenians. Roughly the same is true of life in general. Women who wanted to do away with the competition of slave-girls both in their own houses and in the brothels

[1] P.850. — Philonid. 5.   [2] K.1401, F.1279f.   [3] L.1092.

[4] B.137ff, 707, Pl.155ff, adesp. 12-14, 338-9, Lysias III. Cf. above, p. 100ff.

[5] frg. 700, cf. Xen. symp., passim.

[6] The grotesque enumeration of those who were εὐρύπρωκτοι, all of them, ending with the τῶν θεατῶν πλείονες (C.1089ff), is hardly more than a coarse joke.

[7] L.1105, cf. 1148, 1174. It seems to be essential to distinguish between πυγή and πρωκτός, the latter being used in 1148. πυγή is an element of female beauty (cf. also Liddell and Scott, s. δωσίπυγος in Add.), while πρωκτός generally alludes to paederasty. The meaning of 1174 is rather disgusting, but the obscene explanation of the line is confirmed by P.11 and E.363ff. As far as I know, nobody has yet seen the peculiar tendency of the Laconian woman's words which in her mouth are certainly strange; but all other explanations of the 'Lysistratos' seem to be unsatisfactory. The plot, of course, excludes all possibilities of sexual intercourse except that of legally married couples, but there is another allusion to paederasty (1092).

are hardly more than a joke.[1] But open competition between
free people and slaves, which, as a universal feature of sexual
life, appears ridiculous and is only part of a comic Utopia, has
been regarded as a feature of economic activities in other
departments of life. Even if this were true, all our evidence
points to the fact — a very interesting fact indeed — that it was
no problem. Slave-labour was used by the side of free labour
in craft and manufacture, in a lesser degree also in trade and
least of all in farming.[2] 'Those who can afford it buy slaves
in order to have fellow-workers.'[3] The word fellow workers
is significant. It was as a complement, not in competition, that
slaves worked side by side with free men, citizens as well as
metics and foreigners. It is altogether a mistake to assume a
division of labour between the groups of the population. The
opposite has already been proved to be the case by the well-
known building records and by our investigation of the social
conditions of the metics.[4] Few of these slaves and free labourers
were skilled workmen, and the form of occupation is rarely of
any help in distinguishing between the two groups. It is, for
example, hard to decide whether the mule-drivers, standing
and chatting together in the streets, were slaves or free men
whose only capital might be represented by their animal.[5] The
'man who made a living by anointing', a servant in the palaestra,
was probably a free man who had found a modest way of
earning his living, though one in general more suited to a
slave.[6]

The dividing line between slaves in workshops or on farms
and domestic slaves is not always clear. We do not know, for
instance, whether the slaves with the big collar already mentioned baked bread for a private household or for a baker.[7]
Such border-line cases are frequent. It should be noticed that
the comedians refer to slaves outside the household as single
craftsmen only, not as workmen in a larger shop. However,
the *metalleis*, the mine-slaves, are mentioned. They are called
'sack-carriers', which means that they carried the ore in sacks
out of the pits. In fact, this was only one group of mine-

---

[1] E.718ff. Still, Gorgias (*frg.* 8ª Diels) mentions his love for a slave-girl and
his wife's jealousy.

[2] Cf. the numbers in Gomme, *Population of Athens*, 42f.

[3] Xen. *mem.* II, 3, 3. Cf. Pe. 223f.   [4] See ch. VI.   [5] frg. 633.

[6] ἀλειφόβιος, frg. 740.   [7] frg. 301-2. See pp. 126, 176.

workers, and probably consisted chiefly of boys.[1] Pherekrates wrote a comedy called *Metallēs*, in which a woman descended to Hades and described it as a sort of 'lotus land'.[2] It is easy to imagine that the good and lazy life below was set in contrast with the hard life of the miners; but the few fragments do not allow of any certain conclusion, and the comedian certainly did not advocate better social conditions for such slaves. He may, however, have attacked the rich who bought, that is to say rented, silver-mines, and sometimes employed several hundred mine-slaves.[3] It was, on the other hand, also possible to rent out to the mines one single slave.[4]

On the farms, slaves were chiefly occupied in the house, but also in the fields. When a slave was tied to an olive tree and flogged because he had stolen grapes, he was not necessarily only a worker in the vineyard. And if we find a slave working in the field, while a slave-girl did the domestic work, it does not prove that this was always the case. These two were of the same type as the 'house-slaves in the fields' who got their figs weighed out.[5] On the larger estates real agricultural labourers might be needed, but probably even there at times only when there was extra work to be done; so, for example, hired day-labourers, probably free men, were needed for gathering olives.[6] It was not worth while to feed slaves throughout the year, if they were needed only for a few weeks. We have seen that even small farmers had one or more slaves, but never for agricultural work only, and Aristotle's famous words can be applied to our period too: 'For the poor, the ox takes the place of the slave.'[7] The owner of a big estate had probably a certain small stock of regular workers who were slaves, but it was quite impossible, except in Utopian com-

---

[1] frg. 789. Ardaillon, *Les mines du Laurion*, 23, 91. S. Lauffer, *Abh. Ak. Mainz* 1955/56. In one of the Corinthian *pinakes* (*Antike Denkmäler*, I, 8, nr. 7; my Plate XIIIa) the miners use baskets, not sacks. This may show that they actually were not miners, but digging clay. At any rate, there is no reason to assume the same for the miners of Laureion, as Michell (100) does, giving a wrong translation of θυλακοφόρος.

[2] Pherekr. 108ff.

[3] K.362. — Xen. *Poroi* 4, 4, 14f.

[4] Andok. I, 38. This was one of the μισθοφοροῦντες δοῦλοι hired out for one obol a day.

[5] W.449f. — P.1146ff. — P.1249, οἰκέται ἐν ἀγρῷ.

[6] W.712.   [7] *Pol.* I, 1252b, 12.

munism,¹ to leave all (or even most) of the agricultural work
to slaves.

Free and slave-labour stood on the same economic level, and
hardly any branch of economic life was entirely closed to slaves.
This is the correct view of the part slavery played in the social
life of Athens, and it, too, may be illustrated by the evidence
of comedy. We must not take into account either Euripides'
slave, a perfect sophist like his master, who could be identified
with Euripides' friend and 'assistant' Kephisophon,² or the
two slaves of Demos, who probably represent the *strategoi*
Nikias and Demosthenes, and are sometimes therefore depicted as Attic citizens.³ These are purely figures of comedy.
But the slave of Dionysos persuades his master to take a paid
servant, that means a free workman, to carry the luggage, and
this is not a joke in itself. The joke lies, in fact, in the situation:
a dead man is summoned as a hired servant, and hard bargain-
ing follows.⁴ We see that a free day-labourer might, or might
not, undertake the work of a slave, according to the wage
offered. Many slaves were wage-earners themselves, and even
the wage offered to a free workman would only slightly exceed
the sum regarded as necessary for the upkeep of a slave. There
was no definite distinction, and we find the conclusions we
draw from other sources confirmed. No analogy except one
severely qualified, or perhaps indeed no analogy at all, should
be drawn between ancient slavery and what the modern world
calls 'the international proletariate'.

The evidence of comedy does not throw light on the whole
of the problem of slavery, chiefly because we learn almost
nothing about the slaves who were engaged in trade and manufacture. They were employed in small and large businesses,
but only in the latter can slave-labour have been of economic
importance. We have seen that slave-labour generally offered
hardly any competition to the labour of the free workmen,
since there never was unemployment on a large scale, and it
made no great difference to a man's fellow craftsmen if he kept
a few slaves in his workshop. Thus the question of free and
slave-labour is really the question of manufacturing on a small

---

¹ Cf. E.591f, 651.   ² A.396ff. — F.944, 1408, 1452f, frg. 580.
³ K.320, cf. 81ff. To die by drinking bull blood like Themistokles is certainly
not a slave's plan. They want to die ἀνδρικώτατα, like free men.
⁴ F. 165ff. The dead man was to be a μισθωτός.

or on a large scale. Since we do not believe in the predominant
economic importance of big *ergasteria*, where slave-labour was
generally preferred, we do not believe in the predominant role
of slave-labour in general. It was necessary and needed everywhere, but rather as supplementary and not as part of the
foundations of economic life. Free men never felt slave-labour
as a danger, hardly ever as a disadvantage. That is true of
both citizens and metics, and to citizens, who might feel the
competition of the metics, slave-labour was on the contrary a
help in their endeavours to make money while at the same time
carrying out their political duties.

This raises the question of the treatment of slaves, or to put
it in a more general way, the question of their social position.
Apart from the public slaves already mentioned, we may first
refer to the description of Athenian slaves given by a writer
roughly contemporary with the early works of Aristophanes,
the so-called 'Old Oligarch' or Pseudo-Xenophon.[1] He maintains that the position of slaves in Athens was the same as that
of metics and manumitted slaves, that they wore the same sort
of clothes as the citizens, that they even enjoyed *isegoria*, full
freedom of speech, and that many of them were rich and only
had to pay a fixed sum to their masters. Nobody was allowed
to beat another man's slave, and slaves did not even make way
in the streets.

Let us try to find out what the comedians can tell us of the
accuracy of this description, which is certainly a one-sided view.
We begin with the outward appearance and attire of slaves.
Here we are given a certain number of details. The slaves, for
instance, did not wear their hair long, but this was in any case
done only by noblemen.[2] There were no special clothes which
the slaves had to wear. But it could be said: 'Do dress like a
slave', and the Megarian *chlaniskidion* and the *katonake* were
clearly clothes worn chiefly by slaves, as distinguished from
the fine woollen *chlaina*.[3] The *exomis* also was counted a slave's
dress, and so was the *kyne*;[4] but these garments might also be
worn by poor citizens. The woman, on the other hand, who
complained that she no longer wore light sandals, decorated
with golden flowers, but *peribarides* like a slave-girl, must have
been something of a snob; for the *peribarides* were a quite

---

[1] Ps.-Xen. I, 10ff.   [2] B.911. — C.14f.
[3] Phryn. 2 D. — P.1002. — L.1151, 1155ff, E.723f.   [4] W.444f.

normal, indeed an elegant type of women's shoe.[1] When the oligarch in his pamphlet argues that one could not distinguish slaves and metics from citizens, this complaint was, to some extent, justified, especially when they were engaged in the same kind of work, as craftsmen, for instance, or as sailors.[2]

The master, of course, provided clothing and food for his slaves. Sometimes he gave them old and shabby garments, and different kinds of slaves could be equipped in different ways.[3] Their food consisted chiefly of bread or corn. Two *choinikes* of corn was an unusually large quantity, in fact double the average amount.[4] Besides this there were other cheap foods, such as salted fish, and some fruit, especially figs.[5] On special occasions the slaves got pastry, but the 'lobster sprinkled with salt' is a dish merely due to a mistaken correction of the text.[6] In general, slaves had the same food as poor people.

The treatment of slaves differed at all times, according to the characters of master and slave, for there were always good and bad masters as well as good and bad slaves.[7] After the outbreak of the Peloponnesian War, the treatment of slaves improved, a fact which suggests that many citizens were afraid that the slaves might run away, as, in fact, they did in large numbers, especially after the occupation of Dekeleia, when they could hope to escape without being recaptured.[8] Runaway slaves became a real danger during the war; as brigands they made the whole country unsafe even in the early years of the war.[9] Many of them had been mine-workers who had a very

---

[1] Kephisodor. 4. — L.45, 47, 53, Theop. 52.

[2] Cf. *IG*. II², 2, 1951. Prof. Webster adds that the 'Maison' mask, listed as a slave mask by Poll. *onom*. IV, 148f, was according to Festus, p. 134M, used for 'cooks, sailors, and such like'.

[3] W.444ff. — Xen. *oik*. 13, 10.

[4] Eur. *Alk*. 2, cf. L.1203f. — adesp. 444 (actually Menander, Heros 16), cf. Eupolis 40 P, 15ff.

[5] Plat. 193. — P.1249.   [6] Pl.764ff. — Aristomenes 6.

[7] Xen. *oik*. 3, 4. Eur. *frg*. 529. — Masters were εὔδουλοι (Pherekr. 212) or κακόδουλοι (Kratinos 81). Accordingly there were loyal and faithful slaves, and the opposite. In Euripides as well as the other tragedians particularly the former type is fairly common.

[8] C.5ff. — Thuc. VII, 27, 5. I do not share Westermann's view (*Athenian Studies for Ferguson*, 465) that the pluperfect in Thuc., *l.c.*, proves that the passage about the 20,000 slaves must refer to the whole period between 413 and 404 (in spite of *Hell. Oxyrh*. 12, 4).

[9] A.1187ff. In Euripides' *Herakleidai* the herald, demanding the return of the children of Herakles, speaks of them as runaway slaves (140, 267).

hard life; their iron fetters have been found in the galleries of
Laureion. The life of a slave was not in fact so splendid as the
'Old Oligarch' professes to believe. To run away was to many
slaves worth attempting, though it happened rarely that a
slave tried to murder his master.[1]

Free men and women frequently indulged their pride towards slaves without restraint.[2] The master was always the
absolute lord and owner, the *despotes*.[3] Therefore to kill one's
own slave was not a legal crime, although it involved religious
pollution.[4] It was possible to speak of a yoke for three slaves
as for oxen.[5] A slave was a piece of property, and the master
was its owner;[6] he did not argue, but gave orders.[7] Contempt
for slaves was a natural attitude and very common, but reaction
against it set in at an early date. It was partly an outcome of
the usually good relations between slave and master, but
chiefly and finally derived from a fundamental change of outlook, which is reflected in tragedy rather than in comedy, and
which regards freedom in the light of independence of mind
rather than that of the physical person.[8] On the other hand, the
rich Athenians had very little of that Roman upstart pride in
owning as many slaves as possible. They liked to have 'beautiful weapons, good horses, and splendid furniture', while their
wives spent their money on 'expensive clothes and golden
finery'.[9] Even the gravestones which frequently show the
mistress together with a slave-girl, display her love for jewellery

---

[1] αὐτομολεῖν, K.21ff. — An attempt to murder was once made by a boy of
eleven (Antiphon V, 69).

[2] L.330f, 379, 463f, F.542ff, E.721ff, 941, Eur. *frg.* 216.

[3] e.g., W.67, 442, P.54, 80, 90, Pl.2.

[4] Antiphon VI, 4.   [5] frg. 576.

[6] E.1126, Pl.4, Phyrn. 48, Sannyrion 11, Eur. *Med.* 49, *Hek.* 397. One man,
though, could claim to be κυριώτερος than another (Eur. *Andr.* 580).

[7] adesp. 538. I do not think it is right to say, at least as regards the average
owner: 'the master is ὁ δεσπότης, not merely ὁ κεκτημένος' (G. R. Morrow,
Cl. Phil. 32 (1937), 226). The expression δεσπότης alone does not prove the
point: also a not very masterlike Hermes (P.377, 385, 388, 399, 648, 711), since
he is a god, and a rich man contrasted with a parasite (frg. 491), are so called.

[8] Cf., e.g., Eur. *Ion*, 854ff, *Hel.* 728ff, 1640, *fr.* 511, 831. Both points of
view found striking expression in the *Alexandros*. Cf. also the description of
Kapaneus who was equally courteous towards slaves and citizens (Eur. *Hik.*
869ff).

[9] Xen. *poroi*, 4, 8. I wonder whether this general attitude has something to do
with the fact that slaves are so frequently omitted in lists of property (see above,
p. 167).

rather than any personal relationship such as Alkestis enjoyed, whom her slaves loved like a mother.[1]

On the whole, therefore, the description of Ps.-Xenophon is seen to be exaggerated; we know for a fact that slaves were beaten often enough. Though we may assume that here the comic poets, too, exaggerate, flogging was certainly the usual punishment.[2] A slave might be put in the stocks and whipped, and a comedian coined even a special word for the poor fellow.[3] One of the favourite etymological jokes was to derive the word for 'boy' and 'slave' from the word for 'to strike'; thus even an old slave could be addressed as 'boy', because he was beaten so often.[4] The slaves were subject to their masters' arbitrary desire to beat them, and this is confirmed by a remark like this: 'When the cook has spoiled the food, the flute-player will be beaten.'[5] Comedy as well as other sources affords evidence of the frequent practice of offering to submit slaves to cruel torture in order to prove the innocence of their master in court.[6] Evidence given by tortured slaves was often looked upon as being especially trustworthy, but when offered in a trial, the opponent would normally argue that the testimony of slaves in general and under torture in particular had no value.[7] It was probably a view shared by many, though contested by others, that 'a slave was unable to say the truth, unless it suited his master'.[8] This ambiguity perhaps more than reasons of humanity increasingly prevented the parties from making use of their opponents' offers. The comic situation in the *Frogs*, when the slave offers for torture his master Dionysos with whom he has changed clothes, also gives ground for supposing that torture was seldom actually used.[9] Athens could even pride herself that 'equal law' was applied, whether a citizen or a

---

[1] Eur. *Alk.* 769, cf. 948f.

[2] K.4f, 27ff, 64ff, W.449f, 1292f, 1325, P.743ff, F.745ff, Pl.21, 271ff, 1144, frg. 651 (even for a woman as in Isokr. XVIII, 52ff, and as a threat in Lysias I, 18), Phryn. 36 (?)

[3] κλῳομάστιξ, adesp. 1039. κλῳός = κλοιός is a wooden collar.

[4] παῖς from παίειν. W.1296ff, 1307.

[5] F.547f, 812f. — Philyll. 10.

[6] P.740ff, F.616f.

[7] Antiphon I, 6ff, Lysias IV, 14, VII, 34, Isaios VIII, 12. — Antiphon V, 49ff, VI, 25. Isocr. XVII 15ff.

[8] Eur. *frg.* 313 — belonging, it is true, to the satyr drama *Busiris*.

[9] Cf. J. H. Lipsius, *Das attische Recht u. Rechtsverfahren*, 658ff.

slave had been murdered.¹ There were, under different names, prisons for slaves, and the slave could be called simply 'prisoner' just as the losing bird in a cock-fight was called 'slave'.²

Small wonder that slaves often ran away. If recaptured, they were punished severely and branded;³ but they had an asylum where they could ask to be resold.⁴ All these facts are at least as strong and valid evidence as the typical slaves of comedy, the faithful or the insolent slave who is on intimate terms with the master and sometimes with the mistress.⁵ It is, perhaps, not permissible to neglect one side of the picture in favour of the other, but we must remember that, though both represent comic extremes, the slave who stood on almost the same level as his master was far more of a farcical type than the one who was oppressed.

There was a good chance of social advancement for the slaves who either were hired out or worked on their own account, and had to pay only a fixed sum to their master.⁶ In comedy they are hardly mentioned; but 'the city of slaves, of the wicked new-rich' must have been an imaginary place inhabited by slaves who had grown rich, and that must have been by the pursuit of trade or craft.⁷ It was possible to contrast the impoverished citizen with the slave who had grown rich.⁸ On one occasion a certain Xanthias is said to practise 'the iron craft'; the name shows that the man was a slave, but nothing else is known about this smith or moulder.⁹ The allusions to the careers of certain real or fictitious emancipated

---

¹ This seems to be the meaning of such passages as Eur. *Hek.* 291f and Antiphon V, 48 (cf. also Lykourgos, *Leokr.* 65). The statement is, of course, not true with regard to a man who had killed his own slave (see above, p. 186, n. 4). But in other cases the point can neither be simply denied nor fully confirmed. It was a great thing that in Athens a slave could have legal protection at all; but it was by no means the same as that granted to a citizen. The legal possibilities open to a slave are fully discussed by Morrow, *l.c.*, 218ff.

² frg. 93, Eupolis 348, 19 D, Theop. 63. — frg. 65, 837. — B.70.

³ P.451f. — B.760, L.330f, frg. 64, 97, Eupolis 259, 276, 2, Flat. 187, Andok. *frg.* 5.

⁴ See above, p. 169, n. 3.

⁵ Various situations, W.500, 1352f, Th. 491, F.312, 519ff, 739f, Pl.46, 227f, 319f, frg. 695, 645b.

⁶ ἀνδράποδα μισθοφοροῦντα, Isaios VIII, 35.

⁷ Kratinos 208, cf. Eupolis 197.

⁸ Eur. *frg.* 142.

⁹ Eupolis 263.

slaves or sons of slaves, like Nikomachos,[1] tend to bear out facts known from other evidence, such as, for example, the life stories of the great bankers Pasion and Phormion. The most vivid description given is that of the career of a man who started as a branded runaway slave, was manumitted and became a professional parasite; but he remained a low and disreputable fellow, and on one occasion was thrown out of a dinner-party by the house-slave.[2] Agoratos also, a famous informer under the Thirty, belonged to this class.[3] Exekestides, who is said to have been a Carian slave (this can hardly be true), acquired ancestors and phraters.[4] Wealth sometimes probably enabled a slave to become free, but there were very few slaves indeed who in the end became citizens. Aristophanes mentions those who had fought at Arginusae and so received citizenship; he accepts this as a necessary measure, but he strongly objects to the fact that at the same time genuine Athenians had lost their citizenship; anyway it is clear that the measure was entirely exceptional.[5] In general, very little is said in comedy and tragedy about enfranchised slaves; and as Aristophanes strongly disliked such members of the population, the relative silence about them proves that their number and importance can have been only slight.[6]

No doubt the statement of Ps.-Xenophon that looseness and freedom of speech were both enjoyed by Attic slaves was far from true, even if we do not take 'freedom of speech' (*isegoria*) in its usual political meaning.[7] But the freedom of the slaves, if taken as meaning the degree in which they approximated to the standard of a citizen's life, was considerable. This is proved most clearly by the cults. It had to be said explicitly that slave-girls were not allowed to attend the speeches at the Thesmophoria, a statement which shows that slaves were admitted to many cults and festivals, and, in fact, slave-girls seem

---

[1] F.1506, Lysias XXX, 2; cf. also Plat. 166f.
[2] Eupolis, 159. In comedy he was even thrown into the *barathron*.
[3] Lysias XIII, 18, 64.
[4] B.764f, cf. 11, 1526f.   [5] See p. 174f.
[6] Eur. *Herakl.* 788f, 888ff, also gives the impression that it happened very rarely that a slave was set free. Slaves could be bought back by their relatives and thus become free, but that was something different and simply part of a slave-dealer's ordinary business (Antiphon V, 20).
[7] It is this latter freedom of speech (παρρησία) in which an exile is lacking, and his lot is therefore called that of a slave (Eur. *Phoin.* 391f).

to have attended the general festival of the Thesmophoria.[1] Plutarch once quotes a line from comedy in which 'the thick-legged grinding maid' is mentioned as taking part in processions and sacrifices.[2] We have also spoken of the part which slaves played when they went to Delphi along with their masters, just as slaves attended the Eleusinian Mysteries.[3]

Athens was no slaves' paradise. The fatalistic lament was true:[4] 'Fate does not allow a slave to be master of his own person, but gives it to the man who has bought it.' But if we accept slavery with all its faults as we must, that is to say as a necessary institution and an important element in social and economic life, we must acknowledge that, on the whole, Athenian slaves were treated humanely — frequently, of course, because to do so was in the owner's own interest. Much depended on the individual master, much on the economic situation and activity of the slave. For what we have called the approximation to the standard of a citizen's life rested less on the patriarchal position in the household than on the economic opportunities open to the slave who worked as a skilled craftsman or trader. Both of these types, however, support the view that the organization of economic life at Athens was not based on slave-labour either wholly or even mainly. It is a mistake, although a very common one, to regard slavery in the ancient world indiscriminately in this light, whether in fifth-century Greece or in the Hellenistic world or in Rome. The economic importance of slaves in classical Athens was much smaller than is commonly assumed.[5] Almost the only important exception

---

[1] Th.294. — Th.537, 609, 728, 739, 754.

[2] adesp. 55. The latter statement is not in the quotation, only in Plutarch (de vita sec. Epicuri decreta, 1101F), but it seems unlikely that he would have quoted the line unless it referred to the point in question, that is to say that the maid actually took part in some sort of πομπή or θυσία. Cf. also A. 249, 259.

[3] See page 177. There is no religious motive for Charon's refusal to ferry slaves (F.190). This is invented for the sole purpose of having Xanthias removed from the stage, because Dionysos must row alone in order to become the farcical sufferer he is. Whether the actor who played the part of Xanthias had meanwhile to sing the song of the frogs, as Radermacher believes, is not beyond doubt, if only for reason of the necessary acoustic impression of the Brekekekex Koax which would suggest a choral song.

[4] Pl.6f.

[5] Eur. frg. 1019: δούλοισι γάρ τε ζῶμεν οἱ ἐλεύθεροι must not be taken as a generally true statement, though it certainly reflected the position of part of the citizens.

is the position of the miners. Furthermore, in spite of their considerable number, slaves were never a problem to the population as a whole. Perhaps we may assume that the rise and fall in the numbers of citizens and slaves more or less kept pace with each other, and followed the general economic conditions of the country. The impoverishment which followed the Peloponnesian War was partly responsible for the fact that Attica, in spite of the loss of great numbers of citizens, avoided a dangerous surplus of slaves. Athens was never threatened by the problems and dangers of the Laconian helots. As far as we can see, Athenian economy was never dominated by slave-labour, and Athenian policy never influenced by the number or even the existence of slaves.[1] It remains, however, true that most citizens, and certainly those who really administered Athens, had slaves, at least one or two; without that the political machine would not have worked.

[1] The truth of this résumé on the part played by slave-labour in Greek economics has been challenged by some of my reviewers. I should like to quote the concluding sentences from the frequently mentioned paper by W. L. Westermann, the outstanding expert on all questions of Greek slavery (*Athenian Studies for Ferguson*, 470): 'The slaves were employed at the same work as the free, usually side by side with them and apparently without prejudice or friction. In any sense which implies either that the enslaved population predominated over the free or that the Greek city-state displayed the mentality of a slave-ridden society, Greek culture was not founded upon slavery.'

CHAPTER VIII

FAMILY AND NEIGHBOURS

I

No State in the history of the world was ever such a close community as the Greek Polis. Politically it was organized not simply as the sum of its individual members, nor as a number of co-operating bodies which represented the several classes and professions. The State was subdivided into a gradation of communities to which each individual citizen was bound, and the State was the supreme unit formed out of these subdivisions. We have to deal with these smaller and narrower communities which were, all of them, embedded in the greater whole of the State. We have to speak of the relations of the individual to his family, kinsfolk and neighbours. Hitherto our picture of Athenian life and of the Athenian citizen body has been concerned with its various social and economic functions. We are left with the task of inquiring into the general and common nature of the Athenian people; and a study of the smaller communities, especially those of house and family, can best take us the first steps towards that goal.

The comic poets stage their scenes in the street, in the country, in Hades or in the air, but never inside a house. Nevertheless, we are given some glimpses of life as it was lived there, less by the use of the *ekkyklema* than by the words of the characters on the stage. Almost without exception, they belong to the upper or lower middle-class. In fifth-century comedy we hear almost nothing about life in the houses of the great lords or indeed the rich upstarts. We may almost welcome this lack of evidence. For our main interest is to disclose the outlines of ordinary everyday life, and it is this which is revealed in comedy.

The house is the home of the family, that is to say, above all, of husband and wife. It is not surprising that the comedians sometimes share the attitude of misogyny to which Greek writers had for a long time given expression in fairly strong terms. However, it would be as wrong to accept as absolute truth all the accusations made in the *Thesmophoriazousai* of adultery and even the murder of husbands, procuring, love of drink and gossip,[1] as to accept as real the ideal figures of Lysistrate and Praxagora, and their claims about women. The words attributed to Susarion, according to tradition the earliest of the comedians, in fact repeat only the commonplace that women are a necessary evil, and that getting married is as bad as not getting married.[2] When we try to interpret the social significance of such misogynic remarks, we may assume that they mostly originated among the upper classes. There paederasty was legitimate, and it easily went hand in hand with hostility to women.[3] Never since the days of Hesiod, in spite of occasional anti-feminine utterances, had the urban and rural middle-classes shared these views.

Nobody but a real misanthrope was said to live without wife and child.[4] Marriage was very rarely the result of a love-affair. Match-makers were always busy, and succeeded in bringing together even couples of vastly different social origin.[5]   In tragedy men are frequently advised to marry a girl from a good family, but Euripides speaks also of the disappointments and dangers of a marriage 'above one's station'.[6] The daughter had to marry early, for women outgrew marriageable age more quickly than men.[7] When a girl has just become 'fledged', she is apt to 'fly at men', but generally she had to accept for a husband any man whom her father might choose; if he was dead, she had to marry the next of kin or a man chosen by him, while he had to get the consent of the court.[8] She was normally given a dowry by her father; the ancient custom of buying a bride had disappeared.[9] As a bride the grown-up girl took part in social life for the first time.[10] At the wedding, the *gamelia*, which all

---

[1] Especially Th.335ff, 389ff, 471ff, 559ff.

[2] Susarion 1. Cf. also L.1039, Pherekr. 39 P = 22 D. It is hardly necessary to mention Euripides' misogynic utterances, although they are by no means so uniform and so radical as Aristophanes in the *Thesmophoriazousai* tries to make us believe.

[3] Kratinos 152.   [4] Phryn. 19.   [5] C.41ff.

[6] e.g., Eur. *Andr.* 619ff, 1279ff. — Eur. *El.* 1097f, *frg.* 502f, 16 P, 4f.

[7] L.593ff. Cf. Isaios VI, 14, Xen. *oik.* 7, 5.

[8] frg. 582. — W.583ff, Eur. *Andr.* 987f, *frg.* 953. This is confirmed by many passages in the Orators, in particular Andokides I, 119ff.

[9] Eur. *Med.* 232f, *Hipp.* 625ff, *frg.* 775.

[10] Cf. adesp. *Arch. f. Pap.* VII, 144, where, however, the bride is allegorical.

the family, phraters and friends attended, after the bride's
bath, a good dinner was served, aphrodisiac hymns were sung,
and the young couple, crowned with garlands and anointed
with perfumes, ate together the wedding-cake, and were pelted
with sweets.[1] Happy mothers lit the torch in the wedding-
chamber.[2] Thus marriage was an important event for men and
women, though certainly more so for the latter, and Hera, the
wife of the chief of the gods, 'kept the keys of wedlock'.[3]

References to married life are infrequent, but it becomes
clear that mutual attachment was often strong. With all his
attacks on women and marriage, even Euripides frequently
praises the blessings of a happy marriage, or — from a man's
point of view — of a good wife.[4] Pheidippides was entirely
mistaken in thinking that his father would be quite glad to
learn that he was proposing to beat his mother, and it was just
this which precipitated matters.[5] Sexual relations bound
married couples together. 'I give you Phaidra here as wife,
for I believe fire is going to join fire.'[6] Since it was usual to
speak openly of all intercourse with hetaerae, most likely the
poet refers to married love when he says that 'the pleasures of
love are sweet to experience, but not good to be spoken of'.[7]
A great many jokes and comic situations, some crude enough,
depend upon the sexual intercourse of married people. An
old man was naturally considered 'a shame for a young wife',
unless she was going to play the master's role.[8] Moderation
in sexual love, on the other hand, was regarded as typical of
a decent wife.[9] Marriage as the legitimate form of sexual
intercourse, though grotesquely distorted, is also the pre-
supposition of the whole plot of the Lysistrate: men, refused

[1] Isaios III, 76, 79, VI, 10, 64, VIII, 20. — P. 843, 868, L.378. — P.1195f,
Archipp. 9-12 (although this is the glutton Herakles' wedding-feast). — Pherekr.
12 D. — P.859ff, Pl.529. — B.159ff, Theop. 14. — Cf. also Megara's description
of her imminent death as a wedding festival (Eur. Her. 480ff).

[2] Eur. Phoin. 344ff, cf. Alk. 317.   [3] Th.976.

[4] Cf. Alkestis, also Herakles, besides Med. 14f, Hipp. 836ff, frg. 164, 463,
822-3, 909, 1055-8, 1062.

[5] C.1443ff.   [6] frg. 453.   [7] Krates 2 D.

[8] frg. 600, cf. Eur. frg. 317, 804. — Th.413, cf. E.323f.

[9] Eur. Iph. A. 1159. While the supreme power and tyranny of Kypris and Eros
are a theme on which Euripides harps again and again, 'bed-gluttonness' and
φιλανδρία are Andromache's charges against Hermione (Andr. 218ff, 229), and
Euripides' repeated exhortations to women to be σώφρονες are chiefly directed
against such lack of sexual moderation.

by women, suffer severely; only in his last despair does the man resort to procurers and the brothel.[1] Matrimonial scandals seem to have been rare, or they were at least rarely made public in Athens, though many of the young roués, who are so often shown up by comedy, paid court especially to married women, and sarcastic references to adulterous wives are frequent.[2] We are told that the adulterer is as necessary to women as the dessert to a meal.[3] Possibly, Phaidra's statement that women of noble origin were the first to commit adultery does not only refer to mythological stories, but also confirms the fact that these things happened less frequently in the middle than in the upper classes. What Andokides tells us about Kallias' union with two women, daughter and mother, and the scandalous happenings in his house, seem to have been somewhat exceptional, although Aristophanes also alludes to it.[4] The sufferings of the cutler Panaitios were known only by the peculiar agreement which he concluded with his wife, in the presence of witnesses, in order to be safe from her love-frenzy.[5] Sometimes, women were corrupted by other women,[6] though we never hear of homosexual relations between them. On the whole, if we take into full account the character of our evidence, we may assume that Athenian women were not particularly licentious, and adultery on their part was not more, perhaps even less, frequent than in other societies which can be compared.

It was the privilege of Alkibiades, not only when hardly yet 'a man' to be 'the man' of all the women, but later to take hetaerae into his house while his wife was at home.[7] Apart from such an extreme case, a husband's adultery was rarely taken seriously.[8]   Neither in comedy nor in the forensic speeches is it ever of any importance. Only Euripides, who knew more about female psychology than any of his contemporaries, pictures the effects on a woman of her husband's

---

[1] L.957f. It seems, on the other hand, that the use of the *olisbos* was not infrequent, although regarded as a poor substitute (L.109, frg. 320, 13, adesp. 5 D = 44 P). There is also the evidence of a few vase-paintings; cf. A. Körte, *P.-W.* XVII, 2480ff.

[2] B.793ff. — P.979ff, Th. *passim*, E.225, cf. Eur. *El.* 921ff, Lysias I, III, 23.
[3] frg. 187.   [4] Eur. *Hipp.* 409f. — Andok. I, 124ff, B.286.
[5] B.439ff and schol.
[6] Eur. *Hipp.* 407ff. — *Andr.* 944ff. Cf. the part of the nurse in *Hipp.*
[7] Pherekr. 155. — Ps.-Andok. IV, 14.   [8] Cf. Eur. *El.* 1035ff.

infidelity.[1] The wish that a man might have two wives could
be expressed in Euripides' melodramatic tragedy *Ino*.[2] That
was an idea which could provide a good many jokes; but it
never occurred to any of the comedians, which shows that no
general social problem was involved.

Considering that every kind of sexual scandal was a favourite
subject with comedy, the paucity and general nature of such
indications show that married life was normally stable and
peaceful.[3] House and meals are desolate and dreary, so a husband complains, when the wife is gone.[4] Marriage was protected by the severe law which allowed a man who caught an
adulterer with his wife — or even with his concubine — to kill
him on the spot.[5] There were other unorthodox punishments
as well, intended to put the guilty to shame and give satis-
faction to the outraged husband.[6] Actually, a man who used
force in seducing a woman was less severely punished than the
one who persuaded her.[7] The reason for this surprising piece
of legislation was probably that only the latter corrupted and
destroyed the sacred union on which the duties of legitimate
children — both in their parents' old age and after their death —
were based. A wife, on the other hand, who was caught in
adultery and therefore divorced, would cease to be an object
of affection or even of interest.[8]

The tie of marriage could not be separated from general
family feeling. It might occasionally comprehend even more
distant relatives — for instance, the wife's family; there is a
strong personal bond between Euripides and his relative who
perhaps was his father-in-law.[9] It is a commonplace to praise
the power of the ties of kinship.[10] Naturally, however, we hear
in comedy much more of the closer circle of the family. Thus

[1] Eur. *Med.* 263ff, *Ion* 1090ff. There is, of course, also Sophokles' *Trachiniae*, but cf. my *Aspects of the Ancient World*, 149ff.

[2] Eur. *frg.* 402.   [3] Cf. Xen. *mem.* II, 2, 4f.

[4] L.865ff.   [5] Lysias I, 25ff, 30f.

[6] C.1083.   [7] Lysias I, 32f.

[8] This is clearly shown in Lysias I. The husband, who has killed his wife's seducer, does not speak of her as a guilty person — in fact, hardly as a person at all.

[9] He is called his κηδεστής (Th.74, 210, 584, 1165), but that is a word applicable to both sides in a relationship. Hekabe could even appeal to Agamemnon as a κηδεστής of her son's, as Kassandra was his mistress (Eur. *Hek.* 833f).

[10] Cf., e.g., Eur. *Andr.* 985f, *Herakleid.* 236ff, *Her.* 287, *Tro.* 51f.

Dikaiopolis concludes his private peace for himself, but also for his children and his wife who 'is near to him'.[1] Wife and children were the usual weeping pleaders in court.[2] Mnesilochos, who longs for his wife while he is a prisoner, afterwards hurries home 'to wife and children';[3] a man swears 'by wife and children'; it is of course a joke, when Dionysos, who has neither, does so.[4] Chremylos introduces Ploutos to his wife and only son, while his friend pictures his future wealthy life along with wife and children.[5] A husband gets up in the night and prepares a medicine when his wife is in pain.[6] The parents see that their young children get their meals at the proper time.[7] Strepsiades claims to have nursed his baby son, and he spent the first obol of his juror's payment on a toy for him.[8] Trygaios is an equally affectionate father who promises sweets to his little daughters, while the poor old judge needs his 'small pay' to maintain his family of three, and therefore cannot buy figs for his child.[9] In one traditional custom or another a boy might be valued more highly than a girl,[10] but there is no sign of this in the feelings of the parents. The father is proud of his grown-up daughter, and allows her to kiss the money out of his mouth.[11] One would kiss a small child by holding it by its ears as by handles.[12] Love of children appears in such sentences as this: 'The sun obeys the children, when they say: Rise, dear sun!', or in the poets' descriptions of a game played by boys in the street and of other games.[13] A number of vase-paintings confirm this interest in children and children's games.[14]

Affection for his family did not prevent a man from dining and drinking with his friends, and from kissing the maid when the mistress was out of the way.[15] We have emphasized in various previous passages the great freedom which men usually enjoyed in sexual matters. It may also have happened fre-

[1] A.131f. This is the meaning of the word πλᾶτις used here for the wife.

[2] Pl.382ff.   [3] Th.1021, 1205f.   [4] F.587.

[5] Pl.250, 613ff.   [6] Th.486.   [7] frg. 347.

[8] C.1382ff., 863f.   [9] P.122f. — W.297ff.   [10] Cf. E.549.

[11] A.253ff., Eur. *Hek.* 1101ff. — W.606.

[12] Eunikos 1. Such a kiss was therefore called χύτρα.

[13] Strattis 46. — Plat. 153. — K.855 (with Neil's explanation), W.295f, Kratinos 415, Telekl. 1, l. 14. Cf. Kallias (?), 31 A-D Edmonds.

[14] Cf. L. Deubner, *Die Antike,* VI (1930), 162ff, also his *Attische Feste.*

[15] A.271ff, P.1130ff.

quently that a widower, though he was getting old, manumitted a pretty girl and made her his legal concubine, much
to the displeasure of his children.[1] Isaios, in a very amusing
and characteristic way, describes an old man who was entirely
under the thumb of a hetaera.[2] A son might even buy or hire
a hetaera in order to sweeten the evening of his father's life.[3]
It was not rare for a man to live with a hetaera — Isokrates, for
example, with Lagiska.[4] Concubinage, at least with a free
woman, was a legal union protected, as we have seen, by law
against intruders. A citizen could give his daughter or sister
into concubinage.[5] If a hetaera had become mistress of a
house, it might easily lead to trouble and the house might be
ruled very differently from one in which there was a legal
wife.[6] A man could send his concubine away to a brothel,[7]
an action which seems cruel and beastly; it becomes less so
when we learn what the comedians have to say of the possible
dangers — real or imagined — from such a woman. The
'lecherous goat' could be at the same time a drunkard and a
poisoner, and it can easily be understood that some men — if
not for moral reasons, at least from motives of prudence —
preferred a wife about the house to a poisoner.[8] The fear of
being poisoned was, it seems, frequent and genuine. Women
were supposed to be favourite customers of those who traded
in drugs, particularly in love-potions.[9]

---

[1] W.1352f, cf. Plat. 178.   [2] Isaios VI, 19ff. Cf. Plate XV*b*.
[3] W.738ff, cf. Xen. *oik.* 1, 13.   [4] P.439f. — Strattis 3 (παλλακὴν).
[5] Isaios III, 39.   [6] Isaios III, 13f.   [7] Antiphon I, 14.
[8] Pherekr. 17 D. — Plat. 28 D = 43 P. Page reads (with Schubart and
Wilamowitz, *Berl. Klassikertexte* V, 2, 123) ... γυναῖκα κρ]εῖσσον ἐστ' ἐν
οἰκίᾳ [ἢ φαρμακίτα]ς τῶν παρ' Εὐδήμου τρέφειν, and translates: 'It is better
to keep a wife at home, than antidotes bought from Eudemos.' It is true that this
man was known as a seller of drugs and magic rings (Pl.884, Eupolis 87,
Ameipsias 27); but how can any drug be contrasted with a man's wife — quite
apart from the difficult zeugma of τρέφειν? The fragment seems to make sense
only if we read with earlier editors: φαρμακίδα]ς 'Those from Eudemos' are
the people who have either learned their art or got their drugs from him. The
expression is odd, but it could be supported by ὁ δὲ μετ' Εὐδήμου τρέχων
in Kratinos 299 — unfortunately itself rather an obscure fragment. A more
serious difficulty is that φαρμακίδας does not scan. Thus, the right restoration of the fragment has not yet been found.
[9] Cf. Antiphon I, also Eur. *Hipp.* 478ff, 509ff, *Andr.* 32ff, 157ff, 205ff, 272,
355ff, *frg.* 464. — The preparation of real medicines, however, was, as it seems,
in the hands of men (Th.486, E.404ff, Pl.716ff).

We do not learn very much about the usual number of children in a family. To bear children was woman's natural function, even the most beloved wife was 'a child-bearing consort', children were considered part of a man's wealth, and childlessness often led to marital trouble and divorce.[1] Sometimes a woman 'bought a child' and pretended that it was her own.[2] The frequent lawsuits about inheritance and the many adoptions prove that the mortality of children was fairly high. In the pains of childbirth a woman could be advised to be patient and not to despair, but Medea thought she would rather go three times to battle than have one child.[3] A mother was supposed to help her daughter in her childbed.[4] There existed also a special medicine to make childbirth easier.[5] If we find a family with only one son, this may have sometimes been due to reasons of dramaturgic economy, for instance for the sake of contrasting father and son, as in the *Wasps* and the *Clouds*. On the other hand, the poor farmer Chremylos, following Hesiod's old prescription, has only one son, because he cannot afford more children, and, as he says, does not love even this only child so much as wealth.[6] Nevertheless, Hermes assumes as a matter of course that there are several children in the house.[7] It is hard to say how far voluntary limitation went in regard to the number of children. The primitive method of birth-control by exposing new-born children 'in an earthen crock' could still be used and was not regarded as criminal.[8]

The mutual love of parents and children is a natural fact which can be destroyed by extraordinary circumstances only, whether these are of a personal or a general character. On the whole this is more a theme of tragedy than of comedy. The mother's loving care for her offspring, the father's proud love of his children, the children's devoted love for their parents — all these appear in Euripides' plays. He also speaks of the grief over the death of children, of the sorry fate of orphans, of the evil of having a stepmother.[9] But from comedy too we may, for instance, infer that a good son tried to make his

---

[1] Eur. *Andr.* 4: δάμαρ παιδοποιός. — P.1320ff. — Eur. *Andr.* 904ff.
[2] Th.339f, 407ff, 502f, 564f, Telekl. 41, 2, Eur. *Alk.* 638f.
[3] Plat. 5 D. — Eur. *Med.* 250f.   [4] Eur. *Alk.* 318f.
[5] frg. 872.   [6] Hesiod, *Erga* 376. — Pl.35, 250ff.   [7] Pl.1104.
[8] F.1189f and schol. Cf. A. Cameron, *Cl. Rev.* 46 (1932), 106.
[9] Eur. *Hik.* 1120ff, 1132ff, *frg.* 4.

father's old age easy and pleasant, and that the worst thing
Pheidippides could do was to threaten his father and even his
mother with a beating.[1] Mothers claim that they know best
how to take care of their soldier sons.[2] A son who left his
father's house is aware of his indebtedness to his father for
bringing him up.[3] To honour one's parents was one of the
fundamental commandments of Greek ethics, and in tragedy
particularly there are many examples of the fulfilment or the
claims of that duty. On the other hand, it is known that in
general 'guardians and relatives' did not take much care of an
old man, and a son sometimes behaved in the same way
towards his father.[4] However, family feeling and love of
children were strong among the Athenians, and that could not
have been the case unless women were highly esteemed in
their role of wife, mother and housekeeper. This ideal of
woman culminates in the absurd housewifely perfection of
Ischomachos' 'dear little impulsive wife' in Xenophon's *Oikonomikos*.[5] Tender and gentle feelings for wife and children have
found a more adequate representation, more beautiful and also
more eloquent than in comedy, in the lovely family-scenes of
vase-paintings and the touching sadness of gravestones and
white lekythoi (see Plate XVI).[6]

It was, of course, something of a hindrance to family life
that men's normal life, much more than in our northern
countries, took place outside the house. Frequently the man
spent the whole day in the market, in court or assembly.[7]
By serving in court he earned his and his family's living, and
it was often the man who went to the market and did the
necessary shopping.[8]

This, however, was not always the case. For a larger household a slave, who could be called the 'caterer', made the purchases, and even a citizen of limited means might have a slave-
girl who went regularly to the market.[9] Another man found
fault with his wife, when she came back tired from a women's

[1] W.738ff. — C.1443ff.   [2] E.233f.
[3] adesp. 371.   [4] W.731f.
[5] Cf. T. R. Glover, *Greek Byways*, 159.
[6] Cf. also the charming book by E. Buschor, *Grab eines attischen Mädchens*
(1939).
[7] E.62ff.
[8] W.303ff, E.460ff. — W.493f, B.501ff, L.560, frg. 545, Plat. 190, 193.
[9] ὀψώνης, frg. 503; cf. Pherekr. 126. — Lysias I, 8; 16.

festival, and had bought neither fish nor meat.[1] As a rule the
ladies only used to go for walks, carrying their veils, baskets
and parasols, spinning and talking, and nearly always accompanied by a maid.[2] With the lower classes things were, of
course, somewhat different. Families helped each other out;
there was a great deal of lending and borrowing of household
utensils, and other help of this kind.[3] Women met and
gossiped — as they do everywhere — at the springs or streams
where they washed their linen.[4] When a child was born,
several women-friends at once came to offer their help, expect-
ing to be given a present, especially if the child was a boy.[5]
One of Aristophanes' comedies had the title *Women under
Canvas* or *Women who took their Seats*; they were probably
spectators at a procession or at games, and one of them had
brought with her a big wine-bottle as a 'fellow spectator'.[6] It
is unlikely, as we have seen, that women attended the performances in the theatre.[7] However, women had many and
quite legitimate opportunities for getting out of the house.

And yet, we must not underestimate the extent of women's
bondage to the house, though it has certainly often been
exaggerated.[8] Women and girls, and not only those of the
well-to-do families, spent most of their life indoors; the brother
kept a severe eye on his sister; it was at a funeral or at similar
rare occasions that a woman could be seen by other men;
hardly any woman was used to speak in the presence of men.[9]
Even in small houses a separate part was set aside for the
women, usually on the upper floor, not easily accessible and

---

[1] frg. 318.   [2] Th.279ff, 821ff; cf. L.530ff, F.1346ff.

[3] F.1159, E.446ff,frg. 136(text doubtful). [4] Eur. *Hipp.* 125ff.[5] E.528ff, 549.

[6] frg. 471ff: Σκηνὰς Καταλαμβάνουσαι. The same meaning of σκηνὴν
καταλαμβάνειν is found P.880, where it refers to the Isthmian games. The
seats in theatre are never called σκηναί.

[7] Cf. p. 27, n. 2.

[8] Cf. Gomme's excellent chapter, 89ff, and my remarks in *Aspects of the
Ancient World*, 65f. A curious mistake made by Gomme as well as by his
opponents is that they always regard the social rule that keeps women at home as
inevitably combined with a general contempt for women. Although to some
extent confined to the house, a woman was, as we shall find confirmed in comedy
as well as tragedy, highly thought of if she was a good wife, mother and keeper of
the house.

[9] L.473, Th. 414f, 790ff. — Th.405f, cf. Lysias III, 6. — Lysias I, 8. The
lovers in New Comedy frequently meet at festivals or processions. — Lysias
XXXII, 11.

sometimes locked up by a strong door.[1] The avarice of Aiolos
is shown by the fact that his six daughters share one bedroom
and one bath-tub.[2] Women had pale complexions, unlike men
who, in streets and market, in palaestra and assembly, often
even in the workshop, lived in the open air.[3] If a hetaera lived
in a man's house, she was present at dinner even when other
men were present, but a wife never appeared; nor was a wife
serenaded; men did not quarrel or behave foolishly about her.[4]
In general, this is the picture we should expect to find in a
society so predominently masculine as Greek society was.
The countless suggestions in comedy of women's love of drink,
however much exaggerated, cannot have been without some
real basis; wine might be a consolation in their frequent loneli-
ness. Women seldom knew other men by sight, and they had
to make excuses more or less every time they left the house.[5]

What we have found out from comedy about the social
position of women, follows a middle line between the extremes; it is not refuted by the important part played by
women as characters in some of the comedies. On the contrary, the portraits of Lysistrate and Praxagora get their full
brilliance only by their complete contrast with the background
of women's everyday life. Its seclusion is a fact confirmed by
overwhelming evidence from Euripides, that is to say from the
poet who is generally regarded as the champion of the emancipation of women, and whose Medeas, Phaidras and Hekabes
have strongly influenced Aristophanes when he drew his great
women. Yet it is frequently stressed in Euripides' tragedies
that women ought to be silent, not to argue with men, not to
speak first, not to speak with strangers.[6] Even the old queen
Aithra has to excuse herself when she is about to express her
views: if a woman has something of value to say, it is better
for her to break her silence.[7] It is against good manners if a
woman looks straight into a man's face; it is, in fact, usual for

[1] Th.414f, Lysias I, 9, III, 6, *frg.* 14, Xen. *oik.* 9, 5; cf. D. S. Robertson, *A Handbook of Greek and Roman Architecture* (1943²), 297.

[2] frg. 6.   [3] E.385ff. — Xen. *mem.* I, 1, 10; II, 1, 6.

[4] Isaios III, 13f. Cf. also Eur. *Ba.* 384f, and Winnington-Ingram, *Euripides and Dionysus*, 62, 2.

[5] L.836ff.

[6] Eur. *Herakl.* 476f, *Andr.* 364f, *Her.* 534f, *El.* 341ff, *Iph. A.* 830.

[7] *Hik.* 294, 297ff, cf. also *Tro.* 903f, *Hel.* 1049.

a lady to be veiled.[1] Sensible women are supposed to excel in
'the works of Athena', and to let men act for them.[2] Worst of
all is it to speak to a crowd, or even only to watch a gathering
of men; women ought to remain inside the house.[3] All these
restrictions are even more emphatically imposed on unmarried
girls who should not be seen at all outside, and least of all
among the crowds of an army.[4] A maiden also usually wears a
veil, and it can be regarded as unmaidenly — even in a moment
of threatening death — to perform the usual gesture of a sup-
pliant by clasping a man's knee.[5] There is an almost Victorian
touch about it when we hear that girls must not know of their
marriage beforehand nor talk about adulterous love-affairs.[6]
How weak against this chorus of public opinion seems, for
instance, Medea's cry for a more dignified status for women![7]
Why, we ask, did Euripides testify to such an extent to those
narrow views generally held?   The only reasonable answer
seems to be that he had to do so in order to make his unusual
mythical situations as well as his outstanding female characters
as real and convincing as possible. In Euripides as in comedy
we can trace the realistic background of the plays, and as in
comedy it is this background which gives increased brilliance
to the great individual women on the stage.[8]

On the other hand, if a woman's life was restricted and ruled
by strong conventions, it was by no means useless. Above all,
the management of the household — that is to say, of a large
part of a man's property — was in the hands of the wife.[9] The
importance of the wife and mother in the life of the family and
the maintenance of the house was widely recognized.[10] 'No
house is clean or prosperous if the wife is absent.'[11] Home
duties — care of husband, children, servants — could make it
"hard for women to get out".[12] Naturally voices could often

---

[1] *Hek.* 974f, *frg.* 12 P, 227ff.   [2] *Hik.* 1061f. — 4of.
[3] *Hik.* 1066, *Iph. A.* 187ff. — *Andr.* 876f, *Tro.* 648ff, *frg.* 521.
[4] *Ph.* 88ff, 92ff, 193ff, 1275f, *Or.* 108.   [5] *Ph.* 1485ff, *Iph. A.* 992ff.
[6] *Iph. A.* 671, *El.* 945ff, *Or.* 26.   [7] *Med.* 230ff, cf. also 419f, 429f.
[8] The reality of the background is confirmed by the fact that it needed a period
of continuous lawlessness and the terror of an unbridled and licentious soldiery
to create conditions in which 'women were seen without veils (γυμνάς!) by
crowds' (Isokr. *epist.* 9, 10, written in 356 B.C.).
[9] L.495, 894f, E.211f, frg. 328; cf. Lysias I, 7, Xen. *oik.* 7, 23ff.
[10] Cf. Eur. *Alk.* 415, 825, *Iph. A.* 1159f, *frg.* 13 P, 5ff, *frg.* 822f.
[11] Eur. 13 P, 6f.   [12] L. 16ff.

be heard clamouring for the supremacy of the husband and protesting against any 'dyarchy', although it was hardly possible in real life for the husband to lock up the pantry.[1]   The law introduced by the women's government which allowed no man to dispose freely of more than one medimnos may reflect the fact that the reverse was in fact true and that women depended on their husbands for support.[2]

Women's chief tasks in the house, apart from looking after the children and managing the servants, were cooking and baking, spinning and weaving, and, besides these, the preparation and dyeing of wool (see Plate XIa).[3]   Nevertheless they are said to have found time, while their husbands were out, to anoint themselves and to lie in the sun, though here the situation is due to the plot, and this was hardly a common practice.[4] Of course, clothes and cosmetics, even a razor, jewellery and perfumes, all these 'man traps', played an important part in a woman's life (see Plate XVIIa).[5]   Clothes were kept in large boxes (see Plate XVIIb), and a certain kind of fruit was put in to give a pleasant scent.[6]

Houses were, in general, very simple. The steps leading to the upper floor were often dangerous, a ladder rather than a staircase.[7]   When a good meal was being got ready, the whole house was filled with smoke; in a poor cottage everything was black and dirty with it.[8]   Utensils of gold and silver are often mentioned, so are bolsters and cushions; but, on the whole, very little was done to make conditions hygienic and comfortable.[9]   Vermin were not altogether unknown, but they were more of a nuisance in inns; in the *Clouds* they belong to the plot and are not to be taken as a feature of normal life.[1]   Dogs and cocks roamed about house and kitchen, and the pig-pen

---

[1] Eur. *El.* 930ff, *frg.* 463. — *Andr.* 464ff. — Th.418ff, E.14f; cf. adesp. 710
[2] E.1024f.
[3] L.18f. — E.221ff, frg. 9 D, Pherekr. 22, and elsewhere. — L.735f, E.653f, Eupolis 319. — E.89, 215f, frg. 651.
[4] E.62ff.
[5] In general, see, e.g., L.42ff, 150f, 408ff, E.524f, 732, frg. 17, 320, 632; cf. Eur. *Hipp.* 630ff, Lysias I, 14, 17, Xen. *oik.* 10, 2, *symp.* 2, 3f. — Razor: Th. 218f, E.65f. — Man traps: frg. 666.
[6] W.1055f, cf. frg. 695.   [7] Lysias, I, 9.
[8] Pl.819ff. — Eur. *El.* 1139f.   [9] frg. 19. — E.347, 1059ff.

PLATE XVI

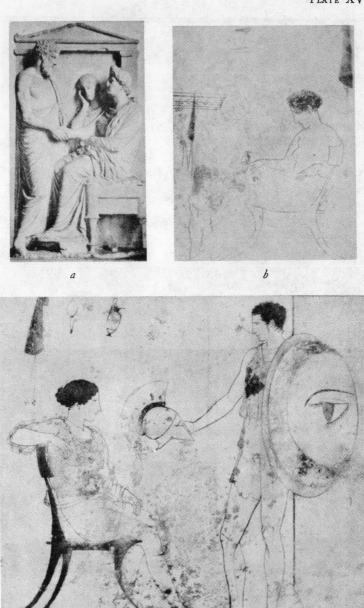

a

b

c

FAMILY LIFE

Plate XVII

a

b

WOMEN AT HOME

could be inside the house.[2] On the other hand, many houses, though chiefly those of the well-to-do, had a bathroom.[3] We also hear of many different kinds of utensils and crockery in house and kitchen, securing a certain amount of domestic comfort and culture.[4] Often several families were living together in a block of houses or a tenement-house.[5] On the other hand, houses could be classed according to the number of their couches; that did not mean beds, but places in the dining-room.[6] Perikles' large and asymmetrically shaped head could thus be called a head of 'eleven couches'.[7] Sanitary accommodation was often provided inside the house, usually by a sort of night-stool.[8] It could be said of a rich man that his house was so full that there was not even a small space left to 'ease one's self'.[9] Frequently the yard, where a primitive latrine might be found, or a small by-street, was used for such purposes.[10] The streets were usually muddy and dirty, especially after rain, and dirty water was thrown from the window into the street.[11]

These houses were the place where the women lived. There is hardly any evidence of Athenian women taking up a profession; women who were innkeepers, bread-sellers and the like, were generally metics or occasionally very poor people of Athenian origin. Certainly, Euripides' mother had never been a greengrocer. Attempts were made to secure some emancipation for women, and we may see them reflected, perhaps not in the ridiculous women's State in the *Ekklesiazousai*, but in

---

[1] F.114f. — C.37, 144ff, 634, 699, 706ff.

[2] W.836ff, frg. 18. — W.844, cf. L.1073, Pl.1106, Eupolis 453, Phryn. 43.

[3] W.141, cf. L.336f. — Houses of the rich even with γυμνάσια καὶ λουτρὰ καὶ ἀποδυτήρια: Ps.-Xen. II, 10.

[4] It seems unnecessary to cite the many passages in comedy in which a great variety of utensils is mentioned.

[5] συνοικίαι, K.1001, Th.273, Ps.-Xen. I, 17, Thuc. III, 74, 2.

[6] Phryn. 66.

[7] Telekl. 44.

[8] τὰ λάσανα, E.1062 (cf. 347, 371), frg. 462, Kratinos 49, Pherekr. 88, Eupolis 224, Plat. 116. A most necessary utensil was, of course, the frequently mentioned ἀμίς.

[9] adesp. 491.

[10] K.888f, P.98ff, 157f, 164f, Th.484ff, E.313ff, 1059ff, cf. P.1230.

[11] W.248, 254ff, 259. — A.616f, frg. 306.

the much more sincere and serious phrases of the *Lysistrate*.[1]
In this play, indeed, though women of all types are depicted,
Lysistrate herself is a woman of true genius, character and
independence, and we may well conclude from her personality
that Kimon's sister Elpinike or the Milesian Aspasia were not
the only women in Athens who met men on their own level,
both personally and socially. But if such women did not stand
alone, they were nevertheless exceptional. That unity among
women of which Euripides sometimes speaks — although he
also knows of their pleasure in talking evil of one another — is
little more than a natural mutual sympathy and allied opposition
to man.[2] What emancipation there was, did not touch the
female sex as a whole and its position in society. It is stated and
at the same time made a matter of reproach that in the tragedies
of Euripides women of every age, as well as slaves, had full
freedom of speech, like men and masters.[3] That is to say, Euripides represents them as individuals and in a more realistic way
than older tragedy. From the passages previously mentioned we
can conclude that Aristophanes' voice was only one in a general
chorus, and that Euripides fully realized the weight of public
opinion against free speech for women. The main burden,
however, of the women's grievances against Euripides is that
he shows up their failings and brings distrust and enmity into
married life.[4] No doubt, in these reproaches there is revealed
both the poet's discriminating psychology and the general
movement towards the emancipation of women, such as was
the natural outcome of an age of rationalist 'enlightenment'.
Aristophanes, however, speaks mainly of the gossipy, drunken
and immoral ways of women.[5] Although Euripides sometimes
talks about the clever woman, the 'learned woman' had not
yet come into existence; comedy is not likely to have missed
the opportunity of depicting her.[6] It remains significant that
Perikles, who was not exactly conservative, either in his views
or in his way of life, is said to have declared that a woman
should not be spoken of among men, either in praise or in
blame.[7] Little more than the first steps had been taken towards
women's emancipation.

---

[1] L.507ff.   [2] Eur. *Hel.* 329, 830, *frg.* 108. — *Ph.* 198ff.
[3] F.949f.   [4] See especially Th.384ff.   [5] e.g., Th.392ff, 476ff.
[6] Woman as σοφή, e.g., Eur. *Hipp.* 640, *Andr.* 213f.
[7] Thuc. II, 45, 2.

The allusions in comedy do in fact suggest that there was a certain competition between husband and wife for the management of house and family. This implies a desire in women for equality of personal, not of course of social or even political, rights. There is also some connection between this development and the first appearance of books dealing theoretically with the management of the household, with *oikonomia*, as a scientific profession.[1] Such books, however, tend to embody the demands and the programme of their writers, and therefore do not give a picture of real everyday life. That, as we have seen, had essentially different features.

2

The relation between parents and children should be discussed also on a wider basis, as the relation between two generations. Old age and youth are naturally opposed, and this opposition has always and everywhere been consciously acknowledged by mankind, though in different ways and degrees.[2] 'Palaestras for old men' are unknown outside comedy, but the view that the old men represented a better and stronger generation than the dissipated youth was no doubt widely maintained.[3] To be sure, when old men are rejuvenated — as might happen either by a miracle or through the influence of a young bride — they are like merry children out to steal bread.[4] Frequently the youthfulness of the old was only senile childishness, as it is expressed in the saying: 'Old age is second childhood', while it is something different when an old man wishes that people might be twice young and twice old in order to correct their mistakes and put things straight in their second life.[5] This is an application of the trivial truth that only the actions of the young and the counsels of the old are valuable;[6] but

[1] F.974ff. For οἰκονομία as an ἐπιστήμη, cf. Xen. *oik.* 1, 1. 2, 12. 6, 4; *mem.* III, 4, 7ff. Cf. also Radermacher, 284.

[2] Cf. Pherekr. 146.

[3] frg. 715. — W.1066ff, Eur. *Hipp.* 937ff, *Herakl.* 325ff.

[4] K.1321ff, P.680ff. — frg. 125.

[5] δὶς παῖς γέρων, C.1417, Kratinos 24, Theop. 69. — Eur. *Hik.* 1080ff.

[6] Eur. *frg.* 508. Thus Nikias admonishes the older generation not to be ashamed of opposing the younger people in their 'ill-starred craving for things beyond their reach' (Thuc. VI, 13, 1), while Alkibiades (VI, 18, 6) pleads for the collaboration of old and young.

behind the commonplaces and the jokes we easily discern the opinion that age and youth are incompatible. This again is an obvious truth, and it remains true although 'the old' are not necessarily old in our sense of the word. The Greeks had no word for middle-aged people of either sex. While we normally think of three generations alive at the same time, the Greeks talk of two only. It is the contrast of these that naturally concerns everybody, but in many cases creates no problem at all. It is most likely to become a problem where the bonds are closest and strongest, that is between parents and children.

It has been shown that the relation between father and son was a stock motif of comedy almost from its beginnings; it appears again and again, and in New Comedy it has become one of the paramount motifs of the plot.[1] It will be wiser, just because of its frequency, not to over-estimate the significance of the actual problem, nor to consider it as especially characteristic of our period. The rivalry, for instance, between father and son for the love of the same girl is simply a typical comic situation.[2] On the other hand, the very fact that the relation between father and son became a typical feature of comedy, shows that a question of general importance is touched upon here. Each age will view this question in a new and different light. The relations between the generations do not always imply opposition and struggle. We may say that in general the opposition grows stronger in proportion to the extent to which change and revolution, internal as well as external, are characteristic of the age.

On one occasion Aristophanes says of an ungrateful son: 'You don't provide for your father being clothed' — a remark which, of course, reveals the son's general, not only this particular, obligation.[3] It is somewhat surprising that elsewhere it seems to be a question of real importance whether a son is allowed to beat his father. In the *Clouds* the son, in spite, or perhaps because, of his sophistic arguments, is proved entirely in the wrong.[4] In the *Birds*, on the other hand, the parricide, though moved to stop beating and indeed killing his father, is not maltreated as the other rascals are who come to Cloudcuckooborough; his eagerness to beat someone turns him into

---

[1] Cf. F. Wehrli, *Motivstudien zur griech. Komödie*, 56f.
[2] Pherekr. 71-73.   [3] frg. 17 D.
[4] C.1409ff, Cf. Heinimann, *Nomos u. Physis* (1945), 122.

a good soldier.[1] The grotesque right of the birds to beat their fathers is contrasted with the duty of feeding the old ones.[2] In the *Frogs* the beating of mother and father ranks with crimes like perjury and offences against hospitality, but it seems to have been no less frequent.[3] We must ask the meaning of all this outside the realm of mere caricature.

At first sight, the whole thing seems to have been little more than an attempt to prove the monstrous nature of all this breaking of family bonds, and thus to reduce it to absurdity. However, there is perhaps something more in it than that. The parricide's desires are prompted by pure avarice,[4] and money plays the leading part also in the quarrel between Strepsiades and Pheidippides. To 'throttle' the father, in a financial sense of course, is typical of the 'sons of our times'.[5] The law grants the father the right to expel his son from the community of the family; on the other hand, in case of mental infirmity, it allows the father to be declared incapable of managing his affairs and the son to take over the whole property.[6] We recall the story of how the old Sophokles was accused by his sons. It seems that both procedures had become frequent by the last decades of the fifth century.[7] In comedy more drastic methods are used. The whole motif is both primitive and burlesque, and it is difficult to take it seriously, though there is doubtless some real background to it. It reflects not only avarice, which played an important part, but also a more profound hostility which was due to different methods of training and education.

In earlier times boys were taught by a teacher, and men by poets. In the *Frogs*, Euripides, being both a poet and a sophist, still approves of this arrangement which is set forth by Aischylos.[8] Everything, however, had been changed by the teaching of the sophists who were chiefly interested in political and forensic rhetoric. Older men now frequently saw themselves disregarded by the modern young men. 'The lads

---

[1] B.1337ff.   [2] B.757ff, 1347ff. — 1355ff.
[3] F.146ff.   [4] B.1352.
[5] E.638f.   [6] C.844ff.
[7] Early evidence for the former action, the ἀποκήρυξις, is scanty, but seems certain. In general, cf. J. H. Lipsius, *Attisches Recht u. Rechtsverfahren*, 355f, 502ff, S. Luria, *Aegyptus*, VII (1926), 268.
[8] F.1054f.

get up and speak before the men.'¹ The older men, when
entangled in lawsuits by the 'young orators', are helpless
against their new methods and sophistic cleverness, and this
is the reason why the comedian proposes to introduce separate
courts for old and young men.² The old jurymen, on the other
hand, have the reputation of being sharp and severe; when
peace comes again, they will be mild 'and much younger'; that
implies, of course, a return to their own youth, not that they
will be like the young men of the day.³ It was a great undertaking for an older man to approach 'matters younger than
himself', namely modern wisdom.⁴ Things seem to be topsy-
turvy when Strepsiades learns the new ways and addresses his
son thus: 'For a young lad you have very old-fashioned ideas',
or when Peithetairos is declared to be old in years, but young
in his views and plans.⁵

A similar kind of contrast can be found between the old
warriors of the Persian Wars and the young profiteers of
democracy, and the poet's dislike of the effeminacy of the
youths and their meddling in politics also reflects the same
opposition between the generations.⁶ The struggle between
Nikias and Alkibiades was partly one between the old and the
young generation.⁷ The contrast between the good statesmen
of old and the bad politicians of today was an often repeated
theme, which in Eupolis' *Demoi* dominates the whole play. It
is at the same time a struggle between the old and the young;
the latter can be called simply 'the gangsters'.⁸ We find complaints of disrespect and of arrogant behaviour, especially
towards older people, of lack of education — in the older sense,
of course — and other similar charges as well as the querulous
complaints of fathers about their sons' keenness on riding or
on writing poetry which they had learned to compose by

¹ Eupolis 310. It is just possible that the μειράκια of this fragment are the same
as the μειράκια κινούμενα of the *Demoi* (Eupolis 100), who have become
στρατηγοί.

² A.679f. — 714f.   ³ P.348ff.
⁴ σοφία, C.512ff.   ⁵ C.821. — B.255ff.
⁶ A.600ff, 676ff, W.1098ff, L.632ff. — Effeminate youth, e.g.: K.1373ff,
1382ff, C.987, 991, 1043ff, 1054, 1073, also Ps.-Andok. IV, 22.
⁷ Thuc. VI, 12f, 17f. Cf. J. de Romilly, *Thucydide et l'impérialisme athénien*
(1947), 176, and above, p. 207, n. 6.
⁸ Eupolis, 40 P, 97: τῶν πανούργων ... τῶν νεωτ[έρων]. Cf. Eupolis
100, 121, and above, note 1.

theory.[1] On the other hand we have the contemptuous remark of the knights that Kleon with his chattering and flattering clearly mistook them for old and senile men.[2] Old age or youth meant more than the number of years a man had lived. At a symposium it was the fashion to tell one's fellow-drinkers one's 'most youthful', 'most dashing', action.[3]

The inconsistent impression which we receive from all these references proves that Aristophanes was no die-hard defender of the older generation, although his stronger sympathies belonged to them. After all, he himself had begun to write comedies when he was still under age.[4] It is only natural that his judgment was at times influenced by his own age, and also by the use of certain conventional types. At least once, he left all the conventions about old and young behind him. In the *Wasps* he is a fervent upholder of youth without seriously defaming old age. There is the fine figure of Bdelykleon who, though he contradicts his father and the other old men, never forgets his filial love, and only prays that his father may become less hard and stubborn.[5] His attitude is the more significant as the son is master in the house, and the relations between father and son are completely reversed in comic absurdity.[6] From our evidence with all its ridiculous exaggerations there emerges as a real fact a change of outlook between one generation and the next, a change, above all, in the methods of instruction, in the nature of education, and in the ethics of political life.[7] Beyond doubt, for good or for ill, the younger generation was emancipated.

3

House and family are revealed as communities based on economic facts and personal attachment. The bonds of family-cult and religion are also touched upon by comedy, perhaps in the prayer to the 'paternal gods', more expressly in Dikaiopolis' sacrifice which is shared by his daughter and slave, while his wife looks on, or in the sacrifice to Hestia which took place

---

[1] C.993f, 998f. — C.916. — B.1440ff. What are the λόγοι 'by which a man is given wings' (1438)? There is no certain answer, but more likely than not they are supposed talks or books on the arts of riding, of writing poetry, or of any other τέχνη, providing theoretical instruction.

[2] K.270.   [3] W.1204f; cf. Neil on K.611.   [4] C.528ff.

[5] W.652, 655, 875ff.   [6] W.67, 442. Cf. above, p. 53.   [7] Cf. chapter X.

inside the house.[1] Public sacrifices usually opened with the invocation of Hestia, and 'to begin with Hestia' acquired the meaning of 'to begin at the beginning'.[2] This pre-eminence of the goddess of the hearth is very significant for the place in religion of hearth and home.

A man's religious activities, whether as the member of a particular cult or as a citizen generally, were, however, mainly connected with the smaller communities, with *genos*, *phratria*, and *phyle*, clan, brotherhood and tribe, apart of course from the State-cults. These communities surviving from the aristocratic period had long lost their specific character. In particular, the old *phyle* had almost completely disappeared since the Kleisthenic reforms, and when a *phyle* is mentioned in comedy, the word always indicates one of the ten tribes which formed the real political organization of the State and also the main cadres of the army.[3] Their eponymous heroes, though created as late as Kleisthenes, were worshipped as *archegetai*, as 'first leaders'.[4] It was the tribes which provided the frame for the public elections. They were also responsible for the choregy; rivalry in producing a good chorus-teacher was strong among them.[5] Sometimes, however, the *phyle* is mixed up with the older forms of communities, in a way which cannot be strictly technical. Only a man, for instance, who is a member of *phyle* and *genos*, is a 'citizen among citizens'.[6] The two Athenians in the *Birds* are called Prokne's kinsmen and tribesmen, because she is the daughter of a mythical Athenian king.[7] We shall have to consider how far the ties of ancient kinship and tribal relationship were still strong besides those of the Kleisthenic order.

It was an unwritten law in Athens that nobody became a citizen until he had registered with phratry and deme, as we know from inscriptions and many passages in the Orators.[8]

---

[1] W.388, A.247ff, Eupolis 281. Cf. also the sacrifice to Zeus Ktesios (Isaios VIII, 16).

[2] B.865, W.846 (ἄρχεσθαι ἀφ' Ἑστίας).

[3] For φυλή = regiment see, e.g., *IG.* I², 1085 = Tod, no. 41, 5.

[4] frg. 126.   [5] B.1403f.   [6] B.33ff.   [7] B.368; cf. Xen. *anab.* VII, 2, 31.

[8] Isaios II, 14 shows that there could be a registration among the ὀργεῶνες, IX, 30 that a child was introduced εἰς τοὺς θιάσους τοὺς Ἡρακλέους. There is no evidence in comedy to illuminate these kinds of associations, though Aristophanes' Δαιταλῆς may have been θιασιῶται (cf. Suidas, *s.v.*). There is ample, mainly epigraphical, evidence, though very intricate, which has been collected in an interesting paper by W. S. Ferguson, *Harvard Theol. Rev.* XXXVII (1944), 61ff.

When a father wanted a child registered, he had to sacrifice a
lamb; but if it was not big enough, it could be refused by the
phrateres, the members of the phratry.[1] 'I only hope', says a
father to the lamb, 'that you won't kick the beam.'[2] By being
introduced into the phratry a son or daughter could be legiti-
mized, and an illegitimate son, a manumitted slave or a
foreign Greek could only thus become an Athenian citizen.[3]
This rule, however, seems to have allowed exceptions, as the
example of Archedemos shows, and this is confirmed by the
fact that, at least in the fourth century, different phratries had
different regulations.[4] Frequently foreigners who had found
their way into a phratry by false pretences were brought before
the court of the *nautodikai*.[5] The *phrateres* who form the chorus
of a play by some second-rate comedian, Leukon, were a real
community, in a much higher degree than the members of
a *phyle*.[6] The phratry granted to its members various substantial advantages, for instance on the occasion of festivals or
the dinners which followed sacrifices. 'Phraters and kinsmen'
met especially on the important days of the Apaturia.[7] The
heliasts, the jurymen at the people's courts who earned the
notorious pay of three obols, are once called *phrateres* of the
triobolon, as members of a true and lucrative community.[8] It
is significant of the conservative element in all the radicalism
of Athenian democracy that in private life, and also as the
necessary condition for the right of citizenship, the membership
of a phratry kept its place.

The *genos*, the 'clan', sometimes mentioned in a general
sense, was no longer of outstanding importance, though in
some of the old noble families its traditions were not dead.[9]
But even the most stubborn oligarchs found their common

---

[1] Schol. F.798.   [2] frg. 286.

[3] B.764f, 1669, Eupolis 40 P, 21ff.

[4] F.588, see p. 160f. — Cf. K. Latte, *P.-W.* XVII, 1069.

[5] frg. 225, Kratinos 233.

[6] Leukon 1ff. — Cf. *IG.* II, 1², 1237.

[7] Xen. *hell.* I, 7, 8. I read (with Dindorf and Hude) φρατέρες instead of the
πατέρες of the codd.

[8] K.255. Cf. p. 230, n. 2.

[9] B.33. — In Euripides' *Herakleidai* (590) Makaria sacrifices herself for the
γένος; Orestes feels the bonds of the οἶκος with deep emotion (*Iph. T.* 693ff),
and Iphigenia will save her brother instead of herself because a man is far more
important for a 'house' than a woman (ibid. 1005f).

ground in their clubs or *hetairiai* rather than in any close relations of birth and origin. The *genos* had ceased to mean anything outside the wider family circle, which had no importance
in politics and little in the structure of society.

The members of a clan, and even those of a phratry, met
only on rare occasions. These communities were therefore of
less importance in everyday life than the neighbours with whom
a man lived in direct contact. It was an old saying, which had
gained new weight, that you must have friends, and not only
relatives.[1] We have referred already to the women who used
to borrow one thing or another from their neighbour, or
helped a neighbour in childbirth.[2] After a birth, there was the
festival of the Amphidromia, when the baby was shown round
to all the neighbours; this was probably the same as the so-
called *dekate*, the name-giving on the tenth day after the birth,
when relatives and friends were invited, even if they lived some
distance away.[3] There are many other examples of neigh-
bourly relations. Neighbours were naturally summoned when
a fire broke out.[4] A man who was always wanting to warm
himself at his neighbour's fire, came to be a proverbial description of a parasite.[5] The god or hero whose sanctuary or statue
stood close by, or in front of, the house, was also a neighbour.[6]
The term 'the neighbours' came to be used with a definite
meaning, and Krates wrote a play with this title.[7] Phrases to
which analogies can easily be found in other languages refer
to the sometimes tiresome habits of people who live near,
whether in town or in the country. 'A man who fries fat is
unpopular with the neighbours.'[8] A poor man would not
easily have friendly neighbours.[9] A thing was a dead secret if
even the neighbours did not know about it.[10] For 'neighbours
have sharper eyes than foxes', and 'it is better to till the rocks
than to live in the plain and have bad neighbours'.[11]

Neighbours in a wider sense than the inhabitants of the
neighbouring houses or farms are the *demotai*, the members

[1] Eur. *Or.* 804ff.
[2] See p. 201. Cf. also, in spite of its obscurity, Hermipp. 29.
[3] L.757. — B.494f, 922f, Eur. *frg.* 2.   [4] Th. 241.
[5] K.780.   [6] W.389, 393, 875.
[7] P.79, E.805, Pl.435; cf. Lysias XVII, 8. — Krates 1ff.
[8] adesp. 608.   [9] Eur. *El.* 1130f.
[10] E.16, Plat. 204.   [11] adesp. 435, 380.

of a deme, the local community in town or country.[1] We find
people addressed or described either simply as '*demotai*',
fellow-demesmen, or 'neighbours and demesmen', 'neighbours,
kin and demesmen', or 'demesmen and friends'.[2] They, besides wives and children, could supply the weeping pleaders
in court.[3] Hermippos wrote a play *The Demotai*, and the
Acharnians as well as Eupolis' *Prospaltioi* took their titles from
the names of individual demes; perhaps Aristophanes'
Daitales referred to a fictitious culinary deme. The chorus of
the old charcoal-burners of Acharnai, which was economically
and politically one of the most important demes of Attica,
illustrates very clearly the close community between the members of a deme, who, inspired by their local Muse, are uniform
and united in thought and feeling.[4] Elsewhere, too, the deme
appears to have a real unity. In danger, a man would call for
help from his fellow-demesmen.[5] A man longed for his deme
when he was away from it.[6] The demesmen met before they
set out on a campaign, and the rich used to give the poor
weapons or money for the equipment they needed.[7] In general
the rich played an important part in the deme.[8] Everybody
knew everybody else, and the circumstances of all the families
were known to everybody. Nobody liked to incur the enmity
of a member of his deme (though this sometimes happened),

---

[1] Cf. Isaios IX, 18: Ἀραφηνίων πολλοὶ τῶν τότε συγγεωργούντων.
The κωμῆται (C.965, L.5), the 'fellow-villagers', were members of the
deme in its character not of a political community but of a residential district.
Thus, the 'fellow-village-girls' and the 'tavern-women' (κωμητίδες and
καπηλίδες) are mentioned together (frg. 274). There is almost no distinction between the villagers and the γείτονες. The δημότιδες in L.333
were hardly members of the same deme (so Liddell and Scott), but female
fellow-citizens. For this use of δημότης see above, p. 82, n. 3. In a political
sense, on the other hand, the States, situated close to Attica, were neighbours (L.698f).

[3] Lysias XXVII, 12.

[4] A.665ff. — 319, 328ff, 333, 349, 675. Importance of Acharnai: Thuc. II,
20, 4; 21, 3; see also the inscriptions in L. Robert, *Études epigraphiques et philo-
logiques* (1938), 293ff, the most important also Tod, 204.

[5] L.685.   [6] A.33.   [7] Lysias XVI, 14, XXXI, 15.

[8] Cf. J. Sundwall, *Epigraphische Beiträge*, 55ff.

[9] Lysias XXIII, 3, Isaios II, 36, VIII, 27.

[10] Eur. *Alk.* 1057ff.

or what was even worse, to go to law with the deme itself.[1]
The demes, governed by the *demarchoi* who were also the
bailiffs, were communities with some degree of independence,
and in a sense assimilated to the old religious communities.[2]
It is significant that the women-*demotai* chose the leaders of
the Thesmophoria.[3] The office of *gymnasiarches* of the deme
gave a man a good opportunity to display his liberality, especially during the political elections.[4] A man who had won
credit both among his fellow-demesmen and among the
whole people might be elected by the members of the
phyle.[5]

Eupolis in his *Demoi* presented a chorus composed of demes,
some of which were perhaps singled out by their names, like
the cities in the same poet's *Poleis*.[6] But even so, they represented a whole, *the* demos of Athens. The individual deme
did not lose its hold even over those of its members who had
moved to another place and, like Euelpides, no longer lived
in their original deme.[7] This is the best proof that the deme
was not only a place of common residence, but a genuine
community. The men from one deme usually had a common
meeting-place in town; for instance, the men from Dekeleia
met in a barber's shop 'near the Hermae'.[8] The demes together were the demos of Athens, represented, not by the old
fool of the *Knights* who personified the assembly, but by all
the men of Attica, who lived in the small communities of town
and country, and were firmly attached to house and land.[9] The
old communities of blood and birth were not forgotten, but
the days when they actually determined the political and social
life were long past. The place of a man's birth, or in some
cases of his father's or grandfather's birth, was in the time of
Perikles as well as later the only small community, within the
State, of genuine social and political importance.

There are sources other than comedy from which we learn

---

[1] C.1218f, Isaios IX, 21. — Isaios XII, *frg.* 5, 1.
[2] Bailiffs: C.37, frg. 484. — Independence: Eupolis 41 P, cf. Thuc. II, 16, 2;
IG. I², 76 (*Syll.*³ 83, Tod, 74), 13, 21, 27, 183ff; II, I², 1172ff (*Syll.*³ 912ff). —
Religious communities: cf. *IG.* II, I², 1138ff, 1229ff, 1237ff (*Syll.*³ 1091,
921).
[3] Isaios VIII, 19.   [4] Isaios II, 42, VII, 36.
[5] Ps.-Lysias XX, 2.   [6] Eupolis 231ff.   [7] B.496, 645.
[8] Lysias XXIII, 3. In a similar way the Plataeans met once a month at the
'Green Cheese' part of the market-place (ibid. 6).   [9] Cf. Eur. *Alk.* 1057 ff.

several facts about house and family and deme. Yet what we learn from them are mostly, though not always, legal facts and formalities, and not facts of everyday life. Painters and sculptors give us other and more intimate evidence. In comedy, although its evidence has to be supplemented from other sources, in particular from speeches by orators such as Lysias and Isaios, something of the atmosphere is revealed in which the Athenians lived in their small communities. And in it, as in the vase-paintings or on the grave-reliefs, there is warm and living breath. What it lacks in beauty and profundity is amply made up in realism.

We had already looked at the people of Athens in their social structure and economic functions: we have now seen them in their private life. In spite of differences, chiefly of wealth, in spite of tensions such as those which existed between the generations or between town and country, we find everywhere the same type of 'small man', occupied in agriculture, trade or crafts, active also in politics, whether as an ordinary member of the assembly or as one of the few leading politicians. From Kleon onwards it was the 'Man in the Street' who ruled Athens. This phrase is much more appropriate and expressive when applied to Athenian life than to our own age and climate. Office-buildings and Houses of Parliament were not the stage of political life, nor house and club that of social life. As already emphasized, almost the whole of a man's life was lived in the open air. The Athenians were men in the street, men in the market, men in assembly and palaestra, men in the groves and sacred enclosures of the gods.

When we speak of the 'Man in the Street' we must include the few larger landowners or businessmen who did not belong to the nobility. Demosthenes' father was one of them. We can trace economic parallels to this type also among metics and even emancipated slaves. We have seen that the distance between the rich citizens and rich non-citizens was not great, except in the political sphere, nor was there, on the other hand, a wide gulf separating the wealthy from the poorer citizens. In the generations after Perikles the 'Man in the Street', the man who belonged to phratry and deme, represented the people in their political and economic activities. His ideal of life was primarily distinguished by the desire to 'live and let live', although with a natural bias in favour of his own material well-being. 'What does wine grant to men?' — in other words, what are the aims of men in conditions of heightened vitality and energy, such as are given by wine, in conditions, that is to say, in which a man is able to realize his ideals? The answer is 'to be wealthy and successful, to win one's lawsuits, to be happy, and to help one's friends'.[1] This quotation is also a convenient bridge from the present chapter to the next.

[1] K.92ff.

CHAPTER IX

MONEY AND PROPERTY

I

THE Athenians would not have been Greeks if money and property had not meant a great deal to them. Here too comedy reflects real life, for it has more references to money than any other literary source. Moreover, it does not weary us with moralizing speeches about avarice, meanness and extravagance, nor with long discussions of complicated legal cases. Money appears in its real function, as the permanent and necessary basis of life for every individual human being. We are left in no doubt that money was in fact the basic factor in Athenian economy. It is significant that money sometimes appears in metaphors, very much as it may occur in modern languages. Sokrates asks: 'What kind of gods do you swear by? You must know first of all that gods are not current coin with us.'[1] The gods of Euripides are called 'a new coinage', and a bad man was called 'of base coinage'; substantially the same phrase was used for a worthless coin.[2] 'Stamp' and 'character' was one word used for coins and men alike, and gold as well as men could be 'adulterated'.[3]

Professional money-dealing, however, the business of the *trapezites*, which included what we call banking, was little developed and entirely in private hands.[4] The so-called 'money-coiner', who obtained and lent money, was quite a well-known figure.[5] Some banking transactions are mentioned in comedy; for instance, the simple changing of money into

---

[1] C.247f. At the same time, there may be a pun here. Θεοὶ ἡμῖν νόμισμ᾽ οὐκ ἔστι reminded the audience of the modern view that gods exist only on account of a mere opinion (νομιζόμενοι). Cf. F. Heinimann, *Nomos und Physis*, 121.

[2] F.890. — Pl.862, 957, cf. A.517f. — F.718ff, 725.

[3] χαφακτήρ: Eur. *Hek.* 379f, *El.* 558f, 572. — κίβδηλος: *Med.* 516ff, *Hipp.* 616, *El.* 550.

[4] Eupolis 125, Lysias, *frg.* 38, 1. We do not know what the δημοσία τράπεζα was (schol. F.367, *IG.* II², 1013, 4; see also *Syll.*³ 577, 12f); cf. Boeckh, II, 319, 2, Laum, *P.-W. Suppl.* IV, 8f.

[5] Kratinos 226, Phryn. 5.

smaller coin, or loans at simple and compound interest, or the
keeping of deposits.[1]   The reliability of the bankers was
generally acknowledged, except for the small moneylenders
and usurers who cannot be regarded as bankers, and of whom
we shall speak below.[2]   It was usual to deposit money by oral
agreement, often even without witnesses.[3]   In a general way
the seeds of the later development of banking were already
sown.

In investigating the part played by money outside the professional handling of it, we ought first to go into the perennial,
if commonplace, matter of prices.[4]   We have, of course, to
take into account the fact that in comedy a price may be
occasionally raised or lowered, simply for the sake of comic
effect.   It is certainly not the usual price when an ordinary
cup is valued at 200 dr(achmai), or when a rich man gives a
dinner for a hundred dr. and the wine costs as much again,
or when a slave pretends to have got for a hundred dr. only
eight bass and twelve gilt-heads, even though these were expensive kinds of fish.[5]   Likewise, the ridiculous haggling
between Dionysos and the dead man about the price to be
paid for carrying the luggage (two dr. or one and a half) is not
about a price which is to be taken seriously, and the seven
obols which are proclaimed with trumpets, probably as a reward, are only a jest.[6]   Any of the prices mentioned in comedy
may be misleading; the general impression will prove to be
right.

[1] W.789, frg. 208. — C.1155f, 1214ff, 1267ff. — frg. 724. — Nothing is said
of that branch of banking which was most important in the fourth century: the
sea-loans. The only possible allusion is provided by the man who looks anxiously
out for the cargo-ships (adesp. 377). He may be an *emporos*, but more likely he is
the moneylender. The chief reason why pure money business plays a comparatively small part in comedy is that the rapid development of this part of economic
life did not begin before the fourth century. Pasion founded his bank in 394; but
even he is partly or even essentially a manufacturer. In general cf. Glotz, 304.

[2] Cf. Calhoun, 82ff. Mere moneylenders, of course, like the mother of Hyperbolos (Th.840ff), were by no means always honest business people; cf. also the
man who gave three minae and charged twelve (Pl.381).

[3] E.446ff, cf. Isokr. XVII, 2.

[4] To the following pages cf. the first chapter of Boeckh.

[5] frg. 71. It is on account of the enormous price of the cup that Pollux
(*onom.* 10, 85), who quotes the fragment, assumes that there were κότυλοι not
only of earthenware but also of silver. — Eupolis 149. — Eupolis 150.

[6] F.173. — Archipp. 19.

PLATE XVIII

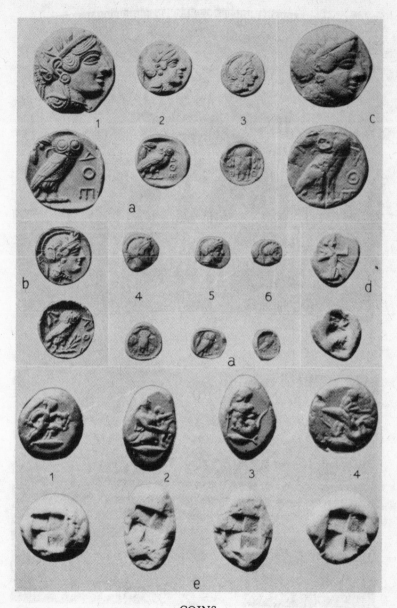

COINS

PLATE XIX

a

b

ARMY AND NAVY

Silver was the prevailing Attic standard, as it was with most of the coinages of the time. Foreign gold coins were being introduced only gradually. The ratio of the value of gold to silver changed; in general gold became less valuable from the time when Persian gold coins began to circulate more freely in Greece, and the output of Laureion decreased, temporarily at least.[1] Nevertheless, in spite even of the occasional minting of gold coins by Athens herself, the monometallic system of silver coinage remained.[2] The *stater* or tetradrachm may be called the standard coin of Athens, but the drachma was the basic unit of calculation, and a sum in drachmas could be given by the mere figure, without the addition of the word drachmas.[3] Anything worth a drachma was called a *drachmiaion*.[4]

Everyday life, however, reckoned in *obeloi* or *oboloi* (obols), the sixth part of a drachma.[5] Foreign money was changed into obols; the 'twelfth part', for instance, which apparently means one twelfth of a *stater* of special value, was worth eight obols.[6] Athenian currency consisted of silver coins of various sizes; some of these coins were not introduced before the fourth century. The whole series included the three-obol piece — the often-mentioned triobolon — the two-obol piece, $1\frac{1}{2}$ obols, $\frac{3}{4}$, $\frac{1}{2}$, $\frac{3}{8}$, $\frac{1}{4}$ and (rarely) $\frac{1}{8}$ obol.[7] All these silver coins, bearing the head of Athena and the owl, were, according to the promise of the Birds, 'the Laureion owls, who will nest in the purses and hatch small coins'; they could also be called 'maidens' or 'virgins' after the virgin goddess.[8] Later, in the fourth century, the bronze *chalkous* took the place of the $\frac{1}{8}$-obol piece, which was almost useless because of its very small size.[9] But there is another small coin sometimes mentioned in comedy, the so-called *kollybos*, probably a copper coin, though it has

[1] Cf. Wade-Gery, *Num. Chron.* X (1930), 16ff.

[2] About the Athenian gold coins see next page.

[3] W.769.   [4] frg. 425.

[5] Cf. M. N. Tod, *Num. Chron.* 1947, 1ff.   [6] Krates 20.

[7] C. T. Seltman, *Greek Coins*, 109, 178f. — Only some of them are mentioned in comedy: frg. 3, 48, F.554. See Plate XVIII*a*. The τετρώβολον (P.254, cf. Theop. 55) and the πεντώβολον (K.798) were, in all probability, not coins but sums of money.

[8] B.1106ff. — κόραι or παρθένοι: Eur. *frg.* 675.

[9] If the χαλκοῦς in adesp. 376 was the same as that coined by Timotheos in the Olynthian War (Ps.-Aristotle, *oik.* 1350a, 23ff), the fragment cannot belong to Old Comedy. In general see M. N. Tod, *Num. Chron.* 1946, 47ff.

been disputed whether it was a real coin at all.[1] In colloquial
language a kollybos meant 'nothing';[2] its money value was
probably a fraction of the *chalkous*. There were perhaps also
pieces of two or three *kollyboi*.[3] When owing to the war silver
was scarce, Athens tried to create more currency by melting
down the golden statues of Nike and making gold coins.[4]
This proved of little effect, mainly, we may assume, because
Athens was accustomed only to silver coinage, and gold coins
could not replace the smaller pieces. Therefore a year later a
real emergency money was minted, thinly plated bronze coins,
which took the place of the silver coins of the same size and
value.[5] This debasing of the coinage represents the earliest
evidence of the usual form of inflation in antiquity; it resulted
in the disappearance of almost all good coins. The emergency
coins, those 'wretched bits of bronze', were therefore suddenly
withdrawn by a decree in 393.[6] Sometimes non-Attic money
is mentioned in comedy,[7] but very few foreign coins had a
good reputation or were current in Athens. Among the few
were especially the electrum *stater* of Kyzikos, the coining and
circulation of which was even encouraged by Athens, the
Persian *dareikos*, and the silver coins of Aigina.[8] The coins
which have been found in Attica confirm the evidence of
comedy on this point.[9]

What was the buying value of drachma and obol? One obol

---

[1] Cf. Regling, *P.-W*. XI, 1099, and the interpretation of Svoronos, *Journ. internat. d'archéol. numism*. XIV, 123ff. Recently Tod, *Num. Chron*. 1945, 108ff.

[2] P.1200, Eupolis 233.   [3] frg. 3, adesp. 1167.

[4] See Plate XVIII*b*. Cf. W. S. Ferguson, *Treasurers of Athena*, 86ff, Seltman, *l.c*., 137f, 177f.

[5] F.720 and schol. F.725. See Plate XVIII*c*.

[6] F.725. — E.815ff. Here Aristophanes is said to have discovered the well-known 'Gresham's Law'; cf. Nicosia, 199. Urbain, *L'antiquité class*. VIII, 195. A more adequate judgment can be found already in Macaulay, *Hist. of England*, VIII, ch. 21. Polykrates (Herod. III, 56, 2) and Themistokles in Magnesia (Seltman, *l.c*., 108) had coined bad money in the same way as Athens did, but it is unlikely that they did so in a state of economic emergency. One should not call inflation what, in fact, was simply deceit by an independent ruler.

[7] For the unusual iron money of Byzantion, see C.249, Plat. 96.

[8] Kyzikos:P.1176,Pl.816f,Eupolis112,233,LysiasXII,11.SeePlateXVIII*e*; note the symbols referring to Athens. — *Dareikos*, E.602, frg. 504, Lysias, *l.c*., cf. Pl 170; see Plate XVIII*d*. — Aigina: Eupolis 141.

[9] Heichelheim, 301ff.

was sufficient to buy 'obolos-bread', apparently a one-obol loaf,
a loaf of average size, and 'ten (or even fourteen) obols' worth
of bread' was a great deal.¹ Meat, of course, was expensive; a
dish for half an obol was certainly a modest meal, though, it
seems, a usual one in the catering trade; the glutton Herakles
swallowed twenty of them.² Salted fish, a cheap and popular
food, cost one obol each, and the same price was paid for a
fair quantity of small sardines.³ It was a vital necessity to the
people that fish should be kept cheap.⁴ Spices were sold for
one or two obols, and three *kotyloi* of wine, a normal but small
measure, were to be had for one obol.⁵ The prices of corn or
flour mentioned in comedy vary considerably, as they did in
fact; once the price of a sixth of a bushel of corn (not quite
sixteen pints), enough to feed a man for eight days, is given
as three obols, while a Boeotian *kophinos* of flour (between
sixteen and eighteen pints) is said to have cost four dr.,
which was certainly an excessive price.⁶ A certain amount,
apparently an average one, of the best honey cost four obols,
a pigeon three.⁷ A jackdaw for one obol and a crow for three
were hardly worth even that price, but the bird dealer, though
a swindler, sells seven finches for one obol.⁸ A small pig, however, cost three dr., while the drachma for a pig's snout may
have included also the belly of the tunny fish mentioned at the
same time.⁹ It is quite impossible for a horse, even a winning
horse, to have been seriously valued at 15 talents (90,000 dr.);
the worth of the horse is in this case jokingly contrasted with
the owner of the horse who was worth hardly a few coppers.¹⁰
But twelve minae, a fifth of a talent, may have been an adequate
price for a 'koppa-branded horse' or one of favourite colour,
while three minae (300 dr.) for a horse constituted a small sum.¹¹

---

¹ frg. 103, 440, Pherekr. 55 (whatever the meaning of this obscure fragment).
The second explanation given by ancient grammarians of ὀβελία, namely that it
means a loaf roasted on a spit, seems unlikely, if only for technical reasons. It may,
however, have been a loaf shaped like an obolos (Poll. VI, 75); Mr. Seltman
reminds me of the normal French loaf. This is also Mr. Tod's view (*Num. Chron.*,
1947, 1f). — W.1391: ἄρτους δέκ' ὀβολῶν κἀπιθήκην τεττάρων. The
ἐπιθήκη refers to obols rather than loaves.

² Eupolis 154. — F.553f.   ³ adesp. 562. — K.649, Aristom. 7.
⁴ Cf. K.644ff.   ⁵ K.676ff, adesp. 562. — Th.743, adesp. 1320.
⁶ E.547. — Strattis 13.   ⁷ P.254. — Phyrn. 51.
⁸ B.18f, 1077ff.   ⁹ P.374, Strattis 4.
¹⁰ adesp. 376.   ¹¹ C.21ff, 1224. Ps. — Lysias VIII 10. — Isaios V, 43.

The prices of other commodities are given. The fuller got three obols for the cleaning of a coat, evidently a fair price.[1] While in the 'twenties a garment was valued at five *staters* (20 dr.), later, though one would expect a higher price, a new warm coat cost 16 or 20 dr., a pair of shoes not more than eight dr.[2] The prices are explained by the fact that the first mentioned garment was an expensive piece of luxury, while the later moderate prices were those of dress worn by ordinary people. Extravagant women are said to have bought dresses for more than a thousand dr. each.[3] A hundred vine-poles did not cost more than one dr., while a toy or a small oil-bottle could be bought for a single obol.[4] A lady could buy white and red cosmetics for two obols, a sum which also represented an adequate payment for an interpreter of dreams.[5] For a ring against snake-bite the druggist charged a drachma, while a signet-ring cost only half that amount.[6] A small chariot and a pair of wheels were together offered for sale at 300 dr., but the price seems to have been thought excessive.[7] While during the war one could get 'hardly a *kollybos*' for agricultural tools like sickles or scythes or water-vessels, after the conclusion of peace, when the peasants were engaged in getting their farms straight again, the sickle-maker could sell his wares for 50 dr. apiece, and the potter for three.[8] The prices charged by the merchants for a breast-plate was ten minae (1000 dr.), for a trumpet 60 dr. and for a helmet 50 dr.; as these things were bought during the war, the usual prices must have been lower, and at any rate 1000 dr. is out of proportion.[9] Finally, we have a special class of prices: to sleep with a hetaera one usually had to pay much more than a drachma.[10] There were, of course, different tariffs, but a silver *stater* was a moderate price.[11] It is by way of a joke that an Attic soldier is said to have bought a mistress for a *kollybos* — and that in Kyzikos

---

[1] W.1128. [2] Eupolis 252. — F.413, Pl.982ff.
[3] adesp. 516. [4] P.1263. — C.863f, F.1234ff.
[5] Ameips. 3, W.52f. [6] Pl.883f. — Th.425. [7] C.31.
[8] P.1198ff. I retain the common reading of the MSS. in 1201 (πεντήκοντα) and do not accept Meineke's correction πέντε γ' αὐτά. The latter would probably have been a reasonable price in normal times; the point here must be that the sickle-maker gets unusually high prices, and the 3 dr. for a rough pot seems also to be a lot.
[9] P.1224ff, 1240f, 1251.
[10] Th 1195 [11] Theop. 21.

with its precious electrum *staters* which were the envy of Athens.[1]

It is obvious that on the basis of these varied prices we cannot construct any sort of price-curve, even if we add all the evidence obtained from other sources. The only certain fact is a general tendency for prices to rise, especially that of wheat. As always with this kind of fragmentary evidence, all we can do is to try to work out a rough impression of the value of money.[2] Apart from the general rise of prices during the war, there were changes in one direction or the other according as times were easy or difficult. Everything that was scarce was expensive, and vice versa; in case of urgent need one had to sell cheaply.[3] The ordinary law of supply and demand ruled. The conclusion of peace, as we have seen, gave the sickle-maker the chance to sell his products at a good profit, while the arms merchant went bankrupt.[4] The soldier's widow, who plaited wreaths for religious purposes, suffered financially from the anti-religious movement which lessened the demand.[5] The Boeotian eel was a favourite delicacy, but three dr. for one was certainly a high price due to war-time conditions.[6] A clever merchant would follow the changes in demand: he tried to buy cheap and to sell dear wherever and whenever the demand increased.[7]

The prices which happen to be given in comedy indicate that many things could be bought for a few obols. The five obols a day which the wealthy grandfather and guardian pretended to have spent for the nourishment of each of his three grandchildren were rightly regarded as an excessive amount of money.[8] If something was to be shown as exceptionally cheap, it was said that one could get 'ten for an obol', while one would get 'of bad things a little for one obol', but even that would be rather expensive. In Hades money-affairs

[1] Eupolis 233.
[2] There were, of course, differences of quality, e.g., between the fine Persian wool and the rough Attic cloth. A Persian coat is said to have been made from wool costing a talent (W.1137f, 1145ff).
[3] A.758f, K.894ff, W.251ff, 491ff, P.252ff. — A.812ff, 895ff.
[4] P.1198ff, 1210ff.   [5] Th. 446ff. This, however, may be nothing but a joke.
[6] A.962.   [7] K.676ff. — A.900ff, cf. Lysias XXII, 8, 14.
[8] Lysias XXXII, 20. The food concerned is called ὄψον which means that σῖτος is not included.
[9] adesp. 763. — Eupolis 185.

were supposed to be on a similar basis.[1] Small change was called by the same word as money on the whole.[2] It was the sum a man had normally to deal with for every-day needs. Thus a drachma was hardly regarded as small coin, and to change it one went to the market.[3] A peasant who had sold his grapes and was going to buy some flour had only small coin with him — some of the coppers which unfortu-nately were withdrawn from circulation at that very moment.[4] He carried the coins in his mouth. This was the general custom, and it was therefore possible literally to stop an orator's mouth by bribery, though 'small coin' would scarcely satisfy him.[5] The poor fellow who had swallowed his only obol was unable to make any further purchases.[6] Someone thought it safer — such a small sum makes it seem amusing — to put two obols and a *symbolon* under his pillow.[7] For larger sums of money, which it was desired to keep for some time, a man had always a purse or a 'bladder', the rich man perhaps even a 'safe'.[8]

On the whole, the prices vindicate our estimate of the value, or rather the lack of value, of the public payments. It is well known that since the days of Perikles 'the Horn of Plenty' had been generous to the 'present-takers'.[9] Payment to the citizens, either for some service rendered to the State or for nothing at all, was more than a necessary result of a democratic system based on the political co-operation of the whole com-munity. In a sense, it was a quite simple and primitive idea, inherent in the nature of the Polis which was a community of citizens, not of subjects; besides, the Greeks always considered private property as the inevitable foundation of the economic

---

[1] Pherekr. 81.

[2] ἀργύριον (frg. 262) or the plural ἀργύρια (B.600, frg. 397, Eupolis 155).

[3] W.788f.   [4] E.817ff.

[5] W.606ff, 791f, frg. 3, 48, 614. — P.645, Pl.379.   [6] B.502f.

[7] frg. 44. According to Poll. IX, 70f the *symbolon* was half a coin, hardly the right explanation. In most cases it means an entrance ticket to court or assembly, which entitled the bearer to receive his fees (E.296, Pl.278). What is important, however, is that it implied a certain small value (Hermipp. 14, 61, Archipp. 8). Cf. Regling, *P.-W.* IV, A, 1092 (unfortunately much too short).

[8] βαλλάντιον: K.707, B.1107, frg. 328, 504, 545, Telekl. 41, 2, adesp. 654, 660. — ἀργυροθήκη: Diokl. 1 D.

[9] Kratinos 244, cf. 128. This probably does not refer to bribery, but to the payment of the jurymen; cf. H. Erbse, *Philologus* XCVII (1948), 189ff.

system. The citizens were, so to speak, entitled to share personally in the surplus revenues of the State, and the Athenians had had experience of this before Themistokles. As pay in the true sense of the word, however, not as the distribution of the public surplus, public payments were first introduced by Perikles. They quickly deteriorated into a weapon of demagogic practice.

The widest form of public payment, the fee paid for attending the assembly, was not introduced until the beginning of the fourth century. For a short time it amounted to one obol, then it was raised to two and finally, about 393, to three obols.[1] At the time when the payment was one obol, the people preferred to hang about in the market; after the three obols had been introduced, there was a veritable rush to the *ekklesia*.[2] The fees of the jurors, instituted by Perikles, as were probably those of the members of the council, amounted to two obols at the outbreak of the war.[3] As early as 425 it was raised to three by Kleon.[4] The citizens, instead of sitting through a whole day, tried to get their money by attending at one lawsuit only, or later, when lawsuits had become less frequent, to be registered under more than one 'letter', thus being certain of at least one sitting; but there was no further rise of fees.[5] Even as it was, the jurymen's pay represented for a long time the heaviest burden on the State, until later on it lost its special importance when everybody who sat in the assembly received the same payment.[6]

Famous, even notorious, throughout the world was the *diobelia*, but what it was is not definitely known.[7] It did, however, not indicate the *theorikon*, a payment of two obols, perhaps introduced by Perikles, perhaps much later, which enabled every citizen to attend the performances of tragedies and comedies.[8] Probably the *diobelia* was on a much larger scale, and is

---

[1] E.183ff, cf. 290ff, 380ff.   [2] E.299ff, Pl.171, 329f.
[3] Members of council: cf. Wade-Gery, *AJP*. LIX (1938), 131ff.
[4] K.51, 255, W.690, frg. 574, Phryn. 63.
[5] K.50f, W.595. — Pl.1166f, cf. 972.
[6] Burden on State: F.1466, cf. W.660ff.   [7] F.140f.
[8] Some late sources, followed by some modern scholars (e.g., Haigh, 329ff), take the θεωρικόν as the entrance fee to the theatre. Although tickets of admission were used — mainly to avoid a rush and secure a fair distribution of seats — the *theorikon* was far more intended to enable a man to leave his work for the days of the festival.

identical with the war-time allowance which Kleophon introduced in 410 as a real help for the poor; it was perhaps replaced
during the siege of Athens by exceptionally large distributions of
corn.[1] Two obols was also the usual payment for rowers and
soldiers.[2] This sum was, however, often raised in war-time,
as we know from the case of the two-drachma hoplite (with
his servant) at Potidaia, or the sailors in the Sicilian Expedition
who received a drachma a day.[3] Tissaphernes threatened to
reduce the pay of the Peloponnesians from one dr. to three
obols, a sum at that time supposed to represent the Attic payment.[4] Cavalry were usually paid a drachma a day.[5]

Sometimes markets are mentioned in connection with military camps.[6] This proves that, as we should expect, the soldiers
had some money to spend during a campaign, although they
often received the pay due to them at irregular intervals, and
sometimes not until after the campaign.[7] It is specially mentioned when troops received their pay or money for provisions
in advance.[8] Besides their pay, the soldiers were given either
food or a gratuity.[9] It is, however, not certain whether the

---

[1] *IG.* I², 304 (*Syll.*³ 109), A,12; Arist. *Ath. pol.* 28, 3. — Ferguson, *Treasurers
of Athena*, 83f.

[2] W.1189, Theop. 55. I consider it impossible that Philokleon (W.1187ff)
should have been a *theoros* with a pay of two obols (cf. Boeckh, I, 271). θεωρεῖν
is used in a double meaning, as is confirmed by 1382: 'to be a sacred ambassador'
and 'to be a spectator'. It is a pun.

[3] Thuc. III, 17, 3. — Thuc. VI, 31, 3. Cf. 8, 1; here we learn that Egesta
offered 60 talents (= 360,000 dr.) for 60 ships (each of 200 men) for one month
(= 30 days); each man received 1 dr. a day, thus: 60 × 200 × 30 = 360,000.

[4] Thuc. VIII, 29, 1; 45, 2; cf. Xen. *hell.* I, 5, 4ff. — Mr. E. S. G. Robinson
has recently found a most interesting tetradrachm of Attic standard with the owl
and the legend ΒΑΣ on the reverse, and the head of a Persian satrap (most likely
Tissaphernes) on the obverse. See now Robinson, *Numism. Chron.* VIII (1948),
48ff. This coin provides a striking illustration to Thucydides' statements that
Tissaphernes paid in Athenian drachmai.

[5] Lysias *frg.* 6, 70ff, Thuc. III, 17, 3. The motion of Theozotides, which is
opposed by Lysias, wanted the knights' pay to be reduced to four obols, and that of
the mounted archers, who were not citizens, to be increased from two to eight
obols. This was pure demagogism.

[6] Thuc. VI, 44, 3; 50, 1, VII, 39, 2.

[7] K.1065f, 1078f, 1366f.   [8] Xen. *hell.* I, 1, 24, V, 1, 24.

[9] It is said contemptuously of the Argives (P.477) that they are μισθοφοροῦντες
ἄλφιτα from both sides. This, of course, does not prove that there were soldiers
who received only the minimum of corn as their pay. For ἄλφιτα, cf. K.1359,
C.106, 176, W.301, also Pherekr. 1.

three Aiginetan obols which are mentioned as *sitos* in the treaty with Argos and were worth about $4\frac{1}{2}$ Attic obols, should be taken as the normal equivalent of the corn allowance.[1] At any rate, the soldiers had to bring with them a minimum of food ('onions and garlic') for the first three days of the campaign.[2] On the whole, the soldiers' pay was hardly large enough to attract many, and the public pension of one obol a day, which was given to total invalids in general, and therefore also to disabled soldiers, was a bonus on the ground of reduced ability to earn one's living rather than a real living wage.[3]

Of the payment earned by the State-officials we know very little indeed. But it is obvious that the great majority, that is to say all those who were elected by lot, earned small fees for every day they were in office.[4] Some of them received, as it seems, their posts by favouritism from higher officials, although it is by no means clear how that was possible.[5] Among the higher posts there still remained a few such as the treasurers or the *strategoi* and *hipparchoi* who were not paid.[6] On the

---

[1] Thuc. V, 47, 6.   [2] A.197, K.600, W.243, P.312.

[3] Lysias XXIV, 13. — The question of the payments to soldiers still involves many uncertainties; cf. the sound discussion by G. T. Griffith, *The Mercenaries of the Hellenistic World*, 264ff.

[4] It was one of the main points in the programme of the oligarchs in 411 that no ἀρχή was to be μισθοφόρος. In the times of Aristotle (*Ath. pol.* 62, 2) the archons received four obols daily εἰς σίτησιν, and out of this had to keep also a herald and a flute-player; but, as the previous sentence suggests, the money was in addition to their μισθός.

[5] Favouritism: W.682f. The charge, of course, may have been made without any justification.

[6] Officers of lower rank such as, e.g., the taxiarch Lamachos (A.607ff, 1073ff) were in a similar position as the paid magistrates. Cf. the interesting short paper by J. A. O. Larsen, *Cl. Phil.* XVI (1946), 91ff. I disagree with his assumption that 'even the generals and hipparchs received some kind of remuneration when on active service'. Ps.-Xen. I, 3, clearly contrasts the elected offices of the *strategoi* and *hipparchoi* with the ἀρχαί which are μισθοφορίας ἕνεκα. Boeckh, I, 152 (more vaguely, p. 340) claims that generals normally received four times as much as the hoplites. This view, which seems widely accepted, is mainly based on Xen. *anab.* VII, 6, 1, a reference to Kyros' payment of his mercenary officers, and therefore hardly applicable to Athens. Prof. Larsen, who sees these points, yet tries to maintain that *strategoi* and *hipparchoi* were paid. Whatever view we accept, the analogy of the ambassadors' fees is off the point. They received their pay (see below) to cover their travelling expenses, and that can be compared with the σίτησις which every officer and soldier received apart from the μισθός, either

other hand, the daily fees of higher officials, so far as they were paid at all, were apparently on the large side. The *synegoros*, who acted as prosecuting or defending counsel, received 1 dr., ambassadors received a travelling allowance, and certain officers, when abroad, a wage of 2 or even 3 dr. a day.[1] These posts aroused widespread envy, the more so as they offered many other chances of money-making, such as did not come the way of the majority of the citizens. The latter were 'the many of the obol', as Aristophanes called them as early as 425.[2] Though there are plenty of sayings to prove that a *triobolon* was of no great value, 'the payment which brings in my living' must have covered the minimum needs,[3] while wealthy people gave their fees to their children as pocket-money or to buy a toy with.[4] For the old man in the *Wasps* the three obols are hardly enough to buy flour, wood and meat for his family of three, probably because of the rise of prices in the first years of the war.[5] As late as 392, on the other hand, the man who sat in court was considered the wage-earner of the family, and the amusing 'rage over the lost *triobolon*' (if Beethoven will allow us the phrase) tells a plain tale.[6] 'What house would not be glad of four obols', runs a fragment which belongs to the last decade of the fifth century, 'if a man now keeps his wife on two obols?'[7]

in money or in kind. On the other hand, any members of the army or navy who did peace-time service (cf., e.g., Arist. *Ath. pol.* 24, 3) — the majority being back in civil life — were paid, though probably less than in time of war. I do not know to what Larsen refers when he says that 'the officers received no pay for normal peacetime activities'.

[1] Synegoros: W.482f, 691; cf. Bonner and Smith, *The Administration of Justice from Homer to Aristotle*, II, 8ff. — Ambassadors: A.65ff, 602.

[2] K.945. These are hardly, as they are usually explained, those 'of whom many make one obol', that is: those entirely worthless. I believe they are those who receive 'the obol', corresponding to the φράτερες τριωβόλου (K.255), those who are connected by the triobolon. Apparently 'the' obol stands for every customary payment, no matter whether of one, two or three obols.

[3] Triobolon: C.1235, P.848, Pl.124f, Ameips. 13, Nikoph. 12. — Quotation: L.624f.

[4] C.863f, W.606ff.   [5] W.300ff.   [6] E.460f. — 380ff, 392ff.

[7] Theop. 55. The reference here is to a soldier's pay and perhaps to the comic possibility that it would be doubled by the women being called up as well. But this flight of fancy does not distort the reality of the general conditions. Another explanation of the fragment is (cf. M. N. Tod, *Num. Chron.* 1947, 16) that 'the rise from two to four obols would make all the difference between straitened means and comparative affluence'. Economically this provides the same picture,

Modern scholars have computed that about 420 two obols meant an ample living wage for a single man, while rather less than a century later three obols barely sufficed.[1] On the other hand, in the last years of the fifth century, a family of four or five could not exist without an income of at least a drachma a day, the usual payment for craftsmen. The three obols for attending the assembly, introduced about 393, were certainly not sufficient to cover the normal cost of living of a whole family. The rush to the assembly was caused by the terrible poverty at that time of a large part of the urban population. What is called a 'living wage' was hardly more than the cost of food alone. Not until the last decades of the fourth century did the members of the assembly as well as of the *boulē* receive, on days of duty, fees of five obols or one dr., sometimes even of one and a half dr. These rises were caused partly by the devaluation of money, partly by the more determined attempts to provide a livelihood for the poorer classes without any regular labour of their own.

In earlier times the purpose of the public payments had been different. They were in no sense 'poor-relief'; they were not a 'dole', as they are sometimes described. For they were given equally to all citizens, no matter whether rich or poor, and on the other hand, these small daily payments, which must have been received very irregularly, could not support a man for any length of time. The jurors' pay is the only one which in a sense was some sort of old-age pension; for the majority of the heliasts — in particular in times of war — consisted of old men, who were unable to earn anything otherwise. The chief, if not the only, idea behind the public fees was to enable every citizen to leave his business for a time and turn his attention to politics, to the courts or to the theatre. This policy was in its nature political rather than economic. The single exception is the *diobelia*, which was an emergency measure introduced in war-time; but even this was due to demagogic and political as well as economic motives.

Every estimate, however, of the economic value of the public payments must take into consideration the extraordinary frugality of Greek life, and the modest demands of the ordinary Greek. If we can believe the evidence of comedy, he owned as a rule only one cloak and one pair of shoes.[2] The fact that

<hr>

[1] Francotte, I, 327ff. Glotz, 286 (somewhat different in details).   [2] E.314f, 353.

the Athenians were content with a very frugal way of living is
plainly shown in the Utopian war-aims expressed by Kleon:
to rule even over the heart of the Peloponnesos, and there to
enjoy one's power as a heliast, not just for three, but for the
unheard-of sum of five obols a day.[1] Such a desire is typical
both politically and financially of the mind of a *petit bourgeois*.

2

There is a strange, perhaps indeed an inexplicable contrast
between the frugality which marks the Greeks, and another
quality equally characteristic, their great avarice and intense
regard for wealth. Not the least proof of this is furnished by
the many lawsuits about disputed inheritance; they were contested by every possible means and in the spirit which animates
the parricide's words: 'I will throttle my father and get all his
property.'[2] Economic needs and desires grew stronger all the
time. A man likes to 'rake together his little bit of money' like
corn or sand.[3] 'Gold weighs more with men than countless
words.'[4] 'Where there is money, everybody rushes after it.'[5]
If wealth is secured, everything is all right: such is the hope
and belief of peasant no less than of townsman.[6] Athens, 'most
beloved by the gods', is at the same time 'the most abundant
in riches'.[7] The birds talk about men: 'Where shall we get
them wealth from? For that is certainly what they desire';
and they promise at last: 'Thus all of you will become rich.'[8]
This reflects the hopes which induced the masses to join up
with such great enthusiasm for the Sicilian expedition.[9]
Health ranks second only to wealth, and it is said to depend
on 'doing well'; this is a play on words, which comes from the
very roots of Greek nature, for 'doing well' involves health as
well as wealth.[10] Even a moderate man, neither miser nor pro-
fligate, loves money intensely, more even than he loves his
own son, if the joke is to be taken seriously.[11] Many, however,
only pretended to be rich; they had, in fact, their money 'in
the air', but they wished to share the credit of the rich.[12]

While the debtor suffers from sleepless nights, the creditor

[1] K.798ff.   [2] B.1352.   [3] Eupolis 113, cf. C.975.
[4] Eur. *Med.* 965.   [5] adesp. 522.   [6] Pherekr. 130, Pl.805ff.
[7] Eupolis 307.   [8] B.592, 736.   [9] Thuc. VI, 24, 3.
[10] εὖ πράττειν, B.603ff.   [11] Pl.230ff, 237ff, 245ff, 250f.   [12] B.822f.

calculates: 'Must a man lose everything he owns? No, never!'[1]
So he tries by every means to recover his money. There were
professional moneylenders, among them the so-called *obolo-
statai*; though it is hardly true, despite the assertions of some
ancient commentators, that they took one obol daily interest
on every mina and thus more than sixty per cent a year, they
were nevertheless usurers who got their name from their
reputation for lending only a few obols at a time.[2] The average
rate of interest was 12 per cent a year on monthly payments.[3]
Thus moneylending was very lucrative; the 'owls', in fact,
hatched plenty of small coins.[4] Borrowing was always a somewhat expensive business, even more so in war-time, when
because of the heavy risks the rate, especially for sea-loans,
increased severely.[5] It is mere sarcasm and mockery when a
comic chorus offers to lend large sums: the man who gets
them need not pay them back, because nobody gets anything.[6]
The popular opinion was that people with 'invisible wealth',
that is capital on loan, had gained their money by perjury.[7]
The distrust of this way of making money was general and is
easily understood; it was probably based on sound reasons.
Frequently a man pawned something in order to be able to
pay interest, and in the ideal programme of the *Ekklesiazousai*
the seizure of goods by the creditor is abolished along with
robbery, envy and poverty.[8]

Wealth had always been an indispensable attribute of the
aristocracy, but that was wealth inherited, not earned, and for
a long time it had consisted of fields and houses rather than
money. Even the sausage-seller, rising to the occasion,
eventually claims to own a two-storied house and two tene-
ment-houses.[9] The social changes which began, as Theognis
shows, as early as the sixth century, and which still dominated
the age of Old Comedy, also changed the general views about

[1] C.420f, 1214f.   [2] C.1155. Cf. Billeter, *Geschichte d. Zinsfusses,* 356.
[3] C.16ff, 1131ff. Cf. Billeter, 10ff. Aischines the Socratic was to pay 36 per
cent interest for working capital he needed, and was satisfied when he got it
somewhere else at 18 per cent (Lysias, frg. 38, 1f).
[4] B.1106ff.   [5] Xen. *Poroi,* 3, 9.   [6] L.1049ff.
[7] E.603. — Capital on loan: cf. Heichelheim, 353. Another explanation is that
invisible wealth meant any property in cash. It is quite possible that ἀφανὴς
πλοῦτος included both meanings, as a general contrast to 'visible' property such
as fields and houses.
[8] C.33f — E.565ff. Cf. M. I. Finley, *Studies in Land and Credit in Anc.
Athens,* 222f.

property and income. The middle classes considered the earning of money no shame. When Isokrates attacks, because of
their money-making, other rhetoricians whom he calls philosophers, this is in his mouth plain hypocrisy.[1] Poets, however,
even Sophokles, earn censure for their avarice, while in tragedy
the same accusation is frequently brought against Teiresias.[2]
The sophists demanded high fees and gave as the chief reason
the fact that they taught matters of immediate value, which
could be converted into cash: for example, how to win a lawsuit by tricks of rhetoric.[3] Sometimes such methods of money-
making were denounced in comedy, and the sophists were
called 'money-coiners of words', men as it were who earned
money by coining new words.[4] The treatment of Sokrates
is somewhat surprising; Aristophanes supposes in the *Clouds*
that he taught for money or money's worth, but he does not
attack him for this reason.[5] On the contrary, he is derided by
the comedians as a starving wretch who robs a pupil of his
coat, a beggar who thinks of everything except where he will
get his food from, a companion at a drinking-party who will
steal a jug of wine while singing a song.[6] Another comedian
adheres more closely to the facts of Sokrates' way of life when
he says that people were surprised to see him wear a woollen
garment, while he walked bare-footed, which annoyed the
shoe-makers.[7] It is clear that the ordinary citizen was greatly
perturbed by Sokrates' indifference to money; his whole property amounted to about five minae only.[8] Sokrates was dis-
trusted mostly because the ordinary man's point of view was
businesslike and realistic. Business, however, very often implied eagerness to make money, and poverty was often nothing
but hidden avarice.[9] The haggling in the *Frogs* between

[1] Isokr. X, 6.

[2] P.697ff.; see p. 21, n. 6. — Sophokles (*Antig.* 1055, *Oid. Tyr.* 380ff) and Euripides (*Ba.* 257) speak of the venal race of seers. It was a typical view deriving,
however, from contemporary opinion rather than mythological tradition. See
p. 260f.

[3] C.98f. — 1041f.

[4] Kratinos 226. The ἀργυροκοπιστὴρ λόγων is a comic counterpart to
Ares called by Aischylos (*Ag.* 437) ὁ χρυσαμοιβὸς σωμάτων.

[5] C.1146ff. I do not think that Strepsiades' gift was purely voluntary (W.
Schmid, *Philol.* 97, 1948, 223, 1).

[6] C.497, 856f, 1498. — Eupolis 352, 361.   [7] Ameips. 9.

[8] Cf. Xen. *mem.* I, 6, 10ff. — *oik.* 2, 3.   [9] adesp. 456.

Dionysos and the dead man, though fantastic in parts, is on the whole a true mirror of the methods and the spirit of Athenian business.[1]

The *Ploutos*, the play which deals exclusively with wealth, naturally tells us more about the importance of money than any other play. 'The love of money overcomes us all.'[2] While to Kratinos the *Ploutoi* were good spirits or *daimones* attached to the Titans, very much like Hesiod's 'wealth-giving spirits',[3] the Ploutos of Aristophanes is not only a beggar, but a sort of money machine. Since everything can be obtained by money, one can never have enough of it. 'For everything is subject to wealth.'[4] The Olympic olive branch, not being of gold, seems worthless to this age.[5] Even Zeus rules only because he owns more money than anybody else, and the same is true of the Persian king.[6] The doctor does not come if there is no money waiting for him; in the same strain, perhaps, another comic writer speaks of the 'one-talent-illnesses'.[7] The hetaerae's greed for money was notorious, and the same was known of some of the minion boys.[8] Even craftsmen and dealers, not excluding thieves and burglars, work only in order to become rich.[9] Rich people want to be richer still, and they live in constant fear for their money.[10] The man who earns just a bare living by the work of his hands is a pauper, though not a beggar — a description which, in fact, may be applied to the vast majority of the people.

This, almost the last of Aristophanes' plays, presents as its chief theme the problem created by the struggle between rich and poor which had been preparing for a long time past.[11] Frugality and the faculty of being content with little were slowly disappearing among the poorer classes, while actual poverty had increased considerably since the collapse of the Athenian empire. Many had to pawn almost all they owned.[12] It is no longer a joke when the poet speaks of those who had neither cloak nor bed nor blankets.[13] Radical poverty was

[1] F.173ff.   [2] Pl.363.
[3] Kratinos, 38 P, a, 9f. — Hesiod, *Erga*, 122ff: δαίμονες . . . πλουτοδόται.
[4] Pl.187ff. — 146.   [5] Pl.583ff.
[6] Pl.130f, 580. — 170.   [7] Pl.407f. — Alkaios 12.
[8] Pl.149ff, 153ff.   [9] Pl.162ff, 510ff, 527ff.
[10] Pl.194ff. — 202f, 207.
[11] In general cf. J. Hemelrijk, Πενία *en* Πλοῦτος (1925).
[12] E.754f, Pl.450f.   [13] E.415ff.

spreading, and the mass of the population, no longer assured of their daily bread, refused to accept 'words for flour'.[1] There had been poor and starving people before in Athens, but what in the *Clouds* could be described as occasional cases providing good fun[2] was after 400 a general and tragic feature. Almost from the beginning of the war it had become necessary to counter the general poverty by public distributions of corn in the form either of cheap sales or outright gifts.[3] This, however, did not prove a final remedy, especially as it was chiefly used by demagogues who hoped to win the favour of the masses. It also caused much ill-feeling that some people were given illegal advantages. Attempts to keep cheap such vital products as, for instance, salt by fixing maximum prices seem to have been ineffective.[4] The Greek Polis of the fifth century had not yet gone very far towards the conception of the Welfare-State.

In earlier times the poor were fairly satisfied if all the rich were included in the register of those who had to pay the extraordinary war-tax.[5] But the usual public services of the rich, such as the trierarchy, choregy and war-tax, though they involved considerable expense, were, above all, an honourable burden, the rich being ostensibly proud to bear them.[6] The poor were therefore less aware of the burden than of the honour. Moreover, many wealthy men claimed, with good reason or without, that they had enough to live on, but not enough to undertake any 'liturgy'; many of them knew how to share such a duty with somebody else, or how to avoid it entirely or in part.[7] The greater the poverty and misery, and the more urgent the public and private demand for money, the less adequate seemed the contributions of the rich to the State.

Money was thrust more and more into the centre of life. All property, no matter whether field or house, furniture or slave, agricultural or industrial products, could be converted

---

[1] Pl.218f, adesp. 687. This reminds us of Goering's 'guns for butter', but the difference is significant.

[2] C.106, 176.   [3] K.1100ff, W.715ff, B.580f, E.422ff.

[4] E.814 and schol.   [5] εἰσφορά, K.923ff.

[6] Expenses: K.913ff. — Pride of the rich: e.g., Lysias XII, 19f, XVIII, 7, XIX, 29, 57, XXI, 2ff, XXV, 12, Isokr. XVIII, 58ff, XIX, 36, Isaios VI, 60, VII, 36, 40.

[7] Isaios XI, 40, cf. V, 36. — Ps.-Lysias VI, 47, Isokr. XVIII, 60. — P.1022, F.1065f, E.197f, cf. Isaios V, 44.

into money, and was esteemed according to its value in money.[1]
A rich family would be called a 'three-talent-house', but even
a 'one-talent-man' was considered wealthy.[2] Fines became the
most usual form of legal punishment.[3] A man who found an
adulterer in his house, preferred money to scandal, divorce
and lawsuit: 'income is better than infamy'.[4] Euphiletos, who
killed the seducer of his wife and refused to accept money,
was probably an exception; we know of no similar case, and
the evidence of comedy mirrors what commonly happened.[5]
Thus a statesman, when attacked by a comic writer, had
in earlier times threatened him with the loss of his freedom as
citizen and poet; so Kleon after the *Babylonians*. Now, however, 'he nibbles off his fees'.[6] A man who was charged with
impiety would rather pay money — probably as a bribe — than
rely on his oath to prove his innocence.[7] Debts, such as those
which tormented Strepsiades and Euelpides, might become
the chief motive for any desperate action, even for civil war.[8]

For some time past the State had acknowledged the necessity of stabilizing its financial policy by the accumulation of
a reserve fund. This is perhaps the most significant part of
the measures by which Perikles prepared Athens for the
threatening ordeal of war. The god of Wealth is the guardian
of the 'Opisthodomos', the part of the Parthenon containing
the treasure of the goddess.[9] The reason why the occupation
of the Acropolis is so important in Lysistrate's struggle for
government, is chiefly that the public treasure was kept there.[10]
This treasure, together with the money in circulation, upheld
the economic prestige and power of Athens. False money was
rare, and the Athenian coins were famous all over the world
for their high percentage of silver; only at times of greatest
emergency during the war were bad coins issued.[11] Criticism
of the use made of public funds was a favourite topic of con-

---

[1] *IG.* I², 325ff (*Syll.*³ 96ff, Tod, 79f), Isaios II, 35, VIII, 35, XI, 41ff.

[2] Isaios III, 18, 25. — Krates 32. The meaning of the fragment seems clear
(see Liddell and Scott *s.v.* ταλαντιαῖος), although Pollux (IX, 53) is not
certain εἴτε τιμὴν εἴτε ῥοπὴν λέγει.

[3] C.758, W.1253ff, B.1052, E.655ff; cf. the ἐπωβελία, Isokr. XVIII, 3, 12,
etc., XX, 3.

[4] Kallias 1, cf. Pl.168.   [5] Case of Euphiletos: Lysias I, 25f.

[6] F.367f, Plat. 133, Sannyrion 9.   [7] Ps.-Lysias VI, 12.

[8] C.12ff and elsewhere, B.115. — Thuc. III, 81, 4.   [9] Pl.1192f.

[10] L.173ff, 420ff, 493f.   [11] F.720ff. See p. 222.

versation, the more so as the decision in such matters was vested in the citizens in council and assembly.[1] It was not the people but a few men of perception who realized in time the danger to the State of distributing so much of its revenues to the citizens, with the result that there was no money 'for triremes and walls'.[2]

All these passages prove that financial questions came to be of ever-increasing importance in both public and private life. This would not have been the case if economics in general had not taken hold of the minds of almost the whole people and even influenced ethics and religion. Wealth was to be the reward of the good and pious people, poverty that of the bad and godless.[3] This is the naive and natural interpretation by unsophisticated people who thought of wealth as a blessing and of poverty as misery.[4] There is a phrase attributed to so fine and idealistic a politician as Thrasyboulos: 'Lucky is he who is killed in battle, for no man, however rich, will have so fair a monument as he.'[5] To combine the idea of *dulce et decorum* with the luxurious graves of the rich may be just a patriotic commonplace, but implicitly it reveals a materialistic outlook. It is in a similar strain that Eupolis complains that it is the victor in sports, and not the good citizen who is better than all the others, who 'gets the washing-basin'.[6] The increasing importance of economic facts was in a sense natural, though it was only after the restoration of democracy, when all the problems of internal politics seemed to have been more or less solved, but when the economic strain grew most intense, that economic questions developed into serious problems.

We may assume that it is not a complete misrepresentation of the facts when Aristophanes asserts that wealth was mostly gained by foul means, while good men were starving.[7] A

[1] Cf. W.656ff.

[2] frg. 220. The transfer of balances to the fund for the building of ships and walls was usual; cf. the well-known decree of Kallias, *IG*. I², 91 (*Syll.*³ 91, Tod, 51), 30. In peace-time, on the other hand, the τριηροποιοί and τειχοποιοί contributed to other public buildings, e.g. the Parthenon (*IG*. I², 342, 40; 343, 90).

[3] Pl.490f, 495ff.

[4] Cf. also Eur. *Kykl.* 316, *Med.* 561, *Andr.* 153, *El.* 1130f, *Hel.* 417ff, *Phoin.* 404f, 438ff, *frg.* 142, 325.

[5] Xen. *hell.* II, 4, 17.   [6] Eupolis 118.

[7] Pl.502ff, 751ff, 804ff.

special word was coined for the man who became rich through wrong-doing.[1] The petty retailers cheated on every occasion, and Hyperbolos had grown rich by selling lamps of bad material.[2] Among the bad qualities attributed to the man un-initiated into the Eleusinian mysteries these are pre-eminent — that he sows the seeds of discord, that he is greedy for personal gain, and that as an official he is open to bribery.[3] Bribery and the embezzlement of public funds, 'wealth from office', are mentioned so often, either as a charge or simply as a state-ment, that, even after allowance has been made for comic exaggeration and for the license of abuse, a very widespread corruption of public life must be admitted.[4] The barber who takes his razor and shaves off the war-tax from underneath the chin probably represents a demagogue who pocketed part of this important public revenue.[5] It seems to have been of very little effect that bribery and theft, or breach of promise to lend money to the State, were punished with the pillory or a written public denunciation; heavy penalties, if not death, could also be imposed.[6] 'The thieves are celebrating a festival', that is to say, they go unpunished.[7] The Athenians had truly learnt to adapt themselves to the new mode; they played no longer in 'Dorian', but in 'Donodorian' style.[8] A saying, which very likely derives from comedy, sums up the story: 'Even on the point of death an Athenian puts out his hand' — for a tip, of course.[9]

Wealth is blind after all. Even the rule of Zeus would come to an end if Ploutos gained his sight for only a short time.[10] The beautiful theme of the old poet's comedy, though

---

[1] ἀδικοχρήματος, Krates 42.

[2] C.1065f, but cf. p. 120, n. 3.   [3] F.360f.

[4] ἐκ τῆς ἀρχῆς, Kratinos 38 P, b, 32, combined by Goossens with Kratinos 160. Cf. also *AJP.* LXVI (1945), 120, n. 23. — Examples of bribery: K.402f, 438f, 472f, 680ff, 834f, 1359f, 1369f, C.591, W.675f, Th.936f, F.360ff, Pl. 379, frg. 100, 219; of embezzlement: A.5f, K.1127f, C.351, W.554, 716f, 1117, B.1111f, L.490f, Th.811ff, Pl.569, Plat.14. But La Rue van Hook, *Class. Journ.* 23 (1928), 275ff, is right in warning us not to take as literal truth the partly inconsistent sayings of comedy about 'Crime and Criminals'.

[5] Eupolis 278.

[6] Usual punishment: K.1046ff, C.591f, Pl.476, 606, Kratinos 115, Plat. 249; cf. Isaios V, 38. — Otherwise, e.g., the case of Perikles: Thuc. II, 65, 3, Plut. *Per.* 35, 4, Plat. *Gorg.* 516 A.

[7] Kratinos 18 D = adesp. 662.   [8] K.985ff.

[9] Diogenian. III, 12.   [10] Pl. 124ff.

not new to Greek imagination,[1] was no mere fancy. It is
something different, when in a comic fragment it is said that
'only in Sparta is Wealth blind like a lifeless picture'. The
meaning is that wealth could not see (nor be seen) here because everybody lived, or at least should live, in accordance
with the law, on the same frugal level.[2] In Athens it seemed
hard not to recognize the bad and blind distribution of wealth.
Though even here certain property could be called 'invisible
wealth',[3] we can hardly speak of any ostentatious luxury, as is
shown by archaeological evidence. Too many, however, who
were rich seemed not worthy of it, especially in the view of the
less wealthy and the poor. Seen from the point of view of those
without it, wealth is usually over-estimated, and to feel superior
to rich men is therefore one of the greatest pleasures the
heliasts can enjoy.[4] The 'men who own', 'the rich and solemn
men', suffer a good deal of criticism, though many jibes are
quite good-natured.[5] The peasant revolts against the wasting
of the results of a whole year's hard work by 'illustrious' men.[6]
If somebody is rich, every means of taking his money from
him seems justified.[7] The remark that service in the navy is
useful for the poor townsfolk, not for the rich and the peasants,
reveals the fact that social and economic matters affected and
threatened the external power of Athens, while the phrase that
the 'orators' look after the common good only as long as they
are poor shows us the same dangers threatening from within.[8]

A fragment from Euripides' *Aiolos*, frequently quoted in
ancient times, runs: 'Do not speak of Ploutos. I do not honour
him as a god, for even the worst man easily takes possession
of him.'[9] The rich were 'brigands, orators, sycophants and
bad men'.[10] The last word reflects the general social change
which had lifted the 'commons' to the top. 'Wealth raises the
worst men among the highest.'[11] This change accentuated the
contrast between long-established and new wealth, which

---

[1] Cf. Hipponax 29, Timokreon 5.

[2] adesp. 410. The meaning is clear from the context in Porphyr. *de abstinentia*,
IV, 4, where the phrase is quoted.

[3] E.602. See above p. 233, n. 7.

[4] W.575. — Over-estimation of wealth: cf. Francotte, II, 339.

[5] K.1295, W.626ff. — e.g., W.1253ff, 1266ff, P.839ff, Pl.594ff.

[6] adesp. 370.   [7] Eupolis 40 P, 65ff.

[8] E.197f. — Pl.567ff.   [9] Eur. *frg.* 20.

[10] ἱερόσυλοι, ῥήτορες, συκοφάνται, πονηροί, Pl.30f.   [11] Eur. *frg.* 95.

found vivid expression in comedy. The 'rich man of olden times' is contrasted with the man 'who is ennobled by his purse' and is one of the 'rascally new rich'.[1] A man like Kallias specified in the list of his inherited goods horses, fields and cattle.[2] Similar statements, which mostly also include houses, slaves and money on loan, are found fairly frequently in our sources. Money in cash was often added, also silver bowls when used as a means of storing wealth;[3] but the immovable property, the slaves included, formed the essential part of inherited wealth. New wealth, on the other hand, came chiefly from 'mines, sea-trade and hidden treasures'.[4] We may leave out the last item, mentioned *ad hoc* because the birds know where they are hidden, and we must not forget that in the whole passage nothing is mentioned that is not somehow aided by the birds, so that craftsmanship and retail-trade are not mentioned at all. Even so the passage is significant. The ownership or tenure of mines had been an important source of wealth for leading politicians at various times; one need only recall the names of Peisistratos and Nikias.[5] But Aristophanes in that passage was thinking rather of smaller people; it was common to make money by owning a mine. This fact is confirmed by archaeological evidence from the mines at Laureion, which goes to show that there were a great many small claim-holders.[6] The most usual ways of making money were, of course, by trade and craftsmanship, and we learn from comedy a good deal about wealth acquired in these pursuits.[7] 'Potter's wealth', on the other hand, meant 'uncertain property', though probably only because the potter's goods were so easily broken.[8] The supposition, however, underlying the phrase is that a store of goods could mean wealth just as much as money or fields, though it was certainly a kind of wealth which could be more easily destroyed.

Criticism of wealth was strong. The verdict of comedy may be taken as largely reflecting public opinion. Occasionally

[1] ἀρχαιόπλουτος, Kratinos 38 P, b, 32. — adesp. 654. — νεοπλουτο-πόνηρος, Kratinos 208.

[2] Eupolis 152-3.

[3] *IG.* II², 1553ff, cf. Pherekr. 129.   [4] B.593ff.

[5] As to possible mining interests of Miltiades cf. my explanation of the Parian Expedition in *Aspects of the Ancient World*, 137ff.

[6] K.362. — E. Ardaillon, *Les mines du Laurion* (1897).

[7] Cf. Chapter V.   [8] adesp. 749; see p. 128.

we find wealthy people appreciated because they have behaved well, like those, for instance, who helped soldiers taking the field, or those who left a good dowry to their daughters but themselves died in poverty.[1] Rich people were expected to organize games and competitions, to keep riding horses or to build public buildings and well-furnished houses.[2] The beautiful houses, however, could be mortgaged.[3] Other rich men were abused, the miser, for instance, who did not give his share to the gods, or the man who did not take on himself the burden of a trierarchy, but dressed in fine clothes and enjoyed good food.[4] The saying that wealth is blind could also be understood in the sense that rich men are blind and unreasonable in their behaviour, and do not see the fate they draw upon themselves.[5] A poet Patrokles was sneered at because of his avarice and the dirt in which he lived.[6] A particularly revolting appendage of wealth were the *kolakes*, or parasites, who curried favour with the rich 'masters', 'picked the hair off their clothes', came uninvited to dinner and did not miss a single meal.[7] They 'made a god of their belly' and were always 'sniffing round the frying-pan'.[8] Among them were such sinister figures as the highwayman and cloak-stealer Orestes.[9]

Most disliked were those who had only recently become rich.[10] They lived in luxury and despised the poor from whose ranks they had sprung.[11] War-profiteers did not impress the public favourably, even if they paid ample taxes and liturgies.[12] Of such men it could be said that 'wealth means boorishness and cowardice',[13] qualities which could easily turn into crude voluptuousness. Though the Athenians saw a distinction be-

---

[1] Eupolis 40 P, 15ff, cf. Lysias XVI, 14, XXXI, 15. — Lysias XVI, 10, XIX, 15ff.

[2] Pl. 1161f. — C.15. — C.815, W.1214ff, Pl. 180, frg. 73; cf. the list in Xen. *oik.* 2, 5f.

[3] Pherekr. 58.   [4] B.1618ff, adesp. 1; cf. Isaios V, 44. — F.1065ff.

[5] Eur. *frg.* 776, though partially obscure.   [6] Pl. 84f.

[7] frg. 167, 491, Eupolis 159, Ameipsias 19. — frg. 657, 714; cf. 410. — frg. 272, Kratinos 44-5. — Eupolis 162. In general, cf. Hug, *P.-W.* XVIII 4, 1384f.

[8] Eupolis 172, 173; cf. 346.

[9] Eupolis 166. The facts remain just as significant if Orestes was a nickname, possibly applied to various persons; cf. Higham, *Cl. Q.* XXVI (1932), 103ff.

[10] W.1309, B.798ff, cf. 1442f, Pl.107ff, Kratinos 208; Eur. *Hik.* 742.

[11] Pl.613ff, 1004f.   [12] Lysias XXVII, 10.

[13] Eur. *frg.* 235.

tween themselves and the proverbial luxuriousness and refinement of Ionia,[1] criticism of the effeminacy of the rich Attic
youth was very frequent. Warm baths, excessive care of the
body, the use of perfumed ointments and the like, also the
idle habit of hanging about in the market instead of going to
the palaestra — all these came in for unceasing attacks.[2] New
wealth and the life of the rich provided often also the ground
for denunciations of tyranny, which was considered especially
hostile to the poor, a significant sign of the general change of
attitude.[3]   The political foe of democracy had become the
economic foe of the poor.

We shall not assess correctly the general verdict returned
on the rich if we fail to realize that the poor were in public
opinion those who were unable to live except by the work of
their hands, but not those who were starving.[4] The absolute
pauper, the wholly destitute, was called a 'beggar', and he was
treated not with pity and charity, but with contempt.[5] One of
the most serious grievances against Euripides is that he brought
beggars on to the stage; Telephos who, though a king, appeared in rags, was a favourite target of the comedian's scorn
and derision.[6] Popular feeling considered the sight of a beggar
on the stage shocking, though even the realism of Euripides
differed from reality to some extent: even in rags a mythical
hero was never an Attic beggar. Euripides, in fact, knew of
the shame of beggarhood, while he preached pity for those
who were in a beggarly state through being exiled from their
native city.[7] In various ways tragedy had included in its pro-
vince the economic side of life.

The painter Pauson, who in the course of many years had
achieved nothing, is mocked, time and again, not because of his

[1] E.883, 918, frg. 543, Kallias 5.
[2] e.g., K.1375ff, C.837f, 991, 1002f, 1044ff, 1053f, frg. 435, Kratinos 100,
Krates 15, Pherekr. 2, 107, 131, Hermipp. 76, Plat. 208, Kephisod. 3, adesp.
56, 338-9, 375.
[3] W.463ff, Pl.946ff, and elsewhere.
[4] Bolkestein, 182ff.
[5] A.558f, 577ff, 593f, adesp. 39. A victim in comedy of this common attitude
is Lamachos. About his poverty, cf. R. Goossens, L'antiquité class. XV (1946),
43ff.
[6] A.415ff, 429, F.842. — Telephos, e.g., A.430ff, 496ff, C.921f, P.528,
L.706f, Th.694f, F.855, 864.
[7] Eur. Hel. 790f. — Hek. 1218ff, Herakl. 318.

apparently poor art, but because of his poverty.[1] The old-
fashioned crook used by old men was at that time called by
some a 'beggar's stick'.[2] The blind god of Wealth is a dirty and
ailing beggar.[3] Zeus created heaven as an immense chimney
for sacrifices in order that the gods might not be called — as
many despised men were called — 'altar-beggars' who had to
beg for the sacrifices.[4] It appears to be a gross misstatement
of some scribblers that the life of beggars and exiled men was
better than that of other people.[5] To eat only dry bread is bad
enough, for even the poor were accustomed to some modest
extra dish;[6] but there were worse things. The children beg
for bread, or even for the 'finger-cleaning crumbs' which otherwise are thrown to the dogs.[7] On entering the bath, the beggar
will be scalded at once, because he comes in rags and out of
the cold.[8] A favourite object of theft in lonely streets or in
the palaestra are cloaks and blankets.[9] This shows what, after
food, the poorest were most in need of.[10] Beggar-poet and
beggar-prophet are most eager to get cloaks, chiton, sandals.[11]
In spite of the Greek climate, which knows, however, very cool
nights, it was hard to have only a thin cloak in which one
shivered with cold.[12] But the cloak-stealers were starving as
well.[13] Vermin, no bed, no food or only 'dried leaves' — that
is a beggar's life.[14] Even at its best, it means that several men
share a common bag.[15] Chionides, one of the earliest comedians, wrote a comedy *The Beggars*, in which they get only
the driest of the cheap salted fish, a frugal meal, though 'if
there is no meat, salted fish is good too'.[16] If one is hungry,
and 'there is no flour in the sack', one must go and steal some.[17]

---

[1] A.854, Th.949f, Pl.602. I believe that Aristotle, *poet.* 1448a, 6, in saying
that Pauson in his pictures made people appear χείρους than they looked in
reality, wished to characterize him as a caricaturist *malgré lui*, that is, in fact,
as a bad painter. Were there ever in fifth-century Greece professional carica-
turists or cartoonists, as it is usually assumed in the case of Pauson?

[2] frg. 127-8.　　　　[3] Pl.266f.　　　　[4] Pherekr. 141.

[5] Isokr. X, 8.　　　[6] ἀρτοσιτεῖν is contrasted with ὀψοφαγεῖν, Plat. 172.

[7] P.120, Pl.536. — K.414.　　　　[8] Pl.535, 952ff, frg. 345.

[9] C.179, B.712, cf. 1490ff, A.1166f, E.544, 565, 668ff, Lysias, *frg.* 9, 1.

[10] Cf. E.408ff, Pl.842ff, 926f.　　　[11] B.933ff, 946ff, 973f; cf. 1421.

[12] adesp. 10 D.　　　　　　　[13] Kratinos 206.

[14] E.415ff, Pl.535ff. — A.469.　　　　[15] κοινοθυλακεῖν, frg. 797.

[16] Chionides 5-6. — adesp. 618.　　　[17] Pl.763. — adesp. 434.

Most miserable is he who after all his hardships leaves no money even for his funeral.[1] Thus even a whole State might be reduced to beggary: Megara starved because of the Athenian decree at the beginning of the war, when it was said that it was impossible to obtain even salt and garlic, commodities of which Megara had ample supply in peace-time.[2]

These are some of the colours in which the picture of beggarly poverty is painted; it is not only a dark picture, but one painted without love and almost without pity. Not mere poverty, but beggarliness, is described in the *Ploutos* as a genuine ground of reproach. Only thrift and work can avail against it.[3] These words form a significant analogy to those of Perikles in his Funeral Speech that it is not disgraceful to admit one's poverty, but that it is disgraceful not to avoid it by working.[4] There is an interesting interpolation in Euripides' *Hiketides*. After some commonplace advice to the rich to con-sider the poor and to fear an equal fate, the surprising counsel to the poor is added to envy the rich and thus be seized by love of wealth themselves.[5] The same spirit is expressed in the fact that there is no reference in comedy to alms-giving and private charity. This is largely due to the fact that Greek civilization as a whole knew very little of that commandment which tells us to love our neighbour as ourselves. Religion had no say in the social behaviour of the Greeks, but the structure of Polis society made this deficiency less damaging. We can assume that one reason for the lack of charity was the small number of beggars. It was only because they represented no real social problem that they could earn contempt as idlers instead of pity and help. 'Pity' to whom an altar was erected in the agora was not an expression of social conscience, but of per-sonal feelings, not towards the poor, but towards every un-happy human being.[6]

Only occasionally, and late in our period, might the com-munity feel itself under an obligation to help its poorer mem-

[1] A.691, E.592, Pl.556.

[2] A. 535, 731ff, 760ff, 813f. — P.246f. — Megarian Decree: see Chapter XII, 3.

[3] Pl.548. — 552ff.   [4] Thuc. II, 40, 1.

[5] Eur. *Hik.* 177f. Actually these lines interrupt the advice given to the rich. A plea for mutual tolerance of rich and poor is made in Eur. *frg.* 21.

[6] Altar of Ἔλεος: Paus. I, 17, 1, Diod. XIII, 22, 7. — Cf. Bolkestein, 112ff. — The chief object of pity were suppliants; cf., e.g., Eur. *Hik.* 190.

bers. We have seen that the public payments were not given for this purpose, and that even distributions of corn and the *diobelia* were chiefly political and demagogic measures. The hardships, however, of the poor became more and more pressing. A genuine concern lay behind the motion brought forward in the women's assembly that during the winter people without beds or blankets should be allowed to sleep in the furriers' shops where enough covering was to be found.[1] The State did provide medical aid,[2] though it was no 'social service' in the modern meaning of the phrase. One of the State-doctors, Pittalos, was consulted by rich and poor alike.[3] Other sources besides comedy speak of these doctors, and we know that some of them were well paid.[4] It is, however, by no means certain whether they had to give free treatment; if they did, it was to everyone, not to the poor alone. It was difficult, on the other hand, to find the right doctor, and it was well known that physicians, presumably those in private practice, demanded high fees.[5] 'Apollo the physician may cure them, since he's paid for it.'[6] Everywhere we find the same outlook, dominated by money, and on the other hand, increasing poverty and pauperization.

3

It is difficult to say how deeply the longing for wealth was rooted in the individual small craftsman or farmer. The testimony of literature begins with Hesiod and Alkman, and the fact that wealth and money are so frequently mentioned shows that poverty and therefore also the desire to make money were always widespread. The poor wanted to be rich, and the rich to have more: 'a purse is insatiable', and it corrupts life.[7] Even the ideal citizen wants to be rich in order, of course, to be good and useful to other people.[8] The varied opportunities of trade both on a large or small scale doubtless gave a big impetus to the general desire. The peasants made little money;

[1] E.408ff.   [2] A.1030, cf. Xen. *mem.* IV, 2, 5.
[3] A.1032, 1222f, W.1432.
[4] Herodot. III, 131. For the public doctors we have also epigraphical evidence, though not from Athens in our period. Cf. O. Jacob, *Mélanges Glotz*, II, 461ff.
[5] E.363ff. — Pl.406ff.   [6] B.584.
[7] adesp. 660. — B.157f.   [8] Xen. *oik.* 11, 9; 11.

they usually exchanged their takings at once for goods.[1] The
real money-makers were the traders, the shopkeepers and
craftsmen, most of whom sold their own products, above all
the retailers, whose sole interest was in buying and selling. It
was among these people that economic competition and social
jealousy found their earliest and strongest expression.

The Pseudo-Xenophon speaks of the people's greed for
money: they had introduced the liturgies 'in order to get
something for themselves and to impoverish the rich'.[2]
Though liturgies and war-tax were heavy burdens, they did
little to lessen the economic tension. The demos was not to
be satisfied with the right of 'gnawing at the offals of his own
realm'.[3] Poverty proved herself no less blind than Wealth.
In times when men might be described as anxious to borrow
money without intending to repay it,[4] the process of bleeding
the rich went on, and finally liturgies ceased to be voluntary
gifts and became compulsory services. Eventually indeed the
rich found themselves in a dangerous situation.[5] The juries
liked to bring in verdicts against the rich.[6] The possession of
wealth became more dangerous than criminal activity, says
Isokrates, who in 354 contrasted this state of affairs with the
situation when he was a boy, thus showing a fact which comedy
confirms, that the decisive change began in the last decade of
the Peloponnesian War.[7] A fragment, which may be of a
somewhat later date, draws the conclusion which was to become
so important for the philosophy and also the religion of the
following centuries: 'There is no one happier than the poor
man.'[8] In our period, of course, this meant chiefly that the
poor could not be drained of their resources. But ever since
Demaratos explained the Greek character to the Persian king
by basing it on the fact that 'Greece had always had Poverty
as her foster-sister',[9] the idea that poverty not only meant
misery, but also strength and aretē, had been alive in Greek
thought. It was a moralistic commonplace that money does
not make a man happy and that the rich are the slaves of their

---

[1] E.817ff.   [2] Ps.-Xen. I, 13.
[3] W.672.   [4] B.114ff.
[5] Cf. Xen. symp. IV, 30.   [6] W.240f, 287f, 575, 626f, and elsewhere.
[7] Isokr. XXI, 12. — XV, 159f.
[8] adesp. 1273; cf. also Xen. symp. IV, 30ff.
[9] Herod. VII, 102, 1.

wealth.[1] On the other hand, the importance and usefulness of wealth were compared with the advantages of noble birth or personal character.[2] It needed only one step further to realize the advantages of poverty.

Nowhere is this view more strikingly expressed than in the scene of Poverty in the *Ploutos*.[3] Poverty, generally condemned as a misfortune and humiliation or even as a cause of crime, is described as forcing men to work, and making them strong and enduring, even better and more pious. Thus poverty became the creator of all human achievement and human civilization.[4] It is typical of the working of the Greek mind that even at a time when the importance of economic factors had become obvious and their impact on social life far stronger than before, the problem of wealth and poverty was essentially regarded as a moral question. Whatever the specific social or economic issue, its influence on the community was primarily one of individual morals. This is probably the chief reason why the Greeks never succumbed to an economic interpretation of political and social life.

The measures taken against the rich did not lead to economic disaster. Though about the end of our period many might think that there was no prospect of economic recovery, as we can see, for example, from a speech by Lysias in 389 B.C.,[5] the following years and decades proved the contrary to be the case. It is most surprising — especially in the light of modern experience — how easily the danger of inflation passed. The copper coins, introduced in 406, could be withdrawn after thirteen years without great difficulty.[6] We must assume that other difficulties of which we know nothing were solved just as easily. Athens overcame quickly enough the grave economic crises of the political collapse and its aftermath, and later there was never a social revolution such as occurred in many other Greek States. This was certainly not the result of Athens being a democracy; for public payments and benefactions

[1] Cf., e.g., Eur. *Hek.* 622ff, 864ff, *Hik.* 875ff.

[2] See, e.g., Eur. *Hik.* 860ff, *El.* 37f, 373ff, 426ff, 941ff, *Phoin.* 404f, 442, *frg.* 248-9, 285, 326.

[3] Pl.415ff.

[4] E.605ff, Ps.-Xen. I, 5, Eur. *El.* 375f. — Pl.510ff, 527ff, cf. Eur. *Alex.* 36, *frg.* 237-8, 248-9, 327.

[5] Lysias, XXVIII, 15; though he obviously exaggerates.

[6] F.720; see above, p. 222. — E.815ff.

brought the finances of the State more than once to the edge
of the precipice. The intention of the oligarchs to abolish all
public fees except army pay was justified from the financial
point of view, but impracticable because of political and social
conditions.[1] The economic stability of Athens rested partly
on her rich sources of income, rich owing to the importance
of Athenian trade even after the break-up of the empire, and
partly on the efficiency of such politicians as Euboulos and
Lykourgos, who pursued a sound financial policy, though
they always had to be on their guard to satisfy the people's
demands.[2] A book like Xenophon's *Poroi* shows the state of
financial, that is of general economic, emergency, as it existed
about the middle of the fourth century before the two men
tried to relieve it. The demos lived on the State's capital, but
its substance was never entirely exhausted; and while the
power of the State over private property was clear and far-
reaching, it was, in the end, the stability of private economy
which saved the State.

We have seen that it became more and more difficult to
fill the assembly and the courts, because the majority of the
citizens preferred to work and thus to earn more than the few
obols offered by the State. This had been the case ever since
the general impoverishment after the Peloponnesian War; it
was this very reason which induced Xenophon in 354 to write
his *Poroi*.[3] In fact, the creative power of poverty was not mere
fantasy or theory, and it might even strengthen the Panhellenic
tendencies of the time. For it seemed worth while to expel
poverty from the whole of Hellas,[4] an idea which, more than
a century later, spread social revolution over a large part of
Greece.

A real social danger was the impoverishment of the peasants,
who were a numerous class; but it did not go beyond a certain
point, owing to the situation of the country and the character
of its inhabitants. Another danger was the growth in the number of poor townsfolk and their equally growing political

[1] Plans of the oligarchs: Thuc. VIII, 65, 3; 67, 3; cf. 69, 4; Arist. *Ath. pol.* 29,
5. For recent discussion of these much disputed constitutional plans see: U.
Wilcken, *Sitzungsber. Preuss. Akad.* (1935), 34ff. M. Lang, *AJP* LXIX (1948)
272ff. L.F. Sartori, La crisi del 411 A.C. (1951). M. Cary, *JHS.* LXXII (1952),
56ff.

[2] Cf. the verdict of Andreades, 376ff.

[3] Xen. *mem.* II, 8, 1. — *Poroi*, I, 1.   [4] Pl.463.

power. There is no doubt that these imminent dangers brought about a certain change in social and political conditions. Nevertheless, in the tirades against the corruption and blindness of Athenian democracy, whether made by ancient oligarchs or by modern scholars, though they are justified in certain details or even to some extent generally, the facts are neglected, that in spite of short periods of economic distress, Athens throughout the larger part of the fourth century was a prosperous community, and that she experienced no grave social or economic crisis in the two succeeding centuries.[1]

This chapter confirms our views based on our investigation into vocational activity and social organization: we realize the unity of a middle class, which spread over town and country, of craftsman and peasant, shopkeeper and trader. Perhaps we should meet one objection. There was a view expressed most clearly in some lines of Euripides that the citizens' body was divided into three parts.[2] Euripides distinguishes the 'useless' rich who only want to be still richer, the people who, owning nothing, are full of envy and therefore easily seduced by the demagogues, and thirdly those between these two groups who represent the backbone of the State. The only basis on which this division is made is that of property. All other distinctions

---

[1] This is perhaps rather a sweeping statement, but I think on the whole it holds good, even though the gap between rich and poor had dangerously widened. For a detailed account of the later periods cf. J. Day, *An Economic History of Athens under Roman Domination* (1942). — As an example of modern deprecation of fourth-century democracy see W. Erb, *Schmollers Jahrbuch*, 61 (1937), esp. 685ff, 693ff. — Rostovtzeff (see p. 4, note 1) has tried (99ff) to make it clear that conditions increasingly deteriorated during the fourth century, chiefly because of the falling-off of trade, especially export trade. He opposes the view that this century as a whole was a period of economic exuberance. In this he is probably right, but a reasonable prosperity of economic life during the fourth century remains a fact in spite of short periods of distress. Rostovtzeff himself considers the crisis of the last part of the century only a temporary decline, though one which brought about 'the necessity of readjusting' economic life. I do not take Menander as a reliable witness for a new improvement in economic conditions (see p. 42, n. 1), and I believe that Rostovtzeff's view of a gradual economic decline in the fourth century is hardly more justified than Beloch's opposite view. There were ups and downs, but at least as many ups as downs. The 'shrinking of the market for Greek products', which R. makes much more evident than previous writers, may, to some extent, have started before Alexander's death, but even then it was mainly due to new political developments, to the opening of new trade routes and finally to the devastating wars of the Successors.

[2] Eur. *Hik.* 238ff.

such as family, profession, reputation, or mode of life, are left out. This makes it clear that the whole exposition is purely theoretical. It is the theory of the Mean, the *mesotes*, which was an important and characteristic feature of Greek political and social thought from Solon to Aristotle.[1] There never existed any distinct social groups or classes to correspond to those three types.[2] It is, of course, always possible to divide the general scale of property, reaching as it does from nothing at all to a great height, wherever and as often as one likes; but the parts which form the living body of society will never be found in this way. It is true that in the Athenian democracy of our period the middle classes played the most important part. We may also admit that economically some of their members rose to the upper classes and others sank below the average level, but that does not alter the general picture; it does not even touch it. The bulk of the population were those moderately prosperous farmers, artisans, and merchants, of whom we have spoken so frequently.

The tension between rich and poor, though intensified after 403, never destroyed the unity of the people. Rich and poor were groups of one society, and there were no strict boundaries.[3] The number of beggars and real paupers, that is of those who were actually below the level of the lower middle-class, remained insignificant throughout the fifth century, but no doubt grew later, in proportion with the generally increasing importance, and the declining value, of money.[4]

[1] Cf. Aristotle, *Politics*, 1289b, 29f, 1295b, 1f, 1308b, 29f. He says that in smaller States sometimes there was no *meson*, but only the two extremes (1296a, 9ff, 1304b, 1, 1319b, 12ff). This, again, must be pure theory. — Solon, of course, does not use the word μεσότης, but many of his verses indicate the same conception (e.g., 4, 7; 5, Diehl).

[2] Newman, *Aristotle's Politics*, I, 471, rightly objects to any confounding of the μέσοι of this type 'with the class which we nowadays group under the comprehensive term "middle-class" '.

[3] Bolkestein, 183, from another starting-point, comes to exactly the same conclusion.

[4] Cf. Bolkestein, 206ff. I doubt, however, whether the existence of numerous foreign workmen is sufficient to prove that there was no unemployment and 'therefore' no beggars. That would be right only if Athens had had an organized Labour Exchange system. There was no law to prevent an employer, even the State itself, from employing foreign workmen who perhaps were more efficient, even if enough Athenian citizens were available. On the other hand, Plutarch's view (*Per.* 12, 5f) shared by many modern writers, that Perikles' building programme

The fact that the policy of Athens was made by men whose
life was not characterized by the passive ownership of property, but by the constant activity of earning — this fact shows
unmistakably the process by which the Polis and its citizens,
no matter whether they belonged to the rich or to the increasing
number of the poor, came more and more under the influence
of economics. The nature of Athenian economics, on the other
hand, was determined by the insignificance of practically all
financial questions. The general standard of life was that of
a modest middle-class, and no capitalism disturbed its moderate
character. Property and work, not capital, were the basis of
economic activity, money was scarce and prices were generally
low.[1]   Men's outlook was dominated by small-scale activity
which resulted, on one hand, in the modesty and frugality of
Greek life, on the other in a greedy desire for wealth and an
almost complete lack of social conscience.

represented a magnificent method of providing employment, hardly holds good
for the conditions of the fifth century B.C. The return of many citizens from war
may have brought a temporary surplus of population, and the sending out of
cleruchies and colonies was intended and probably sufficient to alleviate this
position. Perikles did not build for the sake of the unemployed, although the
whole of the working population, foreigners and slaves included, had advantages
from the work in which they shared. Still less, therefore, is the opposite true that
Perikles spoiled the Athenians by the public payments and left them unaccustomed
to work (cf., e.g., Andreades, 235ff).

   [1] Cf. Gomme, 5of; Michell, 31f, and his ch. IX, *passim*.

CHAPTER X

RELIGION AND EDUCATION

It lies beyond doubt that during the period of Old Comedy the economic factor became steadily more important in the lives and the minds of the Athenians. This fact cannot be explained merely on economic and social grounds. We must seek the general foundation, that is to say, the general development of mind and intellect upon which the economic and social developments rested.

I

Comedy no less than tragedy formed part of a religious festival, either the Dionysia or the Lenaia, both of which were dedicated to Dionysos.[1] If we think of the god Dionysos as he appears for instance in the *Frogs*, we realize immediately how different Greek 'cult' and 'service' was from anything we are accustomed to connect with these words. This, of course, is familiar, and need not surprise us. The spirit of Greek religion is worlds apart from that of all revealed religions. We must realize this essential fact when we try to ascertain what comedy tells us about Greek religion; but this general fact will not of itself suffice to explain its peculiar quality.

The famous scene in Homer in which Hephaistos catches in a net his unfaithful wife Aphrodite and her lover Ares and exposes them to the laughter of the other gods, leads directly to the ludicrous gods of satyr-drama and comedy, such as the glutton Herakles, the rascal Hermes, the debauched and cowardly Dionysos.[2] Travesties of myths, though more frequent in Middle Comedy, occur also in Old Comedy more than once. We must beware of interpreting as rationalizing

[1] On the programme of the Dionysia, which alone contained both tragedy and comedy, cf. A. W. Pickard — Cambridge, *The Dramatic Festivals of Athens* (1953). Cf. also p. 35, n. 4.

[2] *Od.* VIII, 266ff. — For Dionysos, as depicted by Kratinos, cf. G. Méautis, *Rev. ét. anc.* 36 (1934), 462ff.

blasphemy the comedians' mockery of the gods, nor should we, on the other hand, see it simply as Dionysiac exuberance.

There were, however, spheres of religion and cult where reverent awe or at least naive faith and devotion prevailed. Moreover, pious sincerity and grotesque caricature met on a common basis which helps to explain both attitudes. This basis, which is the chief characteristic of Greek religious feeling, was a belief in the presence of, and close intimacy with, the gods. It is, for instance, common to appeal to a deity for help by claiming him or her as a fellow worker.[1] Euripides' Iphigeneia compares her love for her brother Orestes with Artemis' love for Apollo.[2] The comedians depict similar feelings in their own way. In comedy and its various parts it is possible to recognize a considerable survival of old religious rites and ideas. But the *Hieros Gamos*, for instance, the sacred wedding in which the Dionysiac festival culminated, undergoes — if this is the right explanation — a somewhat surprising and profane transformation in the unions of man and woman which form the closing scenes of many comedies. Or, to take a detail, it is rather an amusing example of anthropomorphism when the Athenian women invoke Athena as 'Tritogeneia' (a name which we cannot explain, but which for the Greeks was connected with the sea and water), and beg her to help them in fetching water, if somebody attempts to burn her holy temple. The pious intimacy with the goddess is even stronger here than the comic element.[3] And there is no trace of irony or blasphemy in calling a sweet wine 'The Milk of Aphrodite',[4] nor in the charcoal-burners' invocation of the vigorous Muse of their deme who flashes like the fire on which fish and soup are boiling, nor in Strepsiades' listening to the advice given by the statue of Hermes at his door-step, nor again in Theagenes' consulting the shrine of Hekate every time he leaves his house.[5] These and other examples reveal the affectionate, almost amorous adoration of human beings who actually lived with their gods.[6]

---

[1] συνεργός, K.587f, Eur. *Med.* 395f, *Hipp.* 523, *Ion* 48.

[2] Eur. *Iph. T.* 1401f.

[3] L.346ff; see also K.1189. Cf. Wilamowitz, on l. 349.

[4] frg. 596. Here we remember the *Liebfraumilch* and *Lacrima Christi*.

[5] A.665ff. — C.1478ff, cf. Phryn. 58. — L.63f.

[6] Such a feeling is also reflected in Philokleon's craving for the 'neighbour hero' Lykos whose statue and shrine stood near the courts (W.389, 819ff).

Naturally the close connection between gods and men could find expression also in human fears. Nowhere perhaps are both aspects more strikingly revealed than in Euripides' *Hippolytos*: Artemis is the loving, sister-like companion, Aphrodite the fiendish hater and destroyer. The gods of the myths held intercourse, either friendly or hostile, with men. Euripides used myth to paint the fate to which men have to succumb, and the forces which rule in their hearts. To ordinary men the gods remained gods — near, personal and alive.

This peculiar quality of Greek religious feeling was the ground on which every cult was based. Athens, 'the holy city', was notorious for her many festivals.[1] The 'piety' of the Athenians, no doubt, meant not so much inward vocation and faith as those common bonds of cult which everyone took for granted, the performance of acts which expressed obedience to the foremost of the 'Greek Commandments': to worship the gods.[2] This piety was inseparably bound up with the patriotic pride which the citizens took in their city, and which was largely based on their belief that Athens was 'most loved by the gods'.[3] It also included the natural elation of those who took part in the Panathenaic procession, and the harmless vanity of women showing off on that occasion their best garments and jewels.[4] Greek religion provided ample opportunities for all kinds of 'worldly' pleasures because there was no barrier between religion and ordinary life. What religious worship demanded was in the main ritual service of one kind or another. Ritual acts were often based on routine and formula, but in general that, and that alone, was what the people expected and wanted. Greek religion had little concern for morals or for purely personal emotion. It was left to a few

---

[1] K.582, 1037, P.1036. — Ps.-Xen. III, 2, 8.

[2] 'The Three Greek Commandments' (a phrase of Headlam's) are σέβειν (or τιμᾶν) θεούς, γονέας, ξένους. Cf., e.g., Pind. *P.* 6, 23f, Aisch. *Hik.* 701ff, *Eum.* 270ff, 590ff, Eur. *Herakl.* 236ff, 901ff, *frg.* 311, 853. These 'laws' are now usually called νόμοι ἄγραφοι (after Sokrates in Xen. *mem.* IV, 4, 9f), but I believe this is a misleading name, although it was through ἀνομία that men would cease honouring the gods (Eur. *Her.* 757ff, 779, *Iph. T.* 275ff). On the νόμοι ἄγραφοι cf. my *Sophocles and Pericles* (1954), ch. II.

[3] K.565f, B.826f. — Eupolis 307. Cf. also the polite inquiry of the messenger in Eur. *El.* 795, whether foreigners were allowed to sacrifice together with the citizens.

[4] L.640ff, 1189ff.

outstanding minds to see a deeper meaning and a higher purpose in the world of the gods. Hardly anything of that was
known to either official or popular religion, both of which can
only be discussed in their own terms and their own forms.[1]

The Greek 'Man in the Street' clung firmly to the traditional
forms which were followed in everyday life no less than in
religious festivals. None of these rituals were more sacred
than those for the dead. It is natural that they play such an
important part in tragedy, while they are not even mentioned
in comedy.[2] The comedians provide us with characteristic
examples of other rituals. Thus every citizen took care of his
eiresione, a branch of olives, adorned with sacred bands and
autumnal fruits, which was fixed on the house-door.[3] Everybody knew something about the chief rites, for example that
at a sacrifice the animal's tongue had to be cut out.[4] At the
feast of the Dipolia the worshippers wore in their hair the
gold cicalas which had been the fashion of the sixth century.[5]
Nikias, a representative of the old strict faith, preferred to
invoke the ancient images of the gods; to him and others like
him the statues of Pheidias were without real sanctity.[6]
Meton's reform of the calendar was opposed for reasons of
religion and cult.[7] The runners who came in last in the torch-
race at the Panathenaia were thrashed; originally an old rite,
it had lost its religious meaning and become crude popular
fun.[8] These are a few of the rituals and their implications
mentioned in comedy.

---

[1] G. Keller, *Die Komödien des Aristophanes und die athen. Volksreligion*
(Diss. Zurich, 1931) makes the fundamental (though widespread) mistake of
assuming that there are two exclusive alternatives: the original fertility rites with
their natural obscenity on the one hand, a rational moralism on the other, for
which most of the gods — in particular (of all gods!) Dionysos and Zeus — were
no longer real. There is a good deal between these two extremes. Keller realizes
some of the disintegrating forces, but his picture as a whole is simplified to such an
extent that it is practically false.

[2] The importance of burial in tragedy needs no expounding. Detailed rites
are mentioned, e.g., throughout Euripides' *Alkestis*.

[3] K.728f, cf. W.399, Pl.1054.   [4] P.1060, B.1705.   [5] C.984f.

[6] βρέτη, K.30ff, cf. L.262. They are the ξόανα, the ancient wooden images
of the gods. — There is perhaps an allusion to Pheidias' statue in the sausage-
seller's boast that the goddess has hollowed out 'with her ivory hand' the pieces of
bread which he provides as spoons. 'What a mighty finger you must have, revered
Lady', is Demos' reply (K.1168ff).

[7] C.615ff.   [8] F.1089ff, frg. 442.

Prayers and sacrifices mark the beginning of all important actions. They are often represented in comedy;[1] but there is little of that genuine religious feeling which is, for example, expressed by the chorus in Euripides' *Elektra*: 'Not by moaning but by prayers and by worshipping the gods will you achieve happiness.'[2] Silent prayers are also mentioned. The sausage-seller prays to very peculiar goblins, but we should like to know to what deities Perikles prayed when he was about to speak in the assembly.[3] Sacred rights are mentioned such as that of the asylum for slaves in the Theseion or in the sanctuary of the *Semnai*.[4] We hear of public and private visits to Delphi and other oracles.[5] Women were specially devout and played a great part in religious life.[6] 'Again and again the old women offer sacrifices.'[7] The Eleusinian mysteries were based on deeper religious feeling and higher moral demands than other cults, but there also was a strict ritual for the initiated.[8] The choruses sung by the initiates in Hades, which were similar to the sacred songs of Athens and Eleusis, reveal the spirit of the mysteries and their ethical demands.[9] Herakles knows all about the initiates in Hades — naturally, since he was helped in his fight for Kerberos by being an initiate himself.[10] Dionysos feels 'the most mystical breeze' of the torches, while the slave smells only the whiff of pork.[11] On the other hand, the idea of sacrificing a pig just before one's death and so becoming initiated in order to enjoy the special advantages of another world is a comic exaggeration of a real and generally accepted belief.[12] The torn clothes also, apparently a symbol of the cult, give the chorus a chance to jest about their erotic

---

[1] e.g., W.860ff, P.431ff, 923ff, 1320ff, frg. 165, Kratinos 21, Plat. 174, adesp. 372.

[2] Eur. *El.* 195ff.

[3] K.634ff (cf. 638: φροντίζοντί μοι), Plut. *Per.* 8, 6.

[4] K.1312, Th.224.

[5] K.1229f, 1272f, C.624f, W.158ff, B.188f, 618f, 716, Pl.21, adesp. 460, 8 D.

[6] Cf. L.1ff, 640ff, Th. *passim*, Eur. *frg.* 13 P, 8ff.

[7] Pherekr. 35: πάλιν αὖθις ἀναθύουσιν αἱ γεραίτεραι. The text is doubtful. Liddell and Scott take as probable: ἀναθυῶσιν, because γραῦς ἀναθυᾷ was a proverbial saying, alluding to what is now called the 'dangerous age' of a woman (Diogen. IV, 10; cf. Phot., p. 118 R). In that case the quotation has no relevance to our context.

[8] Cf. Andok. I, 110ff.   [9] F.320, 324ff, 447ff, 454ff.

[10] F.154ff, Eur. *Her.* 613.   [11] F.313f, 337f.   [12] P.374f.

advantages and the god's meanness.[1] Jokes like these do not
touch on the real character of the mysteries, the belief in which
was deeply rooted. The rites of other mystery-cults are also
derided, while, on the other hand, a man could rely on the
prayer of an initiate of the Samothracian mysteries in order to
win the support of the gods of Samothrake.[2] The Orphic
cosmogony is ridiculed, while Aischylos in the *Frogs* mentions
Orpheus as a teacher of mysteries and moral rules, though
only as one of the old poets to whom the Greeks owe their
code of ethics.[3] The deep devotion to the Eleusinian mysteries
and the general religious fervour of the Athenians were most
clearly displayed in the enormous excitement at, and the
dangerous consequences of, the two religious crimes of the
year 415. Years afterwards, the families of the Eumolpidae
and Kerykes, which were closely connected with Eleusis,
opposed the return of Alkibiades.[4] This was no doubt partly
due to personal politics, but their opposition would never have
been so formidable, if the people had not held the Eleusinian
cult in undisputed reverence.

All these passages reveal a significant mixture of pious
devotion, utilitarian consideration and good-natured fun.
Men and gods, profane and sacred matters, were never
separated; they were even connected by the needs of everyday
life and by quite realistic desires. In comedy, as is natural, the
culinary side of cult is stressed above all. Dikaiopolis, for
instance, leads the gay phallic procession of his rural Dionysia
to dinner and a drinking-bout; Strepsiades at another rural
fête fries sausages for his family.[5] Old and poor men soak up
their very frugal soup with small pieces of bread on the festival
of Theseus.[6] Sausages play a great part in the Apatouria also,
and soup does in the Panathenaia.[7] It is important that the
animal, which is to be sacrificed, should be fat and fleshy.[8]
The distribution of meat after the sacrifice is essential for the
citizens, who usually lived on an almost meatless diet, and the
gods could be made to complain that men ate all the good

---

[1] Pl.845 and schol. — F.404ff. Radermacher explains: '*Der Gott sieht auf das
Herz und nicht das Gewand*', hardly to the point. He overlooks ἐπὶ γέλωτι (404),
and does not do justice to the whole tenor of the passage.

[2] C.254ff, 302ff, 457ff. — P.277f.   [3] B.693ff. — F.1030ff.

[4] Thuc. VIII, 53, 2.   [5] A.202, 237ff. — C.408ff.

[6] Pl.627f.   [7] A.146; cf. Th.558. — C.386.   [8] L.83f.

parts of the sacrifices themselves.[1] What would be the advantage of public prayers, if there was no drinking of wine?[2]
'To offer sacrifice' and 'to drink' seemed to be almost the same
thing.[3] When the import of Boeotian eels, a favourite dish at
the domestic feast of Hekate, was stopped, people complained
rather because of the good meal they missed than because a
religious duty was neglected.[4] A man could be called 'fond
of sacrifices', an allusion either to his piety or his greed.[5] The
priests were foremost in enjoying the profits of sacrifices and
the gifts of the devout, and in the *Frogs* Dionysos asks help of
his priest (who sat in the front row of the theatre), since he is
his fellow drinker.[6] We get the impression that, on the whole,
the meal was considered the most important part of the
sacrifice, and the drink the essential part of the libation.

The culinary advantages, however, represent only the most
obvious results, and those most suited to appear in comedy, of
a religious attitude which is called piety, but was a common-
sense and matter-of-fact piety. Men imagined the gods to
feel and behave in the same way as they did themselves. They,
too, liked taking better than giving. 'Gifts sway the gods.'[7]
The notorious 'envy of the gods' derives certainly from the
power and greatness of the gods, who destroy human pride
and arrogance, but also from their immoral greed and selfishness.[8] The wealthy man, who can make larger sacrifices, is
more 'pious', and will therefore receive greater return from
the gods, though on the other hand it is said that only the
good and just make sacrifices.[9] The Roman *do ut des* was, on
the whole, the mainspring of cult and religious feeling among
the Greeks also, although it never assumed the legalistic
rigidity of Roman religion.

There is superstition in every creed, and it is often difficult
to distinguish the one from the other. Usually the attempt to
do so is made from a rationalist attitude. As far as the Greeks
are concerned, we are the less entitled to speak of superstition,

---

[1] K.410, 654ff, 1140, W.82, 654, Pl.227f. — Pherekr. 23; cf. adesp. 460. —
This, of course, does not exclude that the 'table fellowship' of gods and men was a
genuine part of the religious act; cf. A. D. Nock, *Harvard Theol. Rev.* XXXVII
(1944), 148f.

[2] E.140f.   [3] frg. 171.   [4] L.702ff.
[5] W.82, Antiphon *Tetral.* I, 2, 12.   [6] Pl.676ff, 1179ff. — F.297.
[7] E.778ff. — Eur. *Med.* 964.   [8] Cf. Pl.87ff, Eur. *Andr.* 1161ff.
[9] Cf. Hippokr. *de aëre*, 22, also Pl.144f. — Pl.93f, 1113ff.

because to them there was no dividing line between 'true' beliefs and mere superstitions. The divine oracle which was first taught to men by Mousaios and thus considered to belong to the oldest and most sacred traditions of mankind, was not only on the same level as the usual rites of worship,[1] but almost on the same level as the utterances of professional prophets and vagrant soothsayers, or the omens given by birds, by dreams and even by prophetic fish.[2] The Athenian people were, in fact, greedy for omens and oracles, and it is understandable that the comic poet directed his satire against this attitude. He certainly distinguished between the pronouncements of Delphi and the ordinary pronouncements and omens which in the eyes of the people had something of the same validity.[3] When the owl, the bird of Athena, appeared, the goddess and her help were near.[4] The oracles given in the name of Bakis or a Sibyl, and spread by the book-trade, came to have great influence on public opinion.[5] The soothsayers liked to emphasize, if possible, that their words corresponded with some of Apollo's oracles, and sometimes they pretended that their utterances were of Delphic origin.[6] This shows that their patrons still preferred Apollo's authority, but it must have been obvious to almost everybody that most of these pronouncements were not Delphic. Of course, the more ambiguous, the more puzzling and mysterious the sayings were, so much the better; it was then easy to interpret them in the most appropriate way.[7] Sacrifices and prophecies were the natural prelude to any great enterprise.[8] In war-time the practice of consulting the oracles became exceedingly popular with both State and individuals, and Thucydides as well as

[1] F.1033. — Xen. *mem.* I, 4, 2.

[2] C.332, P.1046ff, B.521, 959ff, Eupolis 211-12, 297, Ameips. 10, Kallias 14, Lysipp. 6. — Pherekr. 39, Archipp.15, also B.719ff. On the prophetic fish cf. O. Weinreich, *Arch. f. Rel.-wiss.* XXVII (1929), 57.

[3] Cf. H. W. Parke, *The Delphic Oracle*, 207f, who perhaps overstresses the satirical attitude of Aristophanes towards Delphi.

[4] W.1085f.

[5] K.61, 109ff, 195ff, 997ff, P.1070ff, 1095, 1116, 1119, B.962, 970. Cf. O. Kern, *Religion der Griechen*, II, 140ff.

[6] K.220. — 1015f, 1047, 1072, 1229.

[7] K.202ff, 1041ff.

[8] Cf., e.g., Eur. *Herakl.* 399ff. In 443 B.C. it was the colonization of Thourioi, in 415 the Sicilian expedition, which caused the same kind of activity. Cf. *AJP.* LXIX (1948), 164f.

the comedians speak of the *chresmologoi*, the soothsayers who sang their oracles for a living everywhere in the streets.[1] There were books on the art of prophecy from which a clever man could learn the business' and then make a great deal of money.[2]

Apart from their political character, oracles had wide and considerable influence on the events of everyday life. It was therefore an advantage of the sausage-seller's oracles as compared with those of the Paphlagonian that they were not only political, but were compounded with 'porridge, young mackerel, fraudulent flour-sellers'[3] — that is to say the everyday joys and sorrows of the inquirers, most of whom were much more interested in their own petty economic struggle than in State-affairs. There were methods other than these solemn oracles to influence everyday life. Already Magnes speaks of interpreters of dreams; they charged only two obols, so that they were obviously not quite on the same level as the 'prophets'.[4] Omens by birds were important for enterprises of all descriptions, such as sea-trade, money-making, marriage.[5] Bad omens were numerous; earthquakes, lightning and eclipses were among them, but also a stumbling over the threshold, a cat crossing the road, or

> if a mouse tore through a mud-built altar-stone,
> or gnawed for want of better food a bag,
> or if a cock crew late at eventide.[6]

It is not surprising that more enlightened individuals were ready to joke about all this superstition and to say that it would be much more of a miracle 'if the bag had eaten the mouse'.[7]

---

[1] Thuc. II, 8, 2; 21, 3; cf. VIII 1, 1. — P.1047, B.960.

[2] Isokr. XIX, 5f. This recalls the charges of venality raised in various tragedies against Teiresias; see above, p. 234.

[3] K.1005ff.   [4] Magnes 4, W.52.

[5] B.717ff, cf. Antiphon V, 81ff, Xen. *mem.* I, 1, 14.

[6] Thuc. II, 8, 2, VII, 50, 4. — Eur. *Herakl.* 730, E.791f, adesp. 341.

[7] Arkesilaos 1 D. Mr. B. S. Page suggests that the Arkesilaos of this fragment, quoted from Bion by Clement of Alexandria (*Strom.* VII, 4, 24), may have been the great philosopher, and not a comic poet about whom we do not know anything except the remark in Diog. Laert. IV, 45: γεγόνασι δὲ καὶ ἄλλοι τρεῖς Ἀρκεσίλαοι· ποιητὴς ἀρχαίας κωμῳδίας, κτλ. There is much to be said for this view. The saying in question is reported as a joke of Arkesilaos (παίζων), and it seems to correspond with the general attitude of his scepticism. He was famous for his quick and witty mind; besides, 'he also took up poetry'

On the whole, the comedians abstain from expressing doubts on oracles and superstitious omens, while this is very common in Euripides.[1] It is certain that, in this as in other things, the comic poets were close to the minds of ordinary people. Such a man could ask himself: 'What unlucky thing did I meet when I went out this morning?'[2] Certain omens, though perhaps not that single drop of rain which Dikaiopolis felt, sufficed to close the assembly.[3] Belief in magic powers and ritual belonged to the same sphere of faith. It was a widespread view that the dead man whom one wished to hear one's words had to be addressed three times.[4] Magic was practised in various ways, a favourite tool being magic rings.[5] Miracles were not unknown. Especially famous were the Thessalian sorceresses who could be hired for certain occasions; they were probably also largely responsible for love-potions and similar things.[6]

These incidental examples clearly reveal the considerable importance of the 'lower' forms of religion,[7] and show us that, in that age as everywhere and always, the so-called 'higher'

(Diog. Laert. IV, 30). Belief in the bad omen of a mouse gnawing through a bag was widespread (cf. Theophr. *char.* 16, 6, Cic. *de divin.* II, 59), and the same sort of ironic criticism as here quoted from Bion (who, with all his changing from one school to another, was a sceptic like Arkesilaos) occurs, e.g., in Plutarch (*Lak. apophthm.* 224e), Cicero (*de divin.* II, 62), and as *illud eleganter dictum Catonis* (Augustinus, *de doctr. Christ.* II, 31). It seems not unlikely that the father of this argument was rather the famous philosopher than an otherwise completely unknown comedian. On the other hand, the words ... θαυμαστόν, εἰ τὸν μῦν ὁ θῦλαξ κατέφαγεν seem to be a verse of exactly the kind quoted by Clement some lines previously, describing this very sort of superstitution; and these verses no doubt come from a comedy (adesp. 341). The philosopher wrote epigrams, but it is difficult to imagine that he composed comic trimeters.

[1] Cf., e.g., *Hipp.* 1058f, *Hel.* 744ff, 759f, *Iph. A.* 520, 956f, *Ba.* 255ff, *frg.* 795. Especially interesting is Euripides' characterization of Teiresias in the *Bakchai.* He has little love for this type of orthodox cleric who makes concessions to rationalistic arguments (cf. Grube, 404. E. R. Dodds, *The Bacchae of Euripides,* 87).

[2] F.196.   [3] A.170f.   [4] F.1175f, cf. 184, 305f.

[5] Pl.884, frg. 250, Eupolis 87, Ameips. 27.

[6] C.749ff, — Antiphon I, 17ff, and above, p. 198, n. 9.

[7] Prescriptions such as not to eat figs during the heat (frg. 463, Pherekr. 80, Nikoph. 12), or to avoid onion and lentil soup in winter (adesp. 367-8), hardly derive from superstition, but are based on supposedly dietetic reasons which, however, it would be difficult to discover; they are, in fact, simply humorous, forbidding just the suitable sort of food.

forms did not satisfy all wants and needs. Superstition and magic can arise in other ages from excessive formalism of cult and the consequent starving of certain spiritual desires, which were probably little felt in Athens at this time. What caused the growth of the lower forms in Athens was rather men's attitude to the gods. The fact that the gods could be brought down to a human or 'far too human' level is certainly rooted in the very nature of Greek religion, and there is no doubt that this attitude contributed to the gradual undermining of the old belief in the gods. To make fun of the gods was originally a proof of men's love for them and of their mutual intimacy. To tell immoral and scandalous stories about the gods did not offend average religious feeling; it troubled only advanced spirits like Xenophanes and Pindar in their different — in fact, almost opposite — ways. Stories such as that of Zeus' fatherhood of Herakles were to some people a fact proved by Herakles' great deeds, to others a mere tale or rumour.[1] The successes of Zeus as a lover became a favourite excuse for adultery, but that does not prove much.[2] It is quite different with the terrible archaic story of how Zeus killed his father; for this had become a problem of the general principles of justice, and it is clear that people no longer believed either in the story or in Zeus.[3] Satire and derision progressively attacked even the fundamental and most sacred facts of faith, above all faith in the gods' power, and it was from this that doubt began to grow.

The power of the gods, whose dignity and strength were impressively reflected in most of the tragedies, however different the religious attitudes of the tragic poets were, this same power was on the same festival days belittled and questioned by the comic poets who made fun of the gods and represented traditional and sacred forms in a startling manner.[4] Much, of course, of what comedy makes of the gods is just good-natured fun. Stupidity, for instance, is worshipped and receives libations.[5] The *Agathos Daimon*, the good and luck-bringing power to whom wine was poured, can become a pretext for the opportunity of drinking some unmixed wine, or is replaced by the *Daimon* of the good Pramnian wine

---

[1] Eur. *Her.* 803ff, 826.
[2] C.1079ff, B.558ff, Eur. *Hipp.* 474, *Her.* 1320ff.   [3] C.904ff.
[4] This is expounded in schol. P.741.   [5] K.221.

itself.[1] One man swears by the nymphs, the other by—cabbage;
Poseidon swears by himself, Trygaios by the gods as well as
'by the pots'.[2] Gods are addressed in such terms as the 'devil
of a fellow', 'you blackguard of a man', or 'the biggest coward
among gods and men'.[3] The god of War has a messenger
'Uproar', who is probably a god himself, but at the same time
a slave.[4] Of hero-worship we hear next to nothing. Herakles,
of course, is a figure of crude burlesque, while it is perhaps
significant that Theseus, the traditional and representative
hero of Attica, never appears on the comic stage.

There are other more significant details. It was, however,
the man rather than the god who was mocked when Perikles
was derided as Dionysos or Zeus, or when Philokleon compared the position of the Athenian juryman with that of Zeus.[5]
But it amounts to an upsetting of the divine hierarchy when,
as a reflection of human desires, Eirene is called 'the greatest
of all goddesses' or 'most holy queen'.[6] In general, with only
the clear exceptions of Athena, who even in Cloudcuckooborough remains the revered town-goddess,[7] and the two
Eleusinian goddesses, hardly any god or goddess is safe from
being exposed to comic indecency and coarse ribaldry.
Dionysos in the *Frogs* and Hermes in the *Peace* and even more
in the *Ploutos* are gods depicted without any reverence whatever, and they are made as ridiculous as can possibly be
imagined. Hermes, though he is called 'the wisest of all gods',
yet swears 'by the Lord Herakles' like an ordinary mortal,
and it is significant that the names by which he is worshipped,
sacred titles in actual use, stamp him as the patron of the poor,
of traders and thieves, so that he himself can be thought of as
a retailer, a rascal, a stateless and starving wretch.[8] Karion
says of Hermes: 'What a good thing it is to have many additional names! For he has thus found his little means of livelihood.'[9] Similarly, a sacred cult-name of Zeus is, as it were,
pushed into the gutter, and applied to the dung-beetle.[10] In

---

[1] K.85, W.525, P.300, frg. 35 D, Theop. 40-1. — K.106f.
[2] Eupolis 74. — B.1614, P.376ff: πρὸς τῶν θεῶν — πρὸς τῶν κρεῶν.
[3] B.1638, F.1472, 486.   [4] P.255ff.
[5] A.530f, Kratinos p. 31 D, 107, 109, 111. — W.620ff.
[6] P.308, 974.   [7] B.358, 828.
[8] P.428, 180. — A.816, K.297, P.393, 402, Th.1202, Pl.1139ff, 1151ff.
[9] Pl.1164f.   [10] P.42.

an unknown comedy Zeus, just roused from sleep like the Homeric god, sends Hermes to earth as a kind of farcical peace-maker between Athens and Sparta.[1] Poseidon, as Poseidon Hippios the patron of the knights and their contests, is a snob who puts on airs and sneers at the barbarian god because he wears his coat the wrong way.[2] Apollo 'sharpens his knife' as a reminder of the many sacrifices at Delphi, and as the healing god he is urged to play the doctor's part, 'since he's paid for it'.[3] Aphrodite turns the crudest obscenities into divine powers equal in kind to similar demons known from other sources, to whom men must offer sacrifices and money.[4] Even Zeus is grossly derided; as Agoraios he is the god of the demagogues, as 'the god of the wine cups' he is the patron of drinkers and their speeches.[5] He is threatened with the abolition of all sacrifices, and his own threats and punishments no longer arouse fear; even his death and last will can be discussed.[6] Peithetairos is able to declare a 'Sacred War' not for, but against the gods, and Zeus will rule only as long as he is richer than other people.[7] Some of these remarks may be only jesting, others are more than that.[8]

The knowledge that the gods were almost powerless was bound to spread and to be made even more obvious to worshippers by the utilitarian basis of almost every cult; for prayers and sacrifices led often enough to negative or even undesired results. It was a common attitude to blame the gods whose justice was at fault, who had betrayed and misled innocent and pious people.[9] All kinds of bad qualities and passions were imputed to the gods, and moral feelings came into growing conflict with traditional beliefs. These are well-known facts, and Euripides for one provides ample evidence, for example in the discussion between Theseus and Herakles in the last scene of the *Herakles*.[10] Contempt of gods or heroes

---

[1] adesp. 43.   [2] B.1567ff.   [3] frg. 684. — B.584.
[4] Plat. 174.   [5] K.500. — adesp. 861: Ζεὺς Ἐπικυλίκειος.
[6] B.1236ff, Pl.1113ff. — B.1642ff.   [7] B.556, Pl.130f.

[8] Even if it were true — as I believe it is not — that Aristophanes, in his 'friendly burlesque', was only following the principle that 'nothing popularises like genial ridicule' (G. Lowes Dickinson, *The Greek View of Life*, 47), this would characterize only part of the comic treatment of the gods.

[9] Cf., e.g., Eur. *Hipp.* 1415, *Her.* 339ff, 347, 813, *Ion* 355, 358, 384, *El.* 583f, 971f, *Or.* 162ff, 285ff, 416ff, *frg.* 254.

[10] Eur. *Her.* 1314ff, 1341ff. Cf. my *Aspects of the Ancient World*, 161ff.

could be an expression of human *hubris* as in the case of Lykos, but also of a genuine horror at the immoral behaviour of one of the gods or goddesses.[1] Disbelief in miraculous stories of divine power was equally widespread.[2] It became an attitude not entirely confined to those who were brought up on the modern teaching either to doubt the truth of the mythological traditions or to deny the power and even the existence of the gods.[3] 'If gods do something shameful, they are no gods', was a thought as natural to many as it was illogical.[4] The same trends of thought are reflected in comedy. In spite of all the good fun and travesty, the picture of the gods which the comic poets paint reveals a profound and moving disillusionment. Myth and legend lost credit, and more than that: 'Myth did perish.'[5]

It was not only the myth that perished. Myth is always subject to poetic licence or rationalistic interpretation and scepticism. It was faith itself, expressed in cult and prayer, of which the inner decay was characterized by a great number of parodies of both cult and prayer.[6] Certainly, the gods knew 'how to take a joke', and comic travesty was never considered to be proof of *asebeia*, impiety; in comedy it frequently occurs next to sincere and pious prayers. There is no evidence at all that any of the comic poets was ever accused of impiety. Nevertheless, the natural attachment to the gods and the whole religious sense of the people were, to some extent, changed into an attitude of ironic detachment and superiority. No wonder that those who referred to their divine origin and were proud of long genealogies aroused derision.[7] On the other hand, Euripides and Sokrates can be mocked like gods, and can answer as if they were gods.[8] Even the most sacred festi-

---

[1] Eur. *Her.* 151ff. — *Her.* 669f, 1307ff, *Ion* 436ff, 881ff, *Iph. T.* 711ff.

[2] e.g., Eur. *Hipp.* 195ff, *El.* 737ff, *Hel.* 17ff.

[3] Cf. Eur. *frg.* 286.   [4] Eur. *frg.* 292, 7.

[5] P.131, after Eur. *Iph. T.* 1292.   — Kratinos 59 = Krates 21: ὁ μῦθος ἀπώλετο. It is. not clear what the meaning of these words was in their original context — maybe, something far less general than we have implied. The μῦθος may have been, e.g., the plot of a play. The scholiasts did not know, and therefore tried various explanations. But whatever the right one, the general implications of the phrase remain true.

[6] Much material in H. Kleinschmidt, *Die Gebetsparodie in der Antike* (*Tübinger Beiträge*, 28) (1937).

[7] A.47ff.   [8] A.405f, C.220ff.

vals, mysteries and cult-names could be taken away from the gods concerned in order to bribe greedy Hermes.[1] Religion has lost a good deal of its power, at least for many; good humour and the jests of naive believers have turned into the irony of unbelievers.

The natural consequence was that religious duties often ceased to be taken seriously. People played pranks during the procession of the Panathenaia.[2] A partial purpose of a visit to Delphi could be sightseeing.[3] To Kadmos in Euripides' *Bakchai* the worship of the new god is a matter of opportunist policy and family pride.[4] The wealthy miser envies the gods the sacrifice he is to give them, and offers less than he has solemnly promised.[5] The choregus tries to avoid offering the lamb at the sacrifice.[6] Even the sacredness of the place does not keep the slave Karion from behaving indecently, and further from stealing a pot of soup before the priest can take it.[7] 'Blasphemy by a slave' seems to have been a fairly common thing.[8] It was by no means unusual to ease oneself by the fence of a sanctuary, and the images of Hekate could be soiled by men engaged in religious dancing.[9] We may call all this trivial, or even see in it a sign of 'natural' and unadulterated feeling, but it proves, in fact, that religion had largely lost its hold on men. The Thesmophoria was a holy festival of women, which as a cult included words and rites which were partly obscene; but in the *Thesmophoriazousai* the holy rites and sacred secrets of the festival provide the background not only for a campaign against Euripides, but also for disgraceful and shameful attacks on the women themselves, and for a plot remarkable for its grotesque and rather masculine obscenity as well as for its literary jests. We feel how divorced the repre-

---

[1] P.418ff, 425. — A peculiar kind of sacrilege, which becomes a matter of blackmail, is described in Eupolis 40 P, 65ff, 86. Some foreigner who has drunk the sacred drink (κυκεών) arrives in the market-place with his beard still full of the barley crumbs which the drink contained. 'Clearly an echo of the recent excitement concerning the profanation of the Mysteries . . . a remarkable passage, for Old Comedy carefully avoids the theme as a rule' (Page). But Eupolis differed in his political attitude from the other comedians. Cf. also W. Schmid, *Philologus*, 93 (1938), 426.

[2] Hermipp. 26.
[3] Eur. *And.* 1086ff, cf. *Ion* 182ff.
[4] Eur. *Ba.* 332ff.
[5] B.1618, cf. adesp. 460 (?) — adesp. 1.
[6] P.1022.
[7] Pl.697ff, 673ff.
[8] Eur. *Ion* 1189.
[9] W.394, Pl.1183f. — F.366.

sentation is from its original and from the sacred atmosphere
of the cult. The case of Diognetos, who had been one of the
Hendeka, the famous police commissioners, and then became
a temple-robber, may not have been typical, although grave-
robbers seem not to have been altogether rare.[1] It is, in fact,
not in incidental misdeeds or even crimes that the decisive
weakening of religiosity shows itself, but in a fundamental
change of mind.[2]

Mainly because of the general movement of religious senti-
ment foreign cults penetrated Athens, or rather the Peiraeus,
at this time in ever-growing numbers.[3] Among them that of
the Thracian goddess Bendis was probably the first and was
even officially accepted; others were those of the Phrygian god
Sabazios, the Great Mother and her lover Attis, and, above
all, Adonis.[4] His festival could be mentioned in the same
breath with those of Demeter and Zeus.[5] Eupolis, in the
Baptai, attacked Alkibiades and his friends for taking part in
the orgies of the goddess Kotytto, a Thracian deity to whose
worship the poet ascribes all kinds of magical actions as well
as debauchery.[6] It has been shown that this description is
probably largely fancy and that perhaps no cult of Kotytto
ever existed in Athens, though there was one in Corinth.[7]
Such criticism would make any facts mentioned by Eupolis
rather doubtful, but in all comic exaggeration and fancy there
would still be reflected the general impact which this kind of
foreign cult and its orgiastic rituals made on Greek life. Hyes,
a comic substitute either for the rain-god Zeus or for Dionysos
as the god of moisture, could be called a foreigner.[8] Another
goddess who found adherents even among important people

[1] Eupolis 40 P, 95ff. — Eur. *Med.*1380f.

[2] Sometimes an ancient ritual disappeared, because general views on morality
overcame religious conservatism. Thus, it seems, the method of purification by
destroying a criminal as a scapegoat for the whole people was no longer used
(F.733, cf. Hipponax 7 Diehl). The human scapegoat was called φαρμακός,
but the same word can simply indicate a base or criminal man (K.1405, Lysias VI,
53).

[3] Cf. Kern, *op. cit.*, 224ff.

[4] Bendis: frg. 365, 368; cf. Kratinos' *Thraittai* (71ff). — Sabazios: W.8ff, B.875,
L.387ff, frg. 566; cf. also the evidence on the *Horai*, Cic. *de leg.* II, 37. — Great
Mother and Attis: W.8, 119, B.875f, Theop. 27. — Adonis: P.420, Kratinos 15,
Pherekr. 170, 198, Plat. 1ff.

[5] P.420.   [6] Eupolis 68, 72, 77, 83, 84; cf. also 333, 351.

[7] Cf. S. Srebrny, *Mélanges Cumont*, 423ff.   [8] frg. 878.

of old Attic stock was Isis.[1] It could be said, though with considerable exaggeration: 'You have changed the city from Athens into Egypt.'[2] This is a general reference to religious worship; but the fact that there was at Athens apparently a large community of Egyptians is sufficient to indicate how Egyptian cults had spread.[3] Since the solar and stellar cults of the East had become known, Helios and Selene could be derided as representatives of barbarous religion and foes of the Olympians.[4] Religious desire and yearning, no longer satisfied by the old cults, tried to find new outlets. The Greek Dionysos could appear as the Asiatic leader of ecstatic mysteries which, though frequently nothing but peaceful and pleasant rites, could develop into a form repulsive to the sober ritualism of Greek religion, which occasionally even showed a streak of something like puritanism.[5] It is significant that the opponent of the Dionysian mysteries can describe the god, who is acting as his own prophet, as a seducer and conjurer, and that Theseus sees his son Hippolytos, perhaps pictured as an Orphic, in the same light.[6] The introduction of foreign cults, most of which were of an emotional and even orgiastic character, was in general left to private initiative. It is good fun, but at the same time significant, that in one of Aristophanes' plays someone simply brings to the market the goddess whom he has imported from abroad, and immediately establishes her cult by a sacrifice.[7] New cults were easily brought to Athens, mostly of course by foreigners, and other evidence, for instance the opening sentence of Plato's *Republic*, confirms this.[8] It is

[1] Kratinos 30 (perhaps).   [2] frg. 569, 15.

[3] But Ammon with a ram's skin and horn (Strattis 6 D) had become an essentially Greek god. Dr. Tarn's attempt (*Alexander the Great*, II, 356ff) to make Kallisthenes responsible for the identification of Ammon with Zeus and to discard earlier evidence is unconvincing.

[4] P.403ff. This is remarkably early evidence for something usually ascribed to the Hellenistic age only.

[5] Dionysos' peaceful mysteries: Eur. *Her*. 892ff, *Phoen*. 784ff, *Ba. passim*. — Puritanism: apart from Pentheus in the *Bakchai* see, e.g., *Ion* 552f.

[6] Eur. *Ba*. 233ff, *Hipp*. 1083; cf. 952ff; see also *Rhesos* 943ff. Cf. Winnington-Ingram, *Euripides and Dionysus, passim*. Hippolytos as an Orphic: M. Tierney, *Proceedings Royal Irish Acad*. XLIV, C, 2 (1937), 59ff.

[7] frg. 26 D.

[8] E. R. Dodds, *Harvard Theol. Rev*. XXXIII (1940), 173, well quotes Strabo X, 3, 18 (p. 471) for the fact that the large number of foreign cults made them a stage joke.

difficult to say how far the native Athenian population was affected by the foreign cults. Frequently there were individual conversions rather than mass suggestion, though we hear of processions of women who bewailed the dead Adonis, and the *Bendideia* was a public festival.[1]

Thucydides clearly states that as a result of the plague both fear of the gods and the law of men had lost their power, and that piety and impiety were generally held to lead to the same end.[2] The horrors of those years obviously only strengthened what was already a characteristic symptom of the age. The sanctity of altars was violated more than once at that time, and Theramenes was well aware that the altar would not give him asylum.[3] Even from the position of higher ethics a plea could be made against the indiscriminate right of refuge at the altar for good and bad men alike.[4] So to protect the sacred olives it became necessary to send out supervisors every month and inspectors once a year.[5] Since men began to doubt the power of the gods, the former close intimacy with them and the belief in their vivid presence gave way to an opposite feeling, and the number of those who denied even the existence of gods increased. Demosthenes asks his colleague, the old-fashioned and pious Nikias, the question which was in the minds of many people at that time and which was repeatedly voiced on the stage by Euripides: 'Do you really believe that there are gods?'[6] While formerly the gods lived in each of their statues, they gradually became no more than statues, and the sculptors therefore were the real makers and creators of gods.[7] Hermes pretends to be one of the wooden statues of Daidalos which could both talk and walk.[8] When the gods were like statues, one might soon come to seek one's gods

---

[1] Adonis: Plut. *Nik.* 13, 11, *Alk.* 18, 5. Recent research has shown that worshippers of foreign deities — usually citizens but sometimes foreigners as well — formed associations of the traditional type (ὀργεῶνες or θιασῶται). Cf. W. S. Ferguson, *Harvard Theol. Rev.* XXXVII (1944), 67f., 96ff, 104ff, 107ff; he shows also that Athenian officials were in charge of the festival of the *Bendideia*. — A kind of 'official' reception was given to the worship of Bendis, according to a Boeotian vase-painting, by Themis who, with torch and κανοῦν, greets her, apparently as a newcomer to local cult. Cf. my *Rechtsidee im frühen Griechentum*, 32f, 52f, 140, and plate.

[2] Thuc. II, 53, 4.   [3] Xen. *hell.* II, 3, 53.
[4] Eur. *Ion* 1312ff.   [5] Lysias VII, 25.   [6] K.32.
[7] e.g., C.1478ff and the Eirene in the *Peace*. — frg. 786-7.   [8] Plat. 188.

among real living beings. The man or the woman who was destined to save the State was called Saviour (*Soter*).[1] That is the name which was frequently given to Zeus or occasionally to other gods who saved men or State.[2] The mortal called by this name did not yet enter the ranks of the gods, but the name indicated the first step in this direction, and further steps were to be taken before long.[3]

While Aischylos, who was an initiate of Eleusis, invokes the venerable Demeter of antiquity, Euripides has gods of his own, though largely of Aristophanic origin.[4] Still, there are characters in Euripides who swear 'by the sacred ether, the house of Zeus', and in Aristophanes, Euripides speaks of ether as his 'food'.[5] Ether was a kind of natural father-god to go with Mother Earth.[6] The comedian's mockery, however, was aimed at something more general — at the replacement of the living gods by vague and abstract conceptions.[7] When Hekabe invokes a Zeus who seems to be a collection of different philosophical ideas, it is a natural reaction on the part of Menelaos to speak of her new ways of praying.[8] It is said that because Euripides denies the gods in his tragedies, a poor widow sells only half as many wreaths for religious purposes as before.[9] Every spectator must have realized that much of this was comedy based on erroneous suppositions, for the gods play a most important part in Euripides' plays, from the prologues to the concluding scenes with the *deus ex machina*. But behind the comic insinuation stood the fact, at the time no doubt already quite obvious, that the bonds of religion and cult had slackened, and that this was due, to a large extent, to the views, which Euripides shared, of modern writers, thinkers and teachers. The lawsuits brought on the ground

---

[1] P.1033ff, F.1419, 1436, 1458, 1501. — K.149, P.914f, Pherekr. 187.

[2] Th.1009, F.378, 1433, E.79, 761, 1045, 1103, Pl.877, 1175, 1186, 1189. Aischylos and Pindar provide earlier examples. I cannot explain why our evidence from Aristophanes is confined to his later plays, unless this is because of the general deterioration of the political and economic conditions.

[3] For the self-destruction of the anthropomorphic gods and the demand for living beings instead of dead statues, cf. my *Aspects of the Ancient World*, 187ff.

[4] F.889ff.   [5] Eur. *frg.* 487, cf. Th.272, F.100, 311. — F.892.

[6] Eur. *frg.* 839, 877, 941.   [7] Cf. Eur. *Med.* 494f: καινὰ θέσμια.

[8] Eur. *Tro.* 884ff; cf. also *Her.* 1263, *frg.* 480: Ζεὺς ὅστις ὁ Ζεύς, οὐ γὰρ οἶδα πλὴν λόγῳ.

[9] Th.446ff.

of *asebeia*, which were frequently based on offences against fairly recent and unimportant religious rules, were the answer of those who still firmly believed in the old gods.[1]

Their position was still very strong in the years before and after 400, and the number of citizens who followed the new gods and cults, or were pure atheists, was as yet small. The only opposition which counted was the moralistic or sceptical rationalism taught by the sophists. This is exhibited and derided chiefly in the *Clouds*, though the ridiculous belief in 'Vortex' and the new divine triad of Chaos, Clouds and Language is merely comic and does not give us any idea of the real situation during that important epoch in the history of human thought.[2]

This is far more strikingly reflected in the mind and work of Euripides, though it cannot be the purpose of these pages to give any detailed account of his position in the history of thought and belief. Utterances of criticism of the gods and of unbelief abound in his plays, though they are matched by others which contradict them. The real problem is not that of atheism — rather that of belief or unbelief in the amorality and the power traditionally connected with the Olympian gods. The latter are sometimes superseded by Tyche, an impersonal force of chance and fate which was to gain a predominant position a century later.[3] Tyche is not mentioned in comedy, but it is probably true that in general the religious problems pervading comedy and Euripidean tragedy are of the same kind. The argument that the lightning, which hits sacred oaks and does not hit bad men, is not the instrument of Zeus' justice is relevant and quite seriously meant.[4] Behind the comic presentation we feel the underlying moral energy which, as we know well, gave the chief impetus to the rationalist and ethical criticism of the traditional ideas about the gods, and

[1] Lysias XXX, 17ff, shows that the ancient rituals and rules ἐκ τῶν κύρβεων had been supplemented by many others from public decrees (ἐκ τῶν στηλῶν — a certain correction by Taylor of the meaningless εὔπλων in the codices).

[2] C.380, 828. — 424. It should, however, be noted that 'Vortex' (δῖνος) may have been an allusion to Anaxagoras' principle of περιχώρησις (frg. 12 Diels), and that the νεφέλαι played a certain part in his process of creative separation (frg. 16). — Strepsiades calls the Clouds 'heroines' (C.315), but the 'goddesses great for lazy people' (C.316) are no example of real religion, as is confirmed by the new triad of C.424.

[3] Eur. *Kyk.* 606, *Hek.* 488ff.   [4] C.398ff.

set human reason and wisdom on the throne of Zeus.[1] The comic poet had to be very careful in reproducing such views, as we see from the solemn invocations of the great Olympian gods by the very chorus which represents the new order, the chorus of the 'holy' and 'august' clouds.[2] Aristophanes, of course, is not likely to be simply a detached observer of his time, objectively describing that process of 'enlightenment'. The strength and power of this movement, however, can easily be seen in comedy and its attacks. They prove that an important change was going on and that moralistic scepticism was gaining influence, although the traditions of religious life survived and still dominated the many.

2

Clearly, we do not find sufficient evidence in comedy to understand the social and intellectual importance of the sophistic movement, which in fact was for several decades the most stirring element in Greek thought and life. Neither is the method usually adopted by historians of philosophy sufficient for our purpose, the method which simply explains the sophistic doctrines and compares them with those of earlier and later thinkers. The essential character of the whole phenomenon is to be found in the fact that a considerable proportion of the people was affected by it in that they either came under its sway or were roused to protective resistance. The doctrines of the sophists were no esoteric science. Many of their ideas, well fitted to be treated superficially and thus to be popularized, infiltrated the minds of the people almost without their becoming aware of it. The impact of economic aims and values would not have become so strong, had not the sophists taught the Athenians an essentially practical and opportunist outlook and caused them to doubt many of the traditional values. Instances of one reaction or the other to the teaching of the sophists are found in various authors of the time, in Herodotos and Thucydides, Sophokles and Euripides. But its greatest and most tragic effect has nothing to do with literature; I refer, of course, to the condemnation of Sokrates. No other source makes it quite so clear as the

[1] Cf. Eur. *Her.* 655ff, also *Hipp.* 120, *Tro.* 203, *Ba.* 1348, *frg.* 1018.
[2] C.269ff, 291. — 563ff, 595ff.

Clouds of Aristophanes that it is correct to regard the death of Sokrates as a result of the resistance to a movement which, in spite of considerable internal divergencies, we may treat as one, the activity of 'the sophists'. To a large number, at least, of the Athenian people the spirit of the movement was exemplified most clearly, perhaps also most strangely and in its most irritating form, in Sokrates. It comes to the same thing (though stress is laid on the political aspect) when many years later Aischines addressed the people thus: 'You put to death Sokrates the sophist, because he was shown to have been the teacher of Kritias, one of the Thirty who put down the democracy.'[1]

It is well known that the Platonic Sokrates in his defence referred to that enemy of his who wrote the *Clouds*,[2] while Plato, when he composed the *Symposion*, can hardly have believed that Aristophanes was in any decisive degree an accessory, even an unwilling accessory, to the disaster which befell his beloved teacher. This apparent change of judgment can perhaps be explained by a change in the general mind, in particular in the attitude of the Athenians to Sokrates' teaching.[3] In that respect, the rule of the Thirty made a very great difference. The comedy of 423 became part of the tragedy of 399, but it remained a comedy, that is to say, an essentially irresponsible piece of poetry. Plato never forgot that. We, however, must ask why in the play Sokrates of all men was chosen as the representative of a movement (which incidentally is ill-understood and seriously misrepresented), whereas he is depicted by Plato as the most passionate and most formidable enemy of that movement, an intellectual enemy indeed both to the moderate earlier sophists, such as Protagoras and Gorgias, and to such younger radicals as Thrasymachos and Kallikles —

[1] Aischines I, 173.

[2] Plato, *apol.* 18 B, 19 C.

[3] This view has been elaborated by Wolfg. Schmid, *Philologus*, 97 (1948), 209ff, who finds the picture of comedy essentially that of the true Sokrates. There is some justification for this view, and something will be presently said about it. Schmid is, however, mistaken in assuming that Sokrates at the age of 45, when, for instance, Alkibiades had been one of his pupils, was still, or at least had been recently, devoted to natural philosophy only. Neither can I quite follow B. Snell who suggests (ibid., 125ff) that Sokrates as early as 430 taught that virtue was knowledge, but had not yet realized the difference between his 'true' knowledge and that of the sophists.

the latter a 'great' man and, though a product only of Plato's mind, a spiritual relation of Alkibiades and Kriːias.

The answer to this question has frequently been found in the appearance and behaviour of the real Sokrates. He seems to have lent himself naturally to travesty, the more so since no other philosopher was so well known to the general public as this man, who in streets and palaestra entered into conversation with the most varied types of men and youths, who made himself in fact something of a nuisance to everyone engaged about his own business.[1] This explanation, however, cannot suffice when we recall that the *Clouds* holds up to derision a Sokrates who never existed, and neglects some of the most obvious features, both novel and irritating, of the historical person. It has been maintained that the Sokrates of the *Clouds* is not Sokrates at all, but an example of the comic type of the 'charlatan sophist'; but that, too, cannot be accepted as a full explanation.[2] There are undoubtedly features of the comic figure which, however exaggerated, fit Sokrates far better than the sophists. Only he who never taught for money and liked to walk bare-footed, and not one of the elegant sophists who took high fees, could be depicted as a starving pauper.[3] It is he to whose teaching the 'know thyself' refers which Strepsiades has learnt to use as a maxim.[4] There are a few other allusions, but what the Sokrates of the *Clouds* is chiefly concerned with, has very little indeed to do with the historical person. It is more in fun than with any specially offensive purpose, and at any rate far from the truth, that Sokrates and his pupils are represented as stupidly splitting hairs in argument, or as strange observers of sky and stars, 'star gossipers', out of touch with the realities of life.[5] The sophists, in general, are seen as gossips, or rather prattlers, and their chief art is that of quibbling.[6] Both these activities, however typical of the Sokrates of comedy, 'prattling' and 'measuring the air', are, in fact, sometimes charged against the real Sokrates also,

[1] C.359ff.

[2] ἀλαζὼν σοφός, C.102; cf. Kratinos 380. Criticism of this view goes at least as far back as A. Körte, *Bursians Jahresber.* 152 (1911), 238f.

[3] See above, p. 234. In general cf. W. Schmid, *l.c.*

[4] C.842.

[5] frg. 386. This meaning of μετεωρολέσχης and the evidence of Aristophanes are omitted in Liddell and Scott.

[6] λεπτολογία, Hermipp. 22; cf. frg. 490.

but that may easily have happened under the influence of the *Clouds*.[1] The worship of Ether and Clouds, and the denial of Zeus, are on a different plane. Nothing is more of a justification of the final punishment in the play, and nothing proved more disastrous in determining the actual fate of Sokrates, than the fact that the thinkers 'sinned against the gods'.[2] Significantly enough these words of Strepsiades are the last words spoken before the chorus leaves the stage. All this certainly implies a common misunderstanding of Sokrates, not so much on the poet's part, for he will have known better, but on the part of the audience for whose judgment and taste he wrote, the ordinary citizens with their traditional religious thought and feeling. There can be no doubt that public opinion — and not without some justification — thought of Sokrates as one of those who undermined traditional beliefs. He remembered in his last moment the cock he owed to Asklepios; whatever the meaning of this vow, the man who died with these words was neither an atheist nor did he despise the rituals of public worship. But his ethical rationalism taught him to listen to the voice in his own mind, and it was indeed 'the god within us' who in men like Sokrates and Euripides was working as the great force which gradually destroyed the rule of the Olympians.[3] Without understanding what was happening, the people felt the danger. It is for this reason that there breathes in the *Clouds* the air of the lawsuits in which Anaxagoras and others like him at that period were prosecuted on grounds of impiety.[4]

The identification of Sokrates with the sophists, though at first surprising, becomes somewhat comprehensible if we remember those points in their methods and in their contribution to the evolution of the Greek mind which are in a sense similar — dialectics, aversion from the old religion, attacks on traditional views, the principle of man's own knowledge and

---

[1] C.1480, F.1491 ff, Eupolis 352-3. — C.225.— Xen. *oik.* 11, 3.

[2] C.1509.

[3] This is as far as I would agree with the definition of Sokrates' δαιμόνιον as a religious experience, and of Sokrates (not only of Plato) as an essentially religious mind, as expounded in the deep and stirring book by R. Guardini, *Der Tod des Sokrates* (third ed., 1948; also in English translation).

[4] It is perhaps significant that Plutarch in the same paragraph in which he speaks of Diopeithes' law against philosophers like Anaxagoras also mentions that it was a comic poet, Hermippos, who accused Aspasia of impiety (*Per.* 32, 1).

judgment. Of all this the play gives us hardly more than a few superficial features, but perhaps enough to enable us to understand the poet's real intention. In accordance with popular misconceptions, in accordance also with the comedian's natural desire to make as much fun as possible of the 'philosophers', though at the same time in order to denounce the spirit rather than the man, Aristophanes attacked Sokrates as the true sophist, as the incarnation of all sophists.[1] Thus, for instance, all sophists are said to be dirty and unkempt, though in fact they were not.[2] Both parties are brought nearer to each other and made similar. By adopting this or a like point of view, it has been possible for later writers to draw historical conclusions entirely contradictory of the usual moral judgment. It is well known that Hegel, and many writers since, have sided with Aristophanes, or rather with Sokrates' real accusers, against Sokrates. In doing so they overlooked the fact that the real Sokrates actually fought for the old ideals with new weapons and for new reasons. In part, however, these ideals, too, were filled with new meaning: the ideals of *arete*, *eusebeia* and *sophrosyne*, of goodness, piety and self-control.

All such questions, or rather the one great question of the historic Sokrates, are not only very hard to answer, but they lie, in fact, outside the scope of the problems which we are discussing here. So we may leave this aspect of the question, the more as, no matter to what other conclusions we may come, one fact at least is incontestable: the poet could safely depict Sokrates as a sophist, even as the very embodiment of the sophists, and be sure of interesting the people in this picture. This remains true in spite of the failure of the *Clouds* and its having to be rewritten because the poet found the play

---

[1] This does not mean, as one of my reviewers put it (*American Hist. Rev.* LI, 1946, 293) that I prefer 'to convict Aristophanes of intellectual dishonesty rather than of misunderstanding' (cf. also the similar view expressed by Professor Greene *AJP*. LXV, 1944, 268). Why should the comedian, who could not know what was to happen twenty-four years later, not have chosen to depict Sokrates as the absurd sophist just because the people saw him like that? There was no moral compulsion whatsoever for him to describe in their true colours anybody or anything he wanted to ridicule. It is for this reason that I try in general to find the facts not in but behind the plot. — For Aristophanes' conception of Sokrates cf. also the beginning of the 91st chapter of Lessing's *Hamburgische Dramaturgie* (cited by Meder, note 58).

[2] C.835ff, B.1554f.

too subtle for his audience.[1] The play which won the second prize, while the *Clouds* took the third place, was the *Konnos* of Ameipsias, and this was also an attack on Sokrates. The choice of subject is really more significant than all the details of distortion and caricature. Sokrates was, as it were, in the limelight many years before his trial. He was not only a teacher of some of the best brains among Athenian youth, he was also a popular figure, a man in whose ideas and absurdities the people took a lively interest. The trial of Sokrates is one of the outstanding events of the history of the human mind and the spiritual freedom of man. But our concern is not Sokrates. It is his opponent and executioner, the Athenian people, with whom we are concerned. However strong or feeble the reasons were which induced the court to condemn Sokrates, they will be better understood if we understand the people's mind.

We have seen the peculiar and contradictory part which religion played in the Athens of 400 B.C. The question now arises as to how far the people's attitude to Sokrates' teaching reflected their general intellectual interests. The point is not so much what the people thought of Sokrates, whether, for instance, they believed, because of his alleged lack of cleanliness and physical care, that he was one of the 'Laconisers', a partisan of the oligarchs.[2] It is more important to discover what the average citizen thought for himself, how far, in fact, intellectual problems, questions of instruction and education, were present to the mind of the public.[3] Even contemporary society realized that Athens, 'the most brilliant of cities', stood out among the Greek States for her beauty and spirit.[4] Athens provided the best soil for every kind of intellectual and artistic endeavour. The comic poet derides the man who does not know Athens, or if he knows her, does not love her, or if he loves her, does not stay there.[5] He says in other words what Perikles says in his Funeral Speech when he calls Athens 'the School of Hellas'.[6]

---

[1] C.520ff, W.65.

[2] B.1281f. This is a point which Snell finds also in Ps. Xenophon (II, 19), and he compares Plato, *Prot.* 352 D (*Philologus*, 97, 1948, 125ff).

[3] These questions were referred to in Chapter I and will now be more closely investigated.

[4] adesp. 44, 340.   [5] Lysipp. 7.   [6] Thuc. II, 41, 1.

3

Even acquaintance with a few comedies shows that, in the intellectual sphere, public interest was focused not on abstract thought, but on literary art, above all on the theatre, and equally on tragedy and comedy. This, of course, is understandable, though our impression may be somewhat distorted by the fact that it rests on the evidence of comedy. It is perhaps harder to understand why the most artistic of all people talked very little about sculpture and painting. The Greeks of the fifth century had not yet a theoretical, 'aesthetic', approach to art. We shall see that it was different with literature. Sculptors and painters were to them in general gifted craftsmen, and the questions they asked of a piece of art were less sophisticated, or at least less 'artistic', than we might expect. It is significant that in Euripides' *Ion* the chorus, while admiring the sculptures of the temple, are interested only in the subjects represented, and not in the sculptor's art.[1] When in the *Hekabe* the queen tells Agamemnon 'to stand back like a painter' and thus to view her woes, we feel that the poet is at least interested in the work of the painter, though again hardly in his art.[2]

We turn to the people's attitude to thought and literature. There are a few allusions to the 'present-day sky-philosophers'.[3] Kratinos in his *Panoptai*, the 'All-Seers', attacks the philosopher and physicist Hippon, *inter alia* by quoting the ideas of memory and forgetfulness which play a part also in the Socratic pedagogy in the *Clouds*.[4] Anaxagoras, though he must have been fairly well known after his trial and expulsion, is mentioned only once, as the alleged teacher of Euripides, and so is Damon as the teacher of Perikles.[5] Protagoras is derided as the scoundrel who speaks solemnly about the celestial, but eats with excellent appetite of the terrestrial.[6] Prodikos is considered the most important of the sophists, but is called as pernicious as any book or chatterbox.[7] The 'foreign words'

[1] Eur. *Ion* 182ff, cf. 232f; similarly about the βαρβάρων ὑφάσματα in the temple treasure (1158ff); γραφή in 271 is a book rather than a painting.
[2] Eur. *Hek.* 807f.   [3] C.360.
[4] Kratinos 151ff, especially 154. — C.482ff.
[5] frg. 676 b (Kock, III, p. 725), Plat. 191.
[6] Eupolis 146.   [7] C.360f, B.692. — frg. 490.

which 'deceive the people' seem to refer to the famous Panhellenic speech of Gorgias, though he is not mentioned by
name.[1] Sokrates is once called 'the Melian'; it seems that the
audience knew of the atheism of the poet Diagoras the Melian,
though his trial and banishment took place some years later.[2]
These few passages, apart from the *Clouds*, confirm what we
have so far taken for granted, that the public was acquainted
with the prominent sophists and with some of their doctrines.

We have emphasized that the teaching of the sophists had
a wide influence; but as far as the ordinary people were concerned, it naturally remained superficial. I doubt whether we
are justified to say of the Athenians in general that they were
'enthusiastic about abstract thought'.[3]   Of science most
people knew nothing, and the complete blankness of Strepsiades' mind when he hears of astronomy and geometry
reflects, though in comic exaggeration, the widespread ignorance of what was supposed to be an important part of the
teaching of some of the sophists.[4]   There was, however, one
kind of science which, being the most clearly 'applied' science
of all, made its influence strongly felt, and that was medicine.
It influenced the sophists and various writers and thus indirectly the general public, but it had also its direct effects.[5]
Its impact on the tragedians and on Thucydides is a well-
known fact, and it is not surprising to find Aristophanes, too,
using technical medical terms taken from both Ionian and
Hippocratic teaching.[6] He, of course, does so not because he
wants to show off, but for the sake of comic effect. This shows
that even puns on unusual expressions and allusions to purely
medical issues were received with understanding.[7]   Greek

[1] A.634f.   [2] C.830. — B.1072ff and schol.
[3] Grube, 125.   [4] Cf. Eur. *frg.* 910.

[5] It seems that the antithesis νόμος — φύσις owed its origin mainly to medical
writers; cf. F. Heinimann, *Nomos und Physis* (1945). The medical theory, on the
other hand, of μοναρχία and ἰσονομία (Alkmaion 4; cf. *Historia* I [1950]
535) shows the influence of political life and thought on medical science.

[6] Cf. H. W. Miller, *TAPA.* 76 (1945), 74ff. He has collected the relevant
(and some irrelevant) material from Aristophanes, and the examples in the next
note are quoted from his article.

[7] Puns, e.g., C.74: ἵππερος — ἴκτερος, L.1085: ἀσκητικόν — ἀσκιτικόν;
technical terms, e.g., W.277, L.987; F.1280: βουβωνιάω, suffer from swollen
glands; K.907: ἑλκύδριον, ulcer; L.553, 846: τέτανος, obscene use of 'con-
vulsion'; K.381: χαλαζάω, to have tubercles; F.939ff: medical terms applied on
poetry; and many other passages.

doctors in general did not speak 'doctors'-Latin', and ordinary people were able to pick up something of their language and its technical terms. It was only natural that everybody took an interest in what the doctor said.

Popular knowledge of tragedy and literature in general was based on deeper foundations. According to Greek belief, the poets were originally the true sophists, the 'wise men'.[1] 'To be in the company of wise men' like Euripides is a favourite aspiration of the ordinary citizen.[2] Both tragedy and comedy in themselves prove the high level of understanding and judgment which the poets might expect from their audience, though there was always a grateful public for obscene and crude jokes as well.

The comic poets had their share in sharpening the mind of the people for the subtleties of literary criticism. Wherever one turns in comedy, literary quotations, allusions and parodies abound, some of them unlikely to be intelligible to the average listener, though by far the greater number must have been. It is quite impossible to mention all of them. The number of references to the works of Euripides alone affords a strong proof of his immense popularity. Some of the quotations from him — Alkestis' famous words, for instance — were commonly known even many years after the performance of that play.[3] There are other poets besides Euripides who are frequently quoted or mentioned, censured or praised: Sophokles, Aisopos, who was very popular and whose fables were learned by heart in the schools, but who later almost ceased to be read, and many others, famous or little known.[4] It seems that the model for the sycophant's song in the *Birds*

---

[1] P.700, 798, F.883, Kratinos 2, Eupolis 447, Plat. 140.

[2] Th.21.

[3] A.893f = Eur. *Alk.* 367f; cf. also K.16 = Eur. *Hipp.* 345. On other occasions Aristophanes refers to last year's plays, e.g., in the *Thesmophoriazousai* of 411 to *Andromeda* and *Helena*, performed in 412 (the chorus Th.1015ff. — Th.911 = *Hel.* 365. See schol. Th.1012, 1060).

[4] Sophokles, e.g.: C.257, Eupolis 36, Phryn. 31. — Aisopos: W.566, 1259, 1401ff, 1446ff, P.129, B.471, 651ff, Plat. 68. — Others: A.120, C.534ff, P.803f, 835, 1012f, B.807, 926f, Th.159ff, 168ff, F.661, frg. 151, 32 D, Kratinos 6, 324a, Pherekr. 153, Eupolis 139, 361, Plat. 128. — Gilbert Murray, *Greek Studies*, 24, regards C.534ff, the reference to Elektra's recognition of her brother's hair, as a reference not to Aischylos' *Choephorai* but to the *logos*, the old and famous story. But Aristophanes is expressly looking for 'equally clever spectators'; thus it seems that the allusion is to a play.

can be recognized in a badly damaged fragment of Alkaios.[1] Most of the quotations are parodies, especially those from tragedy; a special word was coined for tragic parody.[2] It was often hard for the listeners to perceive the wit or to recognize the original when a poet's whole style was parodied instead of the actual wording being given and individual characters being misrepresented.[3] Moreover, the quotations were seldom mere repetitions of sayings which might have stuck in the memory or been put down during the performance.[4] Sometimes they were comic and irrelevant recitations, but frequently a vivid interest in literary personalities and aesthetic problems is apparent.[5]

The changes and reforms which a poet has introduced can be described.[6] The tragedian Agathon produces a complete aesthetic theory, according to which the poet is himself to live like the figures of his plays and even to reproduce the details of their appearance.[7] To some extent, Euripides in the *Acharnians* practises the same methods. This theory, which in Agathon's case arises from his lack of imagination, is based on a sophistic doctrine which, of course, was originally to be interpreted quite differently: 'One can only work, that is to say, make poetry [in Greek the word is the same] according to one's own nature.'[8] The tragic poet, from deeper insight, claims that it is Eros who teaches a poet, even if he until then was a man 'alien to the Muses'.[9]

Whole comedies, such as the *Thesmophoriazousai* and the *Frogs*, are mainly concerned with the art of poetry. The subject and intention of other literary comedies defy reconstruc-

---

[1] Alkaios 75 Diehl, B.1410ff, cf. S. Srebrny, *Eos* XLI (1940-46), 104ff.

[2] παρατραγῳδεῖν, Strattis 3 D.

[3] e.g., Th.101ff. Material can be found in A. C. Schlesinger, *AJP.* 58 (1937), 294ff, and *TAPA.* 67 (1936), 296ff. Cf. also the parody of the *Antigone* by Eupolis, 41 P, 14ff.

[4] Cf. C.1369ff, Th.194. — F.151.

[5] Irrelevant recitation, e.g., C.335ff.

[6] frg. 641.

[7] Th.149ff; cf. also frg. 42 (b) P = 33 (b) D: οἷα μὲν ποιεῖ λέγειν, τοῖός ἐστιν.

[8] Th.167. — In a more popular and trivial manner the same theory seems to be expressed in a few lines of Euripides' *Hiketides* (180ff), which, however, are probably an interpolation. There it is said that the ὑμνοποιός must be happy in order to cause happiness.

[9] ἄμουσος, Eur. *frg.* 663.

tion; we do not know, for instance, who were the starving persons who ate the wax of their writing-tablets.[1] Comedies not mainly concerned with literary matters sometimes provide equally significant evidence. At the beginning of an essentially unliterary play like the *Acharnians*, Dikaiopolis introduces himself with tragic quotations, and discourses on various tragic poets and musicians, not in the manner of a professional critic (a profession which did not yet exist), but as a common citizen who took an interest in such matters without being either learned or sophisticated. Aischylos is preferred to the frigid Theognis, one musician to another.[2] Comparisons of earlier and later stages in the development of poetry, or of various individual poets, were always a favourite subject, the most famous example being the great *agon* of the *Frogs* which is interspersed throughout with aesthetic criticisms and is based on the supposition that only a few of the audience would prefer the old-fashioned Aischylos to the modern Euripides.[3] Sthenelos must have had the reputation of being very dull and insipid, since one is advised 'to dip his passages in vinegar or salt'.[4] Euripides came in for criticism because of his schematic use of a participle construction or, on the other hand, of his preference for certain consonants such as s and l.[5] The discussion between Strepsiades and his son culminates in their difference of opinion about the great poets Simonides, Aischylos and Euripides.[6] Such opinions, here as elsewhere, emanate from the personality of the speaker as well as that of the poet, and it is obvious that the views expressed were in many cases simply meant to be funny. Very few soldiers would have had Euripides' *Andromeda* in their knapsack to read while on board a warship — as Dionysos boasts to have done.[7] On the whole, however, the vivid interest of the public in literature is revealed over and over

---

[1] frg. 157. Norwood's reconstruction (p. 290f.) remains uncertain.

[2] A.9ff.

[3] frg. 253-4, Pherekr. 145, 185. — F.78ff, frg. 471, Plat.128 — F.814ff, 830ff, 883. — F.782f. — It is only natural that the criticism expressed in the *agon* does not touch very profound questions. If some modern scholars find fault with Aristophanes because, for example, the contrast between the Aischylean trilogy and the single tragedies of Euripides (and Sophokles!) is not mentioned, this argument is completely out of place.

[4] frg. 151.   [5] F.1206ff. — 1309ff, Plat. 30.

[6] C.1356ff.   [7] F.52f.

again; the spectators also knew how to distinguish between play and performance, and criticized the actors.[1]

A recipe for the preparation of one dish out of the three tragedians combines, it seems, the whole of Sophokles and the whole of Euripides with part of Aischylos, a mixture to which salt was to be added.[2] This would indeed have been a dish to the popular taste. The enthusiasm of the Athenians for their theatre is a well-known fact, and the constant attacks on Euripides would have been meaningless but for the general excitement which he aroused. As the great revolutionary of tragedy, the master of theatrical effects and of psychological insight, he was the natural centre of interest and target for criticism. If Sophokles, as the ideal representative of State and people, was the most beloved poet, Euripides was the most admired and the most discussed. He himself does not hesitate to express criticism of his literary predecessors by occasional allusions probably clear to most of the audience.[3] Among comic writers it was indeed as usual to deride him as to throw nuts to the spectators or to rob Herakles of his meal.[4] The poets felt that in him, in 'his phrases savouring of the law-courts',[5] there prevailed the elements of rationalism and rhetoric. Sometimes Sokrates was held responsible for this, for he was said to have made for him 'those garrulous and clever tragedies'.[6] Euripides was admired by some of the people because of his remarkable and original sayings and the

---

[1] Strattis 1.

[2] ἄλας καὶ μὴ λάλας, adesp. 12 (a) D = 45 (b) P. The last words are translated by Mr. Page — not literally, of course, but most wittily: 'add a pinch — don't pad an inch'. Page assumes that the reference to Euripides is uncomplimentary, but in that case the advice to take ὅλον Εὐριπίδην seems surprising. Webster, agreeing with Page, thinks that this is a recipe for one of Euripides' inferior rivals.

[3] Cf. *Hik.* 846, *El.* 520ff, *Phoen.* 751.

[4] W.58ff.

[5] P.534. I believe this translation of ῥημάτια δικανικά (Liddell and Scott, s. δικανικός II, 2) is much more suitable here than merely 'law terms' (Liddell and Scott, II, 1).

[6] frg. 376, cf. F.1491ff, Telekl. 39-40, Kallias 12. Otherwise Kephisophon, who lived under Euripides' roof, was thought to be his collaborator (F.944, 1407ff, 1452f, frg. 580), though this was little more than a cheap attempt at reducing Euripides' stature. Actually he himself once mentions the idea of literary collaboration in order to show the disadvantages of dual rule as contrasted with monarchy (*Andr.* 471ff).

way in which 'his fine expressions were polished up';[1] it is clear that the 'over-subtle spectator' who 'hunts after sententious phrases' and 'euripid-aristophanizes', was by no means rare.[2] This last phrase, which perhaps belongs to the *Pytine* of 423 and reveals the mind of the older generation, is especially interesting because it includes Aristophanes no less than Euripides in the new generation and new spirit.[3] Both are considered, and rightly so, to be pre-eminently responsible for having made the people acquainted with the new ideas and new maxims. The people's interest and the sophists' influence met and augmented each other; a considerable body of evidence, including the attacks on competitors mentioned previously, suggests that nobody but the Athenians could judge 'the poets' natures'.[4] It is only a slight exaggeration and modernization (in the use of the word 'science') to say, as has recently been said: 'Literary criticism has become a science and evidently a popular one.'[5] As in any other new branch of investigation the experts probably used technical terms of which the comedians naturally made fun. If the audience did not understand the particular meaning of every expression, they knew enough to find it a good joke when, for instance, a poet was called 'productive', or 'to babble' became a serious expression indicating sophisticated talk.[6]

In estimating this side of the Athenian character, we must never forget that the *Frogs*, a conspicuous example of a contest about literary questions, was performed in the last year of the

[1] F.96ff. — frg. 33 (a) D = 42 (a) P. The meaning of the verb [ἐξεσ]μήχετο is uncertain. It would be easy to quote hundreds of gnomic lines from Euripides, and that is exactly what Stobaios, for instance, did.

[2] Kratinos 307.

[3] Cf. A. C. Pearson, Εὐριπιδαριστοφανίζειν (1925). There is much more in this expression than only dependence of Aristophanes' language on that of Euripides (as Schmid, 71, 18, thinks).

[4] F.809f, cf. above, p. 34f.

[5] T. B. L. Webster, *Greek Art and Literature*, 171; cf. already J. D. Denniston, *Cl. Q.* XXI (1927), 113ff. It is hardly a counter-argument to say that the interests of Philokleon's as well as Bdelykleon's companions do not include literature, but are confined to indecent stories and popular fables on the one hand, to talk about politics and sport on the other. The fun is obvious in both cases. Apart from that — what would be the result of an investigation made today, whether in a pub or at a so-called society party?

[6] F.98. — F.91, 839, 954, frg. 376. Denniston, *l.c.*, has collected a number of such terms, mainly from the *Clouds* and the *Frogs*.

great war, at a time of the greatest distress and hardship. But neither must we forget that the real object of the literary competition, and therefore the innermost meaning of the whole play, was to find in the greatest of the tragedians not only the better poet, but also the teacher of the people and the saviour of the State.

Like the beauty of the Acropolis, so the people's love for the theatre, expressed in, and kept alive by, the institution of the *theorikon*, is symptomatic of the spirit which is more characteristic than anything else of all we connect with the name of Athens. The unity between poet and audience, of which we have spoken in the first chapter, would have been impossible unless the audience in general was able to understand the poet's intentions, his literary allusions and parodies. The chorus can even address the audience as those who are experienced themselves in every kind of poetry.[1] In trying to ascertain the general level of education among the Athenians we may quote the famous and tragic saying about one of the soldiers of the Sicilian disaster: 'He is either dead or teaching letters.'[2] Those men who escaped and are here characterized were only a minority, but a fortuitous one and therefore typical of the whole people.[3] Perhaps the 'letters' mean in this case more than only elementary instruction; for it was chiefly by singing the songs of Euripides, famous and popular in Syracuse also, that some of the Athenians saved themselves.[4] The high educational standard of the Athenian people cannot be doubted,[5] and illiterate persons, 'analphabets' — a word apparently coined by comedy — were rare.[6] When in Euripides' *Theseus* a shepherd who cannot read describes the shape of the six letters of the king's name, the audience is

---

[1] K.505f.   [2] adesp. 20.

[3] Cf. Diod. XIII, 33, 1.

[4] γράμματα, cf. Xen. *mem.* IV, 2, 8ff. — Plut. *Nik.* 29, 2f.

[5] But it seems to be a modern habit to do so; cf., e.g., Michell, 363. A generally sound approach can be found in A. Roemer, *Ueber den literarisch-historischen Bildungsstand des athen. Theaterpublikums* (*Abhandl. Bayr. Akad.*, *phil.-philol. Kl.* XXII, 1905), 1ff.

[6] Nikoch. 2 D, Philyll. 2; 1 D. Cf. Körte, *P.-W.* XVII, 346. It is, however, not certain whether the word used by Philyllios is ἀναλφάβητον or ἀνάλφιτον. Against Hasebroek's view that many of the Athenians were illiterate, and that therefore most business was done without written statements, cf. G. Pasquali, *Studi Italiani di Filol. Class.* VII (1929), 243ff.

naturally supposed to be able to follow. The citizens recorded their notes in court on a wax-tablet, perhaps sometimes with their fingers, so that they bring the wax home under their finger-nails.[2] Even the sausage-seller, that pattern of the uneducated, knows, of all the arts of the Muses, at least some writing and reading, though even at these he is bad enough.[3] One man asks to have all the writing in a book interpreted; perhaps he cannot read.[4] Another who cannot read or write knows, it seems, the laws by heart, presumably those of Solon.[5]

The obscure phrase about the spectators 'who all have a book, to learn what is clever' gives proof at least of some general intellectual standard,[6] though the various compliments addressed by comedians to their audience do not mean much, and this one more likely than not is ironical. On the other hand, Aristophanes is no friend of people concerned with books. In the *Birds* the oracle-monger, the inspector, the decree-seller, all carry books about.[7] Euripides is notorious rather than famous for owning many books.[8] A book can corrupt a man just as much as a sophist or an idle prattler.[9] It seems that the word *biblion* covers very different kinds of publications, real literature as well as collections of oracles or laws or, on the other hand, political pamphlets and posters.[10] Aristophanes disliked books because he was hostile to all 'intellectualism', however much he himself was under its sway. His hostility only confirms that books played an important part in Athenian life. Book-trade was on a fairly large scale, a special part of the market was reserved for it, and we hear of booksellers, in particular of a man appearing with a cart full of books.[11]

Along with criticism of literature went that of music, as we have already seen from the beginning of the *Acharnians*.[12] It is hardly necessary to stress the inseparable connection be-

---

[1] *frg.* 382.   [2] W.108, cf. 850.   [3] K.188f, cf. W.959f.
[4] Philyll. 11.   [5] Kratinos 122.   [6] F.1114.
[7] B.974ff, 1024, 1036.   [8] F.943, 1409; cf. Athenaeus I, 4 (3a).
[9] frg. 490.   [10] The last is the most likely explanation of B.1288.
[11] Eupolis 304. — Aristom. 9, Theop. 77, also Nikophon 19. — adesp. 497. Cf. also Xen. *anab.* VII, 5, 14. — Gilbert Murray, *Greek Studies*, 22ff, gives a lively picture of the pre-literary state of affairs in Athens. He dates the decisive change from oral publication to that of books between Herodotos and Thucydides, which is surprisingly late.
[12] A.4ff.

tween all Greek poetry and music. Comedy, like any poetry,
could be called simply the 'art of the Muses', or referred to
by a word which meant both comic and musical.[1]   In the
fourth century the part of the chorus, the chief vehicle of
music and singing in tragedy and comedy, was very much
shorter, though its musical importance outlived its poetical.
With Euripides solo singing became more usual, but some of
the public were apparently bored by this kind of singing, and
'to sing' could become an expression meaning idle talk.[2] The
agon between Aischylos and Euripides, besides being a competition in wisdom and shrewdness, includes both literary and
musical art.[3]   Our sources are not sufficient to make a full
understanding of Greek music possible, and the present writer,
at any rate, is here out of his depth; but we can perceive
a strong sensibility to, and love for, music among the Athenians, and a certain interest in questions of musical aesthetics
no less than in the practical knowledge of lyre and flute.[4]
Only a man who had to flee for his life was excused for 'not
waiting to listen to the sound of the lyre', and a musical man
would object to somebody who was 'in conflict with the
melody'.[5] Music was, as it had always been, a chief instrument
in 'educating the uneducated'.[6] 'May I never live with people
without music', sings the chorus of Euripides' *Herakles*, 'may
I always be among wreaths', that is to say, among men singing
and wearing garlands.[7]   Men sang on their way to work, to
court, to town, and work itself was frequently accompanied by
a song or some other sort of music (cf. Plate XI*b*, a perfect,
though primitive, illustration of 'Music while you Work').[8]
Listening to a bad singer is worse than wearing a wreath of
nettles, and a flute-player Chairis was notorious for his bad
playing.[9] As in poetry, it was possible to distinguish earlier
and later stages in the manner of singing, and Lampros, the

---

[1] μουσική, Eupolis 336; 357,8. — τρυγῳδοποιομουσική, frg. 333. W. B.
Stanford, *Hermathena* LXI, 18, speaks of 'that happy blending of literature and
music'.

[2] F.1329ff. — E.887ff. — frg. 7 D, Eupolis 2 D.   [3] Cf. F.1261ff.

[4] W.269f, 271f. — K.9, Phryn. 2; 6.

[5] frg. 11 D. — Eupolis 6 D.

[6] Eur. *Kykl.* 492.   [7] Eur. *Her.* 676f.

[8] W.219f, E.277f, Telekl. 7. — F.203ff, 1296f, Phryn. 14, Plat. 211,
Nikoph. 17.

[9] Pherekr. 24. — A.16, 866, P.951f, B.858, Pherekr. 6.

well-known music-teacher of Sophokles, could be derided,
because of his music, as a weak and whining 'super-sophist'.[1]
It was the same with dancing. The spectators might be critical
or they might enjoy a dance.[2] Frequently, as we have seen
before, the tragic poet was criticized as the man responsible also
for the dances of the chorus.[3]

It may be regarded as another sign of their musical sense
that the Athenians were extremely sensitive to the use of language and to foreign accents. A highly developed instinct for
language was innate with them. Without language, which
means, of course, the Greek language, a man was a barbarian;
so was Kleophon as a man 'who talks in two languages'.[4] We
must not take into account mere playing with words or jokes
based on omitted consonants,[5] but it is only natural when a
non-Greek is derided for making comic mistakes in the use
of Greek words.[6] Even the Ionian and Boeotian dialects and
their usages are laughed at.[7] Solon had once complained that
those Athenians who had been expelled to foreign countries
had lost their Attic speech or accent.[8] Now the chief reproach
to foreigners recently admitted as citizens was that they spoke
very bad Attic.[9]

The Athenians' sense of language showed in other ways,
too. We have discussed in a previous chapter the fact that
they were conscious of the difference between the town and
country dialects.[10] This difference was caused by a difference
in social and educational standards, and increased by the teaching of the sophists. We have spoken of the illiterate man who
knew the laws by heart; in Aristophanes' *Daitales* the son who
has had an entirely modern education has forgotten the difficult
Homeric words, but is well acquainted with the technical and
even obsolete legal expressions which could be learned by
speaking in court.[11] This indicates that 'linguistic' interest,
following the general trend from poetry to rhetoric, had turned
from literature to the study of law. Besides, the modern young
man knew any number of new-fangled and affected words,

[1] Eupolis 303, Pherekr. 145. — Phryn. 69.
[2] Plat. 130. — W.1524ff.   [3] W.1497ff, P.781ff. See p. 24.
[4] B.199f. — F.679f.   [5] adesp. 393.
[6] Th. 1001ff, frg. 79, Plat. 60.   [7] P.933, Strattis 47.
[8] Solon, frg. 24, 12f, Diehl.   [9] Eupolis 40 P, 23, Plat. 31, 168.
[10] pp. 86ff.   [11] frg. 222. Cf. Isokr. IV, 159. — Lysias X, 16ff.

such as were used by the orators, the sophists and the politicians of the day.[1] These were words which only 'drove by
car', being too big to be carried, a kind of refined and artificial
speech that could be likened to the casting and forging of
bronzes.[2] Among the up-to-date upper classes 'solemn speeches'
were liked, and the usual 'welcome' was replaced as
a form of greeting by an affected 'I greet you', while on the
other hand Kleon was criticized because he introduced the
private form 'welcome' into an official letter.[3] Elegance and
artificiality of speech and style, however, do not preclude vulgar ideas, in proof of which Euripides is cited, who elsewhere
is said to be able to use those 'refined' and 'urban' phrases
which Dionysos expects that both of the competing poets will
use.[4] Dikaiopolis, when he is dressed up in the rags of the
Euripidean Telephos, is glad and proud to be 'filled with pet
phrases'.[5] All these allusions show the importance attached to
language and style.

We have passed from literary to linguistic subjects, that is
to a matter in which the sophists were most keenly interested.
Glotta, 'Language', appears in the *Clouds* among the gods of
Sokrates.[6]   Language was apparently the bridge which
enabled the average citizen to approach, in some degree, the
intellectual sphere of the sophists. Even a coarse fellow like
Herakles learns the importance of speech.[7] The art and study
of speech dominated the educational work of the sophists, as
their aims were chiefly those of political education. We shall
deal in a later chapter with the part the orators played in
political life.[8]   Here it may suffice to point to the almost
innumerable passages in Euripides, in which the poet either
theoretically or by practical application shows the impact of
rhetoric on his poetry as well as on his views. They also bear
strong witness to the general interest in rhetoric. As early as
the end of the 'nineties Isokrates could stress the fact that a

---

[1] frg. 198.

[2] Kantharos 1 D, Polyzelos 1 D, adesp. 836. — frg. 699.

[3] W.1174ff. — χαίρειν replaced by ἀσπάζομαι, Pl.322ff, cf. C.1145,
B.1377, Pl.1042. — Eupolis 308.

[4] K.1375ff. — frg. 471. — F.900ff, 905f.

[5] A.444, 447. This is how Liddell and Scott translate ῥημάτια. The reference
seems clearly to some quotations from *Telephos*, and they would be another
thin disguise of Dikaiopolis.

[6] C.424.   [7] Plat. 51-53.   [8] See Chapter XIII, 2.

number of works on rhetoric had been published.[1] The whole
rhetorical theory of the sophists, who based education on the
individual's natural talents, seems summarized in the sentence:
'To speak is Nature's gift, to speak well Art's.'[2]

The public, in spite of its general interest, had only vague
and often wrong ideas on this subject, and might confuse it
with quite different matters. That, however, does not apply
only to language and rhetoric, but to most of the activities of
those sophists whose character is disclosed when they solemnly
bring out from the depth of their minds some learned stuff,
often only a triviality.[3] The people considered them idlers, and
liked to include, under the name of sophists, not only teachers
and thinkers, but also soothsayers, physicians, astronomers
and their like.[4] Clerks and altar-beggars are said to be typical
of the Athens of the time, a remark which reveals both the
spread of intellectual education and the progress of social
degradation.[5] Many of these men were parasites who got all
they could from State and cult. But they were also 'sophists',
because they made a bargain with wisdom and teaching,
because they lived on their brains. For 'reason is like Prometheus to mankind', says the comedian Platon, with ironical
admiration, in a play which is called *The Sophists*.[6]

The comic poets, in fact, attacked two groups: on the one
hand, the *un*educated men of low origin, the upstarts who
became demagogues; on the other, the *mis*educated ones, the
young men, spoiled by modern education, who considered
themselves wise and clever.[7] Hyperbolos, who took lessons in
rhetoric, was infected by both evils, that of being uneducated
as well as that of being miseducated.[8] A man, on the other
hand, who was both 'wise' and 'inspired by the Muses', if he
really deserved this characterization, was the type which old-
fashioned education tried to shape.[9] Once it had been the
natural consequence of being a citizen to be taught by the
community life of the Polis. Simonides' famous sentence 'The

---

[1] Isokr. XIII, 19.   [2] adesp. 403 (probably Eupolis).
[3] frg. 49 D.   [4] C.316, 331ff.
[5] F.1083ff. An example of this is Nikomachos, mentioned in F.1506, whose
career is disclosed by Lysias XXX: son of a slave, clerk (ὑπογραμματεύς),
member of the commission for law-reform, etc.
[6] Plat. 136.   [7] K.188ff, 217ff. — P.44.
[8] C.874ff, Eupolis 193.   W.1244. — C.961.

Polis educates man' is reflected in the question of the Cyclops:
'What Polis educated you?'[1] The old unsystematic, but sound,
training[2] which aimed at moral discipline and musical education, fought two enemies: rationalistic education which largely
neglected the moral point of view, and lack of education. In
every case, however, education had become a goal consciously
aimed at, and it had therefore to be systematic and deliberate.
To many people in very different ways of life, wisdom and
cleverness (*sophia*), such as taught by the sophists, became an
ideal. Euripides, even more than the comedians, shows how
the word *sophos* 'was constantly upon the lips of the intelligent
Athenians'.[3] Though a rude man might still be called rustic
or boorish, he was certainly 'uneducated'.[4] That means that
the new distinction between the educated and the uneducated,
between the 'wise' and the 'unlearned',[5] opened a new social
gap, which was to influence the conditions of general life to
an ever-increasing extent.

The Old Education is represented by the 'Just Logos', and
the argument between him and the 'Unjust Logos' reflects
most vividly the great social and intellectual struggle which
was going on at the time.[6] It is perhaps surprising that the
weaknesses of the old education, its narrow-mindedness and
prudishness, are not concealed; but only the old education,
as the natural product of the Polis, was based on demands of
universal importance: physical and mental training, modesty
and decency, good manners and good reputation. 'It is an
education for the body and the character, the education of
aristocratic youth.'[7] It was also the education which had given
to Athens the victory of Marathon.[8] The Athenians could
speak of the palaestra as Wellington did of the playing-fields
of Eton.[9]

---

[1] Simonides 53 Diehl. — Eur. *Kykl.* 276.
[2] τὸ σωφρόνως τραφῆναι, K.334.
[3] Winnington-Ingram, *Euripides and Dionysus*, 167f.
[4] Cf. Nikoch. 3, Eur. *Kykl.* 492. Thus Ion dislikes the ἄμουσοι ξένοι (Eur.
Ion 526), and ἀμουσία is described as the first sign of stupidity (Eur. *frg.*
1033). The constant hints in Euripides to the σοφοί and to the implications of
wisdom and ignorance, also to the hostility of ordinary people to the σοφοί,
need no particular quotation.
[5] Cf., e.g., W.1183, 1196.   [6] C.889ff.
[7] Webster, *op. cit*, 99.   [8] C.986.
[9] Cf. W. M. Hugill, *The Phoenix* III (1949), 31ff.

You will excel in the games you love well,
all blooming, athletic and fair,
not learning to prate as your idlers debate
with marvellous prickly dispute.[1]

Health, hunting and moderation go together, as Telekleides puts it, thinking of olden times when the Areopagus ruled the city.[2]

Pheidippides, on the other hand, the faithful disciple of the New Education, turns some words of the selfish Pheres, the father of Admetos, into an attack on his own father: either way the words are an expression of unscrupulous individualism.[3] The rationalist view that it was a matter of knowledge and teaching only to be good was opposed by those who were aware of the strength of human passions; occasionally a conciliatory combination of nature or character and upbringing could be proposed. Euripides allows us to see something of the discussion going on, which naturally was more serious and more subtle than the straight fight between the Just and the Unjust Logos.[4] The answer of the New Education herself is based solely on the idea of personal advantage and enjoyment.[5] 'It is worth more than a thousand staters to take the feebler side and yet to win the case.'[6] The chief advantage of rhetoric as taught by the sophists was its power of influencing decisions in the law-courts, but the new art with all its tricks was to help in every situation of life. The man who had mastered this art was therefore much sought after and well paid.[7] The issues, however, were much larger than that. The boy no longer went to the *paidotribes*, the old-fashioned type of teacher, nor did he undergo the old-fashioned discipline.[8] People were eager for new principles and rules, and the old ideal of moderation no longer satisfied the young.[9] It is one-sided and mistaken to regard the dissipation and effeminacy of youth as the only results of modern education.

[1] C.1002f.
[2] Telekl. 26. Cf. M. Giffler, *AJP*. LXII (1941), 224ff.
[3] κλάουσι παῖδες, πατέρα δ' οὐ κλάειν δοκεῖς; C.1415, Eur. *Alk*. 691. Cf. Grube, 140.
[4] Eur. *Hipp*. 920, *Hik*. 911ff, *Ion*, 247ff, *Or*. 410 (cf. *frg*. 1100), *Iph. A*. 558f, 561ff. — *Hipp*. 78ff, 377ff. — *Hek*. 595ff, cf. Eupolis 91.
[5] C.936ff.   [6] C.1041f.   [7] C.469ff.
[8] C.916, 963ff.   [9] e.g., C.896, 924, 943.

Although it was partly responsible for those moral effects, it resulted at the same time in the free development of the personality. It is not difficult to see even in the praise of the old education that it had become essential to find new methods and subjects, other than the traditional ones of poetry and music, and that undue attention was paid to sports and games. What the poet calls effeminacy and 'politicizing' and alike, means also the enthusiasm for inquiry and knowledge, the liberation of the intellect and the refinement of the spirit. Aristophanes himself belonged to the generation which had been brought up under the first impact of the sophists' teaching. He realized some of the shortcomings of the old methods, but he did not realize that they actually belonged to the past, and he maintained that their weaknesses were negligible, compared with the excesses and the blunders of the modern spirit. Not quite consistently with his general attitude, he also attacked the education described as that given by Sokrates, which included training to endure cold and hunger, though it denounced the palaestra together with other erotic 'nonsense'.[1] Be this as it may (and we must allow the comic poet some liberties), one fact stands out — the change by which the individual mind became the determining factor, both for good and for ill. Euripides even more than Sokrates was regarded by the comedians as the great protagonist of the new spirit. It may be taken as a symbol of his art as well as of his lasting influence that he introduced into literature, and therefore also into myth, erotic psychology and even suicide because of rejected love.[2] Subjectivism and individualism were a danger; they might lead to romantic self-destruction as well as to the destruction of State and society. At the same time they led the way to new heights of art, literature, science, and, above all, philosophy.

The speeches of the Just and the Unjust Logos show that the influence of the new spirit prevailed not only in small circles. The new education, though it demanded an elaborate training and involved longer and more expensive instruction, was not an esoteric movement. We have emphasized this

---

[1] C.414ff. This is not the same as the fairly frequent denunciation of the ἀθλητῶν γένος, known as early as Xenophanes (frg. 2) and violently expressed, e.g., in one of Euripides' satyr dramas (*frg. 282*).

[2] Cf. F.1043ff, 1050f.

already. All the young men whose education would have
been limited to palaestra and gymnasium, were stimulated and
influenced by these ever-spreading new doctrines. The pleasure taken in discussing a matter, even an arbitrary denunciation of a fellow citizen, from both points of view, was widespread and could even be called a philosophical attitude.[1] It
is significant, that, at this time, virtually all departments of
life were subjected to theoretical treatment. Books were published about the State, about farming, household management,
the various arts and crafts and many other subjects. The
mathematician wrote about town-planning,[2] as we know
Hippodamos had done, who flourished about the middle of
the fifth century. *Techne*, the common word for art or craft,
began also to mean a set of rules, a system, a manual.[3] The
authors of many of these treatises argued fiercely against each
other.[4] The whole development of intellectual life was given
a particular colour by the fact that it concerned a large number
of the people, and that the whole population was vitally
interested in it. Thus, the sophists truly revolutionized
education.[5]

Education, however, was and remained fundamentally
political, and the sophists never lost sight of the purpose of
a training whose object was to prepare its pupils for political
life. This is one reason why, when all is said and done, the
working classes were touched rather than altered by the new
teaching. The same can be said of the women.[6] Euripides
even depicts Iphigeneia as unable to write, while the chorus
of the *Medea* tries to make allowances for some women clever
enough to use subtle speech and to deal with important questions.[7] It is obvious that a few women were really educated,
but that this was still rare and exceptional. We must recognize
the limits set to education even in the changing society of the
fourth century, but the decisive factor was that the new ideas
were spread, especially as political individualism and opportunism went hand in hand with the general growth of economic
factors and economic materialism on the one hand, and with
the growing extension of a new class of educated people on

---

[1] Lysias VIII, 11.   [2] B. 1004ff.
[3] Cf. Neil on K.63.   [4] adesp. 345.
[5] Cf. also H.-I. Marrou, *Histoire de l'éducation dans l'antiquité*, 84ff, 96f.
[6] See above, pp. 201ff, 206.   [7] Eur. *Iph. T.* 584. — *Med.* 1081ff.

the other. All this, however, depended on the general interest
of the *petits bourgeois* who filled the seats in the theatre, who
were fascinated by literature, language and other intellectual
matters, who listened to the new ideas. This class, which
formed the bulk of the people, nevertheless firmly rejected the
modern doctrines, and more especially the attacks on the old
religion. It is a great exaggeration, but again one that proves
the interest of the people, when the Just Logos regards almost
the whole audience as belonging to those men 'without brains'
who follow the new false doctrines.[1]

All our evidence points to the strong intellectual liveliness
of the Athenian people. It is only natural that the standards
varied and that 'modern' interests were intermingled with
many trends of traditional thought. But the general level of
education was steadily rising. There is no better proof of this
than the changing aspect of comedy itself. The coarseness and
obscenity both of language and of acting gradually disappeared
in a general process of growing refinement, though also of
diminishing vigour and originality. A large part of the
audience had their full share of literary interests and aesthetic
understanding, but others must have turned to cruder entertainments. The intellectual change, however, was a social
change as well, and while comedy lost much of its particular
appeal to the Athenian people as a whole, it gained universal
appeal to the educated *bourgeoisie* — Athenian as well as non-
Athenian — of the Hellenistic Age.

[1] C.896ff, 916ff.

CHAPTER XI

WAR AND PEACE

THE period of Old Comedy coincides with a period of Athenian history the variety of which seems more obvious than its unity.[1] We realize that there was a unity, and that it was brought about by the fact that the leading actors of the drama were Athens and her empire, with Sparta and Corinth taking important but secondary parts. Seen, however, under the aspects of peace and war, our period has no unity at all, but can be divided into two periods, 460-432 and 431-c. 380. Either of these periods can easily be sub-divided into two parts: 460-446 were years of dangerous tension and some fighting, 445-432 was essentially a time of real peace; again 431-404 was a time of war, 403-380 were years of a very unstable peace. Kratinos and Krates lived in the earlier period, but they lived on to see the first years of the Peloponnesian War.[2] All the other important poets of Old Comedy belong to the second period. It is impossible to understand thoroughly either the social conditions of the age or their reflection in comedy without taking these facts into account. For war and peace do not form the background, against which the facts of normal everyday life stand out — they themselves shape these facts and all the consequent details. Our evidence, however, hardly enables us to describe fully such things as the difference between the economic life of war and of peace, though some details can be recovered, and we have referred to these in earlier chapters. We must, however, try to discover the effects of war and peace on social psychology, and so complete in its essentials our picture of Athenian society.

Perhaps nowhere in our investigation do we meet with such great difficulties as here, for nothing appears more distorted in comedy than the essential features of the war. There was, so it seems, only one possible way for comedy to deal with

[1] See above, pp. 15ff.
[2] Cf. A. Körte, *P.-W.* XI, 1623f, 1647f. For Kratinos cf. especially Norwood, 114ff.

war, and that was to treat it as something unreal. When the
comic poet was pleading for peace, he could not do justice to
the achievements and exploits of the war; and since comedy
was comedy, it could not deal with the horrors. Nevertheless,
we may be able to find some facts behind the silence and
distortion.

One of the outstanding features of comedy is that the
comedians, in order to decry their own generation, recall the
soldierly traditions of the greatest period of the past, the time
of the Persian Wars. This epoch is usually treated as if it were
contemporary. After sixty, seventy, eighty years have gone by,
veterans of Marathon are still brought on the stage, with a
happy disregard of chronology.¹ Various events of the past are
confused: in the general pictures of the *Marathonomachai* are
included the naval war of 480 and some events of about 470,²
the famous runner of the time of the Persian War, Phayllos of
Kroton,³ and the politician Thoukydides who was active in the
'fifties and 'forties of the century, or even, on the other hand,
events of the last decades of the sixth century.⁴ The old men
of the chorus in the *Wasps* boast of having fought in the battle
for Attica; they tell of the sky darkened by the enemies'
arrows, a story that is well known from Herodotos, where the
reference, however, is to Thermopylae.⁵ Furthermore, the old
men in the *Lysistrate*, that is in 411, are proud of their part in
the expulsion of the Spartan king Kleomenes from the Acropolis in the year 508, and even of their part in the battle of
Leipsydrion which took place in 513.⁶ The idea of war was
closely associated with the memory of the past, in particular of
the Persian War, and sleep which overcame a man could therefore be said 'to have attacked him like a Mede'.⁷

For the purpose of our investigation it matters less why and
how Aristophanes used those ancient warriors in his comedies
than to state the very fact of their poetical existence, which

---

¹ A.179ff, 692ff, K.1334, C.985f, W.711, 1060ff, frg. 413, Hermipp. 81.

² A.677. — W.236, 355.

³ A.214f, W.1206. I do not think we should assume that there were two
runners of the same name, the man of Kroton of 480 who did not win at Olympia
(Paus. X, 9, 2), and a later Olympionikes. Rightly: A. Raubitschek, *P.-W.* XIX,
1903.

⁴ A.703. — L.616ff, 630ff, 664ff. In general, cf. my *Ost und West*, 97f.

⁵ W.1076ff. — Herod. VII, 226, 1.

⁶ L.272ff, 665.   ⁷ W.11f, cf. also 1124.

was nowhere displayed more manifestly than in tne chorus of the *Acharnians*. This shows that the chorus is entirely lacking in real 'personality'. The men of the chorus are not men in the usual meaning of the word, they represent the community to which they belong, State or deme or whatever it may be, in its contemporary but also in its historical existence: they embody both present and past. To exalt the heroic and military type of Athenian citizen it was necessary to go back almost a century.

Was this because in a period of war the poets wished to compare their own time with another period of war, and therefore neglected the long, comparatively peaceful period between the two great wars? There may be some truth in such an assumption; it would at least be psychologically understandable.[1] However, there was no lasting peace between 478 and 431. The fifteen years of Perikles' rule (446-432) were peaceful indeed, an age famous for its buildings and not for its battles; but even these years were interrupted by the Samian War and ended with the troubles about Kerkyra and Potidaia. One reason why the land battles of the middle of the century were not taken as examples of military achievements and warlike spirit may have been that they were waged between Greeks and Greeks. Occasionally, however, we find them mentioned, and they are represented by the valiant Myronides,[2] while the naval battles against Persia of the same period such as Eurymedon and Cyprus are never alluded to. The reason for that is clear. Even of the Persian War it is Marathon, and not Salamis, that is glorified. The comic poets were concerned with the old prowess of Athenian hoplites rather than with previous naval successes. The great importance of the fleet in their own time was, as we shall see, reflected by the comedians, but as their comic world was based on an essentially conservative and even romantic outlook, the citizen-soldiers of Marathon became their true ideal, as the product of ancient valour and education.[3]

The 'Marathon-fighters', though in comedy they usually appear faintly ridiculous, are in idea similar to our conception

---

[1] I adopted this view in the first edition to the exclusion of what I now believe is a better explanation.

[2] C.213. — L.801ff, E.303ff, Eupolis 98, 40 P, 51f.

[3] See above p. 292.

of the 'veterans of the trenches', that type of ex-serviceman which twenty years after the First World War was still present to everybody's mind, and even played a rôle in international relations. (Since the Second World War he has been super-seded by whole peoples, as it were, fighting in the front line.) This type of Athenian was an 'active-service-seeker', not a 'full-pay-seeker'; he despised the professional officer, being himself both a good citizen and soldier, *polites* and *hoplites* (see Plate XIX*a*).[1] He did not belong to the 'knights' who were the privileged noble youth,[2] but quite negligible as cavalry in the field, nor to the 'light troops', who as late as 410 did not enjoy a very high reputation, though a few citizens might serve in their ranks.[3] Later on, these light troops came to be regarded very differently, but originally only the heavy-armed hoplite was the true citizen-soldier. The important part which ex-servicemen played in the public mind is brought out by the fact that the phrase 'old campaigners' could be used of those competent to judge the events of a 'war', even if it was one between poets.[4] The pride of the Attic hoplite was his free discipline, which distinguished him equally from the thetes, the poor who could not afford arms of their own and for a long time did not serve at all, from the 'conscript' soldiers of Sparta and from the unsoldierly Ionians who are said to take their wives and babies, and therefore also a bath-tub, with them to camp.[5] The State honoured those of the citizen-soldiers who had been killed in action, not only by a public funeral and eulogy, but also by educating their sons at public expense and equipping them with full arms.[6]

The importance of the hoplites, however, decreased in the decades after the defeat of the Persians. Then the supreme qualification was 'who rowed best'.[7] In fact, every Athenian knew how to row and to sail.[8] Expressions indicating unskilful rowing were used for general ineptitude, 'sea-warfare' could mean any kind of struggle, even one of words only, and the

---

[1] A.595ff.   [2] See p. 95.

[3] Th.232. — For light-armed citizens cf. the τοξόται, *IG.* I², 44; II², 1951.

[4] οἱ ἐστρατευμένοι, F.1113; cf. 1099ff. I do not think that Radermacher's explanation of F.1113 (*der in der Welt herumgekommen ist*) is convincing.

[5] frg. 232. — Eupolis 256.

[6] B.395ff. — Kratinos 171, B.1361; cf. Thuc. II, 46, 1, Lysias, *frg.* 6, 30ff, Aischines III, 154.

[7] W.1097f.   [8] Ps.-Xen. I, 19f.

boatman's cry 'o-op' also came to have a more general application.[1] The Athenians' attachment to the sea is well known.[2]
Athens now owed her political position and widespread power
neither to her hoplites nor, on the other hand, to her trade and
merchant fleet, but to the navy which had command of the sea
and was under Athena's special protection.[3] It is clear that
in Periclean and post-Periclean Athens, 'from which the
beautiful triremes came' (see Plate XIX*b*),[4] the navy claimed
for itself military valour and virtue. The crews of the warships,
'the rhuppapai' as they were called from the rhythmic cry of
the oarsmen, worked hard, and the rhythm and energy of their
rowing were greatly enhanced by this shouting and by music,
just as the greenhorn Dionysos rowed to the rhythm of the
songs of the frogs.[5] 'The rowers who guard the State'[6] played
a prominent part in politics, and as a social group were obviously rising to power. Hence come the attacks on democracy
by Pseudo-Xenophon who, with his peculiar mixture of sarcasm and admiration, admits that the whole company of 'helms-
men, boatswains, captains, mates and ship-builders' gave the
State more power than the rich and the nobles.[7] This is the
democracy which Aristotle later described as of the 'trireme
kind'.[8] The effects were reciprocal: democracy built the navy,
and the navy supported democracy. The demand for the
repatriation of exiled citizens, mainly, of course, the oligarchic
enemies of the existing democracy, was based on two grounds:
one, that even the slaves, who had fought in the battle of
Arginusae, had received citizenship, the other that the exiled
men and their ancestors had often fought in naval actions.[9]
Even noblemen, although either they or their ancestors had
most probably fought as knights, now boasted of their naval
activities; after all, Kimon had given the most outstanding
example. Thus the appreciation of military virtue was turned
in another direction, and this confirms the general social
transformation.

A well-known and typical character in New Comedy is the

---

[1] K.830. — W.478. — B.1395, cf. F.180, 208.
[2] See p. 118.   [3] K.1186.   [4] B.108.
[5] W.909, F.1073, cf. K.602. — F.203ff.
[6] A.162f.   [7] Ps.-Xen. I, 2.
[8] τριηρικὸν εἶδος, Aristotle, *pol.* 1291b, 23; cf. 1304a, 20ff.
[9] F.33, 693f. — F.697ff, cf. Lysias XXV, 12.

boastful soldier who is serving as a mercenary; in Old Comedy
we find the citizen soldier, whether officer (for instance,
Lamachos) or private soldier, in the same rôle of the *miles
gloriosus*. The type (see Plate IIIc) is not simply an invention
of comedy, for it existed frequently enough in fact. There
have always been swashbuckling soldiers, 'taking more pride
in their spears than in their brains', bragging of their glorious
deeds like the cowardly Dionysos.[1] We know, too, that when
Athens was, so to speak, in the front line, it annoyed people
to see men in full armour striding about the market-place.[2]
Such types, or at any rate their more frequent occurrence, was
a necessary result of circumstances, but to some extent also
of the decay of the soldierly and heroic spirit of ancient
Athens. Euripides speaks of the licentiousness and the
malicious gossip of army and navy.[3] The *Marathonomaches*,
the warrior-type, was an ideal from the past, and this ideal
had lost its power; the warrior was no longer either an important or even a conspicuous figure. One of the most significant
features is the almost complete disappearance of the desire for
fame and glory (*kleos*), which had been perhaps the most
important aim in Greek life and literature from Homer to
Sophokles; except for a word of Aischylos in the *Frogs* who
refers indirectly to Homer (and this is a very significant exception), we find in comedy only the ridiculous and unheroic
'sky-high fame' of the skilled sophist and orator, and the comic
glory of the poet which impressed even the Persian King.[4]
This use of the word 'glory', or even its meaning of 'bad reputation', may easily be ascribed to the unheroic nature of
comedy; it seems that in comedy the word occurs only in epic
parodies.[5] No doubt, word and idea lived on in the epic and
tragic traditions, and also as a quality of the State to which the
citizens might contribute.[6] It was, however, different as far
as the individual human being was concerned. There was
another word (*doxa*), but it had a much more civic and even

---

[1] Eur. *Tro.* 1158. — F.48ff.   [2] L.555ff.

[3] Eur. *Hek.* 606ff, *Iph. A.* 1000f. We may mention here also the speech (54)
in which Demosthenes (*c.* 340 B.C.) describes the deplorable behaviour of soldiers
on garrison duty in Attica.

[4] F.1034f. — C.459. — A.646.

[5] frg. 796 (from Photius: κλέος, τὴν φαύλην δόξαν 'Αριστοφάνης). — Cf.
Starkie, in his edition of the *Acharnians*, on v. 646.

[6] e.g., Thuc. I, 25, 4, II, 64, 3; *IG.* I², 943 (Tod, 48), 95; 945 (Tod, 59), 13.

bourgeois character, and the desire for glory commonly deteriorated into petty ambitions and narrow selfishness.[1]

Is it, after all, right to speak of a decline of the soldierly spirit? If we may trust comedy in this matter, the decline or even the absence would be obvious; but it is questionable how far it should be trusted. Many grumbled at having to take with them their three days' provisions, which consisted chiefly of cheese and onions; they hated and grumbled at the whole military way of life.[2] The rich were slothful in equipping triremes, and were even said to commit acts of sabotage.[3] At the very beginning of the war Sparta hoped to acquire the hired oarsmen of Athens by a promise of higher pay.[4] In an emergency the hoplites rowed themselves, but in Sicily the mercenaries, so far as they did not desert, hired slaves as substitutes; order and discipline had become very weak.[5] Dionysos acts like an Athenian who wants to shirk service, when he calls himself 'a non-oarsman, non-seaman, non-Salaminian' in order to avoid naval service.[6] He, the type of effeminate youth, had to be taught military discipline and the rules of tactics by the old hand Phormion.[7] When the men were called up, many of them tried to intrigue with, and to bribe, the officials.[8] A character in Aristophanes' *Georgoi* could pretend that Nikias, well known for his genuine peace policy and at the same time quite a respectable general, had avoided becoming a *strategos* by paying 1000 dr.[9] Citizens were frequently accused of shirking service or of cowardice in the face of the enemy, though desertion was certainly at least looked down upon.[10] An officer stalks about in purple, but in danger he is a pale coward.[11] Young noblemen secure for themselves lucrative jobs as ambassadors while older men do the fighting.[12] Some even know how to disappear with the pay without becoming

[1] Cf. A. D. Leeman, *Gloria*. Diss. Leiden, 1949, 10ff, who also mentions earlier literature on κλέος and δόξα.

[2] A.197f, cf. P.367f. — P.1128f.

[3] K.912ff, F.1065f. — P.1234.   [4] Thuc. I, 143, 1.

[5] Thuc. III, 18, 4. — VII, 13, 2.   [6] F.204.

[7] Eupolis 254. Cf. the somewhat similar scene of Kreon advising the young Eteokles in Eur. *Phoin.* 713ff.

[8] K.1369ff, P.1179ff, cf. Ps.-Lysias IX.   [9] frg. 100.

[10] A.1129, K.368, 443, C.692, F.192, cf. Lysias X, XIV. — Pl.1150; cf. Lysias III, 45, where cowardice is combined with a grave case of insubordination.

[11] P.1172ff.   [12] A.600ff, cf. Ps.-Andok. IV, 22.

soldiers; there was a definite name in use for the 'men who did
not serve', reflecting actual facts and tendencies of the time.[1]
Eupolis, the most virile of the comedians, wrote a play,
Astrateutoi, in which he described the shirkers as androgynous.[2]
The so-called 'conscript knights' also very likely belonged to
this class, chiefly because they wanted to avoid the expenses
of joining up; others would take the money for their equipment as horsemen without being capable of riding; others
regarded ceremonial actions such as to ride in the Panathenaic
procession as their first duty.[3] In brief, there were many who
were 'excellent except in the field'.[4]

Even the State did not always pay regularly the money due
after the campaign.[5] That is probably the reason why the
triremes which please Poseidon are called *misthophoroi*, that is
'carrying [men who have received] their pay'; the god would
not be pleased if as so often the payments were in arrear.[6] At
a later period of the war mercenaries had to be dismissed because of lack of funds;[7] certainly not all the available money
was spent on war purposes.

Some of the passages mentioned are more or less commonplace, due to human and all-too-human nature. Others are
undoubtedly flavoured by the poet's personal attitude. In
spite of such utterances we must not forget that Athens in the
last ten years of the Peloponnesian War won some of her most
remarkable military successes. Many citizens were on active
service and did not see their homes for several months on end.[8]
There is, however, more behind that abundance of evidence.
The last scene of the *Acharnians* shows not only how unfairly
the professional soldier Lamachos could be ridiculed as a
militaristic type, but also how the whole military outlook,
everything virile and active, could be satirized in the same
way.[9] Is this to be set down only to comic licence and the
pleading for peace and peaceful prosperity? At the end of the

---

[1] ἀστράτευτοι, W.1117f, cf. P.526f.   [2] Eupolis 31ff, 3 D.

[3] ἀνάγχιπποι, Eupolis 394, 16 D. — Eupolis 268. — Xen. *hipparch.* 2, 1.

[4] adesp. 451.   [5] K.1366f.

[6] K.555. The explanation given in the text is that of G. Björk, *Eranos*
XXXVIII (1940), 31ff. It seems better to agree with the real meaning of
μισθοφόρος than the explanation that the fleet was 'earning money' by getting
the tribute to Athens.

[7] Thuc. VII, 29, 1.   [8] L.102ff, Th.1168f.

[9] A.1069ff, cf. also 593ff.

play Lamachos returns from the campaign, wounded by a ridiculous accident, while Dikaiopolis returns triumphantly from dinner.[1] One cannot help feeling that the comic poet has here (as in the last scene of the *Clouds*) outwitted his own wit and fallen into an outrageous form of caricature. But since he did so, the audience probably made an adequate response. 'There is a jingoism of peace as well as a jingoism of war.'[2] We are hardly surprised to find that in the very year after Arginusae the word for 'sea-warfare' could be used to indicate sexual intercourse.[3]

There is an unsolved discrepancy in Aristophanes' attitude. At one and the same time he deplores the decline of soldierly virtues and fights the war-mongers. The bellicose spirit of an idealized past finds high praise, but in the poet's own time it is regarded as reckless irresponsibility. The longing for peace, on the other hand, contrasts with his admonitions to look after the fleet, although the lively conversation between the triremes in the second parabasis of the *Knights* is a fervent attack against the war-mongers and their fantastic imperialism.[4] It is not easy to reconcile these conflicting views. To some extent, it may all be due to the fact that serious logic is not a feature of comedy. However true that may be, it seems an unsatisfactory explanation, and we are left to wonder whether in matters which were obviously so near to the poet's heart he could so manifestly contradict himself.

It is probably true to say that all the comedians, as far as they had a definite political bias, turned against the imperialists, though frequently only for the sake of peace and prosperity. Kratinos, who praised Kimon's Panhellenism and attacked Perikles' tyranny,[5] was the first to play that tune. A generation later, it was the same with Aristophanes. In the struggle between war-party and peace-party he knew no compromise and consistently attacked the war-mongers. There is no need to quote all the relevant passages. Criticism extends to politicians and military leaders alike, and this was not merely a privilege of comedy. Euripides, for example, thinks a general ought to look for himself what the position is, and not rely on reports by scouts; moreover, he blames those generals who

---

[1] A.1190ff. Cf. V. Coulon, *Philologus* LXXXXV (1942), 31ff.
[2] Norwood, 205.   [3] F.430.   [4] K.1300ff.
[5] Kratinos 1: 38 P, 15ff. Cf. in general J. Th. M. F. Pieters, *Cratinus* (1946).

rely on high spirits rather than good counsel, who promote war without justification and are tempted by vain hopes.[1] Hope for victory was sometimes based on the firm conviction that one's own side was fighting for a good cause,[2] but frequently that was only a pretext, and sometimes even no pretext was required. Aristophanes' hatred for all war-policy was so strong that his descriptions of the war-mongers certainly do not do justice to them.[3] We could hardly expect anything else from comedy, but then we must draw the appropriate conclusion. Caricature becomes here propaganda. The energetic and daring courage of the Athenians, which the enemy admired, hardly appears in comedy, only the wild expansionist plans of those politicians who were all out for waging war, and, on the other hand, the dangerous eagerness to stop the war, or not to wage war at all, simply because of war-weariness, such as the Spartans were accused of by the Corinthians.[4] However, the bellicose Acharnians at first hate the peacemaker Dikaiopolis much more ardently than they hate Kleon, the demagogue who was the enemy of the agrarian population.[5] The devastation of the countryside, the ruined vineyards, and similar experiences,[6] strengthened the arguments of those who wanted 'to see the thing through to the end', though such arguments chiefly affected the peasants who, on the whole, were not very bellicose. The townsfolk, on the other hand, welcomed the opportunity of adding to the financial burden of the well-to-do.

Menelaos in Euripides' *Andromache* tries to defend the Trojan War and to emphasize the positive values which it had offered to the Greeks. He praises in particular the spirit of

---

[1] Eur. *Herakl.* 390ff. — *Hik.* 161f, 232ff, 479ff. ἐλπὶς βροτοῖς κάκιστον (479).

[2] e.g., Eur. *Herakl.* 755 ff, *Hik.* 304ff, 339ff, 745ff.

[3] e.g., A.305ff, 560ff, cf. 978ff.

[4] Thuc. I, 70, 2. — Thuc. I, 124, 2.   [5] A.300.

[6] A.232, 512. Nothing is said of the olive trees, and the economic recovery of Athens after the war induces one to believe that most of them were spared. A fig tree is mentioned as having been cut down (P.628f). A different opinion is expressed by Michell, 85, but his evidence, which includes even *Deuteronomy*, is insufficient. Thuc. VII, 27, in describing the devastation of Attica after the occupation of Dekeleia, does not mention the olive trees either. Lysias VII, on the other hand, confirms that actually many olive trees, even sacred ones, were cut down during the war, but how far Attic oil-production was crippled by that remains uncertain.

comradeship created by the war in which professional soldiers and civilians had fought side by side.[1] He is not an impressive witness, but his words reflect a reality which has always been manifest in times of war. The comic poets, however, had no use for such militaristic arguments. They speak only — and not in favourable terms — of the solidarity among those who considered war their profession, above all among the army officers. Strategoi, taxiarchs and the rest, some of whom were, as we have seen,[2] connected by birth, were also brought together as members of the same *phyle* — that is to say in this connection, as comrades of the same regiment.[3] It is possible, though only with certain reservations, to speak of a 'military party', and among those who stood for war, the war-profiteers, especially manufacturers of arms, are not lacking, nor are those who had embezzled public funds intended for the prosecution of the war; money was in circulation, and many benefited by this.[4] Some of the demagogues were in favour of the war, not for the reasons given in comedy, but because it provided greater opportunities of satisfying their ambitions; the appeal to patriotic feeling, and often enough in such disguise to baser instincts, usually led to success with the masses.[5] The other side of the picture is seen in the soldier's widow who earns her own and her children's living by making wreaths.[6] Finally we may add to the number of those who stood to gain by the war, the slaves, and among them especially the miners, who seized the opportunity to run away, and the other slaves who, in general, were better treated since the outbreak of war.[7] This, it is true, was a grave drawback for the citizens. Nevertheless, the number of citizens who supported the war and the war-policy for one reason or another was not inconsiderable. As we have already pointed out, it is not true that only Kleon and a few war-mongers were responsible for the continuation of the war-policy. A decisive factor, of course, was that a large number of the townsfolk did not suffer very badly from the

---

[1] Eur. *Andr.* 681ff.   [2] See p. 108.

[3] A.566ff. The *phyle* means here not the political division, but the troops which it supplied (cf. Thuc. VI, 98, 4, Xen. *hell.* IV, 2, 19).

[4] P.447ff, 545, 1210ff. — L.589ff. Cf. Xen. *mem.* III, 6, 7.

[5] Cf., e.g., both Kleon's and Diodotos' speeches on Mytilene (Thuc. III, 37ff, 42ff).

[6] Th.446ff.   [7] P.451. — C.5ff.

war. If, however, Aristophanes thinks that the war-party were actuated, in so far as their motives were not wholly bad, merely by ambition and the spirit of adventure,[1] and not also by serious political ideas and patriotic feeling, we must attribute this verdict to the general character of comedy. Even so, we must remember that the ordinary unimportant citizens were little influenced by high ideals or by more than personal feelings in their attitude to war and peace.

Naturally the picture is not to be painted quite so sharply in black and white as the comic writers would have us believe. We can see this even from comedy itself. To Trygaios the peaceful scent of Eirene's companion is no doubt more fragrant than 'the soldier's knapsack'.[2] It was, to put it mildly, inconvenient and disagreeable, if 'the sheepskin [worn by the soldier in cold weather] was victorious over the kneading-trough made of stone'; the metaphor is rather bold, but its meaning cannot be mistaken.[3] Especially during the years when a large part of the population of Attica was crowded together inside the Long Walls, and the Athenians dwelt 'in casks, nests, and turrets',[4] the morale of the people may sometimes have been rather low. The plague, too, had a very serious effect. All the passages, however, which express a desire for peace and depict the happy life of peaceful times, frequent though they are, speak, in justification of a quick peace, only of the return of the peasants to the country and especially of the material advantages and enjoyments of peace.[5] When specific aims are mentioned, they are, for instance, the re-opening of market trade and the renewed importation of foreign goods.[6] Later, therefore, when the invasions of Attica have ceased, it is the *emporoi* and *naukleroi*, the sea-traders, who are chiefly concerned about peace — even more than the farmers.[7] It was possible to speak of 'peace-profiteers', such as the man who produced agricultural tools and was now able to sell them at high prices.[8] Peaceful 'Reconciliation' (*Diallage*)

---

[1] P.441ff., 450.   [2] P.526f.
[3] Hermipp. 57.   [4] K.792f.
[5] The evidence is well known and ample; cf. A.201f, 971ff, 1048ff, 1085ff, K.1394f, P.324ff, 339ff, 439f, 530ff, 556ff, 566ff, 582ff, 1127ff, frg. 107, 109, 363-4, 400.
[6] A.623ff. — A.916, P.999ff, L.109f.
[7] Xen. *Poroi*, 5, 3.   [8] P.1200f.

belongs to Aphrodite and Eros, and the prayer for peace, significantly enough, invokes Hermes and Aphrodite and her companions.[1] Peace meant business and pleasure.

The economic advantages of peace are, however, seen and admitted from a private point of view only. This is true even of the play called *Peace*, although Eirene was to be the saviour of Greeks everywhere. Not until the drastic financial requirements and financial distress after the collapse of 403 could the 'great illusion' be recognized as it concerned the State. Then it was possible to see that even a victorious war had a much more disastrous effect on public finance than the quiet times of peace.[2] This view, however, is not likely to have been widespread; in general, the public did not much trouble in advance about the economic results of the war. But these results were so disastrous from the financial point of view, that after the war even the ordinary politician had to accept them as a fact.

Once again, we ask whether it is correct to take the evidence of comedy as significant and, to some extent, as true. Athena Promachos stood on the Acropolis — the fighting champion of the city. Had the Athenians ceased to follow her leadership? Perhaps years of peace and the relative easiness of their rule over the Aegean Sea had weakened their fighting spirit. The long and weary war, with its grave disasters, must have had its effects, though it never fully broke the amazing elasticity of the Athenian character. The later years reveal indeed less of that buoyancy which characterized some of the earlier campaigns of the war.[3] The Sicilian Expedition, at least, was guided by a hysterical rather than a sound and soldierly spirit. War and peace, in their influence on the mind of the public, might still be equally effective; but no longer was there a heroic view of war or an idealistic view of peace.

If we look for a higher ideal, ethical or political, as a justification for peace, only one is mentioned — that it would be a good thing at last to end the quarrels among the Greek States,

---

[1] A.989. — P.456, cf. 975ff, and above, p. 55f.

[2] Xen. *Poroi*, 5, 11ff.

[3] e.g., Thuc. II, 31. The view expressed in the text does not contradict Wade-Gery's picture of the fighting spirit of Athens which is chiefly concerned with the 'sixties and 'fifties of the century (*Harvard Studies in Cl. Phil., Vol. for Ferguson*, 153).

and finally 'disentangle the skein'.[1] What is called the Panhellenism of Aristophanes is undoubtedly one of the ideas on
which two of his comedies, the *Peace* and the *Lysistrate*, are
based.[2] It is, however, neither an end in itself nor a constructive
element, but merely the means to a desired result, to secure
peace as quickly as possible. Nor have treaties mentioned in
comedy, such as that of Dikaiopolis, any higher aims. There
is, naturally enough, nothing of that solemnity with which
Euripides describes, for example, the founding of the friendship between Athens and Argos on an oath prescribed by
Athena; its words were to be inscribed on a tripod dedicated
to the Delphic Apollo as 'a testimony to Hellas'.[3] This is
significant. It is, of course, a reflection of current practice into
the mythical plane. A dedication in one of the Panhellenic
sanctuaries was the only possible feature by which a bilateral
treaty could be raised to some Panhellenic relevance. We must
not think of peace at that time, whether in comedy or elsewhere, as a Panhellenic ideal. Panhellenism, though alive in
every Greek when he thought of the barbarians, did not yet
have any substantial impact on politics. In Aristophanes' last
play the Panhellenic idea appears occasionally as an item in
social and economic reform or revolution.[4] In the *Lysistrate* the
struggle for peace among the Greek States is certainly raised
to a higher level by the warm humanity and dominating
personality of the leader, and the ideal of peace is here an
active and dynamic element in the plot, whereas elsewhere it
is simply the expression of quietist hope. To the majority of
the women, however, in this play too, peace is a matter of
private interest and welfare.

Most surprising perhaps in all these expressions of longing
for peace is the fact that nothing is said about the loss of life
caused by war. Not a word is said of the dangers of war,
though mothers are described once as being eager to protect
their sons.[5] It is obvious that the prisoners wanted peace; but
they were powerless;[6] it was well known that a few years back
the Athenians had found the Spartan prisoners a valuable

---

[1] P.993ff. — L.567ff.

[2] P.302, 473ff, 619ff, 993ff, 1082, L.29f, 39ff, 342f, 554, 1005f, 1110f,
1128ff. Cf. W. M. Hugill, *Panhellenism in Aristophanes* (1936).

[3] Eur. *Hik.* 1181ff; quotation: 1212.

[4] Pl.463.   [5] F..233f.   [6] P.479f.

counter in the peace negotiations. Losses in war were an un-
suitable subject for comedy, but for the pathos of the *Lysistrate*
they would have been the perfect argument. Indeed Lysistrate
says: 'We have borne sons and then sent them out as hoplites',
and the *proboulos* answers: 'Be quiet! Do not remember past
evils.'[1] This is generally understood as a brief reminder of the
severe losses during the war which was hushed up as out of
place in a comedy.[2] It may be doubted whether this is quite
the right interpretation. Early in 411, only one and a half
years after the disaster at Syracuse, with no other important
land battle since, the 'sending out of hoplites' would most
naturally indicate the Sicilian Expedition. And it is perhaps
the mind of the timid official rather than the need of comedy
which dictated the answer (though we do not wish to press the
latter point). Anyhow, even here the poet does not refer to
the losses in general, but to a single event of fatal importance
to the State. Other sources, too, only very rarely speak of the
losses which by the significant institution of the official *Logos
Epitaphios* were lifted out of the purely private sphere. An
official epitaph like that on the dead of Potidaia (432 B.C.)
could be written in words as beautiful as these: 'This city and
Erechtheus' people are longing for the men, the sons of the
Athenians, who died fighting in the front line at Potidaia; they
staked their lives as the price of valour, and brought glory to
their country.'[3] It was the Polis which counted, and only
the State spoke of its sorrow. It is true that such an outlook
formed part of the old traditions which were in process of
change and dissolution both then and afterwards. At the
moment these traditions still survived, and we realize that to
archaic Athens, not to speak of Sparta, individuals were almost
nothing but citizens, and citizens might almost cease to be
men.[4]

We get an entirely different impression from Euripides,
and it is this question more than any other — equalled only

[1] L.589f.

[2] Cf., e.g., Wilamowitz, on v. 590: 'An die ungeheuren Verluste durfte und
mochte der Dichter nur von fern erinnern.'

[3] *IG.* I², 945 (Tod, 59), 10ff.

[4] It is in many ways significant that Plato again 'seems to treat war as a normal
incident of political life, not in the least as a public evil to be abolished' (G.
Murray, *JHS.* LXIV, 1944, 2).

perhaps by the religious problems — which reveals how lonely a voice his was. Although public opinion was frequently reflected in his plays by one character or another, he himself rarely followed it. Aristophanes, on the other hand, can time and again be seen sharing the views of a large section of the people. Euripides — together with a few 'modern' thinkers — remained isolated, a man whose single-mindedness was ahead of his time. To show this, it will suffice to point to a few passages only. Though he may have shared the common view that the best thing to do for a man is to be 'hard to one's foes and kind to one's friends',[1] his hatred of war is of a very different kind from that of the comedians. It burns like a fire through such plays as the *Hiketides* and the *Troades*, and the terrible loss of life — of sons, husbands, fathers — is a theme frequently repeated, and sometimes in almost identical words.[2] These plays taught the little-known truth that war spells doom for vanquished and victors alike. Euripides realized the foolishness of war which does not decide anything and only leads to never-ending retaliation.[3] The generals have the glory and the advantages, the common soldiers the hardships and the dangers.[4] Naturally, when it was necessary to ward off a 'lover of war', Athens would defend herself; but peace remained the aim of the government.[5] Peace is praised, frequently in a traditional manner;[6] but the praise is based on the knowledge that peace rather than war can be defended by reason and sensible argument.[7] Surely, Euripides was a pacifist.

The desire for peace expressed in comedy is not pacifism, which is an attitude of mind based on principle. How could the comedians be pacifists, they who at the same time praised the soldierly virtues of bygone days! Nowhere in comedy is there any sign of the view that war is 'a violent teacher', as Thucydides impressively describes it, or that it makes men brutal and savage, and so destroys also the inner peace of the State.[8] At most it is said that war affords ample opportunity for the dishonest practices of the demagogues.[9] Nor do

---

[1] Eur. *Med*. 809.
[2] Eur. *Andr*. 611ff, 1038f, *Kykl*. 304ff, *Hek*. 650ff, cf. 322ff.
[3] Eur. *Tro*. 95ff, *El*.377ff, *Hel*. 1151ff.
[4] Eur. *Andr*. 693ff.
[5] Eur. *Herakl*. 371ff.
[6] Eur. *Hik*. 489ff, 949ff, *frg*. 453.
[7] Eur. *Hik*. 486ff.
[8] Thuc. III, 82.
[9] K.801ff, cf. Thuc. V, 16, 1.

we hear of any attempts to make the methods of warfare more humane. Euripides once emphasizes that the Athenians would not allow a prisoner of war to be killed;[1] but that was a general rule, not confined to Athens, although broken by Athens as well as by other States. Only rarely, on the other hand, is peace depicted in the colours of heavenly perfection and thus as unattainable: 'until wolf and lamb lie down together'.[2] The first signs of rationalistic pacifism can, however, be discovered in the teaching of the sophists,[3] and without them the idea of peace would never have attained the importance it enjoyed throughout the fourth century. It was this idea of peace which again and again men attempted to realize as a constant and 'common' possession.[4] During the Peloponnesian War, none of the small farmers who suffered most severely by the war, nor even the large middle-class as a whole, knew anything of this idea. To them peace meant a 'time without war'.[5] War, though hated, was deemed necessary. Dikaiopolis is well pleased to get a thirty years' peace, and this is the longest possible distance ahead that is thought of in the treaties up to this date; he despises the five years' peace, but a poor peasant might be content even with this.[6] A few years later, peace treaties were concluded for fifty or even a hundred years.[7] Thus the realistic (or pessimistic) view that peace had to be delimited was gradually given up, and politics moved towards the optimistic formula of the fourth century, 'for ever'. This development was entirely independent of the real facts, but it was the sign of a change of mind; people began to look on peace instead of war as the normal state of affairs. War now became a 'time without peace'.

This development belongs to our period, but we can hardly trace it in comedy. Here, as far as I can see, the older view prevailed. The whole idea of peace is simply a matter of prudent opportunism and prosaic self-interest, and it is quite

---

[1] Eur. *Herakl.* 961, 1019.   [2] P.1075f.

[3] W. Nestle, *Der Friedensgedanke in der antiken Welt* (*Philologus*, Suppl. XXXI, 1938), 12ff.

[4] It is well known that the κοινὴ εἰρήνη was a central theme in the political arguments of the fourth century.

[5] adesp. 846.   [6] A.188f, 194ff, 1021.

[7] Thuc. V, 18, 3; 47, 1; 79, 1; but cf. IV, 63, 1 (ἐς ἀίδιον), and Meritt's reconstruction of the treaties with Rhegion and Leontinoi (*Cl. Q.* LX, 1946, 85ff): see also my remarks *AJP.* LXIX (1948), 156, 26.

empty of any higher ideal. People who feel like this cannot
be taken in by high-sounding patriotic phrases such as Dikaiopolis uses in addressing the officials, his voice ringing with the
true indignation of the offended Greek patriot, when the
Thracian ambassadors have stolen his bag.[1] No doubt his
words are an exact and typical reflection of reality. In a sense
the passionate oratory of warlike men, though it frequently
sounds shallow, may have been more genuine, and doubtless
more realistic, than that of the peace-maker. Even in comedy
the warlike type is represented not only by the ridiculous and
tragi-comic Lamachos or his superior officers who were
'stronger in quantity than quality', but in some degree also
by the chorus of the knights, who praise Athens as eminent in
war, poetry and power.[2] After his death the same Lamachos
who had been so cruelly derided in life is praised as a hero.[3]
There was, in fact, a strong political obligation to continue
the war, so long as Athens fought for her empire, and in the
end for her very existence.

Yet the peasants' desire for peace is not a matter of pure
reasoning and opportunism. It results from the specific attitude of peasants who can combine sober and material calculation with an unreasoning devotion to land, to home and garden,
to their crops and their cattle. Among the peasants there was
no room for a war-policy, the more so since in Athens war then
meant naval warfare. Even if the larger part of the crews was
formed by townsfolk, they included a certain number of
peasants, and these naturally disliked this kind of warfare more
than fighting on land, which had sometimes meant fighting on
their soil for their soil.

On the other hand, the bellicose demos did not only believe
in the necessity of warfare; it was also largely influenced by
the idea of material advantage, especially by the chance of
acquiring rich booty, though sometimes the material advantage
might mean simply the soldier's pay.[4] The new century,
however, saw the introduction of mercenary troops with their
good and bad qualities, to take the place of the citizen army.[5]
There had been mercenaries as early as the Peloponnesian
War for certain technical purposes; occasionally they were
employed even as hoplites, and in 403 Lysias was certainly

[1] A.167f.   [2] A.1078. — K.581ff.
[3] F.1040, cf. Th.841.   [4] Cf. E.197f.   [5] Cf. Pl.173.

not the only one who hired soldiers for Thrasyboulos.[1]   It
could, however, be said that by 392 in the Corinthian War
the large citizen armies had been demobilized, and only guards
left in the fortresses of Corinth and Sikyon; 'but both parties
had mercenaries, and with them they fought vigorously'.[2]
The growing importance of mercenary troops went hand in
hand with the declining willingness of the citizens to take the
field.

A certain danger lay in the possibility that the question of
war and peace might gradually divide the population of town
and country. Many honest and wealthy peasants had lost all
their property during the Spartan invasions, whereas in war-
time the townsmen had the advantage in every way. It was
even easier for them to avoid mobilization.[3] As long as sardines
were cheap, the townsfolk did not think of making peace.[4]
This is a joke which expresses in pointed fashion that the town
need not rely on the country for food, and therefore did not
care very much for the interests and sufferings of the rural
population.[5] In 425 Athens, in spite of the unrest of the war,
was full of an intense economic life and industrial prosperity.[6]
The people there were convinced that the war fought through
to a final and complete victory would bring them more
prosperity and more power.

We have stressed a number of features which make the
conflict in Aristophanes' own opinions less absolute and thus
less puzzling. Longing for peace was no pacifism, and hatred
of the war-mongers did not prevent the poet from recognizing
the need of military valour and of a display of Athenian naval
power, wherever it could be brought in line with his predominant general ideas. His criticism, however, was directed
against realities. The irresponsible war-policy of some of the
leaders as well as the general decline of soldierly virtues were
facts, and not only themes of moralistic preaching by a man
who to some extent was certainly a *laudator temporis acti*. The
time had gone when the whole military strength of the State
was founded on the unquestioning submission of its citizens

---

[1] A.153ff, B.1179, frg. 550-1. — Lysias XII, 52f, *frg.* 1, 165. Cf. H. W.
Parke, *Greek Mercenary Soldiers*, 16ff.

[2] Xen. *hell*. IV, 4, 14.

[3] ἀγαθοὶ γεωργοί, Ps.-Lysias XX, 33. — P. 1185f.

[4] K.671ff.   [5] A.1022ff.   [6] A.544ff.

to the military demands of the moment. Earlier than other States of the Greek mainland, Athens, as a sea-power and as the leading State of the Aegean empire, had developed beyond this stage, which, in fact, was the essential basis of the Polis. The unique development of Athens explains the increasing disappearance of the martial spirit; it even forced it on, much as had happened in Ionia a century earlier. Conditions, however, after the breakdown of the empire and her external power turned out to be very uncertain and dangerous, since what the enemy had spared was threatened by the citizens themselves, by their lack of discipline and of common purpose. Athens recovered from her political and economic collapse, but there were now many non-citizens, even barbarians, in the ranks,[1] and never again — even Chaironeia is no exception — did her citizens as a body form a single unit to defend their State and their freedom.

Political events show that, beneath the surface of a petty and narrow-minded attitude, a spark of heroism was concealed, in the friends of war as well as of peace, a spark which might occasionally flare up, but would not grow into a steady fire. The two groups of the people, the two sides of the people's mind, represent two possibilities inherent in the Athenian character, both of them equally dangerous: unrestricted pleasure in power and warlike recklessness on the one hand, abandonment to private indolence and peaceful enjoyment on the other. Perhaps these are general human qualities, and in normal times the troubles they cause may be of minor importance. It was different in a war which was actually a matter of life and death to the whole State. Then, and also during the hard struggle for recovery, the lack of a common and moderate spirit among leaders and people was a real danger. In all the years of the war and its aftermath, Athenian policy swung to and fro between the two extremes. Dangers from outside might still cause the Athenians to rally, but as soon as the danger had passed or only slightly receded, the violent feelings between the various political groups broke into open quarrels again, while the political apathy of the mass of the citizens grew steadily.

It was this curious and dangerous intermixture of external and internal conflicts, combined with the selfish quietism

[1] Xen. *Poroi* 2, 2f.

of many of the citizens, that prepared the soil for revolution
and defeat. The opportunist was the man of the hour, and
nobody typified such an attitude more strongly than Alkibiades. With his splendour and his genius, his utter lack of
character and conscience, and his dissolute life, he both
reflected and magnified characteristic qualities of his people.
In him as in the Athenians generally the old military tradition
lived on; in him as in the Athenians the wonderful lightness of
a great and peaceful civilization survived.[1] The achievements
of Athens during the later years of the war, both in her military
efforts and her works of art, resulted, great though they were,
from a spirit that was losing its unity and strength. There
were still strong reserves which prevented a sudden breakdown and even allowed partial recovery. There could be a
temporary revival of military inventiveness and energy in
Iphikrates' light-armed forces. But the following decades
saw Athenian generals becoming mercenary adventurers, and
the greatest mind of the age banned the freedom of art and
poetry from his ideal State. On the other hand, a book such
as Xenophon's *Poroi*, written as a practical proposal for the
restoration of power and prosperity, shows how fully even a
man who had strong sympathies with military qualities submitted to the demands of pacifist materialism. The two
traditions of soldierly valour and creative culture separated
and were largely corrupted. Perikles had known how to combine martial spirit, intellectual civilization and economic
welfare. He found no successor.

[1] Cf. F. Taeger, *Alkibiades* (1943), the much improved version of an earlier
book, though I still cannot share all his views.

CHAPTER XII

ECONOMICS AND THE STATE

I

ONE of the chief points in the political programme described by Perikles in the Funeral Speech is that all citizens should devote their attention to both house and State, to private as well as public affairs.[1] It can be maintained that at that time, and later even more, the citizens of Athens represented a combination of the political and the economic types of man. Naturally members of the upper class had more opportunity to devote themselves entirely to political life; but democracy demanded an interest in political activity from the great mass of the people. In fact, political leaders emerged from the middle classes at the very time when in these classes political preoccupation was gradually giving way to economic interests. The ordinary citizen then was neither by instinct nor by desire the 'political animal' whom Aristotle's phrase has made famous and who is generally believed to be the true pattern of the Greek citizen.

Let us recall some of the evidence of comedy. The citizen who is exploited by Kleon is depicted as a stupid and wealthy man who is not concerned with politics, but actually afraid of them. He is called *apragmon*, the unpolitical man.[2] Thus Peithetairos and Euelpides, though citizens belonging to tribe and clan, left Athens in order to find 'an unpolitical place', far from the unrest of politics and law-courts.[3] It is, like the ideal of peace, a quietist ideal, but it is here confined to the internal affairs of the State; it springs from the reaction against the agitation and restlessness of democracy. The sycophant who boasts that everything concerning the State lies in his hands is an undesirable type of leader, especially in the view of a good citizen.[4] Nevertheless he rejects a quiet life as inhuman and unendurable, and in this he resembles the

[1] Thuc. II, 40, 2.
[2] K.261ff. See p. 109, n. 5, and my article mentioned there.
[3] B.33f, 44.   [4] Pl.919f.

Athenian statesmen of an earlier generation. During the Peloponnesian War a process began by which the *polites*, the citizen
as a political being, lost his exclusively or at least predominantly
political character. This process was decisive in the further
development of the Greeks.

Aristophanes apparently fights for an unpolitical ideal.
That is, of course, a very different thing from saying that he
is an oligarch, though he seems indeed a sharp critic of democracy, or at least of some of its leaders. He represents a type
of citizen who did not care for party politics. The rich man
already mentioned was neither an oligarch nor of noble family.[1]
Such citizens did not deliberately abandon politics because
they were disgusted with them, as a few may have been. That
rich man was not interested in politics because he was simply
a business man. It is most likely that he himself or possibly
his father had made the family fortune. For in families with
inherited wealth a political career was traditional,[2] though it
might sometimes be a career which involved opposition to the
existing form of State. Our man, however, though doubtless
a member of the upper classes,[3] owed his fortune either to
trade or to manufacture. The heliasts of the *Wasps* might
claim to be the only true autochthonous Athenians — in fact,
all were equally citizens of Athens, 'honest and loving the
State': the farmer, the merchant, the craftsman.[4] The *emporos*
also is a true citizen, and it is quite wrong to maintain that all
citizens who took part in trade were 'proletarians'. Many good
and wealthy citizens were chiefly engaged in the pursuit of
economic aims.[5]

Comedy is a source which discourages all attempts at
idealization, except perhaps in the description of rural life. In
general it is more likely to go to the opposite extreme, and
offer satire and caricature instead of reality. Innumerable passages in all the comedies, for instance, discuss food. Every type
of 'feeder' is mentioned, the refined gourmand no less than the

---

[1] K.261f.

[2] In Euripides' *Andromache* (151ff). Hermione claims her right of ἐλευθερο-
στομεῖν because of her noble origin and rich dowry!

[3] He is μὴ πονηρός, K.265.

[4] W.1076. — Pl.899ff, cf. E.299ff, and elsewhere.

[5] This does not, of course, contradict the view that metics, and in particular
freedmen, rather than citizens came nearest to the pure type of 'economic man'.
Cf. Sir A. Zimmern, *Solon and Croesus*, 132.

'man who likes his porridge', or the ordinary citizen who lunches on bread and garlic, or at the best on half-an-obol's worth of meat and a little cheese.[1] The people's love for food is an eternal joke. The signet ring of Demos has as a seal a particular dish, and the competition of the two rascals for the favour of Demos ends in each of them offering him the most delicious dishes, all given by the goddess.[2] It is also a joke, but one which nevertheless reveals a probably typical culinary materialism, when Peithetairos, the great founder of a new State, at his wedding to Basileia, the queenly goddess from Heaven, remarks: 'Those birds were slaughtered just at the right moment.'[3] Comedy itself is frequently likened to a luxurious meal given to the public, while the play of a competitor is compared to a cheap breakfast.[4] The significance of such passages may be summed up in the phrase: 'Most things exist to most men for the sake of eating only', or in Polyphemos' philosophy: 'to eat and to drink day by day is Zeus for wise men'.[5] The importance of the food problem to the majority of the people is not to be questioned.

Little wonder therefore that fond dreams centred on the subject of food. In the *Acharnians* we hear of Dikaiopolis' elaborate preparations for a magnificent dinner, and there are other similar descriptions, even in tragedy.[6] The comic poets, above all, enjoy describing the miracles of a glutton's Paradise, which might even be situated in Hades.[7] The wonders of fairy-land could be extended beyond the sphere of food; all sorts of things would move of their own, and without having to bother about slaves, everyone would share all possible pleasures of life.[8] Day-dreams of this type, however, do not embody social or economic facts of any importance, nor do they, though they express popular opinion, reflect the whole reality of life. The simple materialism of the land of Cockaigne, the land where every wish is instantly fulfilled,[9] was a pleasant

---

[1] frg. 506, perhaps also 5 D. — adesp. 1190. — A.164, W.679f, F.550ff.

[2] K.953f, 1166ff.   [3] B.1688.

[4] e.g. frg. 333, Kratinos 169, Pherekr. 122 (?), Metagenes 14, adesp. 1330. — K.537f.

[5] adesp. 432. — Eur. *Kykl.* 336f.

[6] A.1040ff. — Eur. *frg.* 467.

[7] B.128ff, E.605ff, Pl.806ff, Kratinos 165, Pherekr. 143, Telekleid. 1, Metagenes 6, Nikophon 13-14. — frg. 488, Pherekr. 108.

[8] Krates 14, 15, Pherekr. 130.   [9] frg. 39 D.

and favourite item in the comedian's stock-in-trade, but in the life lived by real people there were few marvels of culinary art, or other enjoyable miracles. Still, from one point of view those pictures of a materialistic paradise are significant. If everybody has everything he wants, there are no longer rich and poor, and private property has ceased to exist. Thus the comic dreams have a share in that fairly widespread tendency among contemporary writers to outline some new ideal society on a 'communist' basis, as we find it reflected in the *Ekklesiazousai*.

The pleasures of good food and a comfortable life are natural objects for human desires. In comedy, their importance is clearly over-emphasized, though there was some economic reality behind such yearnings. Those fairy-tales were taken seriously enough, probably because they derived from some kind of escapism, to be derided by Eupolis in his *Golden Age* and by Aristophanes in the *Tagenistae* or *Broilers*.[1] They have also some significance for our picture of Athenian society. The thoughts and wishes which lay behind those imaginings form part of a definite outlook, the outlook of the petty citizen, which is common, in some degree, to all strata of society. There were many links between the various groups and levels of the population, between town and country, noblemen and commons, rich and poor. The bulk of the people in town and country were not proletarians, but belonged to the lower middle-classes. It is of particular social importance that the old distinction between men with landed property and those without it, the so-called *thetes*, no longer held good. As early as about 445, when a colony was being founded in Brea, the new colonists were chosen from the *zeugitai* as well as from the *thetes*.[2] Peasant and merchant, craftsman and worker were included in the common type of *petit bourgeois*, but even the day-labourers and other representatives of the very poor were not of an altogether different social type, perhaps with the exception of the 'beggars', who were almost outcasts. Attached to the small local community of the deme, the ordinary citizen, no matter what his vocation, no matter whether he was called

---

[1] Eupolis 276ff, frg. 580, see also 680 (where Meineke's correction αὐτόματ' αὐτοῖς for αὐτομάτοισιν seems necessary). Cf. Gomme, *Hist. Comm. on Thuc.* I, 104f.

[2] *IG.* I², 45 (Tod, 44, *Syll.*³, 67).

'the Man of the Demos' or 'the Man in the Street',[1] was the
true representative of a State which since the time of Kleisthenes had based its political structure on the deme. The
Kleisthenic order, which had at this time been in force for
about a century, with its uniform organization of the State and
its dexterous mingling of the people, formed a framework to
which Athenian society adapted itself only gradually; nevertheless that order had created and moulded the general type of
citizen.

The Athenians did not turn away from politics on principle,
and certainly not in a sudden and general movement. Likewise it is unjustifiable simply to assume, as is frequently done,
that the majority of the citizens lived in and through politics
only. We do not deny that there were many men who lived
more or less on the State;[2] but there were opposing forces,
in both real and ideal life. Let us not forget that large sections
of the people had, in spite of their own occupations, much time
on their hands. Many of them had little difficulty in leaving
their work for a day or even several days, provided they received the compensation of a small fee. The peasants worked
really hard only for about half the year, and the traders did
not put to sea during the winter. Others too were much freer
than men of similar vocation and similar social standards in
other ages. The retailer or artisan, for instance, was his own
master, depending on, and responsible to, nobody else; there
was nothing to prevent his occasionally closing his shop. The
fact that the shops and workshops were so small and so
numerous made it easier for a large number of their owners
to accept public payment, though this did not necessarily
mean that they actually lived on the State. For a long time at
least, political and economic activities remained more or less
evenly balanced.[3] When economic needs became too strong
and the citizens turned away from politics, the State inter-

---

[1] For the δημότης see, above, p. 82 n. 3. ἄνθρωπος ἐξ ὁδοῦ is a phrase actually used by Eupolis 25 D.

[2] This is the so-called *Staatsrentnertum* which plays such a great part in modern
literature, especially in Hasebroek's often-quoted book.

[3] Cf. the lively description by Ferguson, *Americ. Hist. Rev.* XLV (1940), 273:
'As farmers, traders, seamen, contractors, manufacturers, artisans, labourers, the
Athenians had to work for their living, but they took an amount of time off for
public service and, we may add, for talk, sport, and conviviality, which would
have wrecked our economic system.'

vened, as we have seen, and introduced new and higher payments. For a time, therefore, politics defeated economics by economic means — but only for a time.

Economic activity among the Greeks did not only consist, as has recently been said,[1] in 'looking after one's property': such activity could at best satisfy only the upper classes. It was based also on the 'desire for gain', though primarily for the provision of one's daily bread. This is made clear by many passages in comedy. Aristophanes in his old age praised Wealth as the great giver of prosperity and happiness, and approved of, or even glorified, the desire for wealth, in spite of a certain note of satire and the many criticisms which he did not hide — the best example being the splendid scene in which Poverty proclaims her rights and her favourable and important influence on man.[2] We have spoken of the general tendencies which found here their most eloquent expression.[3] This desire for gain was no longer confined to a group that had become more or less proletarian and was therefore compelled to earn a living. The whole people was included, and in their desire to make money took active part in economic life. The great number of small economic units, and the fact that economic activity was mainly in the hands of small people, are proof, in a sense, of the strength of the economic energies which were involved; for the prevailing primitiveness of economic life called for greater, rather than less, exertion.[4] This was all qualified, it is true, by the charming indolence and modest demands of Mediterranean man as well as by the peculiar structure of economic life in the Greek Polis.

2

The question arises whether the growing economic spirit was reflected in the economic activities of the State itself. These can hardly have been confined to the granting of public payments. We cannot understand the economic prosperity of the later fourth century without disentangling the relations between State and economics. Here trade is of decisive im-

[1] J. Brake, *Wirtschaften und Charakter in der antiken Bildung* (1935).
[2] Probably imitated by Pherekr. 130, though only from the agrarian standpoint. Cf. Geissler, 41, 1.
[3] See p. 248f.   [4] Cf. Gomme, ch. III.

portance in our investigation, for it was based on the other economic factors, and *vice versa*. The standard of agricultural and industrial production depended to a large extent on the intensity and vitality of trade.

The comedians tell us little about these problems. This can partly be explained by the fact that the ordinary citizen saw in the State neither an abstract conception nor a personality greater than the individual, but simply a community of men. In comedy, therefore, the people could be personified on the stage, but the Polis could not, unless it was represented not as a social community, but as a factor in foreign policy, as in the *Poleis* of Eupolis. We find in comedy only slight indications of the relations between State and economics. Some of the facts have already been mentioned: the concession, for instance, by which all law-suits in which sea-traders were concerned, were reserved for the winter. We hear of the public supervision of trade and traffic in the market[1] and, of course, of the fundamental importance of the food question. It seems possible to go a few steps further.

The State as a community of men, that is as the people, was embodied in the *ekklesia*, the assembly acting as the sovereign of the State. No doubt, this sovereign people tried to provide as best as it could for its own economic needs and advantages. A large part of the people, and an even larger part of the assembly, was directly interested in trade and craft. Did the State interfere in their activities, if only for their own advantage? In general, it is true, economic life was free from official influence or control, except for the existence of minor officials such as the *agoranomoi* who were responsible for the safety and order of the market-trade, for the accuracy of weights and measures, and similar matters. There are, however, allusions to other and more important connections between State and economic life. The sausage-seller's report about the assembly is no doubt a wild caricature, but the news that cheaper sardines meant the continuation of the war could hardly be given if there was no possible association of ideas.[2] In war-time especially, the rulers had to provide, in one way or another, for both political and economic needs. The import of lantern-wicks from an enemy country is the occasion for a bit of foolery, a grotesque representation of sycophantism in opera-

---

[1] A.723, 824f, 968, W.1406f.   [2] K.624ff, 671f.

tion, but it would have had much less comic effect if an official prohibition of the import of certain goods had been out of the question.[1] If we take into consideration how rarely Athens enjoyed peace, the question of contraband,[2] that is the prohibition of the export of certain goods to certain countries in war-time, must have been of considerable economic importance. Another instance of State interference is the attempt made by the assembly to fix the price of salt at a lower level. It was impossible to carry through the decree, perhaps because of the traders' 'vested interests'; but it is important, at any rate, to realize that this sort of State interference could occur.[3] The ruling statesman, when on one occasion he met with strong resistance from the people, could think of closing the flour-market by way of reprisal.[4] By offering flour to the citizens a politician might win their favour, except when 'the town was full of bread',[5] a contingency which certainly did not often occur. The political leader had to consider 'how long the Polis would be able to live on the corn grown in the country, and how much every year was needed in addition'.[6] All these passages show the naturally close connection between the food question and politics, and we may take it for certain that the mere task of keeping the corn routes free from interference was in itself a matter of high policy and frequent military measures. The necessity and the difficulty of getting grain and other vital supplies for the State and the people afforded a means by which politics could influence economics, and, even more, economics could affect politics.[7]

Kleon was the first who consistently pursued a policy that was dictated by the economic needs and social demands of the middle classes. He was, at the same time, called the collector of customs duties and the 'bottomless abyss of gain'.[8] The

[1] A.916ff. Cf. Boeckh, I, 69. It is interesting to note Herod. V, 88, 2 on the protection which Aigina and Argos afforded their own production of pottery by forbidding the import of Athenian ware.

[2] τὰ ἀπόρρητα, Th.363f, F.362ff, cf. K.278f.   [3] E.814 and schol.

[4] K.856ff.   [5] adesp. 425.   [6] Xen. mem. III, 6, 13.

[7] Much has been written during recent times about the economics of the Polis. The latest book on the food question, which was not yet known to Michell, is: K. Köster, *Die Lebensmittelversorgung der altgriech. Polis* (*Neue Deutsche Forschungen*, Abt. Alte Gesch., Bd. 7, 1939). The author has made good use of the epigraphical evidence.

[8] K.248.

chief demagogue himself had certainly nothing to do directly with the customs; he stands here for the State, and it is clear that customs-duties were a heavy burden, directly to the merchant and trader, indirectly to the consumer. The comedian could speak of a visitor to a brothel in the same way as of a trader boarding his ship: 'before embarking you must pay harbour-dues'.[1] The customs were harbour-fees, to be paid by all ships coming and going, that is to say, they were purely financial measures not based on any idea of economic protection or the like. As has been emphasized already, there were two chief purposes in the economic measures of the State: the feeding of the people, and the creation of fiscal revenue. It may be questioned whether these were the only purposes, but they were predominant. At any rate, if trade in necessities, such as corn or timber for house- and ship-building, represented the bulk of Athenian trade, as it certainly did, it must have influenced the policy of the State in a much larger degree than all the luxury trade. It seems strange that some scholars should assume the contrary. It was essential to all citizens engaged in trade and craft, and, because of the food question, essential to every Athenian, that the sea-routes from the Black Sea and the northern shores of the Aegean to the Peiraeus should be kept open and safe. It seems impossible that the politicians should have been unaware of this fact. Politics and economics were inseparably connected.

We have spoken of the customs. Now we must ask what part they and the other taxes and dues played in economic life in general. It is well known that the Greeks had no system of direct taxation such as today forms the main bulwark of public finances. This is indeed a remarkable fact, but it does not prove, as is sometimes believed, that in Athens, in normal times at least, the State imposed no financial burdens whatever on its citizens. Certainly the so-called liturgies, like the trierarchy and the choregy, were undertaken voluntarily; nevertheless they were a heavy burden on the rich, as comedy quite clearly shows.[2] It is more significant that the State occasionally, as it seems, cheated those who undertook a liturgy; for instance, an old and rotten ship was handed over to be equipped.[3]   In war-time general taxes existed, and they

[1] Eupolis 48.   [2] See above, p. 236.
[3] K.913ff (this, of course, may be merely a joke).

weighed heavily on a large proportion of the people. Again, it is true, the rich bore the chief burden; to some extent taxation may have been an obstacle to business expansion. If there was any tendency for the State to influence economic life, it appeared in some sort of indirect protection for the small shops and workshops. In general, however, this tendency was eventually overruled by fiscal considerations, and the chief object became to secure and enlarge the State revenues. Therefore Euelpides, a typical representative of the lower middle-class, calls Athens a place 'common to all in taking fines from all'.[1] It was not only in the communist State that many revolted against allowing the fruits of their toil and thrift to fall to the State.[2] The difficult times through which the Polis passed inevitably affected directly all sections of the populace. The market-toll, for instance, was imposed, not only on goods from abroad, but on everything sold on the market.[3] Hunger and misery among the peasants are often described, but 'the taxes and the many one-per-cent levies', or even higher levies, among them probably duties on slaves and sales-taxes, fell more heavily on the townsfolk.[4] The citizens contributed quite a considerable sum to the public finances. This contribution was, however, largely influenced by the strength and intensity of general economic life which therefore must have been of the utmost interest and importance to the State and to the politicians who ruled it.

3

Another side of the problem is raised by the question how far the influence of economics can be seen in international relations. The Athenian League, though originally a confederacy formed chiefly for military purposes, was used with the definite intention of establishing an empire, a political unit under the supremacy of Athens. One of the chief means to this end was the creation of economic uniformity based on the exclusive use of Athenian standards of coinage, weights and

[1] B.38. This is not a literal translation. The Greek probably means: 'common to all in that they have there to pay money'.

[2] E. 750f.   [3] A.896.

[4] W.658, E.1007. — Boeckh, I, 395, 402ff. The πορισταί, a board who had created new taxes, were a special object for hatred (F.1505).

measures.[1]   This is not the place for a detailed discussion of
Athenian financial policy, but one essential point must be
stressed. Perikles' policy of providing for a large State treasure
by which the threatening war was to be financed was something
new in Greek economics; Themistokles' use of the surplus
output of Laureion for the building of a fleet was an outstanding precedent, but economically it was not in the same class.
Perikles was in advance of his generation; even later it was
probably left to only a few fully to realize the necessity for
a State to be financially prepared. Thucydides makes it clear
enough how important a factor in public life and especially in
warfare the financial resources of a State actually are; but it is
no accident that the most significant passages on this question,
although of a general and vague character, occur in the
speeches of a few particularly wise and foreseeing statesmen
such as Archidamos, Perikles and Hermokrates.[2]

The knowledge that warfare and finances were closely
bound up with one another was not yet obvious to many even
of the political leaders, and we find only rarely that economic
means were used in the methods of actual warfare. No doubt
the attempts of Sparta to attack Athens through her empire
had economic as well as political aims, and Brasidas' campaign
in Thrace and Amphipolis was, at least partly, intended to cut
off the import of Thracian timber which was so essential to
Athens for ship-building. The purpose of the naval war in the
region of the Hellespont, a strange battlefield to Spartan
soldiers, was to interfere with the Athenian corn trade. Yet,
nobody will assert that Spartan policy and warfare were
influenced to any essential extent by economic aims.

On the Athenian side, the most obvious example of an
action influenced both by political and economic considerations,
an event which also played a rôle in comedy, was the Megarian
Decree. The well-known passages in Aristophanes have been
frequently used to indicate the popular views of the origin of
the war.[3] They may also serve to clarify the meaning of this
famous decree, so far as it is concerned with economic policy,
and it is this aspect of the problem which we propose to dis-

[1] B.1040f. This took place about 449. Cf. Tod, 67 (now best in: *ATL.*
II, D14), also above, p. 157, n. 10.
[2] Cf. Gomme, *Hist. Comm. on Thuc.* I, 26.
[3] A.515ff, P.605ff.

cuss.[1] Incidentally, the whole subject is of special importance from the point of view of method, since it provides an opportunity to check the treatment in comedy of facts known to us from history.

The essential paragraph of the decree, which is known from two passages in Thucydides, runs somewhat after this fashion: the Megarians are not to be allowed to use either the harbours of the Athenian empire or the market of Athens.[2] In Aristophanes this sentence becomes a sort of drinking-song, almost a parody of a poem of Timokreon, 'laws written like *skolia*', forbidding the Megarians to stay 'either on land or in the market or on sea or on the continent', and thus reducing them to famine.[3] The point of this enumeration is to explain, without any logical accuracy, the term 'everywhere', but only the mention of the 'market', put absurdly enough between the words land and sea, alludes to the original wording. Since, however, the Athenians could not forbid anything to the Megarians except in the sphere which they controlled, that is within the boundaries of their empire, we may regard the *skolion* as being essentially in keeping with the original decree.

It has been made a matter of dispute whether the decree indicated a prohibition of trade, following perhaps on an earlier prohibition of import only, or a prohibition of traffic in general. It is hardly justifiable to conclude from the ridiculous situation in the *Acharnians*, when the Megarian is thoroughly searched for various goods, that there existed a specific decree prohibiting all kinds of import.[4] It is, on the other hand, at least as mistaken to describe such behaviour as 'ordinary evasions of customs-duties'.[5] To assume customs-frontiers between Attica and Boeotia or between Attica and

---

[1] Cf. Hasebroek, 122ff, where much other literature on the question is mentioned.

[2] μὴ χρῆσθαι τοῖς λιμέσι τοῖς ἐν τῇ Ἀθηναίων ἀρχῇ μηδὲ τῇ Ἀττικῇ ἀγορᾷ, Thuc. I, 67, 4; 139, 1; cf. also 144, 2; Plut. *Per*. 29, 4. It cannot be proved that Thucydides speaks of the harbours of the empire and the Attic market only because this was 'the most painful feature of the general exclusion' (Hasebroek, 124). He does not mention anything else because the essential phrase of the decree did not and could not mention anything else. Incidentally, I do not believe that there was a Megarian Decree before that of Perikles, as has been reconstructed from A.515ff.

[3] A.532ff. — Timokreon, frg. 5.

[4] A.818ff.   [5] Hasebroek, 123.

Megara, and to try to prove their existence from Aristophanes,[1] is an odd idea; actually they were technically impossible to maintain, in particular during the Archidamian War when Peloponnesian armies crossed the Megarian frontier in invading Attica. The searching of the Megarian could only take place, if at all, at the city-gate or in the market-place. The scene in all its grotesque exaggeration indicates that Athens tried to mark down Megarian traders and to confiscate Megarian goods. This certainly proved to be the safest, indeed the only, way of keeping all Megarians out of Attica. Therefore we interpret the decree as a prohibition of trade as well as of traffic. In fact, the whole distinction seems to be artificial. All prohibition of traffic involved that of trade, and if the inversion of this statement is not necessarily true it came to be so in practice: the only way to paralyse all trade with a place was to deny it all intercourse and traffic; for the ancient State had not the means and methods of modern trade-policy to achieve something similar by treaties or customs.

A second decree, that of Charinos, must be clearly distinguished from that of Perikles;[2] it threatened with death all Megarians who dared to cross into Attic territory. This step, which aggravated, but did not substantially alter, the situation, was taken after the outbreak of war when, of course, enemy traders had no longer any access to the Athenian harbours and market. The second decree is certainly incompatible with the plot of the *Acharnians*, but we know that, if the actual situation on the stage demands it, the poet never keeps to reality, and it is hardly necessary to see here a real contradiction of our other evidence.[3] The prohibition itself and the increased severity of the punishment are beyond doubt. Neither the first nor the second decree, however, should be accepted as 'normal manifestations of Greek alien law'.[4] When Perikles compared the decree with the Spartan *xenelasia*, the official expulsion of foreigners, possible at certain intervals

[1] Andreades, I, 139, 4; 295 (following Boeckh).

[2] Plut. *Per.* 30, 3. I cannot see any possibility of identifying the decree of Charinos with the original decree of Perikles, the less so since the new decree contained regulations concerning two annual inroads into the Megarid. That could not be said before the outbreak of the war. Plutarch, it is true, puts the two decrees chronologically too close together; cf. Ed. Meyer, *Gesch. d. Altert.*, IV, 313.

[3] Cf. Gomme, 98, 2.   [4] Hasebroek, 123.

and known only in Sparta, this was just as much a demagogic
move as his demand for autonomy for the Laconian perioeci.[1]
The great political importance of, and the general excitement
about, the Megarian Decree cannot be explained, except by
its peculiar and unique character which was contrary to all
law and custom.

The enemies of Athens are known to have made the can-
cellation of the Megarian Decree their chief demand in the
final negotiations before the outbreak of the war.[2] The decree
of Perikles, which was then alone in question, went against
the spirit of earlier treaties, especially that of 446.[3] It remains
open to discussion whether a particular paragraph of the former
settlement had been violated, perhaps one that provided for
free trade between both partners and their allies.[4] Plutarch,
however, did not think so when he wrote that 'common rights
and sworn oaths' were broken.[5] I believe the point is this.
Some decades later one could speak of the 'common peace'.
This phrase could not be used at that time, since all treaties
were only bilateral; the time had not yet come for a movement
towards Panhellenic unity. But the primary intention of every
truce and every treaty was to end war and so create a peace in
which trade and traffic were free.[6] It is a misunderstanding
of the very nature of the Polis, a State without formal sovereignty and based not on territory but on men, when a modern
scholar explains the matter by saying that 'each State in virtue
of its sovereignty had the legal right to close its territories
against foreigners'.[7] The prohibition of access to harbours
and market was in no sense a legal act, but a hostile action and
therefore the violation of a peace confirmed by oath and solemn
pledge. The Megarians and the Spartans in their speeches

---

[1] Thuc. I, 144, 2.   [2] Thuc. I, 140, 4.
[3] Thuc. I, 67, 4, and elsewhere.

[4] This is a much-defended view, contradicted by Hasebroek, 123f. He, on the
other hand, is mistaken in denying all formal and legal discrepancy; he speaks only
of Athens 'belying her principle of friendship to foreigners' and the like. Wade-
Gery insists (probably rightly) that Perikles' statement (Thuc. I, 144, 2) is true
that the former treaty did not expressly forbid either the ξενηλασία or an inter-
dict as in the Megarian Decree. Cf. also Gomme, *Hist. Comm.* I, 227 (on 67, 4).

[5] Plut. *Per.* 29, 4.

[6] Cf. H. Schaefer, *Staatsform u. Politik*, 57ff, who, however, overstresses the
point and makes several mistakes of interpretation.

[7] Hasebroek, 124. Also Lysias XXII, 14 does not say this.

make this point quite clear and leave no room for doubt that this is the correct interpretation.

Megara, situated in 'a hopeless patch of stones',[1] depended on supplies from the Black Sea and from Attica or the harbours of the Attic empire. The purpose of the decree was to intercept Megarian trade, to stop all supplies of food and raw materials and thus to force Megara politically to her knees. Since Megara was the doorway to Attica for any Spartan offensive, it is likely that by beating down Megara it was also intended to challenge Sparta and to bring about the war with an offensive stroke. The decree of Charinos proves, however, that the action was equally aimed at Megara herself. The reasons mentioned, such as the reception of runaway slaves or the cultivation of Eleusinian territory near the Megarian frontier, are out of all proportion to the harshness of the decree and are generally acknowledged to be mere pretexts. Athens wanted to turn on Megara, not in order to eliminate a competitor in trade and business, but to gain a political and strategic stronghold. She neither could nor did expect any economic advantages from her action. On the contrary, the complaints of Dikaiopolis make it very clear that the Athenians also suffered from the decree, not only because peace then 'disappeared',[2] but because of its immediate economic effects. The Megarians, of course, suffered much more, as we see from the poor pig-dealer in the *Acharnians*.

To sum up, we may say that a bold measure of political and legal violence was introduced, and one which resulted in economic hardship and misery, but that its ultimate purpose was political. Politics and economics were closely connected, but economic measures were pressed into the service of politics. More than merely economic matters was at stake, but a policy of trade and interference with trade loses nothing of its economic character because it is made to serve the policy of the State and not an economic purpose.

4

The several connections between politics and economics do not perhaps combine to give a clear and uniform picture. No doubt economic questions were important, and the majority

[1] T. R. Glover, *Greek Byways*, 53.   [2] P.614.

of the citizens were involved in them to an ever-increasing extent. The pre-eminence of politics, on the other hand, was at this time still beyond question;·but the policy of the State was no longer determined by the members of a wealthy and leisured upper class, the last heirs of a long and noble tradition who had served the State as officials and officers. 'The happy race of amateurs has come to grief.'[1] The leaders of Athenian policy now belonged to the working people, to those who did not own property, but worked for their living. In their persons the political and the economic ways of life met. Furthermore, apart from the tribute of the allies which ceased after 406 entirely, and the output of the silver mines which had decreased considerably, the State relied for most of its revenue on the harbour-duties, and military, cultural and social expenses were largely met from this source. Thus trade was a very great support to the State finances. It was even more important because it supplied Athens with corn and other essential goods, and there is not the slightest doubt that the State was compelled to protect it. Trade and sea-power mutually supported each other.

The financial position of the State, on its part, influenced domestic politics. The growing cleavage between rich and poor made the well-to-do the natural victims of a State in which the less wealthy had so strong a say. 'When the Council has sufficient money for the administration, they maintain justice; but when they suffer financial pressure, they are compelled to accept denunciations, to confiscate the property of the citizens, and to give way to those orators who make the worst proposals.'[2]

In such and similar circumstances it seems almost impossible that the government should have neglected, and public opinion despised, the economic side of life. In fact, as we have seen, the evidence of comedy confirms our doubts. It might be much more pleasant not to work, and to live on the State; but in spite of public payments which actually sufficed only for some of a citizen's needs, in spite also of the great number of metics and slaves who were active in one line of business or another, in Athens no less than in other Greek towns the main body of citizens was composed of those who in town and

[1] Glover, *l.c.*, 126, though with a somewhat different meaning.
[2] Lysias XXX, 22.

country earned their living by the work of their hands. The comic poets, and doubtless many others too, disapproved of the heliasts and ecclesiasts who lived so largely on public money. This disapproval was based on moral and economic grounds, not on a political, that is to say anti-democratic, attitude. Such citizens could be compared to olive-gatherers who worked for a daily wage, or to hodmen, that is, to men whose activities came fairly low down in the social scale.[1] We see that there were types of labour which were despised; there were vocations which had a low reputation socially, but most of the citizens certainly did not regard sitting in court or going to the assembly in this light. Prejudices against, and aversion from, work have always existed, even more in the happy countries which border on the Mediterranean than in other regions. But there was no contempt for labour in general, especially not for manual labour; the reputation of most of the craftsmen stood much higher than that of the retail-trader. The upper and lower middle-classes had the same desire for money, and money could not be earned if they did not work. On such foundations the economic life of Athens as a whole was prospering and, time and again, overcame the vacillations and vicissitudes of an unstable world.

It is true that, because the democratic State needed a great number of men to keep public life and government going, ideas and feelings of the kind mentioned did actually find public support. From the time of Solon wise statesmen had tried to check them by the influence of law and custom, but they were only partly successful. Aristocratic traditions and popular indolence combined to hold labour in a certain contempt, until the middle classes began to take the lead in politics. This happened during the fifth century, and with it the reputation of labour rose. Afterwards there came a reaction, but one which was confined to a small circle, close and narrow in its social outlook, though in other respects it was most important. The fourth-century philosophers took a step backwards, and by creating ideal forms of the State, full of beauty and deeper meaning, they determined the general judgment on the Greeks down to the present day. With these philosophers the contempt for manual labour, partly resulting from their deliberate idealization of a Spartan kind of State, became

[1] W.712, E.310.

the essential factor in a general programme of political and social life. In reality, however, the people never made the claim to a *dolce far niente*, however honourable and important that might be thought (nor would they have been allowed to).[1] The public payments were necessary both politically and economically, but their social effects, though they increased during the fourth century, have been much exaggerated by modern scholars. Charity in ancient Athens, though it may have begun at home, did not go very far. The children of those killed in war were provided for, and invalids got a small pension.[2] A typical figure is the invalid whom Lysias describes as making a living by some sort of retail-trade, 'a cheerful and witty cockney and possibly a rogue', a true comic character.[3] He is the type of citizen who stakes out his claim to State support, but at the same time tries to earn his living by work of his own. In fact, the ordinary citizen with his desire and ability to earn his livelihood was a decisive factor in bridging the gulf between the citizen of old, who was chiefly a political being, and the demands of a new age, in which the State not only paid and fed part of its citizen body, but also depended on the economic activity of its citizens.

The ideal of the average little citizen of comedy is by no means the ideal of a laborious and hard-working life. Few Greeks, hardly Hesiod himself, had any conception of labour as a moral ideal and a moral programme; on the other hand, they did consider the will to earn money and make a fair profit justified, though they did not approve of certain methods used by fraudulent innkeepers and retailers. Labour in comedy is not a disgrace, but neither is it a thing to be desired; it is simply a necessity, and acknowledged as a necessity, both because of the eternal need for one's daily bread, and because audience as well as poet, even Aristophanes for all his conservatism, belonged and paid tribute to an age which, in an ever-increasing degree, was ruled by an economic attitude of mind.

Not even then, however, did economics overrule the moral

[1] Cf. F. Oertel, *Klassenkampf, Sozialismus und organischer Staat im alten Griechenland* (1942), 24.

[2] An article by A. A. Esser on this subject (*Das Gymnasium*, LII, 1941) was inaccessible to me.

[3] Lysias XXIV. Quotation from Webster, *Greek Art and Literature*, 176. The man looks on himself as a kind of actor in a comedy (§18).

aspects of life. It was, in fact, the other way round. In the very plight of everyday life, and even among the lower classes, the ideal was not so much to become rich as to lead a good life, and it seemed the duty of the State to provide for this. That is why the number of those who were living on the State steadily increased. The ideal of a good life naturally varied according to social and individual circumstances. 'The Greeks never took kindly to wage-earning.'[1] One of the reasons for this was that they hated to be personally dependent on an employer, unless it was the State itself, that is to say, the body of citizens of which each one was a member. The wishful planning of man's good life culminated in the Utopian pictures of an ideal State, and even the philosophers realized that the community had to provide the economic foundations for such a life.

The true background of all this is the very nature of the Greeks, their vigour and vitality as well as their indolence and modesty, in short their immense capacity to live the 'good life', for which comedy is not the meanest witness. In a world of which they knew the sombre no less than the bright side the Greeks lived a full and intense life. It was not laborious nor always honest, and instead of serving the community the citizens had begun to live on it; but in their economic as well as in their political life they always tended to make the most of things.

---

[1] Sir A. Zimmern, *Solon and Croesus*, 159.

CHAPTER XIII

THE PEOPLE AND THE STATE

I

In the previous chapters we have seen the people of Athens in the varied and manifold aspects of their life. Origin, social position, vocation, property, intellectual standing, religious beliefs and economic aims — these things created both the individual citizen and the divisions of the population. We must not, however, forget the unity which lies behind this variety, the co-ordinating forces behind those which divide. The people, in fact, were united in the State, a State whose sovereign power was vested in the people. This sovereignty, so far as the expression is justified, was naturally more apparent in politics than in economics. We are not concerned with questions of political institutions and constitutions, but the aspect of democracy as the rule of the sovereign people is also essential to our investigation. The people ruled, because a constitution, though unwritten and informal, had made it sovereign, and it therefore controlled legislation and executive. These are well-known facts, but they do not suffice for our purpose. We are seeking to discover the social basis and effects of Athenian politics, the social features of the demo-cratic State.

Much of this has been mentioned before in connection with individual points which we need not recapitulate. Nor do we propose to discuss such questions as whether the name of democracy can rightly be applied to a State in which large and important parts of the population had no share in the rights of citizenship. What we have already said about metics and slaves should have made it clear that to put the question thus (and this is often done) is to miss the true nature of the Greek State. Let us repeat: the Athenian State was called neither 'the Re-public of Athens' (like the *res publica Romana*) nor was it called 'Attica' (like a modern territorial State), but 'the Athenians'. The citizens, they and they alone, made up the State which was embodied in the person and idea of Demos, the people. The question of equality was therefore frequently discussed.

The democratic Polis was never fully able to answer the challenge of the conflict between the natural inequality of man and the pretended equality of its citizens.[1]

We may remember the general and, so to speak, symbolic caricatures of the people, given in the figure of the old, doddering master of the *Knights*[2] or in the mad passion for administering justice in the *Wasps*, a passion declared to be an essential and typical feature of the citizen body. We recall these things, not in order to emphasize their reality, but to make clear, once again, the broadmindedness of the Athenians in allowing themselves to be mocked and derided. Dionysos looks for parricides and perjurers among the spectators, the Just Logos sees there only paederasts.[3] The comic poet, just as he often praises too generously, often blames too severely, but always attacks actual faults. On the whole, as we have seen, there is reflected, even in caricature, the real people both in its best and in its worst qualities. This people of sunburnt men, though their vitality and energy were certainly unique, were infected with widespread social diseases, diseases such as the love of gambling, drunkenness and parasitism, or delight, whether in the market-place or in the barber's shop, in gossip and idle chatter, and many others.[4] There were diseases in the political sphere as well.

The comic poets satirize various vices and absurdities in democracy, for instance the honorary decrees, by moving which many citizens sought to win the favour of persons or groups of importance, or the people's passion for change and for the indiscriminate passing of laws: the *nomoi* 'resembled those filmy webs that the spider spins on the walls', and they changed so frequently that after three months one could no longer recognize them.[5] It was usual for the assembly to make its decisions and to cancel them again instantly.[6] Stupid accusations were piled up against such selfless and blameless politicians as Nikias and his like.[7] Naturally, there was very little feeling that an official was someone superior. We need only

---

[1] Typical discussions, e.g., in Eur. *Hek.* 306ff, *Hik.* 406ff, 410ff, 433ff, *Phoin.* 501f, 535ff, *frg.* 1048.

[2] See especially K.40ff.   [3] F.274ff, C.1096ff.

[4] E.63f; cf. Thuc. I, 70. — Diseases: W.71ff. — Gossip: Th.578. — B.300, 1439ff, Plat. 135.

[5] K.267f. — E.577ff, 586f. — Plat. 22, 220.   [6] E.797f.

[7] Eupolis 181, Telekleid. 41, Plat. 185.

think of Dikaiopolis' contempt for the prytanes; they like other officials were nominated by lot, 'the child of chance', and were ordinary fellow citizens, though they themselves might be pompous men feeling superior to the people.[1] To the comedians even the position of those elected to their offices did not amount to much; in the complex process of election the nomination and rejection could follow one another, though sometimes lead to the election of the original candidates.[2] Of the election of the higher officers, above all the *strategoi*, but also the *hipparchoi* and *taxiarchoi*, especially in war-time one of the most important events in the democracy, the comedian says 'three cuckoos have elected Lamachos'; he was at that time probably a taxiarch, but be that as it may, it is clear that both Lamachos and the election were equally derided.[3] Frequently comedy makes fun of the general mistrust shown by democracy towards officials whom the people had themselves elected, or of the citizens' fear of tyranny and conspiracy: 'How you see in everything tyranny and conspirators, when somebody brings in a charge whether large or small! I had not heard that word ['tyranny'] for the last fifty years; now it has become much more common than salt fish.'[4] In comedy a prize could even be offered for the killing of dead tyrants, and people had to suffer for the alleged sins of their ancestors.[5] The comedians ridiculed the outdated hatred of tyranny, which in all debates about State and constitution still took a central position; in tragedy we find the problem discussed repeatedly and seriously.[6] The privilege of comedy was to see, and to laugh at, the weaknesses of the idolized democracy. We should, for example, like to know whether the comedian who called ostracism 'a whip of potter's clay' wished to characterize it as an efficient and dangerous weapon or one which had been blunted; the latter is more likely, as it gives the phrase a comic double-meaning.[7] All the helplessness of democracy, even of the more moderate type, is depicted in the character of the *proboulos*,

---

[1] A.23ff, 40ff. — Eur. *frg.* 989. — *Andr.* 699f.

[2] Archipp. 14.   [3] A.598.

[4] W.487ff. Other relevant passages: K.257, 452, 475ff, W.345, 417, 463ff, 498, 506f, 953, B.1583ff, L.616ff. See also above, p. 110.

[5] B.1074ff. — K.445ff.

[6] To mention a few outstanding examples from Euripides: *Med.* 119ff, *Herakl.* 423f, *Hik.* 403ff, 410ff, 429ff, *Tro.* 424ff, *Phoin.* 499ff, 528ff.

[7] adesp. 33.

whose mind works on the old traditional lines and who is entirely at a loss in an unexpected situation.[1]

The impression, however, that comedy attacks democracy is misleading as it would be misleading in the case of Thucydides. He puts into the mouth of the democratic demagogue Kleon what may be called his sharpest criticism of Perikles' ideal picture of the working of democracy.[2] With Perikles, at least between 446 and 431, success had succeeded; afterwards things were very different. It is only natural that many Athenians, after they had lost Perikles' leadership, realized that democracy was lacking in efficiency, particularly during the war.[3] Neither Euripides who was a loyal democrat as far as he at all adhered to any party views, nor Thucydides who admired Perikles and hated Kleon, but equally despised the revolutionaries of 411, were oligarchs. It was, as we have emphasized before, in the very nature of political comedy to be 'against the government', but not one of the comic poets, as far as we know, was a mere party man, not one of them belonged to the 'oligarchs' as did, for instance, the author of that frequently mentioned pamphlet known as the Pseudo-Xenophon.[4] Kratinos attacked even the 'tyranny' of Perikles

---

[1] L.403ff. Cf. Thuc. VIII, 1, 3. Arist. *Ath. pol.* 29, 2, 5.

[2] Thuc. III, 37.   [3] Cf. Eur. *Andr.* 479ff.

[4] Are we justified in speaking of political parties at Athens? Certainly not in the modern sense of organizations which demand membership and the like. Since Themistokles, by the creation of the fleet, had introduced the lower classes into politics, the division had grown between those who favoured a gradual restriction of political rights, and those who pleaded for complete equality and thus for the rule of the many. There were, after all, 'oligarchs' and what we call 'democrats', both of them 'parties' in the political, though not in any legal, sense. A surprising example of what seems to be the outcome of organized party politics has been provided by the discovery of 'prefabricated' ostraka which were probably to be distributed among the voters (O. Broneer, *Hesperia*, VII, 1938, 228ff). They all bear the name of Themistokles, and the device must be therefore due to his opponents. The date, of course, is not certain, but the 'seventies are a likely guess. It seems that these ostraka were never actually used; thus they were probably left over from an ostracism which may have been the one by which Themistokles was banned, or even an earlier one. (Prof. Gomme has convinced me that I was too definite on this in *AJP.* LXIX, 162.) It is a puzzling story which we cannot fully disentangle; but behind it, there must have been some form of organization, if not a party, at least a *hetairia*. The concentration of the ecclesiasts by Thoukydides, son of Melesias, however, was clearly the result of organized party-politics, and Plut. *Per.* 11 dates from that event — very late indeed — the full division into political parties. Cf. also Wade-Gery, *JHS.* LII (1932), 208.

in the name of democracy.[1]   In his *Nomoi* the chorus of the
Laws appear as old and decrepit men; it seems that Kratinos
tried to preach a return to the neglected laws of Drakon and
Solon.[2]   The lordly Poseidon, horrified at the way in which
the Triballian god wears his coat, laments: 'O democracy,
where do you lead us in the end, if the gods have elected such
a dolt!'[3]   The satire is aimed at the aristocratic opponent of
democracy as much as at democracy itself and its methods of
election.

These various attacks are of an incidental kind.   The main
offensive is launched against the demagogues, 'who swear
upon the speaker's stone', those 'sellers' of low origin who
break with the old traditions — Eukrates, Lysikles, Kleon,
and their like.[4]   They are the terror equally of rich and poor.[5]
Until their old age they are led on by the desire for public
money.[6]   According to the view of comedy, which is put most
vigorously and impressively in the *Birds*, the social change in
the leadership of the State involved a change in the moral
meaning of all service to the State.   Even so, we may doubt
whether it was justifiable to make the 'demagogues' alone responsible for the decline of the public mind. At any rate, among
the demagogues were men of very different political colour.

The public legal payments, which we have mentioned
frequently and which we know to have been a heavy burden on
the finances of the State, might have proved a means of
reducing the illegal attempts to make money out of the State.
But we get the impression that this was not so.   Too many
citizens were dissatisfied with the modest earnings represented
by the juror's fees, the *diobelia* and the *theorikon*, or later by
the payment of officials and ecclesiasts.   All these payments
and also the distribution of corn were for the majority of citizens merely an additional source of income.   They tried to
make money from the State by all means, and there were the
most varied ways of doing so.   Many citizens registered at
court under several 'letters' — that is to say, with different
sections indicated by letters — in order to sit in more than
one court during the day and thus to get more than a normal
one day's payment, or at least to be sure of it if a particular

---

[1] Kratinos 240, 38 P a, 18f.   [2] Kratinos 127, cf. 274.
[3] B.157of.   [4] adesp. 667. — K.129 ff.
[5] K.223f.   [6] adesp. II (parody of Sophokles).

section did not sit.[1] Even men suffering from fever or illness
went to court, though they were certainly not really fit to act.[2]
We have referred to the importance of the meals which followed public sacrifices; meat was scarce and expensive, so the
meat of the victims was much in demand.[3] Even the public
meals in the prytaneion, formerly a rarely awarded honour,
came to have an economic value which many a man made the
most of, and might even sell or buy; the same is said of the
prohedria, though in both cases there may be some comic
exaggeration.[4] Anyhow, times had changed since the days
when nobody made money from public service and everybody
brought his modest portion of food and drink with him.[5]
Now the citizens lived on the public treasure which lay in
Athena's temple, and from which the various fees were paid;
public money served private gain.[6] The thing to do was not
to give but to take, a maxim which in the years after 400 could
even be regarded as traditional and 'deriving from our fathers'.[7]
It remains, however, doubtful (we have mentioned this before
and shall mention it again) how many of the citizens were, in
fact, guilty of such practices, though it is clear that, whatever
their number, many of those who were unwilling to work for
their living were no longer the old easy-going type of citizens,
but men whose chief aim was to make money.

The State sometimes paid out official fees on a higher scale
than the ordinary payments; but often legal and illegal methods
were hard to distinguish. Thus ambassadors received substantial travelling allowances, and might be in no hurry to get home;
moreover they might be bribed by the Persian king.[8] Certain
offices, high or low, afforded ample opportunity for private profit
— for instance, the post of inspector (*episkopos*) of the allies, or
that of contractor for providing supplies for the troops, or that
of a customs official.[9] Competition for a lucrative office could

---

[1] Pl.1166f.   [2] W.813.   [3] Cf. K.410, 655ff, W.654; above, p. 258f.

[4] K.28off, 575f. — An early example is an epigram against Xanthippos found
on an ostrakon and explained by O. Broneer, *AJA.* LII (1948), 341ff.
Xanthippos is denounced as an 'accursed cheat who did violence to the
Prytaneion', apparently because he misused the privilege of having free meals
at the expense of the State. For other explanations see E. Schweigert, *AJA.*
LIII (1949), 266ff, and A. Wilhelm, *Anz. Akad. Wien* 1949, 237ff. They both
take πρυτάνειον as a gen. plur. No definite solution has yet been found.

[5] E.303ff.   [6] L.624f. — E.206f.   [7] E.778f.

[8] A.53, 65ff, 192, 600ff, W.1271ff. — Plat. 119.

[9] B.1111f, Kratinos 38 P, 32. — B.1021ff; W.556f; K.248, F.362ff.

be degraded into a bargain between certain coteries, and people frequently voted without knowing for whom they gave their vote.[1]   There is no doubt that the political leaders occasionally knew very well how to secure their profits; especially in war one man would become powerful and overbearing, while another would be out for his own gains, regardless of the public weal.[2]   The ordinary citizen too could make extra money by proposing a motion in the assembly or as a heliast; it is said to have been almost usual for the jurymen to blackmail the officials when they had to render their accounts.[3] There was also a substantial payment to the prosecutor in cases of public confiscations.[4]   Cases of successful juggling with public funds were well known, and they did not always meet with punishment.[5]   We must, however, not forget that accusations of private profiteering were very common and often without foundation.   The torrent of embezzlement, bribery and blackmail mentioned in comedy must not be taken too literally.[6]   'Kleon the thief', for instance, who is said to have scooped up public money in both hands like soup, kept a careful eye on the tribute of the allies, not in order to make a profit for himself, but because the treasury was empty; and the much-abused Kleophon died a pauper.[7]   Nevertheless, corruption was frequent enough.   What Eupolis said of Themistokles was valid for many of the politicians: 'A clever man, unable to restrain his hand.'[8]

Worst of those who earned their living by exploiting the democratic State and system were the sycophants.[9]   Originally the word ('fig-sayers') may have indicated someone who denounced a man for trading in forbidden goods (why 'figs', we do not know), but it had become a name for any type of informer whose activities made all free talk impossible.[10]

---

[1] L.574ff. — Eupolis 40 P, 31.
[2] K.1127f. — Eur. *Hik.* 234ff.
[3] Lysias XIII, 72. — A.938f, K.258f, 824f, W.102.
[4] δημιόπρατα, K.103, W.659.
[5] C.351ff, Th.811ff.
[6] See above, p. 239.
[7] W.759, K.826f. — K.312f. — Lysias XIX, 48.
[8] Eupolis 13 D.
[9] Cf. the sound description of the whole phenomenon in R. J. Bonner and G. Smith, *Administration of Justice*, II, 39ff, 291f.
[10] adesp. 1186. — A.558f.

Informing went hand in hand with false testimony, bribery
and blackmail no less than the embezzlement of public funds.[1]
The sycophant was 'a happy compound of the common barra-
tor, informer, pettifogger, busybody, rogue, liar and slanderer'.[2]
Naturally he had to thrust his nose into everybody's business;
he was a parasite and busybody (*polypragmon*) of the worst
kind.[3] The peasant's ideal of a quiet and unlaborious life,
certainly not a very high ideal, is in the sycophant's opinion
equivalent to living like cattle.[4] War increased the sycophant's
chances. Then he tried to impute to every possible individual,
especially to foreigners, relations with the enemy, and he
invented the most fantastic tales, which he used for blackmail.[5]
So the profession became lucrative, an easier method than
work.[6] Doro, 'my Lady Bribery of the fig-sandals', and other
heroines of similar type, such as Dexo, the 'Receiving-Goddess',
were invented as the special deities of the sycophants.[7]

During the war and even more so afterwards, but, in fact,
ever since the internal rivalry between the democrats and
oligarchs had been intensified, these men came to be a real
plague.[8] Their number must have been considerable. A
picture of the scandalous activities of such a 'prosecutor' is
given by Andokides in his speech on the mysteries.[9] Another
well-known case was that of Nikias' brother whom persecution
by the sycophants drove into voluntary exile.[10] The sycophants
were frequently young men, and the profession could be
hereditary in a family.[11] The comedians attack men of this
type in the strongest possible terms: they are scorpions and
monsters such as appear in nightmares.[12] The *agoranomoi* are
to expel these rogues from the market-place, which was a step
hardly possible except in comedy; nevertheless the suggestion
is significant.[13] Action by the State against the sycophants was

---

[1] E.561f, Telekl. 41, cf. Isokr. XVIII, 9f. — frg. 219, Plat. 14,   Metagenes
11, cf. Antiphon VI. 42.

[2] Smith, *Dict. of Greek and Roman Antiqu.*[3], s. sycophantes.

[3] B.285. — W.1040f, Pl.906ff, 913, Kratinos 27 D = adesp. 841. The subject
is treated more extensively in *JHS.* LXVII (1947), especially 54ff.

[4] Pl.921f.   [5] A.818ff, 910ff, 920ff, K.278f, B.1431.

[6] Pl.30f, cf. Xen. *mem.* II, 9, 5; 8.

[7] Kratinos 69, cf. K.529. — Kratinos 401.

[8] Lysias XXV, 19, VII, 1. — adesp. 615.   [9] Andok. I.

[10] Lysias XVIII, 9.   [11] B.1431, 1452.

[12] Eupolis 231, W.1036ff.   [13] A.723ff, 824f.

essential. Lucky were those countries in which such people did not exist, but at a later date the poet has to admit that all Greeks suffered from this plague.[1]

In a State in which there was no permanent public prosecutor[2] it was the necessary and proper duty of every citizen to guard the public interest by going to law. In a sense the sycophants were inevitable. But since the majority of the prosecutors were unscrupulous informers rather than honest and patriotic citizens, the whole thing became an evil, tolerated indeed, but therefore still more dangerous. The sycophant always pretended to be a 'public benefactor', a servant of the people and a patriot.[3] It might often have been difficult to distinguish between truth and falsehood. The great part played by sycophants was by no means entirely due to their own lack of morals; it was caused by defects in the general political conditions. The frequently described distrust by democracy of its own citizens contrasted strangely, and was in fact inconsistent, with the freedom which the State allowed the individual citizen and which in an age of 'enlightenment' and dissolution might easily become complete lack of restraint and discipline. No less important was the growing economic and social tension, and the increasing predominance of the economic factor. The poor became aggressive. Insecurity of life and property, brawls and robberies in the streets — all this a legacy of the war and the rule of the Thirty — were a common feature.[4] Plundering the rich became not only the purpose of avaricious individuals; to offer the chance of it to the masses in court and assembly was a favourite item in the demagogues' domestic policy, and the sycophants were the middlemen who by false denunciations provided the victims. The soil was prepared in which the weed grew and flourished. The whole situation is reflected in a significant, though somewhat complex, metaphor:[5] when one day rich and poor wash each other in the public baths (that is to say, support and help each other instead of thinking each of himself only), on that day no one will any longer need, if that is the right explanation, those sponges, soaked full, as it were, with the property of others.

Sycophantism would never have grown so rank, if the

---

[1] A.904f. — Pl.877ff.   [2] Cf. Pl.916ff.
[3] Pl.899ff.   [4] See above, p. 244, and Lysias III.   [5] frg. 55.

Athenian courts had not been open to every kind of personal influence, and if they had not been of such an overwhelming general importance. 'Litigation was the handmaiden of politics.'[1] Athens was not Athens if no jurymen were seen in session.[2] In the country alone the 'seedlings of non-heliasts' might still be found.[3] The courts were a kind of spectacle where men scrambled for the best seats.[4] The demoralization of jurymen and prosecutors, of heliasts and sycophants, was inter-dependent. One of the chief reasons for this demoralization was the fact that so many of the poor, especially old men, sat in court.[5] It led to the worst results that they took the greatest delight in exercising their wide powers, and at the same time were compelled to try to make some extra money.[6] Chiefly for this reason the old men liked 'to bite with the voting stone', and ordinary citizens became 'stinging swarms of wasps'.[7] Sometimes they would listen to a recital by an acquitted flute-player or actor, but on the whole they brought along the necessary 'ration' of anger, and were cruel and keen to persecute.[8] The allies were made to suffer even more than others, and their dependence gave Athenian jurymen the feeling of 'rule over Hellas'[9] — naturally enough, for the courts to which the allies had to bring their cases provided opportunities for interference in their internal affairs and, above all, for an exercise of power in various ways over the subject States of the empire.[10] Many unjust verdicts were given for the sake of shameful gain.[11] The 'bazaar of lawsuits', the only office not compelled to render accounts, damaged law and justice to such an extent that more and more they became, as it were, objects of business transactions.[12]

What is true of the jurymen is also true of the parties to a suit. The Athenians 'were the best of all Greeks in depositing

---

[1] Bonner and Smith, *l.c.*, 43.   [2] C.207f, cf. frg. 210.

[3] B.109ff, adesp. 382.   [4] W.89f.

[5] K.1359f, W.195, 223f, 303ff, 540f, 551, 813, L.380.

[6] e.g., W.552ff, Ps.-Xen. I, 18.   [7] A.375f, W.1102ff.

[8] W.579ff. — W.242f. — K.347, 367, 443f, W. *passim.*   [9] W.577.

[10] See above, p. 157f, and Gomme, *Hist. Comm.* I, 242.

[11] Kratinos 19 D.

[12] δεῖγμα τῶν δικῶν, K.979. — In W.587 the position of a juryman is called ἀρχή as often — with greater justification — the membership of the βουλή; it was not an ἀρχή in the strict sense of the word.

the *parastasis*', that is the drachma which the litigants had to pay at the beginning of the pleading.[1] The spirit of Athenian litigation is depicted in many passages of comedy. 'If you accuse an unjust man, twelve parasites will bear witness for the opposite party.'[2] If a man had been thrashed, he took a witness, who of course had not been present at the incident, and sued for damages.[3] In some cases, for example when a search for stolen goods was made or when an adulterer was caught red-handed, a man could take the law into his own hands;[4] but generally he either went to court or used the opportunity to make some money by blackmail. One lawsuit followed another, and the comedian who warned the citizens and especially the sycophants 'to stop the suits that were eating one another' was more than justified.[5]

These are some of the characteristic methods, most of them well known, by which democracy was exploited by the citizens. Political life apparently depended to a large extent on economic needs and purposes, but its faults were of its own making, too.

2

When Lamachos has to put up with almost too much heckling from Dikaiopolis because of his payment, he exclaims:[6] 'O democracy, can this be borne?' In fact, being an officer, he is entitled to his pay, but his antagonist is the ordinary citizen who envies the officers and ambassadors their higher income, even though it is legal, as well as their other advantages.[7] Lamachos, though hardly a convinced democrat, appeals to the principles of democracy. One of these principles at that time was that every citizen should be entitled and able to live on the State. A generation later thirty thousand citizens will receive 'their meals' from Praxagora's State, a number, most probably, roughly equal to the actual number of citizens,[8] and so of course not the same as the number of those who lived chiefly on the State. The number of these, though much smaller, was still considerable, and the dangers and

---

[1] adesp. 778.   [2] frg. 437.   [3] C.495f.
[4] C.499, 1083.   [5] Telekl. 2.   [6] A.618.
[7] A.607ff, cf. above, p. 229, n. 6.
[8] E.1132f. Cf. Gomme, *The Population of Athens*, 26. Ehrenberg, *The Greek State* (1960), 32f.

weaknesses of such a system are obvious and have often been described. The true facts, however, do not correspond with the view usually held, and we must realize that comedy like other sources tends to give us only one side of the picture. Not one of the important poets or writers of the time came forward to defend the post-Periclean democracy. Even the rejuvenated and glorified Demos in the closing scenes of the *Knights*, though interesting especially as an anticipation of the actual cult of Demos,[1] has no political significance except for the desire to get 'back to the good old times',[2] and he is only one of many to testify to the general tendency, often expressed in comedy, to look back longingly for a better State and better statesmen. Euripides when he praises his mythical democracy of the days of Theseus or his son, is a weak advocate against such powerful and hostile critics as Thucydides and Aristophanes, to say nothing of Plato.[3]

Nevertheless, even allowing for this bias in our evidence, we cannot go so far as to deny the general decline of Athenian politics. Obviously, good reasons lie behind the verdict of those writers. If in some respects the usual view may perhaps be corrected, it can only be done by emphasizing those factors which in part compensated for the decline of politics by an improvement in other matters. The improvement in the economic conditions was noted in the last chapter.

The change in the political situation was chiefly due to a change within a few decades in the political attitude of the people. At one time Athens had been proud of having set up the demos as ruler in every State, and the Athenian demos being the 'monarch' of all Greece; the Attic juryman felt that he held a truly 'kingly' position or *basileia*, which is the name of the divine wife of Peithetairos.[4] In her was embodied the whole scheme of government and politics, both conservative and democratic: she protected all the good elements in political life, 'good counsel' and 'good laws', as well as 'the dockyards, public abuse, the fiscal officials and the public payments'.[5] The decline of political power, on the other hand, the detach-

[1] Cf. H. Kleinknecht, *Hermes* 74 (1939), 58ff.
[2] K.1387, cf. 1325ff.
[3] e.g., Eur. *Herakl.* 389ff, *Hik.* 403ff, 429ff.
[4] A.642, K.1330. — W.546, 549. — B.1634, 1687, 1730, 1753.
[5] B.1538ff.

ment of the individual from traditional bonds, the growing importance of the economic factor — all these weakened the public-spiritedness and the political will of the people. 'Any country in which a man gets on well is his fatherland':[1] the attitude here expressed spread and gradually undermined the citizen's normal, and still predominant, attachment to his State.

The general development found, as a matter of course, its strongest expression in the assembly where the people exercised their political rights most clearly, and where the overwhelming power of the people in controlling market, harbours, and pnyx rendered politically impotent the council, the strategoi, and those prominent citizens who were honoured in the prytaneion.[2] But the sheep were not always prepared to follow their bell-wether and to fill the seats in the assembly; only the prytanes might compete for the best seats.[3] The people, instead of going to the pnyx, preferred to loiter in the market-place where the latest news was to be heard and where most of them had their business. The harsh barrack-yard voice of the herald was displeasing, and the purpose of the 'red rope', to drive the people into the assembly, was rarely achieved.[4] Not before payment of the ecclesiasts was introduced, and subsequently increased from one to three obols a day, did the mass of the people rush again to the assembly, which then once more became a noisy and tumultuous crowd.[5] It could be said of the assembly no less than of the Persian king that it existed 'thanks only to money'.[6]

The fundamental and precious principle of the democratic assembly was *parrhesia* or *isegoria*, free and equal right of speech.[7] It was the foundation of that Golden Age which Eupolis ironically found realized under the rule of Kleon.[8] It was a commonplace to see the combination of freedom and *parrhesia* as the true symbol of Athens.[9] And yet, people's opinions on the value of free speech differed. While some regarded it as 'the most sensible adviser', others thought that

---

[1] Pl.1151, cf. frg. 58 D. See above, p. 147.
[2] K.164ff.   [3] W.31ff. — A.19ff, 25f, 40ff.
[4] A.54, and elsewhere. — A.22, E.378, Plat. 6 D.
[5] E.183ff, 289ff, 380ff, Pl.329f. — E.519, adesp. 45 D.
[6] Pl.170f.   [7] Th.540f, Eupolis 291.
[8] Eupolis 276ff, in particular 290-2.
[9] Eur. *Hipp.* 421ff, *Herakl.* 62, 113, 181f, *Hik.* 438ff, *Ion* 670ff, *frg.* 737.

it gave to every *poneros* a chance to speak, even to an uneducated foreigner or half-foreigner who had become a citizen.[1] The implications of comedy as well as tragedy are that this meant the 'common' man not only in a social, but also in a moral sense.

Such views are, of course, biased, and to arrive at the truth we must see how the principle of *parrhesia* worked in practice. As a rule the people 'listened with open mouth' to whoever spoke, 'gaping up exactly like roasting shell-fish on the coals'.[2] The ordinary citizen had no opinion of his own, but followed those pronounced by the speakers, and probably often the one proclaimed last.[3] The great majority of the people did not use their right of free speech, as we have said before, and this is especially true of the peasants. In general only a few of the better orators rose to speak, usually one 'who hung about the town and was skilled in speech.'[4] The *agon* of the women to find out which of them was the best speaker[5] is a reflection of the fact that it was usually only the better speakers who presented their views in the assembly, and the best speaker is he whose motions are most frequently passed.[6] Oratory was quickly becoming an art, and people began to realize its advantages, to know something of its technique and to enjoy a clever 'battle of words'.[7] The Greeks had always done so, but now they had become something like experts. The people crowded to the place where the speakers could be heard well, and liked to discuss the good points of a speech: the speaker might be said to have spoken very strongly, to have tested all methods, weighed everything and wisely discovered clever and well-chosen arguments.[8] Applause and interruptions were frequent in the assembly, certainly often organized by one or the other of the political factions.[9] Although the principle of

---

[1] adesp. 355-6. — K.335f. — Eur. *Or.* 902ff.
[2] K.752ff, 1118ff, P.635, frg. 68.   [3] adesp. 12 (b) D = 45 P (a).
[4] Eur. *Ba.* 717.   [5] Th.305ff, cf. E.130ff.   [6] C.430ff.
[7] ἀμίλλα (or ἀγὼν) λόγων, e.g., Eur. *Med.* 546, *Andr.* 234, *Hik.* 427f, 465, *Tro.* 907, *Phoin.* 588, *frg.* 189.
[8] Th.292f, E.86f, 588f. — Th.434ff.
[9] Cf. A.37ff, and the whole behaviour of Dikaiopolis in the assembly; K.651, 666, E.213, 399ff, 431ff. — Many of the passages in the text refer to the women at the Thesmophoria, but their assembly — and even more so the dress-rehearsal in the *Ekklesiazousai* — are explicitly copies of the real thing, the Athenian ἐκκλησία (Th.277, 301, 328).

free speech was always upheld, *parrhesia* was largely confined to the 'orators'.

It is evident that the term 'the orators', who were usually identical with those who proposed motions in the assembly, became a fixed expression, indicating a definite group of people.[1] They stood under the protection of Zeus Agoraios, and were thought of as rivals in some sort of competition the victor in which was rewarded with a wreath.[2] In Euripides' *Hekabe* even the sons of Theseus appear as 'orators of opposing speeches', debating the sacrifice of Polyxena.[3] Because of such competition the orator could be compared to a runner or a racing horse; the orators started from the same starting-line, and the mass of the people were simply spectators.[4] Kleon's reproof of the assembly is characteristic: 'In a word, you are in thrall to the pleasures of the ear, and sit like an audience attending a performance of sophists, but very unlike counsellors of the State.'[5] It is most significant that Thucydides puts these words into the mouth of the despised Kleon. It not only proves that Kleon did, in fact, use such words, it also goes to prove the insight of both historian and politician and supports the truth of the observation they make. We find the same idea in a phrase of one of the comedians, who calls the Athenians, the people famous for Athena's owls: 'eared owls, they alone among the Greeks'.[6] In another fragment[7] we are told that people accepted a bad proposal because they believed the speaker of the moment; later, when some new experience taught them better, they blamed the assembly of which they had been members themselves.

The Greeks realized to the full the power of oratory and the dangers of persuasion by mere words. Of all skill and learning it was *Peitho*, or Persuasion, alone that was 'a tyrant for men'; 'there is no other temple of Peitho than speech, and her altar is in man's nature'.[8] Good orators naturally acquired

[1] K.1350, cf. Lysias XII, 72. — A.38, K.425, Th.382, E.244. frg. 198, 4, Eupolis 94, 3; cf. Thuc. VIII, 1, 1.

[2] K.499f. — A.626, K.501f. The award of a wreath is perhaps only an allusion to the fact that every citizen wore a wreath when he spoke; B.463, Th. 380, E.131, 148, 163, 171, Eupolis 21 D.

[3] δισσῶν μύθων ῥήτορες, Eur. *Hek.* 124ff.

[4] C.430, Eupolis 94. — ἀπὸ βαλβίδων, K.1159, W.548.

[5] Thuc. III, 38, 7.   [6] adesp. 47.

[7] adesp. 12(b) D = 45P(a).   [8] Eur. *Hek.* 814ff, *frg.* 170.

great influence over the people, as Perikles did who, it is said, 'carried a thunderbolt in his tongue' and outpaced all other speakers by many lengths.[1] He lived on in public memory as the orator even more clearly than as the statesman and active politician.[2] 'Is there any other orator worth mentioning?' is a question asked in Eupolis' *Demoi*.[3] The critics saw him from the same angle: when the construction of the Long Walls proceeded only slowly, Perikles was said 'to be carrying on with words, but not to be moving anything by deeds'.[4] The 'fiery' Kleon also was a vigorous speaker; he could be compared to a torrent, the fire-spitting Typhon, the hell-hound Kerberos or a scalded pig — all that because of his loud and unpleasant voice and his excited behaviour.[5] Similar descriptions are given of other demagogues.[6] The more uneducated and rustic the assembly, the more easily was it a prey to blandishment and flattery, and the less able to contest any of the speakers' arguments.[7] The 'orators' were responsible for the motions accepted by the assembly, and they could be regarded as standing on a level with the officials who propounded new laws, the *nomothetai*.[8] In the decree on Brea penalties to protect its contents against alterations are imposed on anybody (that is to say any official) who puts to the vote a motion against the decree, and on any *rhetor* who speaks against it or tries to induce others to alter it.[9] The fact that there were many speakers and that many views could be put forward, provided, it is true, a certain control. Nevertheless it was considered especially bad that the orators continually sprang up like the heads of the Hydra.[10] The proverb that under every stone a scorpion might be hidden was used of the orators.[11] There are many examples in Euripides of denunciation of orators and demagogues as a bad lot.[12] Odysseus in particular becomes a

---

[1] adesp. 10, Eupolis 94.

[2] Cf. Kratinos 293, 20 D (= adesp. 37), Hermipp. 46, Eupolis 94.

[3] Eupolis 96.   [4] Kratinos 300.

[5] Hermipp. 46. — K.256, 274f, 285ff, 304, 430f, 511, 626ff, 1030, P.313ff, Plat. 216. — K.137, 218, 311, 487, 1018, W.36, 596, 1034, P.757, frg. 636, Kratinos 186, Pherekr. 51. — Thuc. III, 36, 6.

[6] K.956, P.637, Eupolis 207, cf. also Eur. *frg.* 597.

[7] A.370ff, 636ff, K.1340ff, cf. Thuc. III, 37, 4f.

[8] Lysias XXXI, 27.   [9] *IG.* I², 45 (= Tod, 44. *Syll.*³, 67), 20ff.

[10] Plat. 186.   [11] Th.528ff.

[12] e.g. *Med.* 582, *Hek.* 251ff, *Iph. A.* 337ff, *Ba.* 270f.

kind of prototype of the sly, treacherous and persuasive speaker.[1] In comedy and tragedy alike the reality of politics is intermixed with the exigencies of the plot or other dramatic demands; but the twofold evidence makes it very clear how influential and how dangerous the 'orators' had become.

They played an important part not only in the assembly but also in court, both as prosecutors and as advocates. A man was supposed to have 'a well-balanced [= persuasive or impartial?] language, prepared to answer the speeches'.[2] It was chiefly the older generation which had been concerned in lawsuits; they were pushed out by the 'young rhetors' and the poet was siding with the old men when he said that those who were known for their paederastic connections were considered the best orators.[3] A new social class was rising, the 'bad men' with their lack of tradition, and it soon became clear that selfish men, of low ideals and open to bribery, were using their ability in speech-making in order to achieve personal power and advantage.[4] Only a doubtful security was afforded by the fact that an orator whose proposal in the assembly obviously did general harm was wise to remove himself in time and so avoid legal proceedings.[5] The opposite aspect to this was the notorious tendency of the Athenians, usually incited by one of the orators, rashly to condemn any leader or general who had suffered a setback.[6]

The word 'orator' thus commonly acquired the meaning of 'politician', and the position of orator became a preliminary stage to that of *prostates*, the political leader of the people.[7] There were other, even more dubious, ways of preparing for the highest position in the State, at least according to the evi-

---

[1] *Hek.* 130ff, 254ff, *Tro.* 282ff, *Iph. A.* 525ff.

[2] Kratinos 38 P, 25ff. The text runs: ἔγειρε, θυμέ, γλῶ[ττ]αν εὔ]κέραστον ὀρθουμένην εἰς ὑπόκρισιν λόγων, and Mr. Page translates: 'My spirit, bestir your tongue judicial, roused to action for debate.' My own version owes much to Prof. Webster's. The γλῶττα ὀρθουμένη is probably *pars pro toto*, indicating the man standing up to speak.

[3] K.878ff, E.112f.

[4] Lack of tradition: Pl.186. — Personal aims: K.324f, F.367, Pl.30f, 379, 567ff, frg. 411, 439, Plat. 186, 5 (= adesp. 15).

[5] E.195f.

[6] There is no need to mention evidence for this; but cf. Eur. *Iph. A.* 366ff.

[7] The connection between orator and προστάτης becomes very clear from Eur. *Or.* 907-13 (perhaps an interpolation, and then not datable, but the more likely to reproduce a commonplace).

dence of comedy. Hyperbolos, for instance, boasts that he has learned a lot in the barbers' shops, 'sitting there unsuspected and pretending not to understand'.[1] The lack of tradition among the new middle-class leaders was something of an outrage. The Paphlagonian ruled the house of Demos though he had only recently been bought.[2] Another demagogue has compromised the *hetairiai*, the political clubs, since he had no *phraters* and did not speak pure Attic.[3] This is an allusion to the foreigners who had received citizenship. They as well as other orators might be promoted chiefly because of their ability and insolence, which were characteristic features of the whole type.[4]

The orators opposed the ruling politician who, though himself hardly better than they, had to drive them away from the demos like flies.[5] It seems hard to discover the exact point at which the average orator is to be distinguished from those who grew into demagogues and statesmen. The man who is 'master of the stone on the pnyx', that is the stone step from which the orators addressed the assembly, is, in fact, the *prostates*, the 'leader' of the State or of the Demos, the man in whom the 'people', that is in democracy the masses of the assembly, have full confidence.[6] Kleon was, in the opinion of his enemies, only the most powerful and most evil of the orators, one who always prided himself greatly on his power of rhetoric.[7] But there was a difference between orator and *prostates*. In war-time the contrast between *prostates* and *strategoi* might be even more obvious; the expression for accusing the generals, as a rule unjustly, became proverbial.[8] Generally, however, the *prostates* had to deal with the orators.[9] He had (and this is often forgotten by hostile comedy and by his other enemies) to be more than an unscrupulous dema-

---

[1] Eupolis 180.   [2] K.2.   [3] Eupolis 40 P, 21ff.

[4] K.425f. See above, p. 160f.   [5] K.59f.

[6] P.680, 684. — I believe that the strict distinction between προστάτης τῆς πόλεως and π. τοῦ δήμου, as recommended by O. Reverdin, *Museum Helveticum*, II (1945), 201ff, is too legalistic, at least for the fifth century. But he stresses rightly that 'c'est autour des hommes politiques, plutôt qu'autour des idées abstractes et de programmes généraux', that the assembly usually decided.

[7] K.344ff.

[8] K.355. — διαβάλλειν τοὺς στρατηγούς, K.288; cf. Thuc. IV, 27, 4, V, 16, 1.

[9] K.59f, 358.

gogue; he was bound to take a much higher view than the
rest of the irresponsible crowd of orators. This is obvious in
the case of Perikles, to whose discretion everything was left:
'the tribute of the cities and the cities themselves, to be bound
or unleashed; the walls of stone, to be built or cast down again;
treaties, power, dominion, peace, wealth and happiness'.[1]
Again and again Perikles is called king, tyrant, Zeus, and his
domineering power becomes the target of grim attacks as well
as of good-natured jokes.[2] The later *prostatai*, on the other
hand, were largely the heirs of Perikles. It comes perhaps
from a saying of Kleon himself that he is ridiculed as a sort of
Helios who sees everything.[3] A comparison between the
speeches of Perikles and Kleon, as Thucydides records them,
makes it very clear how strongly the later man tried to follow
his great predecessor. This argument is the more convincing
since Thucydides with equal strength of feeling admires
Perikles and hates Kleon.

If we see the Paphlagonian and the sausage-seller as the
poet wishes us to see them, that is as caricatures of real statesmen, the extraordinary power and importance of the *prostates*
can easily be deduced. It is significant that his position is
described with old-fashioned and high-sounding names like
tagos and *archelas*, or that he is called simply 'the great' or 'the
greatest man'.[4] He is the man who almost alone looks after
the whole of Athenian trade, ruling like Poseidon, as the
'greatest of the Greeks', over a seabound empire.[5] Everything
is full of Kleon's boldness and insolence: country and assembly.
offices and courts and archives, in a word, the whole State.[6]
He is seen surrounded by loathsome sycophants, cheating and
controlling the people by means of oracles and many other
tricks.[7] It may not be easy to decide whether it is really true
that the rich and stupid were exploited by Kleon, or whether
on the contrary, at least part of the people were clever enough
to use and exploit the dishonest *prostates*.[8] In any case, behind

---

[1] Telekl. 42.

[2] A.530f, Kratinos 56, 71, 111, 240, 241, 38 P, 15ff (cf. *AJP*. LXVI, 1945,
120, note 23), Telekl. 17, Hermipp. 41, 46, adesp. 60.

[3] K. 74f, 862f, cf. Eupolis 290.

[4] K.159, 164, 178, 180.   [5] K.176, 837ff.

[6] K.304ff.   [7] W.1033.

[8] K.261ff. The persecution of the wealthy Laches (W.240f) was perhaps
Kleon's work. — K.1121ff, cf. Pl.920.

these attacks on, and jokes about, Kleon and his life, just as behind the half-admiring denunciations we have mentioned of Perikles' activities, lies the reality of the powerful position of the leader of the State.

We can detect somewhat similar features of the *prostates* in Euripides. His democratic mythical kings are frequently examples of ideal 'leaders of the people'.[1] One man with full power provides a better government than a crowd of clever men.[2] On the other hand, Euripides, too, saw the danger of bad leaders, particularly in democracy. 'Terrible are the many if they have evil leaders.'[3]

Demos, though often considered a tyrant, was, in fact, easily led, especially by flattery.[4] In choosing a leader it was necessary to find the man best capable of serving 'Demos and his belly', the 'first man', the 'best man', who could become the saviour of the State and its citizens.[5] Throughout the main part of the fifth century the *prostates* was always a *strategos*, and Kleon, too, was finally elected to that office. The leader was an official, and thus would have to give an account of his administration. Even after 400 the leader of the women's government, who was the leader of a special kind of campaign, had the title of *strategos*, either in the masculine or the feminine form.[6] Ever since the rule of such leaders as Hyperbolos and Kleophon, the leader of the State normally held no office. The exceptions (apart from Anytos) prove the rule. Men like Thrasyboulos and Phokion were primarily generals, and became statesmen in exceptional circumstances. Other generals always remained soldiers, as for example Konon and Timotheos; other politicians who occasionally became *strategoi* did their important political work when they were not in office (Agyrrhios, Kallistratos). The statement remains true that usually at that time the political leader had no legal responsibility.

To be an orator had then become a real profession; that would have been impossible without the training and teaching in rhetoric, given by the sophists, which all the time became

---

[1] Cf. Theseus in the *Hiketides,* also *Herakl.* 206, 826.
[2] Eur. *Andr.* 479ff.   [3] Eur. *Or.* 772.
[4] K.1098ff, 1111ff.   [5] K.1207f, 327, 457ff.
[6] E.491f, 727, 835, 870, adesp. 552.

more subtle and more effective. Rhetoric had become the chief or even the only way of preparation for political life, and there were soon no politicians left other than the orators. It was only human that the political leaders, who had no longer any formal and legal responsibility, often lost all real and personal responsibility as well. The great and hard task of ruling a highly emotional and fickle people had become even greater and harder since it proved so easy to sway public opinion by clever oratory. The temptation was strong to take that leadership to be not so much the uphill work of public service as an easy means for personal ends. Individualism became predominant, above all on the highest level. This is one of the main reasons for the inner decline of Athenian democracy.

There is a further interesting point to be noted. The *prostates* gave to comedy its only chance of describing a 'great man'. Neither the Sokrates of the *Clouds* nor the witty Euripides of the *Thesmophoriazousai* deserve this name, nor even Aischylos in the *Frogs*. And the so-called heroes of many comedies, such as Dikaiopolis, Strepsiades, Trygaios, Chremylos, are not heroes at all; they are unheroic common citizens and insignificant people. That remains true in spite of their part in the plays as, for example, when the chorus maintains that Good Fate has made Trygaios their absolute master.[1] Aristophanes was no hero-worshipper, even if he depicted great men (or women) as he did in three characters of the extant plays: Peithetairos, the ingenious founder of the birds' city, Lysistrate who secures general peace, and Praxagora, the foundress of the communist State. It may be that Lysistrate and Praxagora are to some extent parodies of Euripides' tragic heroines, but they are more than that. Whether man or woman, all three of them are leaders of the State. The great individual, and still more the sophistic idea of the 'right of the stronger', are outside the world of comedy. Only as *prostates*, that is to say, in an almost legal and official rôle, and by virtue of his association with State and people, could the individual human being lift himself above the general level. The great *prostates* was at the same time to satisfy the widespread popular longing for a true leader, which is echoed in particular in the *Birds* and *Lysistrate*.

On the other hand, in both these plays as well as in the

[1] σὲ γὰρ αὐτοκράτορ' εἵλετ' ἀγαθή τις ἡμῖν τύχη, P.359f.

Ekklesiazousai the rise of the individual took place in quite unreal conditions. That may be due to the fact that it all happened on the comic stage. The actual demagogues and leaders were the chief targets of the comedians' hatred and sarcasm. If they were great in reality — and very few, if any, were — the comic poets would certainly not depict them as great, or only as great in their vices and misdeeds, like Kleon in the *Knights*, Hyperbolos in Eupolis' *Marikas* or he and others in Platon's *Hyperbolos*, *Kleophon* and *Peisandros*. Moreover, the unreal setting in comedy of political leadership may also have a deeper meaning. It shows that one of the most important problems of the time, the tension between individual and community, was, if at all reflected by comedy, never touched in its substance. The reason for this is not that the comedian still belonged to a community essentially undisturbed by modern intellectual developments, but on the contrary, that he was entirely a child of his own age. Aristophanes depicts an ideal form of political leadership in Cloudcuckooborough and the women's governments, but wherever he stands on the firm soil of reality, the ideal of an unpolitical life rules supreme.

Aristophanes knew of the struggle of ideas represented in the two words *physis* and *nomos*, nature and convention. When Pheidippides justifies his beating of his father by the analogy of the behaviour of certain animals, he contrasts this with the purely human *nomos*. Thus, without expressly using the word *physis*, he alludes to a doctrine which we mainly know as that of Antiphon.[1] Some indications in the speech of the Unjust Logos point to the same set of ideas.[2] But the *physis* which he generally opposes to the *nomos* of democracy is not that powerful demand of the great individual, which was at the core of the teaching of the later sophists. It is rather some vague idea of 'live and let live', of a human life without problems.[3]

The *Clouds* confirm that the comedian did not and could not enter into detailed philosophical questions and ideas, even if only to make fun of them. The one exception to this rule

---

[1] C.1425ff. Cf. W. C. Greene, *Moira* (1944), 232ff; F. Heinimann, *Nomos und Physis* (1945), 146.

[2] C.1075, 1078; see also 960, 1187. Cf. Heinimann, *l.c.*, 131ff, 140f.

[3] In W.1457f: τὸ γὰρ ἀποστῆναι χαλεπὸν φύσεος, ἣν ἔχοι τις ἀεί, 'nature' is almost the same as 'personal habits', i.e. *nomos*.

is the *Ekklesiazousai*, the only example, as far as I know, of an Attic comedy dealing with one of the fundamental ideas of political philosophy.[1] The silence of comedy, however, must not induce us to forget how intensely political the abstract thought of the Greeks was at that time. As always in later ages, so now when it happened for the first time: the rise of theoretical politics went hand in hand with the decline of practical politics.

The Athenians were passionate patriots, although sometimes in words rather than in deeds. The manifest pride of being an Athenian was there, breaking frequently through all the fun and all the bitter sarcasm of comedy. Despite the inner decline of communal life and the increasing importance of economic aims and means, there was enough tradition left to maintain some of the greatness of the past. And yet, it is from comedy that we can easily discover the limits of that greatness in a changed world. In spite of his general conservatism, in spite of all his patriotic zeal and love, in spite of his sincere appeals for the salvation of the State, Aristophanes was fundamentally a representative of an individualistic materialism akin to the creed he attacked in the teaching of the sophists. Comedy, by its very nature and by its growing incapacity to deal with the fundamental problems of politics, is itself a proof of the growing alienation between people and State.

[1] See above, p. 67.

CONCLUSION

WE propose to summarize in broad outline what Old Comedy has taught us about the life of the Athenian people, and to add some final conclusions.

The life of a citizen in Attica was at this time rooted in the life of his family and deme, that is to say in an emotional and traditional atmosphere which seems to have suffered more from the conflict and contrast between the generations (a conflict which had only recently become apparent) than from the freedom which man enjoyed by the rules of an essentially male society. The contrast of the generations is characterized by two main features: the importance attached to money and property, and the change in the methods and purpose of education and instruction, and both these factors were of significance in various other connections.

The peasants were in grave distress because of the war and the course of economic developments. They were numerous and consequently of economic importance; they also formed a very stable basis in the population by reason of their rural simplicity, their unpolitical desire for peace, their old-fashioned *petit bourgeois* ideal of life. When the tension between town and country grew and the impoverishment of the farmers became more serious, their general importance diminished, but it never disappeared completely. Both peasants and nobility were opposed to the economic and intellectual tendencies of the age. But the nobility was at this time undergoing a process of internal dissolution, brought about by its own luxury and degeneration as well as by the political and social preponderance of democracy and the teaching of the sophists. Athenian aristocracy was dying, and the few men of wealth and standing who existed besides the nobles had no social character of their own.

Traders and craftsmen, in spite of their modest and somewhat primitive methods of business, more and more took over the leadership of the State, politically as well as economically. The whole structure of Athenian economics was on such a large scale that it led to far-reaching specialization and intensification, which were of great importance for future economic developments. Socially these traders and craftsmen belonged to a middle class of which the great majority could only live by the work of their hands. Non-citizens were interspersed in large numbers among the citizens, and there was no social gap between the citizens and those who formed the bulk of the foreigners, the Greek metics. This is true for both the upper and lower middle-classes, for the wealthy and highly-esteemed merchants and owners of large workshops no less than for the poor retailers, artisans and workmen. They were all, more or less, of the same type of petty citizen.

The slaves, quite apart from the domestic slaves, took over from the free men a part, but not a very large part, of the work to be done. If individual slaves rose to wealth and even social esteem, they did so merely by reason of exceptional intelligence and initiative. In fact, some of the slaves injected new blood and new ideas into economic life, but on the whole, slaves did not alter in any essential way the economic position of the citizens.

A community in which the difference between nobles and non-nobles was no longer quite real, and that between rich and poor, though on the increase, was for some time to come of no decisive consequence, represented as a social body a comparatively uniform body, a single unit, the unit of a middle class. Political equality helped to safeguard the unity of the social body, and the farmers, too, belonged to this middle class which at once resulted from, and sustained, the Kleisthenic order and the type of citizen which this order had produced. Much of the opposition to democracy was due to the desire of making political life decent and clean. There were a few idealists, or at least honest politicians, who aimed at a better state of affairs in domestic and also in imperial and foreign policies. Theramenes was perhaps one of them. But the majority of the oligarchic leaders and most likely also of their followers who were members of the *hetairiai*, were little better than desperados and gangsters. That became quite obvious in the upheavals of 411 and 404, which were not attempts of an upper class to regain power. The oligarchs, intent on overthrowing democracy, were a mixed lot, neither a true aristocracy nor a class of the well-to-do. These were not simply social or economic revolutions, it was political strife heralding the break-up of the political community.

A considerable and no doubt constantly increasing number of the people had little interest in politics and political activities. The lure of the official payments was less effective than is generally believed. The number of those who actually lived exclusively on their pay as jurymen, councillors, officials or members of the assembly, was at no time very large, though the burden on the State treasury was heavy, and though of course many welcomed that easily earned money as an additional means of support. The same is true of the distributions of corn. On the whole, those who were in fact 'kept by the State' were in the minority, not only relatively to the number of the whole working population, but also to that of the citizens alone. The age was characterized by an ever-growing urge to find new ways of making money, and the very smallness of the regular public fees proves that the majority of the people could not live on them. The number of those who received public payment in one form or another increased in the fourth century, but Aristotle's estimate of 20,000 men is, if not an 'absurd exaggeration',[1] certainly misleading; it confuses regular and irregular payments, and exaggerates the social and economic importance of both. It is of decisive importance that most of these payments were very modest allowances paid by the day, and that it was impossible to live on them, because there were so many days on which nothing could be earned from the State. It is hardly just to call the Athenians, either these receivers of public money or even the people as a whole, men 'on the dole'; the social question of unemployment never arose. The most we can say is that the very poorest members of the community, and a certain number of crafty and unscrupulous fortune-hunters, relied entirely or chiefly on the State for money, though a great many received some public pay. Everybody realized to an increasing extent the importance of money, and the economic side of life gradually overpowered the political side.

Thus the political consciousness of the ordinary citizen diminished, and the small payments offered by the State were ineffective against this tendency. In the long run, the State could not compete with the possibilities of economic activity, though many citizens tried to make the most that was to be got from politics, and some of them succeeded, frequently by

[1] Aristotle, *Ath. pol.* 24, 3. Bolkestein, 268.

dishonest methods. It is more than an exaggeration when Plato's Sokrates reproaches Perikles, who first introduced public payments, with having made the Athenians 'idle, cowardly, babbling and avaricious'.[1] On the whole, however, it is true that politics were degraded and injured by economics, and could not be saved by essentially inadequate economic measures.

The same development became evident in the decline of the military spirit and the gradual disappearance of the citizen-soldiers. A new type began to predominate, a type certainly not unknown in our own day, the type of man who wanted nothing but a peaceful life and a prosperous business. This type embodied the reaction of a people who after an incredibly rapid and successful rise and after the enjoyment of great power and wealth did not and could not realize the danger which threatened an equally rapid destruction of their power, and finally their very existence. The majority had had enough of war and politics, and did not want to follow their leaders into new adventures. They had enjoyed their 'tyranny' over the allies, but during the war the empire, and the tributes with it, crumbled away. The people themselves were deaf to the voices pleading for a more generous treatment of the allies. By a natural reaction more and more men began to doubt the wisdom of a policy enacted by and for their own Polis only. Thus, the decrease of political enthusiasm was also reflected in the first, as yet vague, signs of Cosmopolitanism, or at least in the clear signs of that Panhellenism which was trying to break down the barriers between the Greek States and to secure universal peace. This policy was, after all, an intelligent movement; several events seemed to justify it, and it might have had greater success, had it not been for the combined destructive forces of Polis individualism and Macedonian power politics.

The intellectual changes which led to these results and which had accompanied the changes in the economic and social spheres were characterized by the activities of the sophists. These men were, perhaps, the outcome rather than the spiritual leaders of the times, but their teaching was of an importance which can scarcely be exaggerated. From the sociological point of view it produced two main results which were to some extent contradictory. There was, on the one hand, the emergence of a growing class of 'educated' people,.

[1] Plat. *Gorgias* 515C.

eager to segregate themselves from the 'uneducated'. A new line of demarcation was drawn through the population, and one which came to be of increasing importance during the succeeding centuries. On the other hand, we see from comedy that the sophistic doctrines influenced very wide sections of the people, and were able to do so because the people took a lively interest in literary, artistic and even linguistic questions. Scepticism in religious matters spread, though it never obtained a real hold on the majority of the people, who were apt rather to fall into the opposite extreme of increased superstition and devotion to ecstatic and mystery cults. Rationalistic criticism even in an 'age of enlightment' was not for the many, and the more difficult and subtle the teaching of the sophists and rhetors became, the more it was confined to a relatively small proportion of the people, to the new upper class of the 'educated'.

The comic poets, although their affection was for the unsophisticated, were concerned with both classes among the people. This shows, especially in that age of change and transition, a certain definite attitude with a peculiar quality of its own. We have used comedy chiefly as an instrument, as a source of evidence. For we saw that it was a social as well as a literary phenomenon; it expressed in a sense views which were generally held, and its mirror reflected the people as a whole. We have not, however, or only incidentally, asked ourselves what spirit comedy can claim as its own. This spirit must have shared in and expressed some general feelings, and cannot have been only the individual spirit of comedy, still less that of the various comic poets. We do not propose to speak of the literary character and high artistic quality of Old Comedy; these are well known and, apart from that, not really our concern. What we do want to stress is in the first place — though this is not the first time it has been said — that comedy was influenced by the economic and rationalist spirit of the age in a much higher degree than one would be inclined to believe in view of its general attitude and especially its criticism of the new tendencies.[1] What does it mean, in fact, all this

[1] This has been proved, for the special but important subject of rhetoric, by C. T. Murphy, *Harvard Studies in Class. Philology*, XLIX (1938), 69ff. Aristophanes, certainly a severe critic not only of the 'orators', but of the art of rhetoric itself, especially in its influence on poetry, is described by Murphy as 'a student and, in some degree, a contributor to the art of rhetoric'.

summoning up of the men and the spirit of the past, if there was actually no way back, and if the comedians never really thought of going back, but were pleading for the ideal of a pleasant and tranquil life and not for the heroic will to liberty and the strong public-spiritedness of the past? What does it mean, all this antagonism to the spirit embodied in Euripides and Sokrates, if the comedians did not spare any of the gods their bitterest satire, if their criticism might attack everybody and everything in social and intellectual life?

There is a second point. The spirit of Old Comedy seems to be characterized by two negative facts: the lack of any clear, detached and more-than-individual standpoint, and the lack of any uncompromising reverence or respect. This twofold 'deficiency' is not simply due to the fact that comedy had to be comedy. Through all the good-natured or bitter fun of comedy, there can be heard the voice of serious and fundamental convictions. Old Attic Comedy, although the wittiest kind of entertainment and merry-making the world has ever seen, was always more than mere entertainment. Just as the Attic tragedian was more than a playwright, so the comedian was more than a jester. Reflecting as it does the spirit of the time and the spirit of the community, Old Comedy was at the same time a product of creative inventiveness and art which easily became, especially in the later stages, pure subjectivism and individualism. We have touched on this point at the end of the last chapter. Comedy was both a product and an active factor in an epoch in which the traditional forms of life had been destroyed without the creation of new ones except within the realm of pure theory.[1] Comedy touched on all classes of the people, not, like tragedy, from a generally accepted but remote platform, standing rather in the midst of the people and the contemporary events and ideas. The poet, who fought passionately against the deterioration of democracy brought about by demagogic leaders, was himself a demagogue. Frequently he used the very methods for which he blamed the political leaders — denunciation, overpraise, and appeal to the greed of the people.[2] Witty and serious, rude and flattering, filled with fantasy and with emotion, Aristophanes, whom once

[1] It is worth while to compare what Hegel writes in his *Aesthetik* (*Werke*, I, 562).

[2] See p. 28ff.

again we take as the representative and the very culmination
of Old Comedy, is one of the greatest seducers in all the history
of literature.[1]   Even in his early comedies, when he was little
more than a boy, his genius led him far beyond the stage of
mere fun-making, however gorgeous.   Comedy is permeated
by the same spirit as that which led the people to the decisions
about Mytilene, about the victors of Arginusae and about
Sokrates.   It is this spirit of demagogy which persuaded the
citizens to consider it intolerable if they were not allowed to
do exactly as they pleased, even to the extent of cancelling
laws and decrees sanctioned by themselves.   It is the spirit
which turned the sovereign people into a tyrant proud of not
being accountable to anyone, either as jurymen or in the
assembly.[2]   In the end, the people became the fool of their own
sovereignty, and democracy was undermined for the sake of
democratic principles.

Athens succeeded during the Peloponnesian War in the
most magnificent and most astonishing achievements, both in
the military and the cultural sphere.   On the other hand, by
her own fickleness, distrust and arrogance she brought about
her eventual collapse.   Democracy was responsible for both the
one and the other, but it is difficult to decide how much of what
happened came about because Athens was a democracy.   The
negative consequences, of course, were more obvious, still
more so the character of the State after the collapse.   The
democracy of the beginning of the fourth century, based on,
and justified by, the expulsion of the cruel tyranny of the
Thirty, was a State of some power and vitality; but it no longer
followed the trend of the time, which tended towards the rise
of larger territorial States.   The 'petty State', with its character
of provincialism, so anxiously predicted for a long time past,
became to a large extent the reality.[3]

This development is, in a sense, reflected in the development
of comedy.   The spirit of comedy, its very nature, depended
originally, even in its criticism, on the spirit of the whole

----

[1] After I had written these words, I read the fine sentences of Fr. Schlegel
which follow almost the same lines (*Vom künstlerischen Wert der alten griechischen
Komödie. Sämtl. Werke*, IV, 25ff, especially 34).

[2] W.587, Thuc. III, 43, 4.   Cf. J. A. O. Larsen in: *Essays in Political Theory,
pres. to G. W. Sabine* (1948), 10ff.

[3] The Athenians as μικροπολῖται, K.817, frg. 819.

people and the democratic State. Later the tendencies we have characterized, above all the quietist ideal defined again and again in the middle of a terrible war, show the path which comedy took, a path which led finally to a somewhat dull and wholly unpolitical atmosphere. The two latest extant plays of Aristophanes, and especially the *Ploutos*, with their narrow and materialistic dreams based on 'wishful thinking', are witnesses to a period of weakening and transition. The fantastic and Utopian exaggeration of reality in Old Comedy has vanished, while the artistic subtlety and the deeper psychology of New Comedy have not yet been achieved. So the historians of literature divined or discovered the existence of Middle Comedy which, seen from a general point of view, includes the period when poetry had left the sphere of politics. In a world in which, even at its best, wealth, good manners, and intellectual education had replaced the old standards of austerity, physical prowess and patriotism, comedy too had to change in manner as well as in matter. The topical question, for instance, of whether rhetorical or philosophical training provided the better kind of education, was no subject for the comedians who turned against every kind of intellectual education. Consciously or not, they adapted themselves to a new *bourgeois* audience and its standards of decency, materialism and private interests.

Aristophanes opposed a development in which he was himself unconsciously involved. This development with its doubtful and tragic as well as its more positive features went further. The social demands of a stratum of petty citizens, partly almost proletarians, gained ground, and men accustomed themselves more and more to new economic ideas and methods. The whole change in social life, both in the material and in the psychological sphere, proved to be an important, indeed an inevitable, stage of historical development. With the increase of the economic dependence of the citizens on the State, Athens undoubtedly went beyond the boundaries of a sound social and financial policy. This process, however, did not go so far as is often supposed, and the effects were balanced to some extent by the fact that contempt for trade and craft decreased rather than increased. The vast majority of the people continued to live by these pursuits, and, on the other hand, State and citizens derived much advantage from the work of non-citizens. All this was far from being a good and sound system, either politically or economically, but as a joint effect of economic development and public support, social life reached a stability which should not be under-estimated.

During the fourth century the decline of the Polis, both as a political form and power and as an unquestioned moral and intellectual community, went hand in hand with a slow but clear increase in economic prosperity and in the number of the population, and an even more obvious rise in the standard of technical and intellectual civilization. There were setbacks and temporary crises, but on the whole we can maintain that the loss of political influence together with that of political traditions and wisdom, which can easily be recognized in all the decades up to and beyond the times of Demosthenes, was the price, and certainly a very high price, of economic prosperity and social consolidation. These, however, could not have been achieved if economic thought had not been all-pervading and predominant. Nobility had lost its meaning and dignity; the peasants were impoverished, though they never entirely lost their importance; the townsfolk with the metics and slaves became an economic organism of consider-able strength — of many weaknesses, too, but these were to a large extent overcome by the system of State payments and distributions of corn. In spite of all its political blunders and its general economic unsoundness, the whole system worked fairly well by reason of a peculiar mixture of social equity and social corruption. Though far from setting a good example in government, the democracy of the fourth century yet revealed, from the domestic point of view, strength and efficiency. 'La démocratie qui travaille ne laisse pas mourir de faim ses enfants.'[1]

Some modern scholars uphold the view that its financial system was the real cause of the destruction of the Athenian State.[2] We cannot accept this line of thought. The financial system was bad, but it worked not too badly. The prosperity of economic life and the relative equilibrium of social con-ditions during the fourth century categorically refute the claim that the unsound conditions of public finances were in any

[1] Francotte, II, 357. I should like to refer here in general to the vivid picture which R. J. Bonner gives in his *Aspects of Athenian Democracy* (1933).

[2] Cf. Andreades, 363, quoted, e.g., by Michell, 393, as his last summing-up.

way decisive. In a sense, economics were the reason for the decline, not because of overwhelming poverty and disorganization, but just because economic life flourished. The victory of the economic outlook and the preponderance of 'Economic Man' were the true reasons for the deterioration of politics and morals.

Is this the final result of our investigation? I believe not. We must, once more, look back on the whole development which caused the decline of political comedy, because it reflected the decline of the Polis community. Athens did not die either in 404 or in 385 or even in 338. Neither the decay of political life and power, nor on the other hand economic aspirations, social achievements or social hardships, should blind us to the fact that the Athens of the fourth century was also, and above all, the Athens of philosophy, and that Hellenistic Athens remained the educational centre of a world which had grown in size. It was not economics but its own spirit which survived the political Polis. The comic poets could know little of that, and they misunderstood even such essential facts as they knew; but the people, without whom all this spirit would have been empty and void, really lived in comedy, and its evidence is witness of the people's capacities. Buoyancy and alertness in the average citizen joined with an innate sense of beauty and of pleasure in life on the one hand, with a gradually spreading, though superficial, rationalist education on the other, to form the foundation on which the temple of the spirit was to be erected. Its architects, it is true, looked down upon the lower people with aristocratic contempt. But right and justice were the ultimate social goals of the great philosophers, and, in spite of all their aristocratic opposition to democracy, they built on the basic fact that justice was embodied as an idea in a people who lived in political equality and far-reaching social unity, even though it was not embodied in the practices of democratic politics and in everyday life.

The Greeks themselves, and the Athenians more than anyone else, believed in the overriding importance of constitutions. The survival of democracy was, however, less due to the working of assembly and council or the power of the lawcourts than to the fact that the Athenians had become, as it were, natural democrats. Institutions, however obsolete, lived on because there were still men steeped in an old and great tradition.

In proclaiming justice as the true goal of the State, Greek philosophy at the same time defeated the attempts of both democrats and oligarchs to proclaim the 'Right of the Stronger'. The comedians, as we have seen, did not deal with this idea,[1] but Thucydides, in the dialogue between the Athenians and the Melians, shows how in external politics the democratic State followed the idea of 'Might is Right', and thus became a perilous threat and danger to the other Greek States.[2] The oligarch Kritias, on the other hand, who was a clever sophist and an unscrupulous politician, applied the same principle to domestic politics and established the savage rule of the Thirty. In a sense, Thrasyboulos was the predecessor of Plato, for when he led democracy to victory, the statesman overthrew the government of those who later, on the intellectual battle-field, were finally exterminated by the philosopher. Both worked in the service of the Polis when they defeated the practice and doctrine of the 'Superman'. Though even the sophists never believed that *physis* as opposed to *nomos*, nature as against convention and tradition, meant the innate superiority of one people or one race over another, their belief in the right of power, in the case of both the State and the individual, challenged the right of man. Victory was due not to democracy or aristocracy, but to the true spirit of State and people, and it will always be the same whenever the same challenge is made.

In recognizing the close connection between the political philosophers and the Polis (and no understanding of them is possible without this recognition), we indicate by the abstract conception of the State something which at the same time was a lively group of human beings, who suffered from many faults and shortcomings and who, it is true, became more and more alienated from the State. The people of Aristophanes had once been the people of Perikles, and would soon be the people of Demosthenes. By the same development an upper class, distinguished partly by tradition and partly by education and wealth, was being destroyed, while its individual members were led to the sophists, to Sokrates, to philosophy and political theorizing, and finally to the ethical or eudaemonistic individualism of the Stoics and Epicureans, while the bulk of the

[1] See above, p. 358.   [2] Thuc. V, 84ff.

citizens became a people without political direction, and gradually an essentially unpolitical body. The type of the *apragmon* was nothing but 'a private person', no matter whether the individual was concerned with business or intellectual enjoyments or a general *laissez-aller*. Nevertheless, and indeed because of this people, Athens continued to exist. Behind all the storms of politics (and they were not to die down for a long time to come), behind the loss of political strength, wisdom and self-sacrifice, immortal Athens lived on and with her her people of petty farmers and petty townsmen.

Social disintegration, however, was going on all the time, and its chief result was the formation of a new upper class, distinct from the majority of the people by prosperity or sometimes even great wealth and also by education, a *bourgeoisie* which, as the economic masters of a multitude of employees, tenants and slaves, took over the task of government.[1] The intellectual interests and civilized enjoyments of the new upper class rested on economic security. We have seen how in the late fifth and early fourth centuries this new form of life began its career in all kinds of economic activities.

It is at this point that a peculiar problem arises. The chief trend was clearly towards an upper class guided by selfish materialism and unpolitical individualism. There always was, on the other hand, an intense political activity, and at least part of the people were still living in the old traditions of Polis life, its patriotism and also its religion. Exactly the same contrasts are described in the most authoritative work on the social history of the Hellenistic age. Rostovtzeff[2] realizes both sides of the character of that *bourgeoisie* which governed the Hellenistic Polis; but he finds the traditional ways of life by far the stronger force, and he goes so far as to see in the citizen of the third and second centuries B.C. the true heir of the *homo politicus* of the classical age. This cannot be correct, unless there was round about 300 B.C. a complete break and volte-face in the development of the Polis, for which, of

---

[1] Cf. M. Rostovtzeff, *Social and Economic History of the Hellenistic World passim*, in particular II, 1115ff.

[2] *Op. cit.*, 1119ff, 1125f. I was able to discuss the matter with Professor F. W. Walbank, and I am glad to say that he, coming to the problem from the Hellenistic side, seems fully to agree with my own views. Cf. also Walbank, *Cl. R.* LVI (1942), 81ff, and *JHS.* LXIV (1944), 13, and Momigliano, *JHS.* LXIII (1943), 116f.

course, there is not the slightest evidence. Rostovtzeff's own attempt to bridge the gulf between the two contrasting pictures and to subordinate everything to the predominance of tradition and patriotism is very weak indeed and not convincing.[1] The solution, which can here be outlined only very briefly, will be found in a complete shifting of emphasis from the one side to the other.

In the course of the fourth century there occurred the frequently mentioned disintegration of a fairly uniform society into the two classes of *bourgeoisie* and proletariate as heralded in Aristophanes' latest plays. The members of either class lived as members of their class and no longer — or at least only partially — as citizens of the State. In a long and gradual process the Polis had changed from a true political community into a society of the educated and well-to-do who enjoyed a fairly comfortable life at the expense of a poor rabble which was not interested in either politics or matters of the intellect. To some extent, the *bourgeoisie* preserved the middle-class body which had been at the core of the citizen body of the previous two centuries, and thus naturally received a legacy which they were bound to cherish. The heirs retained considerable pride in the past glory and present beauty of their city. They displayed a local patriotism which, fighting as it usually was against hopeless odds, now and then gained the appearance of the true Polis spirit; in the end, however, it was less concerned with politics than with gymnasia, games and festivals. The 'political' life of the Hellenistic city was essentially determined by two largely contrasting facts: the lack of real power and the insistence on autonomy. As there was so little power, the autonomy more often than not was only nominal, and at any rate remained a purely parochial affair. There were no true heirs to the political citizens of the classical age.

Once more, we return to the earlier period which is the framework of this book, and to the people who are its subject. The Athenians were a great people, and this greatness was certainly not confined to the short period from the Persian wars to Perikles' death. The inner disintegration, however,

---

[1] Walbank thinks that Rostovtzeff's picture of the Hellenistic *bourgeoisie* is coloured largely by his observation of the American *bourgeoisie* of today. That is probably true, but the incongruity of the conflicting characteristics remains, whether applied to ancient Greece or modern America.

had begun under, and partly even through, the rule of Perikles. Though the Athenians were still capable of great military exploits, shrewd political designs and high artistic achievements, both during the Peloponnesian War and in the succeeding decades, the social structure was changing at the same time, and we are entitled to ask whether the people of Demosthenes, or even that of Aristophanes, was the true representative of the Polis of Athens, in the same sense as the people of Perikles had been. The people, previously discordant on issues of constitutional and foreign policies, but united as the social body of citizens, gradually disintegrated into a class-conscious society. When the masses were no longer led by aristocrats but by men of their own stamp, the standards of 'the people', that is to say of its majority of *petits bourgeois*, became predominant and general. A people, however, of 'small officials and cunning beggars',[1] a people distinguished by economic egotism, narrowness of outlook and good-natured love of pleasure, will never create true and eternal things, either in the political or the spiritual field. It will make no decisive difference if this people is excited by its leaders to fanatical devotion or outrage. The peasants and artisans, merchants and workmen represent an often pleasant and lovable part of the people, but they were and are unable to maintain and carry on the traditions of a great past. This can only be done by the famous 'creative minority', an aristocracy of intellect and morals, an upper class, not mere individuals, of a higher level of intellectual and moral education. It is the undying merit of democracy to have found the means for the necessary aristocracy to receive continually new blood from the whole people, and at the same time to have controlled this aristocracy by public opinion. But no democracy, and no State whatsoever, is fit to live if the ruling class is formed by the *petit bourgeois*, still less if these men are guided by misleading and demagogic propaganda. This also was not more true two thousand years ago than it is today.[2]

---

[1] F.1084.

[2] I have left the last sentences as they stood in the first edition, although they have been open to misunderstanding. Therefore I better add that when in 1942 I wrote of the *petits bourgeois* misguided by propaganda I was naturally thinking of the Nazis and their followers.

CHRONOLOGICAL TABLE

Except where actual dates are given, the chronological position is approximate; if a ? is added, it is quite uncertain. Names of poets without the title of a play indicate little more than a sort of *floruit*. Since the Lenaia and the Great Dionysia fall roughly in February and April respectively, the performance of a comedy always belongs to the second half of the official year. I have, however, put down both years to which the official Athenian year belonged in order to cover the period when the play was actually written. For the latter cf. A. Ruppel, *Konzeption u. Ausarbeitung der aristophanischen Komödien*, Diss. Giessen, 1913, and in general Geissler's frequently mentioned book.

First Generation of Old Comedy	Second Generation of Old Comedy	Other Dates
	460-446 B.C.	
Kratinos: victory (454/3)		
Krates: victory (451/0)		
Kratinos: *Archilochoi*		Death of Aischylos
Chionides		First Performance of
Magnes	Birth of Eupolis (446)	Euripides
Ekphantides	Birth of Aristophanes	*IG.* I², 40, 44
	445-432 B.C.	
?Kratinos: *Drapetides*		Peace with Sparta
? „ : *Nomoi*		*IG.* I², 45
„ : *Cheirones*		
„ : *Ploutoi*		?Arrival of Protagoras in
„ : *Pylaia*		Athens
„ : *Thraittai*	?Pherekrates:	Sophokles: *Antigone*
„ : *Boukoloi*	*Doulodidaskalos*	
„ : *Malthakoi*		Euripides: *Alkestis* (439/8)
Kallias : *Kyklopes* (435/4)		
Kratinos : *Euneidai*		
? „ : *Panoptai*		
Telekleides: *Sterroi*		
„ : *Hesiodoi*		Megarian Decree
	431-428 B.C.	
Kratinos: *Dionysalexan-*		Outbreak of war
dros (431/0)		Euripides: *Medea* (432/1)
? „ : *Nemesis*		

374

First Generation of Old Comedy	Second Generation of Old Comedy	Other Dates
	431-428 B.C. (*cont.*)	
Telekleides: frg. 43, 44 (431/0)	Hermippos: *Moirai*	
	„ : *Stratiotai*	
Kallias: *Atalantai*		
? „ : *Pedetai*		
?Telekleides: *Amphiktyones*	Hermippos: *Theoi*	
	Phrynichos and Eupolis: First performances	
	Eupolis: *Prospaltioi*	Death of Perikles (429)
Telekleides: *Apseudeis*	Pherekrates: *Tyrannis*	„ „ Herodotos
Kratinos : *Horai*		Euripides: *Hippolytos* (429/8)
„ : *Seriphioi*	Pherekrates: *Automoloi*	Revolt of Mytilene

	427-421 B.C.	
	Aristophanes: *Daitales* (428/7)	Ps.-Xenophon: *Athenaion politeia*
	Eupolis: *Taxiarchoi*	
	Hermippos: *Phormophoroi*	Embassy of Gorgias of Leontinoi
	Aristophanes: *Babylonioi* (427/6)	
	„ : *Acharnes* (426/5)	
	Pherekrates: *Petale*	
	Phrynichos: *Satyroi*	
	Eupolis: *Aiges*	
Kratinos: *Deliades* (425/4)	Aristophanes: *Hippes* (425/4)	
	? „ : *Georgoi*	
	Eupolis: *Chrysoun genos* (425/4)	
	Aristophanes: *Holkades* (424/3)	Thucydides goes into exile
	„ : *Nephelai* (α) (424/3)	
Kratinos: *Pytine* (424/3)	Ameipsias: *Konnos* (424/3)	
	?Eupolis: *Astrateutoi*	
	Aristophanes: *Proagon* (423/2)	
	„ : *Sphekes* (423/2)	
	Leukon: *Presbeis* (423/2)	*IG.* I², 76 (423/2)
	Eupolis: *Poleis*	
	Pherekrates: *Krapataloi*	
	Eupolis: *Marikas* (422/1)	Death of Kleon
Death of Kratinos	„ : *Kolakes* (422/1)	
	Aristophanes: *Eirene* (α) (422/1)	
	Leukon: *Phrateres* (422/1)	Peace of Nikias

Second Generation of Old Comedy	Third Generation of Old Comedy	Other Dates
	420-416 B.C.	
Pherekrates: *Agrioi* (421/0)		*IG.* I², 84 (421/0)
Eupolis: *Autolykos* (421/0)		
Aristophanes: *Geras*		
„ : *Eirene* (β)		
Platon: *Nikai*		
Platon: *Perialges*		
Hermippos: *Artopolides*		
Aristophanes: *Daidalos*		
„ : *Danaides*		
Platon: *Hyperbolos*		
Hermippos: *Kerkopes*		
Platon: *Syrphax*		
Aristomenes		Ostracism of Hyperbolos
Lysippos		
Aristophanes: *Horai*		
„ : *Anagyros*		Capitulation of Melos
	415-404 B.C.	
Platon: *Peisandros*		Euripides: *Troades* (416/5)
Eupolis: *Baptai*		Antiphon V.
Pherekrates: *Ipnos*		
Aristophanes: *Amphiareos* (415/4)		
„ : *Ornithes* (415/4)		Siege of Syracuse
Phrynichos: *Monotropos* (415/4)		*IG.* I², 325ff
Ameipsias: *Komastai* (415/4)		*IG.* I², 329 (414/3)
?Aristophanes: *Heroes*		
Platon: *Heortai*		
Eupolis: *Demoi* (413/2)		Euripides: *Helene* (413/2)
Aristophanes: *Lysistrate* (412/1)		
„ : *Thesmo-phoriazousai* (412/1)		
„ : *Lemniai*		
Platon: *Sophistai*		Revolt of the Four
Death of Eupolis		Hundred
Archippas	First performances of	
Hegemon	Metagenes, Polyzelos,	
Philonides: *Kothornoi*	Strattis, Nikophon	*IG.* I², 113
		Ps.-Lysias XX
Aristophanes: *Ploutos* (α) (409/8)	Kantharos	Andokides II
„ : *Phoinissai*	Strattis: *Phoinissai*	
„ : *Gerytades* (408/7)	„ : *Chrysippos*	Alkibiades' return
„ : *Thesmo-phoriazousai* (β)		Death of Euripides and Sophokles (406)
„ : *Batrachoi* (406/5)		Euripides: *Bakchai* (406/5)

Second Generation of Old Comedy	Third Generation of Old Comedy	Other Dates
	415-404 B.C. (cont.)	
Phrynichos: *Mousai* (406/5)		Euripides: *Iphigeneia*
Platon: *Kleophon* (406/5)	?Theopompos: *Kapelides*	*en Aulidi* (406/5)
„ : *Skeuai*	Sannyrion: *Danae*	
	Metagenes: *Homeros*	
	Demetrios: *Sikelia*	End of the war
	403-390 B.C.	
Platon: *Hellas or Nesoi*		Lysias XII, XXXIV
		Isokrates XXI, XVIII
	Archippos: *Ichthyes*	*IG.* II², 10 (401/0)
	Strattis: *Kinesias*	Lysias XXI
Aristophanes: *Pelargoi*	„ : *Makedones*	Lysias XXV, ?XXXII
	„ : *Potamioi*	
	Theopompos: *Althaia*	
	Nikochares	
	Philyllios	?Isokrates XX
	Kephisodoros	Andokides I (399/8)
	Sannyrion	Death of Thucydides
	Diokles	Lysias XXX, XIII, XXXI, XVII
		IG. II², 1237 (396/5)
Aristomenes: *Dionysos* (395/4)		Isokrates XVI
		Lysias XIV, VII
Platon: *Presbeis*		Andokides III
		Isokrates XVII
		Isaios V
Aristophanes: *Ekklesia- zousai*		
Platon: *Phaon* (392/1)		Lysias III, XVI
		Isokrates XIII, XIX
		?Lysias IX
	398-380 B.C AND AFTER	
		? Xenophon, *Anabasis*
		Lysias XXVIII, XXIX, XXIII, XXXIII
Aristophanes: *Ploutos* (β) (389/8)	Theopompos: *Theseus*	
	Alkaios: *Pasiphae* (389/8)	Lysias XIX, XXII
	Nikophon: *Adonis* (389/8)	Isokrates X
Aristophanes: *Kokalos* (387/6)	Nikochares: *Lakones* (389/8)	
„ : *Aiolosikon* (β)		Antiphanes (Middle Comedy): first perform- ance
Platon: Αἱ ἀφ' ἱερῶν		
	Theopompos: *Admetos*	Lysias X, XXVI
Death of Aristophanes	„ : *Hedychares*	
	„ : *Pamphile*	Isaios
	„ : *Medos*	Xenophon
	Strattis: *Atalante*	

GENERAL INDEX

Names of writers quoted as evidence only, or of stage characters, as well as such general items as Athens, Old Comedy, people, Polis, economics, politics, religion, are not mentioned here. Ordinary figures refer to pages, raised figures to footnotes, Roman figures to chapters.

ADDENDUM

to page 27, note 2.

In Hibeh Pap. II 182 a (c. 280-250 B.C.), the story is told which we also find in Diog. Laert. II, 5, 34, partly in different and partly in identical words. At Sokrates' house important guests are expected; in fact, they have already arrived: [ἤδη ἥκ]ουσιν οἱ ξ[έ]οι. Xanthippe is fussy about the preparations (στρώματα καὶ π[οτ]ήρια), and Sokrates tells her not to worry: εἰ μὲν γὰ[ρ], ἔφη, εἰσὶ χαρ[ίεντ]ες, οὐθὲν αὐτοῖς διοίσει μετέχε[ιν] τῶν παρόντων· εἰ δὲ μή εἰσι χαρίεντες, ἐμο[ὶ] αὐτῶν οὐθὲν μελήσει. Later we read:, ἡ δὲ Ζανθίππη βουλομ[έ]νη εἰς Διονύσια ἐξελθεῖν [. . .]. If this means that she was going to the theatre the disputed question whether or not women attended theatrical performances would be decided. But the evidence rather points to something else. It was late in the day; the time for dinner could not be much before sunset (in April). Xanthippe was in a hurry, not because she wanted to go to the theatre, but because she wished to be in time for some event in the evening. That would probably be the κῶμος, the procession in which, at the end of the first day of the festival, the figure of Dionysos was brought back from the grove of Akademos to the theatre. This procession provided opportunity for drinking and revelling (A. Mommsen, *Feste der Stadt Athen*, 439. L. Deubner, *Attische Feste*, 139ff). It is well known that women took part in Dionysiac processions, and there would be many among the spectators.

SCHOCKEN PAPERBACKS